ERNST MACH

Ernst Mach at Vienna
(Courtesy of the Ernst Mach Institute)

ERNST MACH

His Work, Life, and Influence

John T. Blackmore

University of California Press

BERKELEY · LOS ANGELES · LONDON
1972

University of California Press
Berkeley and Los Angeles, California
University of California Press Ltd.
London, England
Copyright © 1972 by John Thomas Blackmore
ISBN 0-520-01849-4
Library of Congress Catalog Card Number: 79-138514
Designed by Elsie Nahem
Printed in the United States of America

Contents

Contents

Preface

This book was written with several purposes in mind. First, I wanted to present as much new biographical information on Ernst Mach as possible. My reason was to help make him much better known to the educated public. Second, I wanted to clarify the full range of his contributions to science. Mach was not merely a physicist. He also did important work in psychology and physiology and wrote extremely influential books on both the history and philosophy of science. And third, and most important, I have tried to write this book in such a way as to emphasize the central and controversial influence of Mach's philosophical ideas on the development of twentieth-century physics and philosophy of science. Mach's chief greatness lay in his attempt to base modern physics on a presentationalist epistemology within the philosophical tradition of Berkeley, Hume, and Kant. This ambition is the primary reason why Ernst Mach remains so controversial a figure today. Many people, myself included, reject the Berkeley, Hume, and Kant tradition in philosophy and think that it has seriously interfered with the development of twentieth-century science. But while I oppose almost all aspects of Mach's philosophy, I have nevertheless tried to be informative and fair. Mach was a good scientist, an important philosopher, and on the basis of his scientific and philosophical influence alone should be mentioned in the same company with Max Planck and Albert Einstein. In addition, Mach had a strong and in later years even a courageous temperament.

But if Mach is so important why has he been so obscure for so long to the educated public? Why has no full-scale biography been written about him up to now? First, Mach did not want a biography written about him, and second, his central role in the philosophical "power

vii

play" to interpret physics within a presentationalist epistemology has not been sufficiently emphasized to catch the attention of most scientists and philosophers, let alone educated laymen.

Ernst Mach's son, Ludwig Mach, gathered material for a biography of his father during the 1920s and 1930s but apparently destroyed his material during World War II. H. D. Heller, a resident of Prague who later emigrated to Israel, began to write a biography but his early death cut the work short and it appeared in 1964 limited in scope and completeness. My own interest in Mach grew slowly and fitfully. Professor John G. Burke, historian of science and Dean of the Social Sciences at the University of California, Los Angeles, first encouraged me to write on Mach, and I prepared a fifty-page paper during a seminar in the history of science in 1965. When I mentioned that substantially more material was available, Professor Burke suggested I write my doctoral dissertation on Mach. At that time I declined, arguing that I preferred not to write a "negative" work. I felt that it would be more suitable if someone basically sympathetic with Mach's philosophical ideas wrote about him.

During the next year I concentrated on a "positive" dissertation in the philosophy of history in which I developed my own ideas. My doctoral board, however, preferred a research dissertation. This fact along with the realization that a biography of Ernst Mach was critically needed finally persuaded me to undertake what gradually became an awesome task.

Three and a half years later I finished a 1,200-page doctoral dissertation hopefully balanced between biography, science, and philosophy. My own stylistic deficiencies and tendency to overwrite on secondary figures persuaded the publisher to ask me to cut the work in half. This has been done with consequences best judged by the reader.

The surviving condensed version is organized chronologically but in a way that requires explanation. In general, biographical chapters alternate with ones on science or philosophy, with the science or philosophy chapters covering the same chronological period as the preceding biographical chapters. In the second half of the book, however, except for short sections describing events between 1895 and Mach's paralysis in 1898 and between 1913 and his death in 1916, the narrative focus shifts away from Mach's outward life to the inward and outward happenings in the lives of his friends and philosophical opponents. In that section Mach's psychological reactions to these happenings pro-

vide a unifying thread from chapter to chapter. Ultimately, these intellectual and emotional reactions become the central concern of the book
as Mach desperately attempted to rise above the philosophical controversies that threatened to destroy both his life spirit and what he felt
were his most important contributions to the philosophy and methodology of science. In short, the second half of this book should be understood as a biography only in a very qualified and largely indirect sense,
even though some of the later chapters may well outweigh the earlier
chapters in elucidating what is crucial to an understanding of Mach's
life.

A striking feature of Mach's early scientific work was his anticipation
of later discoveries. Mach's interest in microphotograhy, use of multidimensions in interpreting atomic behavior, investigations into what
came to be called "Mach bands," and pioneer work on Gestalt phenomena all took place roughly half a century before rediscovery by
others of his own work and its further development.

Ernst Mach acquired a modest scientific reputation long before he
became widely known as a philosopher. Indeed, he never considered
himself a philosopher, denied he had a system, and preferred to think
of himself as a physicist with an interest in the history and methodology of science. He even considered his epoch-making criticisms of
Newton's ideas on mass and "absolute" space, time, and motion as
basically scientific rather than philosophical in character, in spite of the
close resemblance of his views with those of the eighteenth-century ✓
philosopher George Berkeley. Mach's attitude in this respect profoundly influenced even great scientists into unconsciously adopting
not merely Mach's ideas as a scientific methodology, but more important, Mach's epistemological assumptions. Understandably, when
these scientists finally awoke to the actual character of Mach's philosophical crusade, bitter controversies erupted which tormented Mach's
last years and which have never really ceased.

Mach's later life was a painful Götterdämmerung. The suicides of
Heinrich Mach, his brilliant second son, and of his colleague and
philosophical opponent Ludwig Boltzmann, together with a stroke
that disabled the right half of Mach's body for the final two decades
of his life combined to make him physically unable to meet the storm ✓
of philosophical protest against his ideas which peaked between 1909
and 1911. But answer these criticisms and in the eyes of his followers
triumph over them Mach did. With the aid of his first son, Ludwig

Mach, the seventy-year-old scientist-philosopher launched an unbelievable counteroffensive which included a host of articles and books, all
typed with only one finger of his left hand.

Space limitations have forced me to omit several of the controversies,
including Edmund Husserl's rather one-sided attacks, but I have tried
to detail his wars with the leading physicist of the day, Max Planck,
the most prominent psychologists of the time, Carl Stumpf and Oswald
Külpe, and with the subsequently famous revolutionary Vladimir
Lenin. Mach became embattled on all fronts, and even an early ally,
Albert Einstein, gradually turned against him.

Mach had always supported his own philosophical "theory of relativity," but under the drumfire of constant criticism at the very end
of his days Mach flatly rejected both the atomic theory and Einstein's
physical theory of relativity as "dogmatic." Mach's followers, however,
refused to believe his own words, and since his death in 1916 they have
used one argument or testimony after another to persuade themselves
that Mach "really" accepted atomism and physical relativity. Are their
arguments legitimate? Have they proved their case? If this book can
help provide the answer I will be more than satisfied.

Far from scientific and philosophical disputes lay an idyllic world
of peace and "the general public." For most people "Mach" means
"Mach-I" or "Mach-II"—expressions that became popular in the 1940s
when airplanes first broke the sound barrier. Ernst Mach's most important contribution to experimental physics was his work on shock
waves and his photographs depicting bullets breaking the sound barrier. As with so much of his other work, this investigation took place
many decades before the results were given extensive attention. Mach
first successfully photographed shock waves in 1886. In view of his
importance in the field it is only appropriate that his name has been
applied to so many different aspects of aeronautics and gas dynamics:
for example, "Mach number," "Mach angle," "Mach effect," "Mach
reflection," "Mach stem."

On the other hand, it would be fitting if Ernst Mach the man were
eventually to become better known. Ernst Mach, the philosopher of
science, along with most of his controversial ideas, is still very much
with us, and the time for his comparative anonymity to disappear is
long past due.

To clarify and occasionally criticize Mach's philosophical ideas especially those of a phenomenalistic or Buddhistic drift, I have often

Preface

contrasted his point of view with what I call "common sense." I mean
the representationalist views of Galileo, Boyle, Locke, and Newton—
ideas widely accepted and used by practical people today and the only
epistemology compatible with a reasonable understanding of the process
of perception as accepted by most scientists in the field. I do not mean
by "common sense" either the "Scottish realism" of Thomas Reid and
his allies or G. E. Moore's so-called common-sense philosophy and least
of all contemporary "linguistic analysis" or "ordinary language philosophy." Nor do I equate common sense with "naïve realism." The latter
is primarily presentationalist in epistemology, that is, it identifies the
physical world with sensory objects, while Galilean common sense,
which is what I mean, is representationalist in that it assumes the
validity of the representative or causal theory of perception and identifies the physical world with causal objects and agents that exist outside
all conscious and sensory objects or impressions. It is from this seventeenth-century and practical approach that most of my criticisms are
made.

Followers of Berkeley, Hume, and Kant along with more recent presentationalists such as Mach and Rudolf Carnap have tended to misunderstand representationalist or "common sense" philosophy as if it
were presentationalist and merely used a peculiar linguistic approach.
To understand representationalist philosophy it is necessary to assume,
contrary to Rudolf Carnap, that reference does not imply the existence
of what is being referred to in any way, shape, or form. Galilean "common sense" philosophy, unlike modern presentationalism, assumes that
reference is an intentional act of allowance and is neither a form of
cognition nor in any way subordinate to cognition. In other words,
representationalist philosophy, properly understood, is not merely another "language game" but offers a genuinely different epistemological
approach, and hence has value as a foil with which to compare and
better understand the ideas of presentationalist philosophers such as
Ernst Mach.

Major limitations in this book include insufficient coverage of Mach
as a historian of science and of his influence on very recent work in
philosophy and science. My excuse is partly the technical nature of
many of these problems, partly space considerations, and partly a desire not to criticize living philosophers. A second limitation concerns
my very sketchy treatment of the "Mach principle." In astronomy it

has become an issue of major proportions, but frankly, as understood in modern discussions it has very little to do with Mach's original conception. Even more spurious are philosophical uses of this term and the so-called Mach criterion, both of which curiously relate Mach's views to the hypothesis-deduction-verification approach to science which Mach firmly rejected!

In light of Joachim Thiele's remarkable bibliography of Ernst Mach's works (over 400 entries), and in view of my own space problems I have decided not to attempt an exhaustive bibliography, but instead to complement Thiele's list by providing a select, not a complete, bibliography. I refer to every source read on Mach which has substantially aided the writing of the original dissertation and this published version, not to every source used, much less to every source perused or known.

A second point of clarification concerns the use of publication titles in the main text. Since some readers may not know German or other languages I have tried to put in English all book titles that appear in the main body of the work. Important books and articles on Mach are also given in the original language of publication in the footnotes, bibliography, or both.

I am deeply indebted to many individuals and institutions for helping me to improve the quality of this book.

I would like to acknowledge, above all, the advice and assistance of my parents, Brigadier General and Mrs. P. G. Blackmore, my doctoral advisor Dean John G. Burke, and Professor Emeritus Otto Blüh. Without them this book would never have been written.

I wish to acknowledge the receipt, use, and value of a National Science Foundation Grant for archive research in Europe. Without that opportunity it would have been very difficult or impossible for me to rely heavily on primary source material.

I also wish to express my appreciation to the other members of my doctoral board who kindly and wisely advised me on what to add and delete from my original manuscript: Professors Truesdell Brown, Raymond Fisher, Francis Crowley, and Wade Savage.

I would like to acknowledge the indispensable cooperation of Ernst Mach's living relations, in particular, Frau Anna Karma Mach and Dr. Ernst Anton Lederer. Their kindness with respect to documents and photographs is most appreciated.

I am deeply indebted to a number of prominent historians and philosophers of science for their willingness to read and criticize my manuscript: Stephen Brush, Gerald Holton, Max Jammer, Friedrich von Hayek, and Martin Klein.

Most welcome has been the complete cooperation of the Ernst-Mach-Institut in Freiburg im Breisgau, Germany. Led by Frank Kerkhof and Wolfgang Merzkirch, they have made their vast collection of Mach documents and correspondence available for examination and study. I remember my months there with marked pleasure.

I further wish to express my unreserved thanks to the large number of ladies and gentlemen whom I interviewed concerning their remembrances and/or ideas on Ernst Mach and his colleague the philosopher and kinetic theorist Ludwig Boltzmann: Josip Boncelj, Engelbert Broda, Rudolf Carnap, Dieter Flamm, Lili Hahn, Viktor Kraft, Victor Lenzen, L. B. Loeb, E. S. Pearson, and Hans Thirring.

Nor can I overlook the generous assistance given me by the entire staff of the reference desk of the Research Library at the University of California, Los Angeles, between 1967 and 1971, in particular Mrs. Ann T. Hinckley. I also wish to thank Dr. Horst Müller of the Universitäts Bibliothek der technischen Universität Berlin-Hochschularchiv; Dr. Paul Geyer, Stadtsarchivar Stadthaus Zürich, Helen Dukas, Einstein Archive, Institute for Advanced Study, Princeton, New Jersey; and the following libraries: Center for Research Libraries (Chicago), Houghton Library (Harvard), Bancroft Library (Berkeley), Open Court Archive (Southern Illinois University, Carbondale, Ill.), Jacques Loeb Archive (Library of Congress, Washington D.C.), Physics Department Library (Zagreb, Yugoslavia), The Historical Institute, Archive of the Academy, Archive of Czech Literature, and the Central State Archive (all in Prague, Czechoslovakia), Hugo Dingler Institut für methodologische Forschung (Munich), Die österreichische Akademice der Wissenschaften, österreichische National Bibliothek, and österreichisches Staatsarchiv (all in Vienna), and the Akademie-Archiv, deutsche Akademie der Wissenschaften (East Berlin). I am further indebted to the staffs of the following university libraries: Bonn, Cologne, Oslo, Copenhagen, Freiburg, Hamburg, Munich, Graz, and Vienna. I also appreciate the assistance of the National Museum in London.

I feel very fortunate and grateful for the valuable aid and advice of a number of excellent Mach scholars: Joachim Thiele, Erwin Hiebert, Friedrich Herneck, Dieter Herrmann, Robert Cohen, Peter Bergmann,

Elek Tibor, Bela Juhos, Theodore Kneupper, Floyd Ratliff, Jaroslav Pachner, Josef Mayerhöfer, and Raymond T. Seeger.

During my visits to Vienna and Prague many people were instrumental in helping me to find the type of source or firsthand information I was looking for. These considerate and knowledgeable guides include Dr. Neider, Dr. Julius Kroczek, Irena Seidlerová, the family Pfeiferova, Dr. Havranek, and Dr. Strouhal.

In order to be more accurate in my work I often found it necessary to correspond with experts and eyewitnesses about particular events or with people who had important correspondence in their possession or who knew where it was. Among such people I would like to especially thank Herbert Feigl, Martha Dingler, Josef Sajner, Karl Przibram, Eugene Freeman, and Helga S. Hacker.

Let me acknowledge my appreciation to the following magazines and publishing companies for the use of quotations from articles or books: *Journal of Chemical Education, Psychological Review, Synthèse, Boston Studies in the Philosophy of Science, Philosophia Naturalis, The Personalist, Isis, American Journal of Physics, Physikalische Blätter, Physics Today, Bulletin of the Atomic Scientists, Journal of the History of Ideas,* George Allen and Unwin Limited, Rowohlt, Akademische Druck und Verlaganstalt Graz, Verlag Wissenschaft und Politik, Simon and Schuster, Inc. Harvard University Press, Springer Verlag, Dell Publishing Company, Holden-Day, McGraw-Hill Book Company, Little, Brown & Company, The Open Court Publishing Company, Prentice-Hall, Appleton-Century-Crofts, Doubleday & Company Inc., Praeger Publishers, Harper & Row Publishers, Alfred A. Knopf Inc., The Macmillan Company, The Johns Hopkins Press, The American Philosophical Society, Princeton University Press, Abelard-Schumann Ltd., State University of New York Press, Southern Illinois University Press, and Oxford University Press.

I would like to thank the Austrian National Library of Vienna, the German Museum in Munich, Holden-Day Publishing Company and Miss Nancy Martsch for permission to use selected photographs and diagrams.

And finally, I want to express my gratitude to Mrs. Eleanor Little for typing the final version of this work as a dissertation and to Mrs. Teresa Joseph for editing the copy being prepared for publication.

John T. Blackmore

Los Angeles, May 2, 1971

An Abbreviated Mach Genealogy

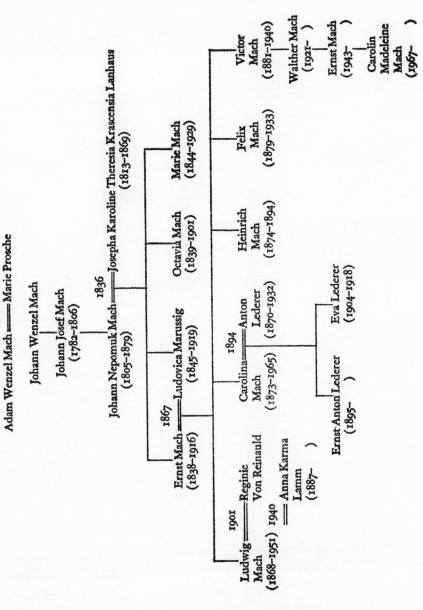

Adam Wenzel Mach ══ Marie Prosche
1688

Johann Wenzel Mach

Johann Josef Mach
(1782–1806)

Johann Nepomuk Mach ══ Josepha Karoline Theresia Krascensia Lanhaus
(1805–1879)   1836   (1813–1869)

Ernst Mach ══ Ludovica Marussig   Octavia Mach   Marie Mach
(1838–1916) 1867 (1845–1919)   (1839–1901)   (1844–1929)

Ludwig ══ Reginie   Carolina ══ Anton   Heinrich   Felix   Victor
Mach   Von Reinauld   Mach   1894 Lederer   Mach   Mach   Mach
(1868–1951) 1940   (1873–1965) (1870–1932) (1874–1894)   (1879–1933) (1881–1940)
         ══ Anna Karma
            Lamm
            (1887–   )

Ernst Anton Lederer   Eva Lederer   Walther Mach
(1895–   )   (1904–1918)   (1921–   )

                                                                               Ernst Mach
                                                                               (1943–   )

                                                                               Carolin
                                                                               Madeleine
                                                                               Mach
                                                                               (1967–   )

Chronology

1838	Born in Chirlitz/Chrlice, Moravia
1840	Moves to Untersiebenbrunn east of Vienna.
1853	Attends secondary school in Kremsier/Kroměříž, Moravia.
1855–1860	Attends the University of Vienna.
1861–1864	Privatdozent in Vienna.
1864–1867	Professor of mathematics and physics (1866) at the University of Graz in Styria.
1867	Marries Ludovica Marussig in Graz.
1867–1895	Professor of experimental physics at the University of Prague.
1868–1881	Birth of four sons and one daughter.
1879–1880	Rector of the University of Prague.
1882–1883	The University of Prague split into German and Czech institutions.
1883–1884	Rector of the German University of Prague until his resignation in January 1884.
1886	First photograph of projectile shock waves.
1886–1919	Publication of physics textbooks used in German and Austrian secondary schools.
1890	Co-editor of educational journal.
1894	Suicide of Heinrich Mach.
1895–1901	Professor of philosophy at the University of Vienna.
1898	Stroke permanently paralyses the right half of his body.
1901	Official retirement from university position and appointment to the Austrian House of Peers.
1901–1913	Lives in retirement in Vienna.

1908   Max Planck's first public attack on Mach.

1909   Vladimir Lenin's book *Materialism and Empirio-Criticism* criticizes Mach's phenomenalism and philosophy of science.

1909–1913   Mach-Einstein correspondence.

1913   Moves from Vienna to Vaterstetten, Bavaria.

1913   Mach attacks Einstein's theory of relativity in the preface to a posthumously published book (1921).

1916   Death from heart disease.

Abbreviations

WORKS BY ERNST MACH

(Arranged chronologically by date of original manuscript completion or book publication)

MANUSCRIPTS

1880 Auto.   A four-page, handwritten autobiographical manuscript. Austrian Academy of Sciences, Vienna.

1910 Auto.   A seven-page, typed autobiographical manuscript. Open Court Archive, Southern Illinois University Library, Carbondale, Ill.

1913 Auto.   A thirteen-page, typed autobiographical manuscript. German Academy of Sciences, East Berlin.

GERMAN BOOKS

EDA   *Die Geschichte und die Wurzel des Satzes von der Erhaltung der Arbeit.* Prague, 1872.

Mechanik   *Die Mechanik in ihrer Entwicklung historisch-kritisch dargestellt.* (Leipzig, 1883).

Beiträge   *Beiträge zur Analyse der Empfindungen.* Jena, 1886.

PW   *Die Principien der Wärmelehre.* Leipzig, 1896.

PWV   *Populär-wissenschaftliche Vorlesungen.* Leipzig, 1896.

Analyse   *Die Analyse der Empfindungen.* Jena, 1900.

E & I   *Erkenntnis und Irrtum.* Leipzig, 1905.

K & M   *Kultur und Mechanik.* Stuttgart, 1915.

Leitgedanken	*Die Leitgedanken meiner naturwissenschaftlichen*
Sinnliche Elemente	*Erkenntnislehre und ihre Aufnahme durch die Zeitgenossen. Sinnliche Elemente und naturwissenschaftliche Begriffe.* Leipzig, 1919.
Optik	*Die Prinzipien der physikalischen Optik.* Leipzig, 1921.

Books translated into English

SOM	*The Science of Mechanics.* Chicago, 1893.
PSL	*Popular Scientific Lectures.* Chicago, 1895.
CAOS	*Contributions to the Analysis of Sensations.* Chicago, 1897.
S & G	*Space and Geometry.* Chicago, 1906.
COE	*History and Root of the Principle of the Conservation of Energy.* Chicago, 1911.
AOS	*The Analysis of Sensations.* Chicago, 1914.
POPO	*The Principles of Physical Optics.* London, 1926.

OTHER ABBREVIATIONS

Symposium	*Symposium aus Anlass des 50. Todestages von Ernst Mach—veranstaltet am 11/12 März 1966 vom Ernst-Mach-Institut Freiburg im Breisgau.* Freiburg, 1967.

Publications of the Austrian Academy of Sciences

SW	*Sitzungsberichte der kaiserlichen Akademie der Wissenschaften.* Mathematisch-naturwissenschaftliche Classe. Vienna.
SW—Almanach	*Almanach der kaiserlichen Akademie der Wissenschaften.* Vienna.
SW—Anzeiger	*Anzeiger der kaiserlichen Akademie der Wissenschaften.* Mathematisch-naturwissenschaftliche Classe. Vienna.

PART I 1838–1895

CHAPTER 1

Childhood

I

The earliest known members of the Mach family were German-speaking peasants from the mountains north of Prague in the old Habsburg crown land of Bohemia.[1] The traditional family home was house number 64 in the town of Liebenau.[2] While we can trace names back to the marriage of Adam Wenzel Mach in 1688, perhaps the first interesting figure was Ernst Mach's grandfather, Johann Josef Mach. This enterprising young peasant not only worked the family holdings but also bettered himself, partly by becoming a wealthy weaving master and partly by marrying Johanna Hörbe (1804), the daughter of a local probate judge. But two years later, shortly after the birth of a son, tragedy struck. A large fire broke out in Liebenau burning over 150 houses and more than 50 other buildings. The young father joined in the fire fighting, and was so badly burned that he soon died.[3]

According to one story, the wealthy widow was much sought after and finally married a nobleman from an established Bohemian family with the name of Jedek or Dedek. But he soon went through her whole fortune while adding three more children to her care. After her death in 1817 the twelve-year-old son born of the first marriage was sent to a Piarist school and apparently was forgotten by all. According to a second story the orphan may have received some of his inheritance but through youthful misadventures supposedly lost it. The child, Johann Nepomuk Mach, was Ernst Mach's father.[4]

Johann Nepomuk prospered at school, receiving marks of "excellent" in all his subjects in the Jungbunzlau Gymnasium until his graduation.[5] In the following year, 1824, he entered the old and renowned Charles-Ferdinand University in Prague. Unfortunately, that very year the government of Prince Metternich had passed a law reducing the philosophy or liberal arts program to a mere two-year preparatory stage for entering the law, theology, or medical faculty; that is, it was no longer possible to receive a doctor's degree in a nonpractical or non-applied field.[6]

Johann Mach studied in the philosophy faculty the allowed maximum of two years. Again he received the grade of "excellent" in all the courses for which we have records. Indeed, he was so proficient that he was awarded an academic scholarship and was excused from paying fees. The variety of subject matter to which he was exposed is revealed by the titles of his classes: Greek, Educational Science, Pure Mathematics, Universal History, Latin, Theoretical Philosophy, Religion, Greek Literature, Physics, Practical Philosophy, Latin Literature, and Applied Mathematics.[7]

Johann Mach's mother had hoped that he would join the Piarist teaching order. On leaving the university he entered his novitiate and began teaching in a Piarist school.

The next ten years of his life were rather obscure; nonetheless, a few stories have survived. Our first tale concerned his future wife. One of his students invited him to spend Christmas Eve (1826) with his family. On seeing the student's sister for the first time Johann Mach was supposed to have said: "If I ever marry, I have today seen my future bride." And ten years later he married her.[8]

A second story was about his long and mysterious *Wanderjahre*. He had journeyed to Vienna with 40 gulden in his pocket to study medicine. On the first evening of his arrival while returning to his lodging he was accosted by a beggar who so moved him that he allegedly gave away all his money. The next morning, penniless in his room, he heard a knock at the door. He had been invited to lunch by a Baron Brethon. The nobleman proposed during lunch that Johann Mach undertake to educate the baron's two sons. Mach's father agreed and continued to teach them until both entered the University of Olmütz several years later.[9]

Johann Mach married Josephine Lanhaus in the village of Turas near Brünn on October 18, 1836. Her father was *Rentmeister* for the archbishop of Chirlitz. Her recent ancestors had been professional people. To support his bride Johann Mach began to look for a teaching post, but his old employer and friend Baron Brethon wanted to retain him, so he stayed on, though whether still in the position of tutor is not clear. This situation, however, created a problem, for Baron Brethon lived in Zlin, some 60 miles to the east, while Josephine stayed with her parents in the archbishop's palace in Chirlitz, a few miles south of Brünn, the capital of Moravia; hence the recently married pair were separated for long periods.

Josephine Mach had an interest in music, painting, and poetry. Her son remembered her as cheerful and gentle. Her youngest daughter, on the other hand, thought her nervous and weak.[10]

II

Ernst Waldfried Joseph Wenzel Mach was born in house number 1 in Chirlitz, that is, in the archbishop's palace, on February 18, 1838, and was christened in the neighboring village of Turas on the same day.[11] He was the first of three children and the only male child, but death long threatened the infant.

Ernst Mach's own story was that his step-grandmother thought he was not being fed enough and insisted on stuffing him between meals when no one was looking. As a result, he became so sick that his life was despaired of. Mach's father, however, who was a tenacious believer in what was called the "Priessnitzian water cure," refused to give up. The "cure" was to wrap Mach in wet sheets that were as cold as possible. Somehow, he survived both the "disease" and the "cure." [12]

Ernst Mach's first memory was of fur-coated men standing in a waiting room. He later determined that he must have been two years old and that the scene took place in the Lundenburg station while the family was moving from Chirlitz to an isolated farm in Untersieben-brunn east of Vienna in 1840.[13] He next remembered two farm experiences: the sun disappearing over a hill and his chasing it up and down from one high meadow to the next until it vanished altogether; and how frightened he was when the elastic seed capsule of a garden balsam plant opened on being pressed and pinched his finger. It had seemed alive, like an animal.[14]

At the age of three Ernst Mach was plagued by perception problems. He had trouble grasping both perspective and shading. He could not understand why tables in pictures had one end wider than the other, when in real life, opposite ends of tables were the same length. Apparently, regardless of how far away an object was, he "saw" it as the same size as when it was close. He also had difficulty understanding the purpose of pictures. Mach wrote: "But that the picture of a table on a plane surface was not to be conceived as a plane painted surface but stood for a table and so was to be imaged with all the attributes of extension was a joke that I did not understand."[15] Nor did Mach even in later years fully abandon his resistance to perspective art. He still tended to consider it misleading and unnatural.

The relation between shadows on sensory objects and shading in pictures completely escaped him. He failed to notice the former and objected to the latter. He considerd shading a pointless distortion and much preferred mere outline abstraction. "When I began to draw I regarded shading as a mere custom of artists. I once drew the portrait of our pastor, a friend of the family, and shaded, from no necessity, but simply from having seen something similar in other pictures, the whole half of his face black. I was subjected for this to a severe criticism, on the part of my mother, and my deeply offended artist's pride is probably the reason that these facts remained so strongly impressed upon my memory."[16]

Ernst Mach also had difficulties with causal explanation: ". . . I myself heard while still a child of four or five the hissing of the sun as it apparently plunged into a pond, and on stating my observation was thereupon laughed at by the grown-ups."[17] And: "When I first came to Vienna from the country as a boy of four or five years, and was taken by my father upon the walls of the city's fortifications, I was very much surprised to see people below in the moat, and could not understand how from my point of view they could have got there, for the thought of another way of descent never occurred to me."[18]

Even though Mach's perceptual and causal confusions were probably rather common for children of that age and his remembering of them not too uncommon, nonetheless, his tenacious retention of many aspects of his childhood understanding does merit some close analysis. A basic cause of this retention probably lay in his isolation and loneliness. Young Ernst and his sisters had no playmates. Their father, who was a tutor in Vienna, was almost always gone. There was virtually no contact with neighbors, and visitors rarely came to their house. Even the occasional discourse at home may have tended more to mystify than clarify their relations with the world. They had an old female servant who could tell fascinating fairy tales and who also, like

6

Mach, had great difficulty in recognizing or understanding wall pictures as perspective representations of real three-dimensional objects.[19]
When Johann Mach was home he also compounded some of young Ernst's bewilderment by amusing the children with demonstrations of magic and by his own excellent storytelling. One consequence of this was that when Ernst Mach had his own children he forbade them to be taught fairy tales.[20]

He remembered a first major step in his escape from noncomprehension in a windmill experience:

If we call to remembrance our early youth, we find that the conception of causality was there very clearly, but not the correct and fortunate application of it. In my own case, for example—I remember this exactly—there was a turning point in my fifth year. Up to that time I represented to myself everything I did not understand—a pianoforte, for instance—as simply a motley assemblage of the most wonderful things, to which I ascribed the sound of the notes. That the pressed key struck the chord with the hammer did not occur to me. Then one day I saw a windmill.[21]

We [Ernst and his sister Octavia] had to bring a message to the miller. Upon our arrival the mill had just begun to work. The terrible noise frightened me, but did not hinder me from watching the teeth of the shaft which meshed with the gear of the grinding mechanism and moved on one tooth after another. This sight remained until I reached a more mature level, and in my opinion, raised my childlike thinking from the level of the wonder-believing savage to causal thinking; from now on, in order to understand the unintelligible, I no longer imagined magic things in the background but traced in a broken toy the cord or lever which had caused the effect.[22]

That Mach had developed a form of causal explanation was clear, but the particular kind has given the impression of having been within the context of his "childhood phenomenalism." For example, he mentioned the experience once again in a letter: ". . . an accident, the looking at a windmill from the inside, first taught me causal thinking, or more exactly functional thinking." [23] This qualification was critical. When the adult Ernst Mach approved of "causal explanation," he meant constant relations between sensory appearances, relations that he believed could best be expressed in terms of mathematical functions. When he opposed "causal explanation," as he normally did, he meant appealing to transphenomenal "laws" or "entities," which in terms of his ontology simply did not exist.

Mach's aversion to the notion of force was both ontological and ethical and was grounded in his childhood upbringing and health. Mach was physically weak, frequently ill, engaged in no contact sports, is not known to have been physically punished, and always disliked military "heroes" and people who triumphed by "force."

The practical consequence of his preference for "functional" over force-oriented explanation was to dispose Mach toward mathematics and science and away from narrative history and the humanities. Looking for contrast relations was fine for trying to understand idealized types of happenings or for understanding particulars as examples of types, but in history, the humanities, and practical life, explanation meant not laws or constant relations but discovering the most important variables or swing factors understood as particular agents or forces at particular places and times. For common sense, forces were causes. For many scientists, laws or functions were causes.

III

Johann Mach introduced his son to science when the boy was seven years old, but the introduction was effected so well that young Ernst remembered it with pleasure for the rest of his life. First, his father showed him an empty flowerpot and asked him what was in it. The boy, somewhat disconcerted by the question, answered: "Nothing." Then his father put a small cork in the hole in the bottom and told Ernst to push the pot face down into the water of a nearby rain barrel. When the pot was some distance under the water the cork popped out and air bubbles came up. In this way Ernst Mach learned about the existence of air and the nature of air pressure.[24]

Mach's father carried out other simple experiments with a tumbler and a garden tub, equally clear, and equally fascinating to the young boy. Ernst became so interested that he soon began to experiment on his own, but not always with sufficient care. For example, he once tested camphor to see if it would burn. The result was singed eyebrows.

Mach was equally attracted to mathematics, and indeed, progressed so rapidly he soon could be left to learn on his own. At eight, he overheard another of his father's pupils, a boy of fourteen, learning algebra and picked up a lot just listening to them, though he later admitted his comprehension had been incomplete and superficial.[25]

Ernst Mach began his classical, humanistic education at the Benedictine Gymnasium in Seitenstetten west of Vienna in 1847. The nine-year-

8

old child, however, did not fare well. In particular, he had difficulty learning Greek and Latin grammar. Declensions and conjugations were simply too hard. He especially remembered resisting the sentence "Initium sapientiae est timor domini" (the beginning of wisdom is the fear of God). The only class he later recalled with pleasure was geography, which seemed easy to him. Indeed, he later claimed: "Even now I have the forms of the continents so well in my head, that without ever having studied geography again I can still carry out imaginary trips without a map." [26]

The Benedictine fathers considered him completely without talent ("sehr talentlos") and literally unteachable. They allowed him to pass the year, but recommended that he learn a trade or be prepared for a business career. Mach later admitted that under the circumstances it was a correct judgment, and that he would never have made a good jurist or paragraph-memorizer such as many of his colleagues became.[27]

Johann Mach, deeply upset, took his son home, and shortly began the toughest and most significant turoring job of his life. He began to teach his son Greek, Latin, history, the elements of geometry, and algebra, and when progress was slow he often shouted at him "Norse brains!" or "Head of a Greenlander!" [28] With gruesome difficulty the boy learned. Eventually, when able to read the classics with some fluency, and after he discovered that all ancient works were not merely about aggressive kings and war, Ernst actually came to enjoy some of them. He also eagerly listened to his father's stories about Archimedes, Vitruvius, and other early scientists. In the long run, Mach was to read through a vast part of classical literature, indeed much more than would have been likely in a regular school. Wilhelm Jerusalem, who taught Classical philology for many years, said of him: "How astounding it was to be shown that the physicist and physiologist, Mach, was better acquainted with the old classics than many a specialist." [29]

Judging from Ernst's later excellent grasp of French and English and from the fact that his youngest sister Marie later taught French—even though she never attended school a day in her life—it is highly likely that Johann Mach also taught his children modern languages as well as "dead" ones.

Indeed, it was a family habit to read foreign novels to one another at night, though whether in the original language is not clear. Marie Mach recalled: "Also winter had its agreeable hours. In the evening after our frugal night meal father would read aloud. I was taken to bed early because I was still too young to understand anything. I would then press myself into my pillow and be as still as possible and would not lose even a single word of what was read. I was given the most pleasure by *Tales of a Grandfather from Scottish History* by Sir Walter Scott." [30]

IV

Johann Mach had become a "freethinker," and his son accepted similar views as a matter of course.[31] Both disliked the post-1848 "clerical-reactionary" political regime in Austria. To escape such "oppression" Ernst Mach asked his father to have him apprenticed to a cabinetmaker for two years so that he would have a trade when he emigrated to America, "the land of my deepest longing." [32] His father acquiesced, so that for two full days every week for more than two years Ernst learned cabinetmaking from a skilled master in a neighboring village. Mach remembered this time with pleasure. He came to enjoy working with his hands, and the tired feeling at the end of the day, often coupled with visions of flying machines and other future inventions, was quite agreeable. Also, much that he learned came in handy when he came to set up his own laboratory in later years.

Mach remembered only shortly afterward a turning point in his philosophical development: "I have always felt it as a stroke of special good fortune, that early in life, at about the age of fifteen, I lighted, in the library of my father, on a copy of Kant's *Prolegomena to Any Future Metaphysics.* The book made at the time a powerful and in-effaceable impression upon me, the like of which I never afterward experienced in any of my philosophical reading." [33]

Before continuing with young Mach's views, let me clarify three different epistemological positions that must be understood in order to obtain perspective in understanding the development of Mach's philo-sophical ideas. Most people normally behave as *naïve realists,* describing nature in presentationalist terms (apparent physical objects are physical objects) and explaining in representationalist terms (innate forces are causes). Most people's best or most consistent understanding, or what I call "common sense" in this book, is *causal realism* which is representationalist in both description and explanation (conscious experience provides evidence and allows us to infer the characteristics of physical objects and causes that lie entirely outside conscious experience). *Phenomenalism* is presentationalist in both description and explanation. Like causal realism it identifies *apparent* physical objects with sensations, and like naïve realism it is presentationalist in describing nature, but unlike both naïve and causal realism it rejects causes as forces or agents in favor of explanation in terms of "laws," "mathematical functions," or "regular sequences of events."

Mach claimed that Kant ended his "naïve realism," but in fact, Mach had never accepted the naïve realist's approach to causal explanation in the first place. What Kant did was merely to change Mach's particular form of epistemological presentationalism from a sense-physical-objects to a sense-sensations identification. In short, Kant helped overthrow those aspects of naïve realism which Mach had only incompletely or reluctantly accepted as improvements over his "childhood phenomenalism."

Two or three years after his Kant experience, Mach made an even more overt return to his childhood "solution of noncomprehension" by augmenting his epistemological with an ontological phenomenalism (his theory of cognition with a theory of reality):

"The superfluity of the role played by the 'thing-in-itself' abruptly dawned upon me. On a bright summer day in the open air, the world with my ego suddenly appeared to me as *one* coherent mass of sensations, only more strongly coherent in the ego. Although the actual working out of this thought did not occur until a later period, yet this moment was decisive for my whole view." [34]

v

Ernst Mach made a second attempt to match wits with an Austrian Gymnasium. He passed an entrance examination and in the fall of 1853 was admitted into the sixth class of the Public Piarist Gymnasium in Kremsier, Moravia. He had both social and academic problems. In his own words: "With respect to social relations and the like I must have seemed extremely immature and childish. Apart from my slight talent in this direction, this is to be explained to some extent by the fact that I was fifteen years old before I ever engaged in social intercourse, particularly with students of my own age. . . . At the beginning things did not go especially well, since I lacked all of the school cleverness and slyness which first have to be acquired in these matters." [35] Also, Mach's attitude may have left something to be desired. His al-

Ernst Mach

ready developed strong interest in mathematics and the mathematical sciences influenced him merely to try to endure and survive the rest of his academic subjects. "My dislike of the language disciplines and especially grammar had the result that in spite of considerable fluency in reading the ancient authors I became only an average student." [36] "All in all, I can only say that the direction of my life had already been determined before I entered the public Gymnasium. I felt oppressed by the school and treated it merely as an obstacle, while on the other hand, I must have seemed like an ungrateful object of their endeavors to my teachers." [37]

After two years Mach graduated and received his *Matura* but decided not to emigrate to America. Shortly afterward, his father sold their house in Untersiebenbrunn and with the money bought a farm in what is now the northwestern part of Yugoslavia where he struggled for several years to raise oakleaf-eating silkworms. Unfortunately, the quality of silk was poor and there was no market. As a result, the farm went ever deeper into debt. Josephine Mach died in 1869, and Johann Nepomuk Mach, tutor extraordinary, but stubborn and visionary to the last, died on December 8, 1879.[38]

Young Scientist

I

Ernst Mach entered the University of Vienna in the fall of 1855 where
he was finally free to concentrate on his favorite subjects, mathematics
and physics. Unfortunately, his courses presupposed a knowledge of
integral and differential calculus, and neither introductory classes nor
easy textbooks on the subjects seemed to be available. Self-instruction
and tutoring from his meager 30-gulden allowance per month gradually
enabled him to learn the subjects well enough to keep up with his
courses. Nor was Mach satisfied with his courses. "I never had a
teacher of importance outside of the great dead classical authors, for my
student days preceded almost all of the reforms of the Austrian universities, which had been allowed by Kaiser Franz to go to the dogs.
Since I had no money to attend a German University, I remained a
stranger with respect to all of my professors, an 'outsider,' someone they
mistrusted and against whom they visibly tried to excite mistrust."[1]

Nonetheless, Mach did become skilled in laboratory technique under
Andreas Ritter von Ettinghausen (1796–1878), the successor of the renowned Christian Doppler as head of the Vienna Physical Institute.

Perhaps the most interesting of Mach's professors was the mathematician Josef Petzval (1807–1891). His scientific fame came primarily
through his design of the first achromatic double objective during the
early days of photography. He also lectured on the oscillations of electric bodies. His popular reputation was based largely on his peculiar
manner of living and fearsome manly talents. According to one story
he rented an abandoned monastery and lived there in complete isola-

Ernst Mach

tion, except for his horse which he put in a neighboring room on the same floor. He liked to ride his magnificent Arabian stallion through the streets and parks of Vienna up to the very door of the university lecture hall.[2] He was known as a superior boxer and as the best fencer in the city. He was also considered indolent and rather unapproachable, indeed, far too much so for Mach, who was especially dissatisfied with the state of his own mathematical understanding. Mach was not taught and was never to learn many aspects of advanced mathematics. He later wrote, for example: "Set theory has long been beyond me. The reason goes back to the weakness of my youthful training in mathematics, which, unfortunately, I have never found the opportunity to correct."[3]

II

Mach received his doctorate in 1860 and became a privatdozent or unsalaried lecturer the following year. He wanted above all to study under Franz Neumann (1798–1895) at Königsberg, the physicist who had helped to establish the mathematical laws of the induction of electric currents and who had done research on a dynamic theory of light. But Mach simply lacked the financial means, nor could he even afford to buy the equipment necessary to carry out satisfactory physical experiments in Vienna. Thus financial pressure drove him in two directions: first, to introduce popular, remunerative lectures, and second, to find a way to carry out inexpensive laboratory experiments.

He attempted to solve the first problem by lecturing to the large numbers of medical students in Vienna. For example, in the fall of 1861, besides offering a course in "Methods of Physical Investigation," he taught "Physics for Medical Students" and "Higher Physiological Physics." He was respected as a good teacher, and in 1863 he published some of his lectures under the title *Compendium of Physics for Medical Students*.[4] The book, however, was not a commercial success and soon became a rarity.

In the summer of 1862 Mach gave lectures on "Mechanical Principles and Mechanistic Physics in Its Historical Development," a title that anticipated his later book on the history of mechanics (1883).

Mach developed an increasing interest in physics as applied to physiology and psychology. The reasons for this were severalfold: first,

14

Mach's attraction to Gustav Fechner's recent book *The Elements of Psychophysics* (1860); second, the work of the leading physicists Hermann von Helmholtz and Emil du Bois-Reymond, in physiology and psychology; and third, the presence of outstanding physiologists in Vienna at that time. Mach was especially impressed with the lectures of Professor Ernst Wilhelm von Brücke (1819–1892), the brain physiologist and a close associate of Helmholtz.

Mach's interest in the new field of psychophysics soon resulted in a series of public lectures on the subject which he gave in the winter semester of 1862/1863 and in the summer of 1863. His presentation was a popular success, but in spite of this he soon became quite dissatisfied with his teaching. "Inspired by Fechner's book, I delivered some very bad lectures on the subject [on how the qualitative variety of sensations can arise from the variation of the connections and from mere quantitative differences], the value of my lectures being still further diminished by the fact that I soon came to see that Fechner's theory of formulae of measurement was erroneous."[5] He published the lectures in the form of separate articles scattered through the same issue of a scientific journal in 1863.[6] But again, no stone ever sank with less noise or trace of a ripple; no review, no criticism, nothing.

The winter of 1863/1864, his last semester as a privatdozent, saw a series of Mach lectures on Helmholtz's latest acoustical discoveries. The lectures were titled "Acoustics as the Physical Foundation of Music Theory."[7] But once again, Mach's published lectures, *Introduction to Helmholtz's Theory of Music* (1866), met with no professional recognition. The book simply fell on deaf ears.

III

Mach did not solve his second major problem, finding satisfactory inexpensive laboratory equipment, but by shifting at least part of his experimental interest to physiology he was able to make some progress, even with the most primitive instruments and apparatus or with none at all. Some of Mach's experimental work was quickly successful and gained a measure of recognition; some of it was too far ahead of its time, and the remainder was of minor or transient importance or was unsuccessful. In brief, Mach was concerned with the following approaches and subject areas:

15

A. Oral Suggestions (1860–1864)
   1. Microphotography (1860)
   2. Perceptual sensitivities of the mentally ill (1861)
   3. Why geometrically similar figures are also optically similar (1860s)
B. Experimental Work (1860–1864)
   1. Doppler Theory (1860)
   2. Fechner's logarithmic law (1860)
   3. Construction of an improved blood pressure measuring device (1862)
   4. Molecular behavior of liquids (1862)
   5. Attempts to improve and go beyond Helmholtz's work on acoustics and ear structure (1863–1864)

Microphotography

In Mach's own words:

About 17 years ago [1859–1860] while still a student I discussed a project to develop microphotography [micro *sized* photographs, not microscope photography] with Herr Auer, who at that time was director of the state publishing house, but he rejected it as impractical. . . . under particular circumstances microphotography seems to be a valuable tool for the spread of literary material and as superior to printing as printing is to handwriting. I cannot object to the complaint of lack of practical experience in this field, and that this project cannot be immediately put into practice, because of immense difficulties which are still present. But I cannot reject the idea in principle, since it has developed from my own undeniable needs, of having had a very limited library while having to work on a farm.[8]

It seems clear that Mach anticipated both the need for and the possibility of microfilming. We do not know if either his oral suggestion or his 1876 article contributed to or helped hurry the development of microphotography as applied to reading material; nonetheless, his early support and efforts deserve to be rescued from oblivion. He was clearly a pioneer and well ahead of his time.

Sense Perceptions of the Mentally Ill

Mach suggested that there might be value in examining the perceptual sensitivities of mental asylum patients. He first proposed this before a group of colleagues in 1861 and in the following year before a gathering of the Austrian Society of Doctors.[9] Unfortunately, his idea made little impression at the time.

Geometrically and Optically Similar Figures

Another verbal foray was even less successful—were that possible—though the ideas presented appear today to have been a remarkable anticipation of some of the basic notions of Gestalt psychology. Mach remembered: "Some forty years ago, in a society of physicists and physiologists I proposed for discussion the question, why geometrically similar figures were also optically similar. I remember quite well the attitude taken with regard to this question, which was accounted not only superfluous, but even ludicrous. Nevertheless, I am now as strongly convinced as I was then that this question involves the whole problem of form-vision." [10]

We may add that Mach did not drop the issue, but soon began to write articles on it. Indeed, many of his later books included chapters or at least groups of paragraphs on this subject and on related problems.

The Doppler Theory

Christian Doppler (1803–1853) noticed in 1841 that the frequency of sound waves as measured by pitch changed as the source approached or receded from the listener. Two years later he extended this observation to light waves as measured by changes in color. By 1845 he had generalized what might be called the Doppler theory to all wave motions from moving sources. In 1845 the Dutch meteorologist Buys Ballot had also conducted some railway experiments which seemed to confirm the Doppler effect, at least with respect to sound.

Doppler's colleague, however, the eccentric Professor Josef Petzval, attacked the Doppler theory on theoretical grounds from the standpoint of his own "Law of the Conservation of the Period of Oscillation." He denied the reality of the Doppler effect. Professor Anders Ångström of Uppsala in Sweden also claimed that he was unable to measure the Doppler effect with respect to light.

Shortly after Mach received his doctorate, Von Ettinghausen encouraged him to construct an apparatus that could help settle the Doppler controversy. The young scientist's first attempt failed, but a second apparatus was able to demonstrate the Doppler effect, at least with regard to sound.

This apparatus (diagram 1) "consists of a tube *AA'* 6 feet (183 cm) in length, capable of turning about an axis of BB' at its center. At one end is placed a small whistle or reed *G,* which is blown by wind forced along the axis of the tube. An observer situated in the plane of rotation hears a note of fluctuating pitch, but if he places himself along the axis of rotation, the sound becomes steady." [11] Also, the faster the tube is rotated the greater the difference between the two tones. In this way Mach was able to show that Doppler was right, that the change in pitch varied only with the direction and speed of the sound source, given a stationary listener.

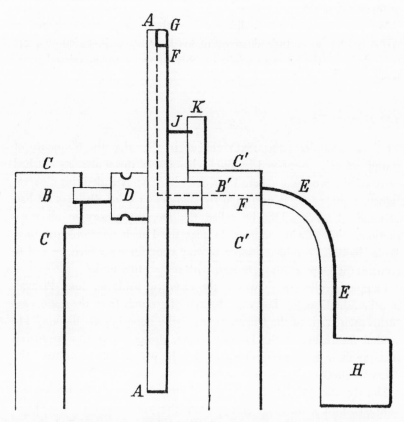

DIAGRAM 1. Ernst Mach's Doppler instrument

Mach's apparatus became a frequently used class demonstration device throughout Central Europe for many years, but this should not be construed to mean that all opposition to Doppler's theory thereby ceased or that there were still not problems with respect to interpreting star colors and color changes.

In any case, Mach was convinced, and he remained an adamant supporter of Doppler's theory for the rest of his life. Meanwhile, however, in the same year, 1860, Petzval renewed his attack. Mach, in his reply, attempted to show that both Doppler and Petzval were right in their opinions, but that Petzval had misunderstood the Doppler theory and the range of application of Petzval's own mathematical "law." In fact, there was no conflict between the two notions at all. Petzval remained obdurate but at least refrained from using all the means at his disposal for settling the controversy. We do not know Von Ettinghausen's reaction to Mach's work, but presumably it was favorable. On the other hand, as we shall see, it was unfortunate that Mach became involved in a conflict between two of his professors in such a way as could easily harm his own academic career.

Mach eventually became a party to other Doppler controversies as well. In the 1870s a Professor Mädler, an astronomer from Dorpat (Tartu) in Estonia, reopened the controversy with blasts at both Doppler's and Mach's ideas. Mach countered by reissuing (1873) his earlier Doppler articles, writing a new one (1878), and by carrying out three public demonstrations. In the dead of winter in 1878 Mach dragged a group of Prague professors and students outside into the cold, sat them on a hill, and made them listen to whistles from approaching and departing trains. On their return they signed prepared statements supporting the Doppler theory.[12] Even as late as 1913, when a scientist had written him a letter asking his opinion on a possible incompatibility between Einstein's special theory of relativity and the Doppler theory, Mach went through the experimental evidence once again in an effort to show that Doppler's ideas were still valid.[13]

Mach also made the first clear proposal to determine the movement of the fixed stars by examining spectral lines, but it must be admitted that he was unaware of Armand Fizeau's prior work in that area.[14] Mach's 1861 suggestion was followed by impressive results in 1889 when Edward Pickering described the first spectroscopic double star Ursa Maioris and H. C. Vogel in 1892 determined the radial components of the peculiar motion of the fixed stars by spectroscopic means.

Ernst Mach

Fechner's Logarithmic Law

Mach read both Gustav Fechner's 1858 paper and his 1860 book attempting to give mathematical expression to Ernst Weber's 1834 law relating physical stimulus to mental response. "Fechner's law" in its mathematical form ran: $S = K \log R$, and in words: *The magnitude of a sensation is proportional to the logarithm of its stimulus.*

If this law was valid, it could help put psychology on a scientific basis and establish a new science, "Psychophysics," the study of relations between psychical and physical phenomena. Mach's interest led to laboratory tests. "My first series of experiments in the summer of 1860 were undertaken above all for the purpose of determining whether the so-called Weber Law of Fechner was also valid for the perception of time." [15]

By the fall of 1860 he had set up an experiment that seemed capable of giving decisive results. "Two pendulums of variable lengths were so arranged, that I could only see them behind each other. Both . . . had their lengths gradually changed until I noticed the difference in the duration of the swings. It then became clear that the first noticed difference in the time of the swings was proportional to the overall time." [16]

This result increasingly bothered Mach until he finally concluded that it was sufficient to refute the law. Later, Mach's switch from Fechner's version of "psychophysical parallelism" to his own served as confirmation. The relation between "physical" stimulus and "mental" responses was not logarithmic but merely proportional, nor was it subject to exact mathematical measurement.

Measuring Blood Pressure

Carl Ludwig, one of Brücke's physiological colleagues in Vienna, constructed the first "Kymograph," an instrument to record blood pressure, in 1847.[17] Vierordt and Étienne Marey developed a "Sphygmograph" as an improvement on that. In early 1862, Mach, perhaps with the encouragement of Ludwig himself, attempted to make still further improvements, but was only partly successful. He was unable to find a needle both firm and flexible enough to measure accurately pulse beats and changes in blood pressure on a graph. While he considered

Mach followed Brücke and
Ludwig

his testing sufficient to justify recommending Marey's Sphygmograph
to medical doctors, nonetheless, he hoped that less complicated instruments could be developed in the future, in particular, devices that relied
more on photographed wave patterns and less on frequently untrue
and easily disturbed needle wanderings.

Molecular Behavior of Liquids

To understand more about blood pressure and circulation Mach experimented on forcing liquids through tubes. Unfortunately, however, the
fluid simply moved too fast to be measured satisfactorily with his own
primitive equipment. Furthermore, his attempt to understand liquid
motion in terms of the movement of molecules also went astray. In
particular, he failed in his effort to identify chemical elements by means
of spectral lines. This experimental failure was later used by Mach as
an argument against the utility of the atomic theory.[18]

Acoustics and Ear Structure

Mach gravitated toward these fields by following the interests of
Brücke and Ludwig, and the recently published work of Helmholtz.
He apparently hoped to compensate for his lack of anatomical knowledge by his keen sense of observation and his command and knowledge
of music. He was, to say the least, optimistic. He later wrote: "I should
like to close with a reminiscence from the year 1863. Helmholtz's *Sensations of Tone* had just been published and the function of the cochlea
now appeared clear to the whole world. In a private conversation which
I had with a physician, the latter declared it to be an almost hopeless
undertaking to seek to fathom the function of the other parts of the
labyrinth, whereas I in youthful boldness maintained that the question
could hardly fail to be solved, and that very soon, although of course I
had then no glimmering of how it was to be done." [19]

IV

Ernst Mach formed two close and long-lasting personal friendships at
this time, one with Josef Popper-Lynkeus and the other with Eduard
Kulke.

Edmund Reitlinger, a Vienna privatdozent in physics, introduced

Ernst Mach

Mach to Popper-Lynkeus in 1862. The friendship immediately took hold. Josef Popper ("Lynkeus" was a literary pseudonym referring to the mythical helmsman of the *Argonaut*) soon became Mach's first and for a long time his only known philosophical ally, and this in spite of the fact that both men had very different personalities. Mach was normally modest, careful, and unemotional, while Popper was notoriously enthusiastic, imaginative, and polemical. Nonetheless, they shared numerous interests and both men made significant contributions to a variety of fields.

Josef Popper (1838–1921) was Jewish and graduated from a Technical Hochschule in Prague before they were recognized as academically equal to universities. Overcoming numerous obstacles, however, he became a successful inventor and original theoretician. He is perhaps best known today for his ideas of a guaranteed annual wage and government labor service for the unemployed. He also wrote books and articles on physics, mathematics, aeronautics, machine technology, Voltaire, anti-Semitism, Tolstoy, Goethe, human rights, and individualism.

Popper was probably responsible for extending Mach's interest in social reform, in Voltaire, and in the Enlightenment. Two of Popper's better-known admirers from a later period were Albert Einstein and Theodor von Kármán.

Mach's second major friendship began as follows:

I became acquainted with Kulke, who was then a journalist and music critic for a large newspaper, in 1863, and quite by accident. In the Cafe Griensteidl some musicians, who were sitting at a nearby table, were arguing over a mysterious and beloved topic: What were the real characteristics of musical tones? Someone observed my interest and drew me into the discussion. I took Kulke's side, who had represented his views in a clear and sober way. From then on we saw each other almost daily, until about a year later when my profession took me to Graz. . . . Our friendship lasted for 34 years until Kulke's death on March 20, 1897. I never came to Vienna without looking up Kulke and joining his circle of friends, every member of which knew how to unite a cheerful conception of life with serious goals, and who all became my friends.[20]

Eduard Kulke (1831–1897) was also of Jewish ancestry as were many of Mach's "freethinking" friends. He was known chiefly as a music critic and theorist and as the author of *On the Transformation of Melody* (1884) and *Critique of the Philosophy of Beauty* (1906). Under the influence of Darwin's ideas, Mach encouraged Kulke to write a book on how there was also a "survival of the fittest" in music. Kulke obliged and published a work in 1868 with which, however, he was not satisfied.[21]

A fragment from an undated article by Ludwig Karpath during the 1930s has supplied the information missing in Mach's own account, namely, the prominence of his own role in Kulke's group.

A close relative has told me a lot about a Vienna coffeehouse which I can no longer remember, the "Cafe Elefant," which was located in a narrow passage between Stephen's Place and the Graben.

Every day, scholars, artists, and doctors of medicine and law would gather together. The regulars [Stammgaesten] included such later famous people as Professor Mach, Lynkeus (Popper), a group of Wagner-oriented musicians: Peter Cornelius, Heinrich Porges, the music critic Graf, the composer Goldmark, and many others.

People wandered in around 2 P.M. and stayed until 2 in the morning, that is, some were always leaving while others were arriving. Unbroken wit and argument on philosophical, scientific, and artistic matters kept the discussion sharp and stimulating.

To a certain extent the young Dozent Ernst Mach presided over the gathering. His profound understanding and reflective manner impressed everyone. According to my relative he was one of the first to occupy himself deeply with the recently published work of Helmholtz on tone perceptions about which he formed many interesting and instructive conclusions.[22]

v

It is possible, however, that Mach was not making friends in the right places. So long as Von Ettinghausen was in active charge of the Physical Institute all went well. Indeed, in 1861/1862 Mach's former teacher even became Rector of the university, but this favorable situation came to a rather abrupt and unexpected end. In 1862, the sixty-six-year-old Von Ettinghausen became ill. An acting head of the Institute was needed, someone who if he did well might be in line to get both a university chair and the Institute job permanently. The leading candidates for the temporary post were all privatdozents at the Institut. The three with the best chances were Josef Stefan, Ernst Mach, and Edmund Reitlinger. But Reitlinger's health was already failing. This left Stefan and Mach.

On the face of it, Stefan had the more imposing credentials. He was three years older. Mach was only twenty-four. Stefan had already been elected a corresponding member of the Austrian Academy of Science, the most important scientific society in the country, while Mach had not been elected to anything. Stefan got along better with most of the Vienna science professors, in particular with Petzval. Mach dedicated his textbook, *Compendium of Physics for Medical Students,* to Von Ettinghausen, but this one academic ally or would-be ally was not enough. Mach's rival won; that is, Stefan became acting chief of the Physical Institute while Von Ettinghausen remained the legal head.

Josef Stefan (1835–1893) was born in Klagenfurt in southern Austria of poor, illiterate Slovenian parents. As a gymnasium student he published Slovenian poetry. His best-known physical contributions were to be in radiant energy and in electrotechnology. The major significance of his victory over Mach was that it brought an end to the Doppler, Ettinghausen, and Mach approach to physics in Vienna and replaced it with the attempt of Stefan's associates, Josef Loschmidt and Ludwig Boltzmann, to introduce the atomic theory into all branches of physics. Stefan's triumph meant that for the next thirty years the University of Vienna was to be an atomistic stronghold in physics, and that if Mach and his point of view were to prosper they would have to do so elsewhere. Vienna physics had found a new orientation.

Ernst Mach's difficult financial situation and understandable emotional depression were relieved about a year later: "By a happy accident I was appointed in 1864 to fill the vacancy in the chair of mathematics in the then somewhat neglected University of Graz at a salary of ten hundred and fifty gulden. This appointment came just as my strength was almost to fail me, but I now soon recovered when thus relieved from actual want and privation." [23]

VI

Mach taught in Graz, the capital of the Austrian province of Styria, from 1864 to 1867. Remembering his own difficulties in learning calculus by self-instruction and tutoring, he started by giving introductory lectures in integral and differential calculus. During the next three years he taught a variety of courses in mathematics, physics, physiology, and psychology. His winter 1864/1865 lecture series "The Elements of Psychophysics" attracted a large audience, including many of the university professors.[24]

24

Young Scientist

Since Mach published no articles on mathematics or mathematical theory, but a great many on experimental physics and physics applied to experimental psychology and physiology, it was clear where his interests lay. Hence, when an opportunity developed to exchange his mathematics for a physics chair in early 1866, Mach readily accepted it.

It would be hard to exaggerate Mach's pleasure at finally obtaining his own laboratory and having enough money to afford more satisfactory equipment. From 1864 to 1867 he was able to publish three books and twenty-seven articles.[25] Most of his work, however, was only a continuation of earlier research and was not to reach fruition for many years. His most important scientific discovery during this period was what are now called "Mach bands," psychological phenomena that only recently have begun to receive the attention they deserve.

Mach's two most significant philosophical personal contacts while at Graz were with Gustav Fechner and Emmanuel Herrmann. Fechner's philosophical and psychological ideas largely inspired Mach to write a psychology book and to dedicate it to the Leipzig professor. An inconclusive correspondence between the two men was gradually supplemented by personal meetings.[26] The negative reaction of Fechner to many of Mach's ideas so badly discouraged him that he put the manuscript (*Analysis of Sensations*) aside for twenty years. The break led Mach into a closer examination of just where his ideas differed from those of Fechner and were in need of increased clarification.

Emmanuel Herrmann (1839–1902) was a privatdozent in what was then called "national-economy." His attempt to see an "economic" aspect in the most disparate fields and actions of life helped Mach clarify his own general theory of "economy." Mach wrote: "Through my intercourse in 1864 with the political economist, E. Herrmann, who, according to his own specialty, sought to trace out the economical element in every kind of occupation, I became accustomed to designate the intellectual activity of the investigator as economical." [27]

We may add that Herrmann was more than just a theorist who influenced Mach's philosophy. He also had practical ideas. Among other things he was known as the inventor of the postcard, whose "economic" function has become familiar to virtually everyone.[28]

CHAPTER 3

Philosophical Development

Mach & Berkeley for long time w/o belief in god

I

We have already touched on Mach's childhood problems in perception and causal explanation, his windmill experience, his reading of Kant's *Prolegomena* at age fifteen, and his first strong suspicion two or three years later on a warm summer day that the world consisted only of sensations. But many problems still needed his attention.

1. How could he relate Darwin's ideas to his phenomenalism?
2. How could he reconcile his use of the atomic theory in physics with phenomenalism?
3. What form of explanation could he use which would be valid in all the sciences?
4. Was phenomenalism solipsistic?
5. What were the logical consequences of ontological phenomenalism on religion?

Most of this chapter is an attempt to show how Mach tried to solve these problems and put some of his doubts to rest.[1]

Mach seems to have done little reading in philosophy as an undergraduate (1855–1860), but from then on he worked on solving the problems enumerated above until about 1875 when he found answers that were to satisfy him in very large measure until his death almost a half century later. He had read George Berkeley, Georg Lichtenberg, and Johann Herbart by the early 1860s. Mach recalled that his views resembled those of Berkeley for some time, though without his belief

26

in God or in a divine causality. He also shared for a while Berkeley's belief in an ego or self not identical with sensations.

Karl Popper wrote an article in 1953 which asserted that Mach's criticisms of Newton's ideas on space and time were very similar to those of Berkeley almost two centuries before. John Myhill reiterated this point in an article in 1957.[2] Karl Menger suggested in his introduction to the 1960 English-language edition of Mach's *Mechanics* that Mach's reticence in discussing Berkeley's influence on his philosophy might have been connected with a desire not to be labeled as an "idealist" or have his ideas condemned merely by such an association.[3] Mach's position is doubly understandable in light of his sincere belief that he had left Berkeley's opinions behind.[4]

Mach claimed that his reading of books by the German philosophers Herbart and Lichtenberg helped him to reach a point of view similar to that of David Hume, whom he was not to read firsthand until the 1880s. Herbart also put forward a number of ideas on which Mach was later to build. He suggested that psychology could be a science and could profitably employ mathematics. He also speculated on multidimensions and on the primary concern of the human soul for self-preservation.

Three events occurred in the year 1860 which were to influence Mach in one direction and most physicists in another. First, Charles Darwin's *Origin of Species* was widely read in Germany and Austria in this year. Second, Gustav Fechner published his *Elements of Psychophysics* and attempted to present a philosophy that would hold for both physical and mental reality. And third, a chemical conference at Karlsruhe heard a speech supporting Amedeo Avogadro's long neglected hypothesis concerning the number of atoms in gaseous molecules.

Mach attempted to use his Darwinian-influenced theory of "economy" to justify his underlying phenomenalism. He argued that only epistemological phenomenalism could give the certainty science needed and that only his theory of economy could ensure the particular collection of certain information (science) that could be of most value for satisfying human biological needs. In short, phenomenalism was justified only insofar as it helped human beings to survive and prosper. Also, except in descriptive statements of "immediately given" sensations, Mach rejected what most people understand by "truth," that is, a reliable correspondence between an assertion and a past, present, or

27

Ernst Mach

future reality or happening. He preferred the pragmatic notion that an assertion was true only to the extent that it satisfied "human purposes," "human biological needs," or contributed to the "survival of the human race or species."[5]

Mach was neither a lover of knowledge in the sense of "knowledge for knowledge's sake" nor a lover of power in the Baconian "knowledge is power" sense. Nor was he even a rigid "survival of the fittest" Darwinian. He rejected the "immoral" features of natural selection in favor of Lamarckian progress via the inheritance of ever more advanced acquired moral and intellectual characteristics. He believed that the survival of human civilization could be accomplished only by rational, educated individuals subordinating their particular purposes to aims beneficial to the species as a whole and that the survival requirements of the species on a civilized level determined morality.[6]

Mach's theory of "economy" played a double role in his philosophy of science. He described the purpose of science as the simplest description of the appearances, but this was merely an internal purpose and an internal application of his theory of "economy." That is, it provided a goal and an orientation for himself and other scientists, but it was merely half the story. He also described the purpose of science as ultimately to help satisfy "biological needs." That is, science's external purpose, and ultimate justification was its Darwinian function of aiding the survival and welfare of the species. And the internal purpose was only justified to the extent that it contributed to the external purpose. Furthermore, Mach's theory of "economy" tended to shift meaning from the "internal" to the "external" purpose. "The simplest possible description of the appearances" tended to make logical simplicity a goal, though the saving of time and effort was surely a desirable means. But the "external" purpose of satisfying biological needs in the simplest or most economical way possible idealized practical efficiency as a goal. In other words, while the influence of Darwin's theory and of Mach's own theory of "economy" permeated his whole philosophy, they were applied in different ways at different points such that the complexity of these two influences in his philosophy should not be underestimated.[7]

The second major 1860 event to influence Mach's philosophy was the publication of Fechner's revolutionary book. His *Psychophysics* seemed not only to put psychology on a scientific basis, but also to eliminate the unwelcome shifting in philosophical assumptions which Mach had felt compelled to make when doing work in physics and then in psychology. Fechner attempted to put forward a scientific methodology which, by assuming only a single kind of reality, might apply to both physics and psychology and to his created field "psychophysics," which had the task of relating "mind" and "body." Fechner claimed that this single type of reality had two "sides," a physical "outside" and a psychological "inside" which were related to each other not by means of interaction but by means of a parallelism of behavior which could be reliably described and understood by means of mathematical equations and functions.[8]

Since the seventeenth-century Cartesian controversy between interactionism and parallelism may come to the reader's mind—and in this case confuse his understanding—some clarification is in order. Descartes's problem concerned the causal relationship between experienceable and nonexperienceable types of reality, while Fechner was interested merely in the relationship between different kinds of conscious appearance, one called "physical" and the other "mental." From Descartes's point of view both of Fechner's "sides" were mental and neither had anything to do with physical reality. Furthermore, Fechner's reliance on mathematical functions to link "mental" and "physical" behavior—precisely because parallelistic—was not genuinely causal at all.

But regardless of what Descartes and his followers might have thought about Fechner and his philosophy, Mach did become enthusiastic about it. Mach later claimed it set him free from "the greatest intellectual discomfort of my life." Also, Fechner's point of view not only justified and encouraged the use of mathematics and physics in solving psychological problems, but it even set up a new field, "psychophysics," which fit exactly the kinds of interests and problems Mach wanted to investigate further. In addition, Fechner reinforced the influence of Herbart on Mach as to the wisdom of using "functional explanation" in place of traditional "force" explanation.

Mach, however, was unable to remain satisfied with Fechner's approach. Not only did he soon question the validity of Fechner's "psychophysical laws," but the monistic character of the Leipziger's theory of reality also began to seem dubious. Was Fechner really a phenomenalist or not? Some of Fechner's other books suggested much more the *Naturphilosoph* than the experimental physicist or psychologist.[9]

Mach finally concluded that Fechner believed not in one kind of reality with two sides, but in three kinds of reality, the two "sides" and the unknowable "metaphysical" something which had the sides. Mach's eventual reaction (1875) was to retain Fechner's parallelism, but with a different meaning, and to identify "mind" and "body" not with different sides or kinds of sensations, but with the way in which the sensations were related.[10] That is, the same sensations could be both "physical" and "mental." In one group of relations an appearance was "physical" and in another "mental."

Perhaps the most interesting aspect of Fechner's influence concerned philosophy of science. Under his spell Mach came to believe that the traditional gulf between "mind" and "body" had been overcome, even to the extent that the future of physics lay in close conjunction with that of psychology.[11] Mach retained his confidence in the legitimacy of "psychophysics" as a science to the end of his life.

The third major 1860 event bearing on Mach's philosophy may have gone almost completely unnoticed by him at the time. Some German chemists had called a conference at Karlsruhe to help solve the problem of element valences. An Italian delegate, Stanislao Cannizzaro (1826–1910), argued that the problem had already been solved almost fifty years before by his countryman Avogadro. A pamphlet which the delegates took home with them was persuasive enough to reopen the issue, with the result that soon Avogadro's ideas were accepted.[12] The success of his law in giving the definitive atomic weights of elements not only led to more support for the atomic theory within chemistry, but also influenced more physicists to take an active interest in chemistry and to try to introduce the atomic theory into more aspects of physics. Eighteen sixty meant Fechner's psychophysics for Mach and the attempt to bring physics and psychology closer together on the basis of a phenomenalistic philosophy, but 1860 meant the rediscovery of Avogadro's law to most other physicists and the need to bring physics and chemistry closer together on the basis of the atomic theory understood in terms of a materialistic or mechanistic philosophy. Mach had long admired Helmholtz as a physicist who had made significant contributions to physiology and psychology, but about 1866 even Helmholtz moved his interests and work back in the direction of bringing physics and chemistry closer together in terms of the atomic theory. Mach became increasingly isolated. For most physicists "elements" were types of minute chemical entities. For Mach "elements" referred

30

Epistemological phenomenalism
" Knowing"?
Can only know ideas & sensations
Also ontological phenomenalist

to Fechner's book *Elements of Psychophysics* and meant types of sensations.

believed in relations

II

Mach has normally been considered a phenomenalist, a sensation as opposed to an "act," "relation," "whole," or "experience" phenomenalist. He avoided the term himself, nonetheless, in more than one sense he was a phenomenalist, hence, the need arises to clarify some distinctions.[13]

Epistemological phenomenalism was the view that we could "know" only ideas and sensations, with the infinitive "to know" sometimes meaning *to experience,* sometimes *to be certain of,* and sometimes an ambiguous mixture of both. People who doubted that we could be absolutely or infallibly certain of anything tended to question the legitimacy of epistemology as a field of study. Mach accepted "knowing" in both senses, as "immediately experiencing" and as "being absolutely certain of." He did not question the legitimacy of epistemology or *Erkenntnistheorie,* and he did restrict knowledge to ideas and sensations, hence, it seems quite just to label Mach an *epistemological phenomenalist.*[14]

Mach was also an *ontological phenomenalist,* that is, he restricted reality to ideas and sensations. He did augment this with a belief in the reality of "relations," but he never clarified what he meant by "relations."[15]

Mach was normally not an *immanent phenomenalist,* that is, he normally did not hold that sensations had to be consciously present to be real, but he was very reluctant to allow talk about "unconscious sensations" in scientific discourse. For example, he expressly rejected Heinrich Hertz's appeal to "hidden motion" as a legitimate approach in physics. Mach defined consciousness not as a quality or as an entity, but merely as a particular kind of relation between sensations. This definition, however, created two serious problems which plagued Mach until his death. First, if consciousness were a relation and could be absent, then sensations could exist unperceived. Mach as mentioned above accepted this conclusion, but he did not like it. Second, if consciousness were a relation, then he would have to leave the term "relation" undefined. For if relations were sensations, then consciousness would be a sensation, which was either a contradiction or at best involved a circular argument. On the other hand, if relations were not

31

sensations, then Mach was faced, if not with an unwanted ontological dualism, at least with having to shift from a "sensation" to a more inclusive "experience" form of phenomenalism.

Mach was frequently if not normally a *referential phenomenalist,* that is, unlike Kant and John Stuart Mill who were also epistemological phenomenalists, Mach often assumed that it was only possible to refer "meaningfully" either to what was being consciously experienced or to what could be consciously experienced. In short, reference implied existence, at least sensational or phenomenal existence. This point of view was in very sharp contrast with the everyday opinion that we could refer to anything real or unreal, experienceable or not experienceable, past, present, or future, and so on, that reference in no way implied existence.

In practice Mach alternated so often between referential phenomenalism and a common sense approach to reference that most of the key terms in his philosophy were defined in at least two different ways, making sense only when the proper theory of reference was used. For example, critical terms like "fact," "metaphysics," and "atom" all had double definitions depending upon the theory of reference used at the time.

A *fact* for Mach was normally a conscious sensation, that is, when he was following his referential phenomenalism, but a *fact* was simply a historical happening, not necessarily conscious or even experienceable, when using an everyday or common sense theory of reference. The most regrettable feature of this particular double definition was that he applied it in a misleading way with respect to how other people used the term. For example, Mach frequently criticized Newton for not living up to his intention to deal only with the "facts." But clearly, Mach, presupposing his referential phenomenalism, not only himself meant facts as conscious sensations, but falsely supposed that Newton intended the word in that sense too, whereas, it seems reasonably evident that Newton meant it in the ordinary sense of a mental or physical happening or a reliable statement about that happening, without anything necessarily being experienceable, a "sensation", or in any way connected with epistemology.[16] In other words, Mach's referential phenomenalism tended to make him foreshorten his understanding of what other people were talking about to conscious sensations, regardless of what those people were under the impression they were talking about.

32

Mach usually defined "metaphysics" in what he supposed was a Kantian sense, that is, as the study of what existed outside experience.[17] But Mach also defined it, when using his referential phenomenalism, as the study of those ideas whose source or history we could not clearly trace.[18] If an idea could not be intelligibly related to the history of other ideas, then it was "metaphysical." And in general, the fewer relations a referent had with other objects or ideas the more "metaphysical" it was. From this definition one could easily understand why Mach considered himself a "relativist" and opposed "absolutes" or what he thought were completely "metaphysical" since they presumably lacked all relations to anything else.

Many scientists, then and now, believed that it was both possible and desirable to eliminate "metaphysics" from science. By "metaphysics" they normally meant speculative, unverifiable theorizing. The more philosophical scientists also tended to use the word as a justification for rejecting the Galilean or common sense purpose of science (i.e., "to understand reality") in favor of Mach's goal of "describing and relating the appearances." We may add here, however, that it was Mach's second definition of "metaphysics" which provided a major justification for his interest in the history of science. That is, if we could make ideas less "metaphysical" by tracing down their historical connections to other ideas, then by all means we should become more historically minded ourselves and should encourage other scientists to become interested in the history of science.[19]

Mach's double definition of the word "atom" has resulted in a great deal of confusion and controversy. It has sometimes been alleged that Mach accepted the atomic theory during the period of his early scientific experiments, that is, between 1860 and 1863, but while there was a sense in which this was true, nonetheless, the assertion has been quite misleading. Mach never believed in the reality of atoms or in the indispensable value of the atomic theory in any normal sense.

In terms of Mach's referential phenomenalism he meant by an atom an idea, that is, a theoretical construct. He foreshortened reference to what could be experienced, and since no one had ever perceived an atom, it must be a mere thought or idea.[20] In other words, when following a phenomenalistic theory of reference, he felt compelled to identify everything talked about with those conscious impressions or sensations which for most people have merely symbolized or imperfectly represented what was being referred to. For most people our idea of an atom is neither the atom nor what we are referring to when we talk about atoms. From the common sense point of view referential phenomenalism has confused symbols with what are symbolized, though to reverse the situation, the referential phenomenalist has claimed that common sense tries to refer to things that in fact could not be referred to.

To be sure Mach "believed" in the reality of atoms as ideas, but this was a trivial sense, and has hardly deserved to be considered a belief in the reality of atoms at all.

Mach's occasional assertions that he did not believe in the reality of atoms has suggested that he was capable of understanding and using a nonphenomenalist theory of reference.[21] The very act of denying the reality of atoms presupposed the legitimacy of reference to what did not exist. For if he could not refer to atoms, then he could not deny their existence. In short, in terms of Mach's second definition of atoms, that is, not as "ideas" but as what lay outside experience, we lack evidence that Mach at any time believed in their reality. And because this has long been the normal or customary use of the word "atom," we may rather flatly state that Mach did not believe in the reality of atoms. (See appendix for a further discussion of Mach's stand on the reality of atoms.)

On the other hand, there was a difference between believing in the reality of atoms and believing in the value or utility of the atomic theory. Mach did believe that the atomic theory as he understood it, or rather misunderstood it, had "provisional value" in science, but except for the period between about 1860 and 1863 he denied that it had permanent value or was indispensable to science.[22] His two major objections were: First, the atomic theory could not be successfully introduced into all the sciences, particularly psychology and the social sciences; and second, it was not as "economical" in terms of describing the appearances as the use of mathematical functions could be.[23] But while we must admit that Mach was an atomist to the extent of allowing that the atomic theory might have transient value in science, nonetheless, even this quasi-support could hardly mean much since Mach meant one thing and most people another. Most people understood the atomic theory as a group of ideas referring to entities outside experience. Mach misunderstood it, as if the theory both was, and merely referred to, a group of ideas. (See appendix for further discussion of physical atomism.)

I have now discussed Mach's ideas to the extent that they could be interpreted in terms of epistemological, ontological, immanent, and referential phenomenalism, but still to be discussed is the most important and influential type of phenomenalism, namely, the phenomenalistic conception of the purpose of science. Galileo helped establish the common sense purpose of science as the most reliable and informative understanding of reality possible.[24] His opponent, Cardinal Robert Bellarmine, presented the phenomenalistic conception by arguing that the purpose of science was merely to describe the appearances in the simplest way possible, and that questions of reality should be left to the church and theology.[25] The essentials of Bellarmine's phenomenalistic position were revived by Berkeley, Hume, and Kant, and were introduced into the social sciences by the founder of "Positivism," Auguste Comte, and into physics primarily by Ernst Mach. The point of greatest significance has been that many scientists who rejected the other aspects of Mach's phenomenalism have, nonetheless, retained his phenomenalistic conception of the purpose of science. Remarkably few scientists, however, have realized that this was merely Mach's "internal" purpose of science, and that to understand it properly, it must be subordinated to Mach's "external" purpose, which was the satisfaction of human "biological needs" in such a way as to help the human species survive and prosper.[26]

III

We do not know exactly when Mach became satisfied with his understanding of the relation between the self or "ego" and the rest of the world of sensations. His reading of the eighteenth-century philosopher Georg Lichtenberg, had the most influence on him in this respect and this probably took place during the early 1860s.[27] Lichtenberg substituted the notion of "It thinks" for Descartes's "I think." This stimulated Mach to frame another double definition. In terms of his common sense theory of reference the "ego" did not exist at all. There was no "I" or "self." There were merely sensations related in different ways. This "definition" served as Mach's justification for denying that he was an "idealist" or a follower of George Berkeley. Mach's second definition, which was in terms of his referential phenomenalism, allowed for two "egos," a "narrow" one and an "inclusive" one.[28] The narrow ego consisted of those sensations which phenomenalists identify with a particular person, while the "large" or "inclusive" ego meant the totality of all sensations. In other words, while there were many "narrow" egos there was only one "inclusive" ego. Also, he did not think it possible to demarcate with complete clarity between a "narrow" ego and the physical environment around it.

Mach now had a defense against the possible charge of solipsism, a criticism often thrown at phenomenalists and certain kinds of idealists. For if there were no "ego" (and there was none in terms of his common sense theory of reference), then there was no "self" to be alone in the universe and hence no solipsism. Also, if there were a great many "narrow" egos (and there were in terms of his referential phenomenalism), then this very plurality of "selves" obviated solipsism.

But while Mach as a person adjusted to the modest status of being merely "a group of sensations," there was a problem about other people. Assuming that other people were also merely groups of sensations, how could it be that they could sense conscious impressions which were not aspects of what we sense about them? and which could not be conscious to us? Mach's answer had two parts. First, we knew by an "irresistible analogy" that other people had thoughts and sensations that we could not experience just as we knew that we, ourselves, had thoughts and sensations that they could not experience. And second, we should not try to locate or confine the thoughts and sensations of other people to their brains. The relation between "mind" and "brain" was not a geographical one. Just as the causal relations between our own thoughts and actions were to be understood in terms of "psychophysical" relational constancies and mathematical functions and not in terms of geographical "forces" or some kind of alleged interaction, so should we interpret the relations between other people's thoughts and actions.[29]

Unlike Fechner, Mach was unwilling to push his "psychophysical parallelism" to the point of attributing thoughts and sensations to plants and other vegetation. It was plausible to argue that for everything mental there was some kind of accompanying, parallel physical activity, but in spite of logical pressure, few people were willing to hold the reverse, namely, that for every physical action there was also an accompanying parallel mental response. Mach's reticence on this point should probably be attributed more to fear of ridicule than to anything else. Fechner was certainly criticized for his "logical" stand that if relational constancies could be found between ideas and the behavior of plants or even of stones, then "minds" should be attributed to them.[30]

IV

Mach accepted some of the antireligious consequences of his philosophy. If there was no "I" or individual soul then clearly there could be no individual salvation or survival of the "soul" after death. Also, death itself was merely a relational realignment. Furthermore, his position suggested either atheism or pantheism, that is, either there was no God or "the appearances" were God. Though Mach occasionally made side references to his antireligious point of view, for practical reasons, if for no other, he normally chose to remain silent.

He did, however, accept a kind of impersonal immortality. He claimed that the important ideas that a person discovered or believed would become conscious for other people as well, and in this way ideas as a form of sensations could linger perhaps forever in the consciousness of successive persons.[31] He held that it was this hope which spurred on many scientists and scholars.

A further consequence of Mach's "egoless" position was not so much logical as emotional. He hoped that it might discourage unduly aggressive "egotistical" behavior. For if "I" were nothing, then how could "I" be anything to brag about? Concerning the objection that personality meekness and self-effacement were inconsistent with Mach's Darwinian "survival of the fittest" belief he would probably have answered that individual restraint and social cooperation normally had a better chance of leading to the survival and progress of the race as a whole than any form of self-assertive arrogance at the expense of other people, and that it was the civilized progress of the human species which should come first.

What might be called the positive religious logic of Mach's phenomenalism with its rejection of both the human "ego" and "force" explanation seems to have escaped him for some time. First, he was a strong believer in scientific and technological progress and often thought of religion as "reactionary"; second, he was a strong Darwinian and admirer of Voltaire and the "Enlightenment"; and third, he apparently associated religion with a belief in God. It was only in his last years that he began to notice the similarities between his own underlying philosophy and Buddhism.[32]

CHAPTER 4

Prague Professor

I

Mach arrived in Prague in April 1867, as a professor of experimental physics. The incoming scientist did not forget his first impressions. Prague was so remarkable, even exotic, a divided city at this time as to etch some rather acute and deep-hued memories. The chief fact of life was the growing Czech nationalism and the stubborn efforts of the German minority to defend themselves and especially German as the dominant instructional language in the University of Prague. Following are some of Mach's Prague reminiscences and some of those of his daughter and the Mach biographer, K. D. Heller.

It was in April 1867, when I moved from cheerful, friendly Graz to beautiful, gloomy Prague where my profession called me.[1]

The city is rich in medieval and modern buildings, rich in historical mementos, the place where I was to follow my profession for several decades. It is also rich in talented people, inventors, reformers, characters, and oddities of all kinds, indeed, one can call the city itself an oddity.[2]

Street signs normally serve for orientation, but that they can also serve for disorientation, for the purpose of angering opponents, the wanderer must one day experience for himself. On the same street one can find Czech, German, French, Russian, Turkish, and even Greek street signs.[3]

Prague was and doubtless is a beautiful city. The view from the Charles Bridge toward the "Kleinseite" and its Baroque buildings, and above all from Hradschin and the Dome of St. Veit, for those who have seen it, is unforgettable. But also the expression . . . "depressing" was not inappropriate at that time. It was the city which one meets in Meyrinck's *Golem*, it was Rilke's birthplace.[4]

One experiences little that is pleasant, and much that is saddening in such a city.[5]

With respect to sanitation the city left almost everything to be desired. The small grocery stores were dirty. Ice cream was often wrapped up in notebook paper or even wastepaper. But by far the worst was the lack of good drinking water. Most of the available water came from old wells and as a result of bad pipes and plumbing had become totally infected. Typhoid fever was endemic, and yearly took its toll of victims. Everyone was also afraid of smallpox. Prague even had its own special smallpox hospital, which was filled the whole year round. Anyone who wanted to escape typhoid fever had to drink boiled water or mineral water from one of the resort springs to the north, Giesshübel or Krondorfer. Also, connections between different parts of the city were greatly lacking. If one was not able to master long distances by foot, only so-called droshkies were available, dubious two- or four-seated coaches with only an old cart horse hitched on. These droshkies also served in place of ambulances to take infected people to the hospitals.[6]

One of the first things Mach had to do in his new "home" was to make a call on the Rector of the university. He began by taking one of the vehicles mentioned above.

I chose a coach and wanted to get in, when the driver called out, at that time still in German, some friendly advice "Watch out for your silk hat!"— "I'm already aware of that," was my answer. The friendly coachman replied "Oh no, Professor Halla always gets his knocked off." He had named the Rector, whose absentmindedness had already become proverbial, and he had sized me up at once as a teacher from whom something similar could be expected.[7]

The audience with the Rector would have made an extremely comical impression on any casual bystander unaware of the situation in Prague. I thought he was Czech because of his name [Dr. Josef Halla], and he thought the same of me because of mine. Thereupon we both started—because neither one of us wanted to begin by quarreling over politics—by very cautiously probing each other out.[8]

Nor were Mach's initial contacts with other Prague professors always free from this same threat of nationalistic unpleasantries. One of the reasons Mach may have wanted to come to Prague was to meet the famed physiologist and idealistic philosopher, Jan Purkyně (1787–1869), who among other things was concerned with light and dark adaptation in the human eye, a problem related to Mach's then current investigations into what we now call "Mach bands," but alas, the old man had other things on his mind.

39

A letter from Mach to Purkyně (June 14, 1867) regretted a missed opportunity to get together.[9] But when they finally met it became clear that there had been another misunderstanding. "Purkyně, the famous physiologist, whose optical work had aroused Goethe's interest, . . . was known as a strong Czech nationalist and believed that he had found in the new professor of physics, who was born in Moravia, a friend who shared his political point of view. When Mach first came to visit him, Purkyně spoke Czech and said 'I have heard that you speak Czech.' Mach answered in German and refused to be drawn into a political discussion." [10]

Mach saw no reason to get involved. He took the position of Joseph II and Franz Grillparzer against nationalism. He simply did not believe in it. He considered it emotional and reactionary. He wanted to remain detached and silent on the whole issue of Germans *vs.* Czechs. It was not a matter that could be solved in a scientific way. But his Czech "countrymen" were hard to discourage; they wanted him on their side. Mach continued to dodge and evade, but in the early 1870s he was to encounter the heaviest artillery piece in the Czech arsenal.

The single man most responsible for the Czech Renaissance of the nineteenth century was probably the historian Palacký, whose books published in the 1830s and 1840s opened the eyes of many Czechs to the glories of their own past, in particular to the victories of Jan Žiška and Prokop the Great over the numerous German "crusades" launched against the Hussites in the fifteenth century. According to G. P. Gooch: "But by far the most celebrated [scholar] was Palacký, the greatest of Slav historians and the creator of the national consciousness of Bohemia." [11] Mach now had to face him.

"When Mach was elected to the Bohemian Scientific Society, he had to pay a visit to the historian, Palacký, who at that time was president. He energetically urged Mach to place himself on the Czech side, for in critical times everyone had to take a position. Mach decisively rejected this advice and remained what he was, namely, a German-speaking Austrian who wanted to dedicate himself entirely to science and who did not want to trouble himself about politics." [12]

Fortunately for Mach, the times, while depressing for linguistic Germans in Prague, were not yet critical and he was able to survive this early grilling and get on with being a reasonably happy and successful professor of physics. Indeed, he was shortly to have a number of highly appreciative Czech students in his classes, some of whom were even to become close personal friends a few year later.

II

Ernst Mach married a cheerful orphan, Louise Marussig, in Graz on August 1, 1867.[13] They settled in Prague and slightly over a year later their first child, Ludwig, was born. The family continued to grow until there were four sons and a daughter. Each child soon acquired at least one nickname. If we have guessed correctly from existing correspondence, Ludwig (1868) was "Flaxl," Carolina (1873) "Lina" and "Katzl," Heinrich (1874) "Schrupp," Felix (1879) "Sultl," and Victor (1881) "Azzorl." Besides the children there were also numerous successive cooks, nursemaids, servants, and visiting relations, as well as a swarm, a whole menagerie of animals. Louise liked Dachshunds best. Mach's preference was for half-tamed sparrows.

Mach's laboratory was located at 562 Obstmarkt, in a structure adjoining the oldest and most important building in the University, the "Carolinum," which faced a large public square in the very center of Prague. Mach and his family lived above the laboratory on the fifth floor. Concerning instruction, his lectures covered a wide range but gradually narrowed until by the 1880s he rarely taught more than one course in experimental physics five days a week along with laboratory exercises. His teaching was normally oriented toward the needs of medical and pharmaceutical students and prospective Gymnasium men.[14] His classes on experimental physics stressed an historical approach to each physical topic and after the first few years were combined with class demonstrations using instruments and equipment frequently designed by Mach himself and constructed by his talented *Mechaniker,* Franz Hajek.

Original laboratory inventions included a special pendulum to demonstrate the dependence of the duration of a swing on its acceleration, a tobacco smokebox to help give a visual demonstration of light refraction through prisms into color, and a polarization apparatus with a rotating analyzer. Many of these mechanical devices were used in physical laboratories throughout Central Europe for over half a century. A collection was kept in Prague at least as late as the outbreak of World War II.[15]

The most famous of all his instruments was surely his "wave machine." This device could make progressive longitudinal waves, progressive transverse waves, standing longitudinal waves, and standing transverse waves.[16] Mach recalled: "My laboratory instrument maker,

F. Hajek, made by chance a very pertinent remark that one could obtain a right pretty progressive transverse wave if one struck a series of pendulum-like suspended lead pieces at well-timed intervals, one after the other." [17]

III

Between 1867 and 1879 Mach published four books and at least sixty-two articles.[18] Most of these contributions were on scientific subjects, but one work, *Conservation of Energy* (1872), was at least as much philosophical as scientific, thereby introducing its author to the academic world for the first time as a philosopher. The book, however, attracted little attention. It was loosely written, and its speculative attack on the mechanical theory of heat and the atomic "hypothesis" did not impress many physicists. Nor did philosophers take significant notice of it.

Three books, largely based on Mach's experimental work, were published within the next three years: *Optical-Acoustical Investigations* (1873), *Contributions to Doppler's Theory of Tone and Color Change through Movement* (1874), and *Outlines of the Theory of the Motor Sensations* (1875).[19] Among the numerous experiments that Mach was carrying out at this time those he conducted on motor sensations were probably the most important, and are covered in the next chapter. His ballistic work and pressure pattern investigations are touched on in the chapter on shock waves.

IV

Mach was fortunate in several of his students. Čeněk Strouhal (1850–1922) studied math and physics at Prague between 1869 and 1873.[20] During his first year he attended Mach's classes. "Mach, who was then 31, fascinated Strouhal with his clear and fundamental lectures. At that time [1869] there was no *Praktiker* to conduct experiments during the lecture, and the listeners were happy when afterward the assistants would carry out demonstrations with some of the various laboratory equipment available. Mach came to like Strouhal so much that a very cordial relationship developed." [21]

Strouhal continued to work under Mach after he received his doctor's degree. His *Habilitation* thesis on frictional tones clearly revealed Mach's continuing influence. After a short stay at Würzburg, Strouhal returned to Prague in 1882 and became the professor of experimental physics in the new Czech university. Indeed, Strouhal even became known for the similarity of his teaching style to that of Mach. The Czech professor became Rector of his university in 1903/1904. Strouhal is best known in science for joint publications with the American, C. Barus, on the magnetic and galvanic properties of steel. "These publications contained the ingenious method of calibrating bridge wires for the manufacture of permanent magnets for measuring instruments which were used for many decades." [22]

Another young Czech that Mach got along with very well was Čeněk (Vincenc) Dvořák (1848-1922). "[He was] one of my first and most gifted students." [23] Dvořák recalled those early days in a letter to his former teacher: "Thank you very much for your photograph which I remember from the time we were in Prague, where I, who was as yet so little skilled in city culture, came to your laboratory to receive a mass of new ideas and to learn how to experiment with few means or mechanical assistance. It was truly a wonderful time!" [24] According to Mrs. Irena Seidlerová, a noted Czech historian of science, "Č. Dvořák gained world fame by a number of experimental studies concerning the mechanical effects of acoustic waves which demonstrated the analogy between acoustic and electromagnetic events, and proved the correctness of the mechanical theory of the ether. However, later on it was proved that the whole subject was far more complex." [25] Dvořák was also known for his "acoustic reaction wheel" and for his attempts to improve on striation photographic devices.

Dr. Seidlerová has commented on Mach's influence on the development of Czech physics:

Optics and acoustics became first grade disciplines due mainly to E. Mach who established a thematically specialized school.[26]

Mach also supplied the impulse to Koláček's development of Maxwell's theory. Almost simultaneously with Hertz's experiments, i.e., at a rather confused situation, F. Koláček proved the correctness of Maxwell's conceptions of his electromagnetic theory of light dispersion, the explanation of the dispersion of axes, dichroism and circular birefringence.[27]

She also has criticized some aspects of Mach's influence, however.

The prevailing philosophical views, Machism on the one hand, the denial of the atomic theory (Seydler) based on Fechner's philosophy and culminating in Wald's energeticism on the other, often acted as retarding influences on the work of Czech physicists.[28]

Perhaps Mach's most curious influence on a student was on Wilhelm Kienzl (1857–1941) who studied acoustics under him in 1876. The young man dutifully read Helmholtz's *Theory of Tone Perceptions* and Oettinger's *A Harmony System in Dual Development,* and learned how to operate the resonators and monochords in Mach's laboratory. He even gave a successful *Kolloquium* on acoustics, which happened to mark his nineteenth birthday, but apparently Mach was not deceived. "This good and wise teacher recognized well the nature of my gift as overwhelmingly artistic and not scientific. He looked on my conscientiousness with interest . . . and well-meaning smiles." [29]

One day Mach showed young Kienzl a dramatic poem by the Indian dramatist, Kālidāsa, and suggested that *Urvasi* as it was called could be adapted into a successful opera. "He gave me a copy of Lobedanz's free translation of the imaginative Indian work. I was so enthusiastic and carried away that although I was no way capable of composing a great musical piece at the time I eagerly began to learn fundamentals in order to prepare myself." [30] Five years later Kienzl started the actual composition. The work was completed in 1884 and "first staged in 1886 at the Hoftheater in Dresden under Ernst Schuch, who experienced at that time the first of his many brilliant and successful productions. Both of these "Ernsts" [Mach and Schuch] were therefore quite seriously the founders of my career as a dramatic composer." [31]

The success of *Urvasi* encouraged Kienzl to write other operas, including his best-known one, *Der Evangelimann,* which continues to be frequently staged in Austria today. The Mach-inspired *Urvasi* was itself revived in 1910, 1912, and in 1932. Kienzl also composed the national anthem for the First Austrian Republic in 1919.

Fine as Mach's relations were with many Czech and German-speaking students, there was at least one relationship which became decidedly unpleasant and which helped seriously to undermine his never too stable health. Below is a translation of a strange Mach document found among those of his papers sent to the Ernst-Mach-Institut in 1967. Apparently it was originally intended to be read in case of his death, but later he apparently forgot about it. Actually, there are four documents, two of which are relevant here.

In the year 1876 my assistant J. *Wosyka* was discharged at once from the institute because of bookstealing. I have replaced the books. I have fallen, because of this behavior of Wosyka's, who was indebted to me for many things, into an emotional depression which has made me for years incapable of work. First after several years I was so far composed that I could persuade myself that equipment was also missing. If I should die before everything has been replaced this will serve for explanation. I myself took care to lock up the Institute every evening. [But] naturally this does not suffice against a thief in the house, who in a clever way steals never used and therefore seldom contested things. These proceedings have robbed me of my joy in life, [but] one should not condemn him too hard. [Dated 1886.]

I have given respect to Wosyka. When he arrived again at a position after many years I held myself obliged to tell his superior of his past behavior. Also Wosyka is aware that one knows and watches him. He is said to have been upright until now. I don't know anything else detrimental about him. Since I have taken care of all of the damage which could be traced back to this source there is no longer any basis on which to prosecute him. But the facts shall not remain unknown. [Dated 1894.]

The discovery of Wosyka's behavior, besides depressing Mach, led to the onset of fortification scotoma, an abnormality of the eye associated with high blood pressure and migraine headaches. Here are two references to Mach's ailment.

"Thus, years ago on a number of successive days, a bright red capillary net (similar to a so-called enchanted net) shone out upon the book in which I was reading, or on my writing paper." [32] A letter from Paul Carus to Mach went into more detail: "I am very much obliged to you for communicating your experience to me, concerning blood pressure. I will say in reply that I had the same kind of phenomenon in my left eye which you describe. The spots in the eye are as you say fortification designs and in one case like latticed leaves, only the leaves were not green but grey. But finally the whole eye became grey. The film became clear but the center of vision is still blind." [33]

A number of points should be added to help clarify this generally unknown, but in some respects important incident. First, even as early as 1868 there was a letter from one of Mach's assistants protesting to Mach that he had not stolen anything from the laboratory. Apparently even then Mach had such thoughts on his mind. [34] Second, the University of Prague bulletin listed "Wossica" as Mach's assistant a year after the incident is supposed to have happened. Hence, presumably, either the bulletin was wrong or Mach misdated the happening. [35] Third, there is the question of the actual effect of the incident on Mach's experimental work. That he continued some laboratory investigations in subsequent years is evident enough, but it is true that after 1875 there was a marked decline in the number of his published articles per year on experimental activity, that the few articles he did publish were almost all coauthored with his students, as if they did the actual laboratory work, and that from the middle 1880s on, most of his investigations and experiments were clearly carried out by such men as Professor P. Salchner in Fiume on the Adriatic or by his son, Ludwig.[36] But regardless of how much he may have felt hindered from personally conducting such experiments, there is every reason to believe that he continued to direct and supervise those laboratory investigations in which he was most interested.

CHAPTER 5

Psychology

I. EARLY MACH CONTRIBUTIONS

Gestalt Qualities

Ernst Mach is often credited with having first brought attention to Gestalt qualities, that is, to experienced wholes that do not merely equate with the sum of perceived parts. Different observers, however, refer to different Mach articles and observations. In fact, Mach's "holistic" impressions seem to go back at least to the age of three when he "saw" tables as rectangular, and refused to accept either direct visual images or wall-picture representations that tapered at one end as legitimate. His first adult concern with "visual holism" may well have been his 1861 analysis of visual symmetry. Christian von Ehrenfels, who is sometimes considered the first person to write on gestalt qualities, once wrote to a friend: "I sent Mach 'Gestalt Qualities' [an article published in 1890] and he replied in a friendly manner that he had already given the main thoughts in 1865 in volume 46 of Fichte's magazine, and had expressed them in a more psychological way." [1]

But Ehrenfels seems to have considered another Mach article as the real start of gestalt analysis.

The theory of gestalt qualities began with the attempt to answer a question: What is melody? First and most obvious answer: the sum of the individual notes which make up the melody. But opposed to this is the fact that the same melody may be made up of quite different groups of notes, as happens when the selfsame melody is transposed into different keys. If the melody were nothing else than the sum of the notes, different melodies would have to be produced, because different groups of notes are here involved. Mach, who was struck by this fact, drew from it the conclusion that the essence of melody must reside in a sum of special sensations which as note sensations (*Tonempfindungen*) accompany the notes.[2]

Patrick J. Capretta in his *A History of Psychology: In Outline* (New York, 1967) has argued that while Mach may have been a pioneer of Gestalt psychology, nonetheless, he was on the wrong path and may actually have hindered the development of this new orientation and school in psychology.[3]

Ernst Mach 1885), an eminent Austrian physicist by profession, probably presented the first clear exposition of the Gestalt phenomenon as it applied to perception. He argued that certain arrangements of elements—for example, lines and angles in a geometric figure—cause the emergence of different "totals" reported by the observer as squares, triangles, circles, etc. Paradoxical as it may seem, Mach's stand in conceiving of the new or different totals as still another sensory content (in keeping with the Wundtian tradition) represented a theoretical position in psychology that was for all intents and purposes antithetical to the eventual developments in Gestalt Psychology. It must be emphasized that Mach favored a psychology of sensation, the doctrine that all knowledge is sensorial.[4]

Were Mach and Ehrenfels, as historian Gardner Murphy suggests, engaged in the futile gesture of buttressing a tottering structuralism by the addition of superordinate elements? [5]

Alexius Meinong, best known as the founder of the first Austrian psychological laboratory at Graz in 1894, actually came somewhat closer to the Gestalt position than did either Mach or Ehrenfels in recognizing the importance of the perceptual act itself as giving rise to form-quality, or as Meinong preferred to call it "founded content." [6]

Mach Bands

Mach's phenomenalism has been criticized so often that we may tend to overlook those occasions when it may have significantly contributed to important scientific discoveries. An ontological phenomenalist by identifying the external world with sensory impressions often tends to be more alert to sensory peculiarities than ordinary people who commonly dismiss them as sense illusions or misidentifications of some sort. What we now call "Mach bands" probably could have been noticed thouands of years ago, and perhaps were, but Mach seems to have been the first to take them seriously. They can be noticed all around us and at almost any time, but the natural tendency is simply not to believe what goes so contrary to our expectations. As a good phenomenalist, however, Mach insisted on believing what he saw, not as a symbol or as a sensory stand-in for something else, but as simply a particular arrangement of sensations. But what are "Mach bands"? And what is so strange about them?

One day Ernst Mach took a white color wheel with a tapering but irregular black nick in it and spun it. According to the then generally accepted "Talbot-plateau law" (1835), the rotating disc should have been gray on the outer edge becoming constantly if irregularly lighter toward the inner edge. In fact, however, there appeared two color bands that were not supposed to exist at all.[7] Toward the darker edge there was a band that was too dark and toward the lighter edge there was a band that was too light (diagrams 2, 3). How could this be explained?

Mach wrote five articles between 1865 and 1868 to help solve the problem. He soon came to the conclusion, using diagrams to show color intensity, that the peculiar bands probably reflected neurological inhibitions and that they were merely "subjective," in that measuring instruments not using the human eye would not record them.

Unfortunately, not enough was known about neurological "inhibition" at the time to test Mach's hypothesis properly, hence, like his discovery of gestalt qualities, his work on these strange bands was neglected and generally forgotten for some thirty years. It is possible that this neglect may have been a factor together with the Wosyka experience in influencing Mach gradually to abandon his experimental psychological work during the 1870s.

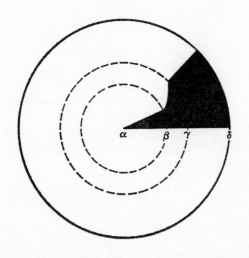

DIAGRAM 2.
Black-white color disk
with nick
(and superimposed
dotted lines
and Greek letters).
(*Courtesy of Holden-Day
Incorporated*)

A number of scientists independently rediscovered these bands during the 1890s but were more mystified than not by them. An astronomer wondered why the earth's shadow seemed larger than it should be during a lunar eclipse; two scientists were perplexed by unanticipated "interference" fringes on X-ray pictures.[8] C. H. Wind made strides toward clarification and for a while thought that he had been the first to discover the bands. In 1899, however, he accidentally learned of Mach's work and in generous fashion both admitted Mach's priority and gave them their current name, "Mach bands." [9]

This renewed interest in the bands and in Mach's old work soon came to Mach's attention. It so encouraged him that he returned to the subject and in spite of physical disability published yet another article to expand and further clarify his views.[10] In fact, however, the full significance of these intensity lines was still by no means fully grasped. Mach bands gradually became recognized as phenomena that the careful observer would have to watch out for so as not to be confused as to what was "objectively" there. The connection with neurological inhibition and excitation, however, continued to be ignored almost completely.

Georg von Békésy (1899———), the future Nobel Prize winner, suggested in 1928 that there might be "subjective" phenomena similar to Mach bands outside the visual system. And indeed, just such phenomena were eventually discovered in auditory reception, and they too have been related to neurological inhibition.

In 1951, after a meeting with von Békésy, Floyd Ratliff was encour-

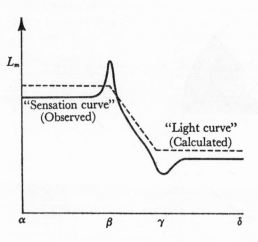

DIAGRAM 3.
Mach bands as
graph deviations
between observed and
calculated color intensity.
(*Courtesy of
Holden-Day Inc.*)

aged to inquire further into the mathematical relationships between Mach bands and neurological inhibition. "The reason for this seemingly belated development of interest is that only within the last quarter century or so have the techniques of electrophysiology finally become sufficiently advanced to provide a sound empirical foundation for such studies." [11]

Professor Ratliff has recently written *Mach Bands* (San Francisco, 1965), a very informative book on contemporary investigations into these odd phenomena. The book also includes English translations of Mach's hard-to-get articles, as well as a lengthy account of Mach's life, philosophy, and other scientific work.

Labyrinth Functions and Sense of Motion

Mach's early "psychophysical" attempts to relate hearing with ear structure and sense of motion with human physiology were not successful. He tried, for example, to find out if middle ear muscles had auditory as well as mechanical functions. He was disappointed.[12] In one experiment he even poured atropine and carbonic acid into the ear of a patient to paralyze the muscles temporarily, but in his own words even this "Hamlet scene" failed to bring results. Little of Mach's work in this area was ever published.

Mach developed two successive theories on motion as a feeling. He first became interested in the subject "on the occasion of a series of experiments on liquids which contained suspended particles [1865?], which one of my pupils performed at my instigation." [13] Mach's apparent discovery that the measurable characteristics of the particles, including perhaps their weight, were at least partly dependent on their acceleration, led to his first theory, that the whole human body contributed to the sensation of movement.[14]

Apparently, Mach had no suspicion at this time that a particular bodily organ might be responsible. His "psychophysical" tendency to look for mere relational constancies instead of for particular physical connections did not serve him well at this time. For about eight years his progress in this area was slight.

Mach remembered the beginning of his breakthrough well:

> On rounding a railway curve once, I accidently observed a striking apparent inclination of the houses and trees.[15]

> For the popular explanation by unconscious inference [Helmholtz's theory] the matter is extremely simple. We regard the railway carriage

as vertical and unconsciously infer the inclination of the trees. Of course the opposite conclusion that we regard the trees as vertical and infer the inclination of the carriage, unfortunately, is equally clear on this theory. . . . [Rejecting Helmholtz's theory] I inferred that the direction of the total resultant *physical* acceleration of the body reacts *physiologically* as the vertical.[16]

In other words, he thought that the direction of acceleration determined not only what we feel is vertical but also what we see and otherwise sense is vertical.

But as so often happens in science, the original brainstorm that stimulated his thinking and experimentation toward significant discoveries was itself unsound. In this case, Josef Breuer and Alois Kreidl were later to show that the optical distortion of the vertical depended on an involuntary reflex wheel-like movement of the eyes. In other words, neither the explanation of Helmholtz nor that of Mach turned out to be adequate. Mach, however, in the blissful enthusiasm of his own idea, decided to put it to an experimental test (1873) and from this much that was unexpected developed.

Ernst Mach constructed (or his laboratory mechanic Franz Hajek constructed it for him) a whirling chair made of wood within a double wooden frame. It vaguely resembled today's Link trainers and astronaut centrifuges.[17] When the seated observer was spun on the secondary axis of rotation his impression of visual verticality seemed to change in a way to support Mach's theory, but when he was rotated on the primary axis Mach began to notice a different phenomenon. A paper box was placed over his head and when the speed of rotation was either increased or decreased he felt a sense of motion. When the speed was constant, however, he ceased to feel any motion at all, no more than he would have had he been at rest. Mach was intrigued. He had discovered a sense of motion, a "sixth sense," though of course this sense and dizziness had naturally been noticed by other people before. Not stopping with describing its characteristics, he then inquired about its "parallel" physical counterpart or cause.

The question now arose what particular organ might function in such a way as to arouse a feeling of motion only when there was bodily acceleration or deceleration. According to Mach, he experienced "a perfect illumination." [18] "My juvenile experiences of vertigo occurred to me. I remembered Flouren's experiments relative to the section of the semicircular canals of the labyrinths of doves and rabbits, where the observer had observed phenomena similar to Vertigo, but which he preferred to interpret, from his bias to [Helmholtz's] acoustic theory of the labyrinth, as the expression of painful auditive disturbances." [19]

Furthermore, Mach vaguely remembered that F. L. Goltz, about 1870, had asserted that while it was uncertain whether the semicircular canals are auditive organs or not it was at least clear that they were necessary for bodily equilibrium. They were, so to speak, "the sense-organs of equilibrium of the head and indirectly of the whole body."

Mach now attempted to study the structure of the semicircular canals themselves, but here he ran into a serious problem. Mach was not an expert in anatomy or human physiology, and furthermore, he was an antivivisectionist. But without skillful surgery how was he going to understand the exact characteristics of a tiny organ located deep within our heads? Surely animal vivisection was an indispensable tool for scientific investigation. But Mach would not budge. He denied both its necessity and desirability.[20]

Presumably, Mach learned the requisite structural information on the labyrinth from books written in large part by authors who themselves had engaged in vivisection and learned many things from it. But in any case, he soon arrived at what he thought was the answer. It was inertia helping to press semicircular canal liquid against receptors in the ampullae which caused the feeling of motion. When there was no acceleration or deceleration, inertia ceased to force the liquid and there was no feeling of movement at all.

In spite of the plausibility of Mach's explanation, however, it aroused a good deal of criticism, especially from scientists who favored vivisection, or at least who saw no satisfactory alternative to it.

On the other hand, Mach's priority of discovery turned out to be only a matter of days. Mach's paper was received on November 6, 1873, by the Austrian Academy of Science, Josef Breuer's paper on November 14, 1873, by the Austrian Imperial Society of Doctors, and that of Professor Crum Brown of Edinburgh on January 19, 1874.[21] All three men worked independently, with Breuer especially using a different type of approach. Mach was interested in the "psychophysical" relation between a feeling and a bodily organ while Breuer emphasized comparative anatomy, and carefully examined organ structure. It is possible that this experimental work helped persuade Mach finally to abandon Fechner's particular understanding of "psychophysical parallelism" in favor of a different conception of that parallelism. From this time on it was the type of the relational constancy and not of the sensations related which determined the parallelism for Mach.[22] In practical terms, Mach's first theory of motion was Fechnerian and his second, and more successful one, merely parallelistic in his later and more nominal sense. His second theory facilitated closer attention to particular structural connections in the human body.

Mach followed up his experimental success with a number of closely related ventures. He sent an electric current through his own labyrinth to find something new, but found nothing shocking. He stunned fish to test their sense of equilibrium and balance. And he constructed an ingenious windmill-like model to show how semicircular canal liquid affected receptors and helped cause the feeling of motion.

Mach put his results together and published *Outlines of the Theory of the Motor Sensations* in 1875. This book terminated his research in this area, except for a brief addition in 1886. Joseph Breuer, however, pursued his investigations into the labyrinth and inner ear even further. Later, he helped clarify otolith function and our sense of equilibrium.

Mach probably turned away from further labyrinth investigations partly because his interests were more with sensations as sensations than with bodily structure, and partly, because he may have anticipated that it was possible to study organ structure and function only so far in an informative way without having to rely on vivisection.

The results of Mach, Breuer, and Brown were amended somewhat a few years later by the discovery of J. R. Ewald that, after the removal of the labyrinth from some animals, they gradually find ways to move about again and apparently even feel motion, presumably using substitute organs.

In light of the importance of the work of Mach, Breuer, and Brown in relating our feelings of motion, unbalance, and dizziness with particular parts and actions of particular bodily organs, it is quite remarkable that their investigations have gone, comparatively speaking, so unrecognized, especially in light of the need for such information in this the Space Age with its problems of gravity pull and weightlessness. But, in fact, the obscurity of their discoveries was of course never as complete as their roles in making the discoveries, nor was the obscurity shortly after they made the discoveries much less than now. The first Nobel Prize in the field went to Robert Bárány (1876-1936) in

1914, who had studied in Vienna and who presumably had learned a good deal from Breuer, who was also there.

Hering vs. Helmholtz

Johannes Müller (1801–1858) is often considered the father of German physiology. His investigations helped open up the whole field of sense physiology to scientific examination and discovery. Mach read his *Handbook of the Physiology of Man* (1833–1840) and was impressed by many aspects of it, particularly his "nativistic" theory of space, a notion that fitted in well with ontological phenomenalism.[23] "Nativism" as a psychological theory of space held that space "like other sensations was immediately given in consciousness," that is, space was not something inferred from sensory qualities or somehow interpolated from memories, past associations, or reasoning.

Mach also accepted Müller's theory of specific nerve energies. This theory was an attempt to replace a particularly crude interpretation of the representative theory of perception, namely, the view that physical objects transmitted images that were received by the eyes and were then literally transmitted in unaltered form by the optical nerves into the brain where the soul consciously noticed the images. Müller's (1826) approach, which went back to Charles Bell and was by no means original, was that we directly perceived nerve qualities and that these qualities differed from nerve to nerve. Mach, together with Ewald Hering, held tenaciously to this view. Even as late as 1896 Mach defended Müller's opinion against what has now become the common view, namely, that most nerves seem remarkably alike in both structure and function, and apparently differ primarily in quantity of message load carried.

Müller's "theory of innervation," that the brain sent instantaneous messages to the muscles, likewise attracted Mach for a long time, perhaps it seemed to support "mind-matter parallelism" over interactionism. Mach, however, began to change his mind with the reading of some of William James's work (1880) and that of Hugo Münsterberg. (James was an "interactionist.") Mach finally came to think that Müller's "sensations of innervation" simply did not exist.

Mach also was intrigued by Müller's book *The Phantasms of Sight* (1826), which further stimulated Mach's already avid imagination and interest in hallucinations. Most phenomenalists presumably distinguish between perceptions and "phantasms" just as ordinary people do, nonetheless, one gathers from their writings that they tend to consider distinguishing between the two more a problem than most people would probably admit. Apparently, Mach and many other phenomenalists cannot distinguish between the two in many cases except by means of noticing different relationships. Qualitatively sensations and hallucinations must frequently seem the same to them.[24]

But while Mach retained a lifelong admiration for Müller's work, and accepted much of it longer than scientific advance warranted, this cannot be said with respect to the contributions of Helmholtz. Here there was a comparatively rapid shift in Mach's overall opinion. Within a decade, from the early 1860s to the early 1870s, Mach had changed from being an active supporter, who even wrote a book sympathetically explicating Helmholtz's ideas on music, into a determined philosophical opponent who also increasingly rejected more and more of Helmholtz's individual scientific theories and ideas.[25]

Hermann von Helmholtz (1821–1894) was so outstanding a scientist and one who made so many important contributions to so many fields that it would take pages merely to list them all. But for practical reasons I confine myself merely to those which interested Mach and which he later came to oppose in part or altogether.

Helmholtz was born in Potsdam outside Berlin, in the heart of Brandenburg-Prussia. He was trained as a medical doctor, loved music, became associated with Müller's group of students, became a professor at Heidelberg and eventually Berlin, and quite early began to apply mathematical and physical methods to problems of psychology and physiology. Helmholtz's approach seemed so successful by the early 1860s that Mach simply gravitated into admiration for him and into trying to follow in his footsteps.

Helmholtz attempted to unite Müller's physiological tradition with the kind of atomism that Justus Liebig had so successfully introduced into organic chemistry during the 1830s and 1840s. His 1845 agreement with Brücke and Emil du Bois Reymond that "No other forces than common physico-chemical ones are active within the organism" and his 1847 paper on the conversation of energy were landmarks in midcentury science. Helmholtz was a leader in the fight against German philosophical idealism, vitalism, and those traces of *Naturphilosophie* still lingering in science. He also opposed the crude monistic materialism that Ludwig Büchner, Karl Vogt, and Jakob Möleschott advocated during the 1850s. Helmholtz attempted to steer a middle path between philosophical idealism and materialism by claiming that sensory impressions neither copy nor are physical reality, but merely somehow indicate in a reliable fashion what the real physical world outside the appearances is actually like. This modest symbolic realism, though admittedly a kind of compromise, suited the generally acknowledged leader of German science, and as long as Mach still flirted with the atomic theory he did not openly oppose this aspect of Helmholtz's philosophy.

Mach's 1863 rejection of the atomic theory and his disbelief in the reality of atoms coincided closely with the high point of Helmholtz's philosophical influence on other scientists. Most physicists seemed to be following Helmholtz toward representative realism and the atomic theory while Mach was going in the opposite direction. That Mach should begin to take a more critical look at some of Helmholtz's scientific contributions at this time should not unduly surprise us.

After initial enthusiasm Mach gradually developed a very mixed attitude toward Helmholtz's *Theory of Tone Perceptions* (1863). He admitted that it seemed very important when it appeared and that it undoubtedly encouraged further research and discovery; nonetheless, it simply included too many mistakes. Mach split his criticism as follows: He accepted from Helmholtz; that noises and composite sounds could be resolved into musical tones; that for every distinguishable rate of vibration there corresponded a particular nervous end-organ; and Helmholtz's theory of audition.[26] He rejected Helmholtz's notions: that the labyrinth was an acoustical organ; that the ear consisted of a series of resonators that singled out numbers in a Fourier series, corresponding to the form of vibration presented and heard them as partial tones; his theory of harmony; and his two definitions of consonance.[27]

Mach also came to oppose some of the best known of Helmholtz's theories in psychology, in particular, his theory of "unconscious inference" and his familiar three-color theory. According to Profesor Boring, "Helmholtz adopted this theory [unconscious inference] while he was at Königsberg, for it is an essential phase of his empiricism. He expounded its essentials in a lecture that was published in 1855. He used it in the second volume of the *Optics* in 1860. In the third volume in 1866 he gave the first full exposition. . . ." [28] Mach's first dated opposition to it also appeared in 1866.[29]

Helmholtz's choice of language was perhaps unfortunate. Apparently he did not mean "inference" either as something voluntary or as something we merely take for granted. By "unconscious inference" he apparently meant those associations that come from past experience which we think we see when we look at something but which are not actually sensations. Mach did not deny the reality of such "inferences," but rather their explanatory value. In particular, he felt that such a theory could be used to "explain" events and appearances in contrary ways. In modern terms, it lacked a criterion for falsifiability.

On the other hand, to allow "unconscious inference" introduced the suspicion that sensations may be neither "immediately given" to consciousness nor entirely free from psychic, nonsensory associations. Furthermore, it suggested an alternative to "nativistic" theories of space, namely that in both physical and physiological contexts space was a relation and not a sensation.

Mach rejected Helmholtz's adaptation of Thomas Young's (1807) color theory which allowed for red, green, and violet as primary colors in favor of his own theory. He also rejected Helmholtz's (1863) attempt to relate colors to nerve fibers.[30] Mach's own color theory was first published in 1865. Here he assumed six primary colors: white, black, red, yellow, green, and blue, plus six different corresponding processes in the retina.[31] He was not very satisfied with his own theory, however, especially with the relation between black and white. Hering, however, showed quite an interest in it.[32]

Mach has sometimes been considered close to the psychological school of Wilhelm Wundt (1832–1920), presumably, because both men were deeply interested in describing sensations. Both called sensations "elements," both relied heavily on introspection and self-experiment, and both have often been accused of psychological "atomism." But while there is no denying much of their closeness in experimental approach, little of it seems attributable to Wundt's influence on Mach or vice versa. Both men were influenced by the same tradition in psychology, and most important, both were heavily influenced by the work of Helmholtz and Fechner. Each tried to make psychology a science and took much of his methodology from physics. With respect to the term "element" to describe sensations it is possible Mach got it from Wundt, but more likely both men were indebted to Fechner.

The accusation of psychological "atomism" requires comment. For a

long time Wundt and Mach did treat sensations as psychological ir-
reducibles or "atoms," but there is an explanation for this. Also, when
both men realized they were under attack for their position they both
increasingly emphasized the importance of relations. During the
1860s and early 1870s both Wundt and Mach in their efforts to make
psychology scientific wanted to deal only with observable, measurable
referents. Sensory impressions seemed capable of exact measurement,
but concepts and other psychic referents did not. Hence, even though
both men acknowledged their reality, for example, all thoughts were
treated as "images," they wanted to exclude consideration of them from
psychology until suitable means for reliable observation and measurement could be found.[33] In philosophical terms, Mach refused to graduate from a "sensation" to a more inclusive "experience" phenomenalism
(such as William James and John Dewey were to accept) or to a
"whole" or gestaltist immanentism. His reluctance, however, was
based on what he believed were scientific rather than philosophical
grounds.

Ewald Hering (1834–1918) was born in Altgersdorf in Prussia south
of Berlin. He studied medicine under Weber and Fechner at Leipzig
and taught several years in Vienna before coming to Prague. According to Professor Boring: "He belongs in the tradition of Goethe, who
had such confidence in what trained observation can see, and of
Purkyně, another famous physiologist-observer, who dedicated his book
on vision to Goethe." [34]

Hering is perhaps most famous for his two major conflicts with
Helmholtz, which developed roughly as follows: Hering presented his
version of "nativism" in *Contributions to Physiology* (1861–1864). Mach
outlined his six-color theory in 1865. Helmholtz came out with both
his three-color theory and his "unconscious inference" approach in 1866.
And Hering, shortly after his arrival in Prague in 1870, carefully
studied Mach's color theory, reorganized and added to it, and in 1878
published his own color theory as an answer to Helmholtz. The color
theories of both Hering and Helmholtz have had their advocates to
the present day.

Hering's theory took Mach's six colors and converted them into
three antagonistic pairs: black-white, red-green, and yellow-blue. Professor Boring described the result:

In this theory he supposed the retina to have in it a "red-green" sub-
tance, a "yellow-blue" substance and a "white-black" substance, each of
which can be excited with either of two opposing reactions, dissimilation

(or catabolism) and assimilation (or anabolism). The dissimilative reaction gives white, yellow or red respectively in the three substances. Assimilation accounts for black, blue and green—the quieter or less "violent" colors. There were many other refinements that had to be included in this theory, but its historical importance nowadays is that it represented for almost fifty years an effective alternative to the Young-Helmholtz theory.[35]

Mach accepted Hering's revisions of his own ideas, and very modestly never attempted to claim any credit for Hering's final product. It seems only fair, however, as Professor R. Jung has recently suggested (1967), that Mach's role in the matter should be given a little more prominence than it has received in the past.[36]

Hering, in 1870, the same year he took over Purkyně's chair in Prague, gave a significant lecture before the Austrian Academy of Science: "On Memory as a General Function of Organized Matter." This lecture had a major influence on Mach, dovetailing remarkably with his Lamarck-Darwinian view of evolution.

Fechner's theory that all living creatures had "minds" including plants apparently influenced Hering to attempt a rather sweeping generalization. Until then, Jean Baptiste Lamarck's theory of the inheritance of acquired characteristics had normally been applied to the inheritance of physical characteristics. If, however, everything physical had a "parallel" mental counterpart, then mental characteristics, especially ideas, might also be inherited. Normally we suppose that ideas are conscious and that they vanish with the death of particular people; hence, if ideas, and in particular "acquired" ideas are to be inherited, then evidently some kind of unconscious memory is required, and this of course was the hallmark of Hering's theory.[37] He wrote:

The whole history of individual development, as observed in higher organized animals, is, from this point of view, a continuous chain of reminiscences of the evolution of all the beings which form the ancestral series of the animal.[38]

The conscious memory of man dies with his death, but the unconscious memory of nature is faithful and indestructible.[39]

Mach tended to place "memory" in quotation marks, but on the whole he accepted Hering's theory. His last written article, published after his death in 1916, reaffirmed his confidence in Lamarck, Hering, and in unconscious "memory." [40] On the other hand, there is no evidence that Mach accepted or would ever have accepted C. G. Jung's not unrelated "unconscious world soul." [41]

Wundt vs. Brentano

Ernst Mach not only curtailed much of his experimental activities during the middle 1870s, but at least as far as psychology and physiology were concerned, he never significantly resumed them. Equally important, he ceased from then on to attempt to keep up with all the latest theoretical developments in the two fields. This was unfortunate. For, just as Mach was slacking off, Franz Brentano with his new approach to psychology was just getting started. In spite of the fact that the lives of the two men were to cross more than once, that they corresponded with each other in later years, and that the philosophical followers and disciples of both men were in frequent conflict with each other, still, there is no evidence that Mach ever read any of Brentano's psychology or philosophy books prior to 1907.[42] Admittedly, the books were not particularly easy reading, but Mach unnecessarily handicapped himself by not reading them. It meant that he would not be in a good position to answer the criticisms of Brentano's followers, but would have to rely on the knowledge and wisdom of his own supporters, which frequently was not equal to the task.

Franz Brentano (1883–1917) was born in Marienburg (Marlbork), on the Rhine, was descended from an old Italian family, and was related to Clemens Brentano and Bettina von Arnim, the literary figures. He began training for the priesthood at sixteen, studied at the universities of Berlin and Würzburg, and had a number of outstanding teachers. Friedrich Trendelenburg interested him in Aristotle; Ignaz von Döllinger advocated a liberal Catholicism; and Rudolf Lotze among other things helped him to become a professor at Vienna in 1874.

In this same year both Wundt and Brentano published important psychology books: Wundt, *Fundamentals of Physiological Psychology*, and Brentano, *Psychology from an Empirical Standpoint*.[43] From then on one may speak of the two men as leaders of rival psychological schools, Wundt's "Content Psychology" *vs.* Brentano's "Act Psychology."

Wundt's approach was normally labeled "introspective" and "experimental," two terms that sometimes may seem incompatible or contradictory. The solution or "synthesis" lay in the type of experimentation. Wundt, like Mach, believed that the experimental subject or person with the use of proper equipment could not only reliably notice his own sensations, but also in many cases could reliably measure them. To be sure this took training. And Wundt gradually became known for his "trained introspectionists" who could cancel out enough individual differences to get a reliable picture of normal human sensations.

Brentano, on the other hand, denied the applicability of psychology to sensory content altogether. For him, psychology studied the acts of sensing and experiencing and physics studied the content or objects sensed. Brentano helped to lead psychology in two opposite directions. First, his emphasis on acts was a step in the direction of behaviorism, and away from so-called introspectionism. But second, he retained such a concern with sensations and observation as to help influence many of his numerous followers into "superintrospectionist" psychologies like Gestalt psychology and Edmund Husserl's phenomenology.[44]

Brentano published comparatively little after his 1874 book, especially in psychology, but he easily made up for this with his lectures and personal influence over a host of talented students including: Ehrenfels, Freud, Husserl, Lipps, Marty, Masaryk, Meinong, and Stumpf. Nonetheless, in spite of Brentano's undoubted influence, most experimental psychologists remained closer to Wundt's approach than to that of Brentano. According to Professor Boring: "The historical fact is that content has lent itself persistently to experimentation, whereas act has not."[45]

Brentano's personal life was dominated by an extreme and uncompromising scrupulousness, combined with gradually shifting views about the Roman Catholic Church. He became an ordained priest in 1864 and entered a Dominican monastery. Five years later, he wrote an article against the proposed doctrine of papal infallibility. In 1872 papal infallibility became dogma. The next year Brentano resigned his university post at Würzburg and also quit the priesthood, insofar as this was allowed in Germany in those days. He fell in love in 1880, but as a former priest was not allowed to marry. He resigned his Vienna professorship, married, and returned to Vienna to teach as a privatdozent. His wife died in 1894, and his eyesight began to fail. He resigned for the last time in 1895, explained his action in a book *My Last Wishes for Austria* (1895), and then retired to Florence, Italy, where he remained intellectually active for some time. Several of these events influenced Mach's life; in particular, it was the availability of "Brentano's Chair" in Vienna in 1895 which allowed Mach to make his triumphant return to the Habsburg capital. Brentano died in 1917 while his influence in psychology and philosophy was still great, and that of his students was still largely ahead of them.

III. HIS PHENOMENALISM AS A DESCRIPTIVE PSYCHOLOGY

Nature of Psychology

Many basic aspects of Mach's philosophy, his Darwinian "biological needs" approach, his theory of "economy," and the various senses in which he was a phenomenalist, have already been covered, but there were a number of descriptive details of his phenomenalism I have not dealt with yet which as aspects of a "descriptive psychology" would probably be of interest more to psychologists than to either philosophers or physicists. Hence, I consider these details in this chapter.

Mach wrote most of these details for the first time in his Fechner-influenced manuscript of 1866 (see chap. 2). Unfortunately, we have no way of knowing what was in the manuscript for its location is unknown. Presumably, he made a number of changes when he resumed work on it almost twenty years later. Mach published his *Contributions to the Analysis of Sensations* in 1886. This book is normally considered the most readable and popular presentation of his philosophy, but, in fact, as much of it concerned psychology as philosophy, and it has long served as a primary source for his opinions on psychology.

First, what did Mach mean by "psychology"? Until at least 1872 he seems to have followed Fechner's distinction as this quotation from his *Conservation of Energy* shows:

1. The determination of the connexion of presentations. This is psychology.
2. The discovery of the laws of the connexion of sensations (perceptions). This is physics.
3. The clear establishment of the laws of sensations and presentations. This is psychophysics.[46]

Apparently, at this time he still distinguished between sensations and presentations, with the latter presumably meaning "ideas" and perhaps "relations." In other words, he still viewed psychology as the study of a particular kind of data. But this 1872 opinion was radically different from his 1886 understanding which appeared in his *Contributions*.

Thus the great gulf between physical and psychological research persists only when we acquiesce in our habitual stereotyped conceptions. A color is a physical object as soon as we consider its dependence, for instance, upon its luminous source, upon other colors, upon temperatures, upon spaces, and so forth. When we consider, however, its dependence upon the retina . . . it is a psychological object, a sensation. Not the subject-matter, but the direction of our investigation, is different in the two domains.[47]

In short, Mach came to the view that both physics and psychology studied the same sensations, but merely in different relationships. He held what we now call "neutral monism," a particular type of phenomenalism which reduced ideas and perhaps relations to sensations, such that the world consisted only of sensations. But what is troublesome to the historian is that Mach developed an unexpressed third definition of psychology, which was actually more basic than the others. Pieced together the definition ran as follows: Physics dealt with the dependence of "external" sensations on each other. Physiology dealt with the dependence of "external" sensations on measurable sensations of the human body and the latter sensations on each other. Psychology merely dealt with those bodily sensations (ideas, moods, dispositions, and so on) which were not yet subject to scientific measurement.[48] In other words, in terms of his own highly singular third definition, he admired physiology more than psychology. Indeed, he seems to have hoped that psychology in this sense could be abolished in favor of physiology.[49] The primacy of this third definition came from the fact that from the 1860s on, his definitions of both space and time were in terms of it, and were clearly inconsistent with his explicit 1872 and 1886 definitions of physics and psychology. In a sense, this third definition (or rather series of definitions) suggested a sophisticated retention of Fechner's parallelistic "sides" as opposed to his theory of "elements," in that once again both fields studied different types of conscious experience.[50]

To the philosophically unsophisticated, Mach's third definition of "psychology" might seem the rankest sort of materialism, an attempt to reduce all "mental" phenomena to "physical." But the impression is misleading. For Mach all four terms "psychological," "mind," "physical," and "physiological" referred to sensations and must be understood in terms of his ontological phenomenalism. Also, by "physiological" Mach did not mean "physical." For Mach, in terms of his third definition, the physical world was the world of physics, that is, an abstract world where math and geometry were used to "relate the appearances."[51] It was the physiological world, the world of green trees and white houses related to the particular observer, which was the real "external world," but strangely enough, it was also the science of physiology which provided the ideal "internal" or "psychic" world for Mach.[52] In this sense to make psychology scientific was to turn it into physiology, but this did not mean monistic materialism, but monistic phenomenalism.[53] Also, he did not believe in the reality of atoms and molecules as entities outside the appearances, hence, it would not be reasonable to consider him a "materialist," in spite of his choice of language, except in the religious sense where the word is used to mean someone who is not a "spiritualist" or a believer in God.

Elements

Mach's three definitions of physics and psychology placed different limits on the scope of what he meant by "sensations." In 1872 sensations were distinguished from presentations or ideas. In 1886 sensations were labeled "elements," and they exhausted reality; the term "sensation," however, was reserved for those elements related to the human body. In Mach's third definition, which increasingly foundationed his views from the 1860s on, "measurable sensations" were distinguished from "not yet measurable sensations." Nonetheless, Mach's use of the terms "sensation" and "element" was not intrinsically ambiguous. With the three sets of definitions above in mind one could normally determine what he meant. The problem was merely that Mach, in frequently shifting between different definitions without realizing it, facilitated the rejection by many psychologists not only of his "elementist" approach, but in some cases, of his entire theoretical psychology. On the one hand, he wanted to define sensations (in the sense of "elements") in such a way as to make clear their measurability and certainty, and on the other hand, he wanted to include everything that could be "meaningfully" referred to. There was no logical way, however, to have a single definition include everything and not include everything.

If we mean by "sensations" or "elements" merely sensory qualities related to the five senses, then surely modern psychologists are right in alleging that we experience more than "sensations," but at least in terms of Mach's second and third definitions he never intended such a restriction. Not only did he include space and time as "sensations" (in the broader sense), but everything else as well, including a great many things for which we evidently have no sensory organs with which to "sense" them. In short, especially in terms of his third definition, he did not define what could be reliably measured in terms of sensations, but defined sensations in terms of what could be reliably measured! In other words, if it could be reliably measured (and related to other things), then regardless of what else it might be, and regardless of how we might experience it, then it had to be a sensation.[54] The questionable stretch in Mach's third definition was not that he restricted "elements" to sensory qualities, which he did not do, but that he did not make his distinction between "measurable sensations" and "not yet measurable sensations" overt, and kept suggesting that all sensations were "immediately given" in consciousness and were "certain," as if their character were independent of the way in which they were identified, or misidentified.[55]

Space and Time

Mach distinguished between a number of different kinds of space and time. *Physiological space* was the space we notice "out there"; it was "immediately given" and as much an "element" as colors or sounds; it was what Mach meant by "nativistic space." *Physical space* was a "functional dependency" used in physics to help relate sensations to one another in the most "economical" way possible. *Metric space* was an idealized construct developed by geometricians which might have as many dimensions as could suit the human imagination.

These distinctions between different kinds of space were apparently first developed in the early and middle 1860s. In 1862 and 1863, while Mach was trying to reconcile the atomic theory with his phenomenalism, he began to speculate on what kind of space would suit atoms as ideas. He came to the conclusion that only an ideational space of more than three dimensions would be adequate.[56] But he argued against the practicality of his own hypothesis on the grounds that "real" space (i.e., what he later called "physiological" space) had only three dimensions, and that in science it would be "uneconomical" to use a space of more than three dimensions. Mach later considered his notion of more-than-three dimensions an anticipation of Riemann's multidimensional geometry. Mach's rejection of the atomic theory as "uneconomical" was at least partly related to his similar rejection of the use of multi-dimensions in physics as "uneconomical." [57]

Mach's own interests, especially in his later years, were directed primarily toward "physiological space." And here he made a number of further distinctions. He held that besides *visual* physiological space there were also *tactile, haptic,* and various emotionally felt types of physiological spaces.[58] He also believed that they were somehow related or coordinated with one another.

Mach made some largely verbal changes in his ideas on space during the 1890s and early 1900s. According to his new definitions *primary space* was what a fixed, immobile animal would notice, a bounded, asymmetrical, three-dimensional, visual world (i.e., "physiological" space). *Secondary space* was what a moving animal or person would see who constantly corrected asymmetrical and bounded features in terms of symmetrical, geometrical, and unbounded features (i.e., a "metric" correction of "physiological" space).[59] But Mach also added: "Primary space cannot be absolutely supplanted by secondary space for the reason that it is phylogenetically and ontologically older and stronger." [60]

Ever since Saint Augustine made his famous searching and unsuccessful analysis into the nature of time, philosophers, and especially phenomenalists, have been dissatisfied not only with the understanding of other philosophers concerning this question, but even with their own understanding. Mach was not an exception. He had his own theories of time, but they pleased neither his critics nor himself.[61]

Physiological time was a feeling accompanying the labor of attention "closely connected with periodically or rhythmically repeated processes." [62] He added, however, "It is of course only for small times that I hold that there is an immediate sensation of time." [63] *Metric time* was a "chronometric concept" which arose from comparing physical events with one another and unlike physiological time was the same for everyone.[64] *Physical time* was "the dependence of changes on each other." [65]

It would be a mistake, however, to exaggerate Mach's confidence in his understanding of space and time. Physically speaking both were relations, but as mentioned before, Mach declined to clarify what he meant by relations. With respect to physiological space and time, he always felt that they had never been examined exhaustively enough to exclude the likelihood of major future discoveries.

Phenomenalistic Reduction of Categories

Mach's phenomenalism forced him to understand a number of concepts and categories in some rather strange ways.

For Mach, the *will* was almost identical with "psychic attention," but was neither a cause nor a power, nor was it any more free than "magnetic attraction." People who thought the will was a cause or power were guilty of primitive "animism" or "fetishism." He also added: "Schopenhauer's conception of the relation between will and force can quite well be adopted without seeing anything metaphysical in either." [66]

Purpose was an "interior pressure" and *volition,* "nothing more than the totality of those conditions of a movement which enter partly into consciousness and are connected with a prevision of the result." [67] Nonetheless, Mach admitted "Man is pre-eminently endowed with the power of voluntarily and consciously determining his own point of view." [68] A *concept* was "an impulse to some accurately determined often complicated, critical, comparative, or constructive *activity."*

Mach proved that he could at least initiate a sensationist reduction of psychological referents and categories, but as should be fairly evident from the easy understandability of most of his writings, his supple and limpid style, Mach rarely employed this reduction either in his scientific work or in his popular lectures or in everyday life. To define all ideas in terms of experienced sensations was an interesting goal, but ideas so defined were not yet suitable for purposes of human communication and lacked practical value.

IV. CHILD AND ANIMAL PSYCHOLOGY

Mach is often considered an "introspectionist" in psychology, but his ideas on child and animal behavior escaped this stereotype more than one might expect. Also, his interest in dreams and hallucinations and his stress on the importance of childhood experiences have suggested an anticipation and possibly an influence on Sigmund Freud and his followers. In other words, Mach had a wider range and was more "modern" than he has sometimes been given credit for in psychology. This does not mean that he was a Freudian or even a behaviorist in Watson's sense which he surely was not, but it does mean that his interests, especially in his last years, were turning more toward problems of psychological and anthropological behavior, and that he was trying to advance beyond the limitations of so-called introspectionism. The mainsprings of this late activity, however, seem to have come from a desire to substantiate and utilize Lamarck's theory of the inheritance of acquired characteristics and Hering's theory of "unconscious memory" in the face of August Weismann's chromosome theory and recent criticisms of the ideas of Lamarck and Hering.[69]

Mach attempted to recall his childhood past and study the behavior of children and animals to distinguish between which reactions were learned and which instinctive, and also to distinguish between which "instinctive" reactions were most likely inherited as "unconscious memories" from former generations and which not.

He concluded that the child's fear of darkness and ghosts and the sparrow's increased irritability and defensiveness at night were instinctive reactions and most likely had been inherited from acquired reactions of distant ancestors. He extended this argument in his last book *Culture and Mechanics* (1915). Here he pointed out that careful observation of the behavior of children when they construct and attempt to repair toys can give us insight into how primitive people first developed tools and the techniques for making tools. But even if we reject "unconscious memory" and the possibility of "inheriting" techniques from primitive man, nonetheless, the point that we may be able to learn something about how primitive man constructed things from observing the behavior of children seems well taken and worthy of consideration.

Mach apparently thought that the bodily and mental natures of men and animals were essentially the same and that most differences were more quantitative than qualitative. He claimed that man's primary advantages over animals lay: first, in the richness of man's mental life; second, in his broader range of interests; third, in his ability to reach biological goals by more indirect and subtle means; fourth, by his capacity to make use of the experience of his fellow creatures; and fifth, by the extent and rapidity of changes in his mental life. He also felt that the similarities between human and animal emotions allowed us insight into the psychic life of animals through the emotions, for on the side of feeling and will, man and beast came closer together than on the side of the intellect. But conversely, he thought that animals were naturally of an egoistical nature and that they lacked the capacity to form general or altruistic goals. He qualified his understanding of animal intelligence, however, by distinguishing between "higher" and "lower" types and by stressing that we should not overestimate the intelligence of the "lower" types.

Perhaps the most basic difference between the behavioristic approaches of Mach and Watson went back to a philosophical dispute. Mach accepted the study of "introspective" phenomena as legitimate, and Watson, following the position of Auguste Comte, the founder of Positivism, did not.[70] For Watson, psychic data were private and incapable of public verification, hence, could not be treated in a scientific way. Mach's "neutral monism" and elimination of the "self" or "ego" undercut the problem, but in such a way as to repel the lingering naïve realism of most so-called positivists.[71] In other words, then as now, few "positivists" have actually used their much-vaunted "empiricism" in a manner as consistent and thoroughgoing as might approach Mach's phenomenalism. On the other hand, even if Watson's behaviorism from a philosopical point of view must be considered a mess, nonetheless, its practical and historical value with respect to the development of psychology as a science probably outweighed Mach's more consistent position with a good deal to spare.[72] The reason was that Watson unintentionally came much closer to common sense than Mach.[73] Behavioristic "stimulus-response" explanation by seeming to introduce mechanistic understanding into psychology seemed much more practical than Mach's reliance on abstract mathematical functions as "economic" descriptions of the "appearances."

Failure to distinguish between Comte-Watson "positivism" and Mach's epistemologically more coherent brand has led to such unfortunate contemporary statements as the following: "The methodology of the science of animal behavior is, in the now accepted technical sense, *behavioristic*—i.e., it is founded on the psychological positivism of Ernst Mach. It is concerned with the annotation and causal analysis of the overt and recordable behavior of animals, not with their passions, hopes, and fears." [74]

If the author of these lines had substituted the name "John Watson" for "Ernst Mach" he would have come closer to the truth. To praise

Mach is fine, but perhaps his real contributions to animal psychology, even if considerably more modest than the paragraph above suggests, should be emphasized rather than a misunderstood version of his philosophy and an exaggerated conception of its influence. Mach was interested in animal behavior and he was in many senses a "positivist," but he was not a follower of Watson, and animal psychology is not based on Mach's "positivism." Nor did he refuse consideration to the "passions, hopes, and fears" of animals.[75]

Mach's Darwinian tendency to think that ideas and other psychic phenomena were subject to "natural selection" and a kind of "survival of the fittest" helped lead him to a form of teleological explanation, or justification by means of ostensible purposes. In particular, he came to the opinion that if psychic phenomena satisfied no "biological need," then to that extent they were "purposeless" and even "pathological." In his own words: "All marked and independent appearance of phantasms without excitation of the retina—dreams and the half-waking state excepted—must by reason of their biological purposelessness be accounted pathological." [76] But what if a reader should go beyond Mach and suppose that all dreams and phantasms, whether pathological or not, might satisfy biological purposes? What might we call such a person? Might we not call him Sigmund Freud?

Ernst Mach and Josef Breuer successfully attacked some of the same problems concerning the human "labyrinth" and "semi-circular canals" during the 1870s and knew each other reasonably well.[77] During the 1890s Breuer published studies on aphasia and hysteria in collaboration with Sigmund Freud. More than likely Breuer interested Freud in some of Mach's ideas. It is also probable that Freud was indirectly influenced by Mach through his reading of Popper-Lynkeus's book *Phantasies of a Realist* (1899).[78] Freud directly referred to Mach's point of view in a letter to Wilhelm Fliess, dated June 12, 1900: "When I read the latest psychological books (Mach's *Analyse der Empfindungen*, . . . etc.) all of which have the same kind of aims as my work, and see what they have to say about dreams, I am as delighted as the dwarf in the fairy tale. . . ." [79]

What Freud overlooked, however, was that the first edition of Mach's book came out in 1886, which was several years before Freud had developed his own ideas on dreams and hallucinations. We lack factual evidence that Mach influenced Freud in any way, shape, or form, nor did Freud ever acknowledge any debt to him, but the fact that both men were deeply interested in the significance of childhood experience and dreams, that Mach's written account preceded Freud's by several years, and that Freud had ample opportunity to soak up Mach's ideas in a variety of direct and indirect ways, has strongly hinted that at least in these respects Mach *did* influence Freud.

CHAPTER 6

Mach's Two Rectorates

I

Ernst Mach's first public recognition came neither from his work as a scientist nor from his philosophical ideas but from his position and behavior as head of the University of Prague. Mach did not enjoy the notoriety, however, and his last sixteen years in the Bohemian city were increasingly troubled and unhappy with only occasional bright spots such as major publications, the visit of William James, and the discovery of a philosophical ally in Richard Avenarius.

Ernst Mach was elected *Rector Magnificus* of the University of Prague in the same year (1879) that Count Eduard von Taaffe (1833–1895) came to power in Vienna with his program of reconciling Slavic minorities to the Habsburg state. The Czechs immediately demanded full language parity in the University of Prague.[1] Taaffe supported this request, which placed Ernst Mach squarely on the spot.

The new Rector's response was to consult with the four university deans (December 1879) and openly propose that the Czechs establish a separate university.[2] As the Czechs were unwilling to abandon the old "historic" buildings, however, he then made a secret recommendation that the five hundred-year-old Charles-Ferdinand University be split, and each "historic" structure be partitioned literally into two halves with separate German and Czech entrances.[3] Unfortunately, while Taaffe eventually accepted and gradually implemented this so-called solution, neither language group was satisfied with it. An incident late in "Solomon" Mach's first rectorate completed the emotional discord and political polarization.

73

II

The German Burschenschaft Carolina, a nationalistic student group, decided to celebrate the twentieth year of its founding, and invited the Rector, Ernst Mach, and a large number of other professors and dignitaries. They even invited special groups from Germany itself. Thirty-five students arrived from a Berlin technical *Hochschule,* and the Burschenschaft Arminia-Breslau also sent members.[4]

The celebration began at 8 p.m. on May 12, 1880, in the *Convicthall* somewhere in Prague. An estimated three hundred guests were there.[5] The festivities included a number of speeches and presumably a great many songs. Some of the more popular students ones at the time seem to have been Joseph von Eichendorff's "Nach Süden nun sich lenken," Schenkendorff's "Wenn alle untreu werden," and "Frisch auf zum fröhlichen Jagen."

Ernst Mach as Rector of the University gave a speech on the importance of moderation and realism. The following fragment has survived.

You have spoken of your ideals. With your allowance I will add some general words on ideals in principle and on their realization in practical life. It is in the nature of the situation, that the interval in which we can devote ourselves to them in an unhindered way, the happy, cheerful celebration in which you are now, is relatively short as opposed to the following period of serious practical life. There we first learn to know the difficulties which stand in the way of the accomplishment of our ideals. And the older we become, the more we have the occasion to notice the difference between the desirable and the achievable. . . .[6]

But Mach's sober note was soon forgotten in the flood of nationalistic oratory. Perhaps the most extreme came from Professor Klebs, Dean of the Medical Faculty: ". . . Just as the Burschenschaft Carolina will, so will the great Carolina, the University, always remain German. The enemies of Germandom do not even want their own university which has been offered to them, because they know they are incapable of maintaining it. . . ."[7] The proud Burschenschaft then made Rector Mach and Dean Klebs honorary members of their student group.[8]

The gay, defiant celebration continued for two more days, when it was switched to a summer theater where a happy stage presentation finally brought the student festival to a noisy close.

The Czech newspapers were not amused. The humorous side of

Dr. Klebs's speech and the presence of the *Rector Magnificus* gracing the glorified beer hall scene escaped them. Two nights after the Carolina *Fest* was over, Czech students gathered by the hundreds before Professor Klebs's house, shouted insults and criticisms, and then threw stones to break as many of his windows as they could. They broke ten, but unfortunately they belonged to a neighbor's apartment.[9]

But the night was still young, so before the police arrived the students transferred their activities to the large market square before Mach's laboratory and house. Again they shouted curses and verbal abuse, but Czech aim had not improved. Two windows were broken, but both belonged to the apartment of Mach's laboratory mechanic, Hajek.[10]

Mach immediately reacted to the Czech student excess by posting a notice on the main student bulletin board the following morning to the effect that such student demonstrations as that of the preceding night would not be tolerated. The German-language but pro-Czech newspaper *Politik* replied to Mach's notice as follows:

> Professor Dr. Mach, Rector of our local University, published a warning on the bulletin board for students not to repeat the occurrences that have just taken place. That was quite in order . . . , but we cannot understand how his magnificence could be so naïve as to assert in his ukase that the "regrettable incidents are the result of agitation by local newspapers." How have the newspapers done any "agitating"? Doesn't the Herr Rector know, that they have only repeated what he and his speech-happy colleagues bellowed forth so loudly during their "Carolina" drinking-bout? [11]

As for the prime instigator, the newspaper continued:

> Dr. Klebs, an exotic great, over whose significance in learned circles there is at the very least divided opinion, dared to slander the Bohemian nation to its face, *that they were not even able to maintain a university!* These impudent words have insulted the national feeling of the Bohemian students and the constant calling attention to his German standpoint has irritated the Austrian [i.e., Czech] students against this foreign [i.e., German] professor. Nothing is more natural than that this continual German national agitation should bring forth *an Austrian* [i.e., Czech] *counter movement.*[12]

The Carolina incident was widely reported in Central European newspapers, and it was at this time that Mach first began to develop his reputation as a "defender of German rights." [13]

Two months later, perhaps on scientific grounds or perhaps for political reasons, Mach received an overdue and treasured reward:

regular membership in the Austrian Academy of Science, the most prestigious scientific society in the now slowly disintegrating Dual Monarchy.[14]

III

Mach remained quite busy between the end of one rectorate in 1880 and the beginning of a second in 1883. Besides teaching, laboratory work, and supervising the construction of a new science building and laboratory away from the center of Prague and the likelihood of student riots which had now become the order of the day, he concentrated on writing a carefully argued, lengthy book on the history of mechanics.[15]

During this same period a number of events conspicuously encouraged his interest in philosophy. A special lecture "On the Economical Nature of Physical Inquiry" attracted the avid support of the Classical scholar and historian of philosophy, Theodor Gomperz.[16] Thomas Masaryk, the future president of Czechoslovakia, began teaching positivistic philosophy in the Czech University. And Mach entered into personal relationships with a pair of talented and later quite influential thinkers.

In the fall of 1882 an expected visitor arrived from America and boldly announced his desire to speak with Stumpf, Mach, and Hering. William James, the Harvard psychologist and philosopher, who had earlier studied in Germany, wrote to his wife about his welcome as follows:

I have rarely enjoyed a forty-eight hours better, in spite of the fact that the good and sharpnosed Stumpf . . . insisted on trotting me about day and night, over the whole length and breadth of Prague, and that (Ernst) Mach (professor of physics) genius of all trades, simply took Stumpf's place to do the same. I heard (Ewald) Hering give a very poor physiology lecture and Mach a beautiful one. I presented them with my visiting card, saying that I was with their "Schriften sehr vertraut und wollte nicht eher Prague verlassen als bis ich wenigstens ein Paar Worte mit Ihnen umtauschte." They received me with open arms. I had an hour and a half's talk with Hering, which cleared up some things for me. He asked me to come to his house that evening, but I gave an evasive reply, being fearful of boring him. Meanwhile, Mach came to my hotel and I spent four hours walking and supping with him at his club [the Deutsche Casino?], an unforgettable conversation. I don't think anyone ever gave me so strong an impression of pure intellectual genius. He apparently has read everything, and has an absolute simplicity of manner and winningness of smile when his face lights up, that are charming." [17]

Mach and James corresponded and remained friends for the next twenty-eight years until the latter's death. Mach even dedicated a book to him.[18] Nor were Mach's ideas without influence on William James's subsequent philosophy, as we shall see.

Richard Avenarius, professor of philosophy in Zurich from 1877 until his early death in 1896, independently developed a phenomenal-istic and "economy"-oriented philosophy very similar to that of Mach. The two men began to correspond in 1882, and three years later Mach tried in vain to arrange a professorship for Avenarius in Prague.[19] The latter called his form of phenomenalism "Empirio-Criticism," a label that had a certain vogue until World War I.[20] Mach was especially impressed by Avenarius's notion of "introjection," a descriptive criti-cism of the process of imagining the mind and consciousness into the human brain.[21]

Avenarius's influence, however, while long equal or even greater than Mach's, began to fade after the turn of the century, partly because of his early death, but mostly owing to Mach's increased scientific reputation and the fact that Mach's philosophy books—being free from Avenarius's technical jargon—were much easier to read.

IV

Mach never finished his second rectorate. His reign was short and turbulent. But interesting as some of his actions were in themselves, perhaps most interesting is the question of his resignation. Just why did he resign?

In the first place, it was no small honor for Mach to have been chosen again to lead the University only four years after his last term in office. The Academic Senate chose a rector for one year, and the office was rotated among the four faculties, so that, in effect, Mach was reelected at the first opportunity. Apparently, the shrunken German University wanted to start out with its best man. Ewald Hering was the first rector after the split that took place in 1882 and Mach the second.[22] Both men were considered the leaders of German professor-ial opposition to Czech demands in Prague.[23] Mach's academic repu-tation had also risen in the interim between his two rectorates with the publication of his *Science of Mechanics* in 1883.

Mach's inauguration introduced the first problem leading to his resignation. The German University insisted on retaining and using the old, traditional symbols of investiture and was reluctant to let the Czechs have them to inaugurate their own rector.[24] Also, there was only one seat in the Bohemian Landtag for a rector and the Germans claimed it. It finally required legislation from the "Czech-Feudal" majority in the Landtag and from the government in Vienna to give the Czechs their "rights" in the matter.[25] But the "humiliated" Czechs did not have to wait long to find a way to get even with the German professors and their current rector.

The Czechs focused their attention on the one faculty that was still undivided, the Theology Faculty, which had remained attached to the German University, even though most of the students were Czech.

The big and final blow fell on November 7, 1883, just as Mach and other prominent guests were preparing to attend a gala German University evening of speeches, singing, and drinking.

The Minister of Education in Vienna announced that theology students would henceforth be enrolled, take their oaths, and presumably receive their degrees, not from the rector but directly from the dean of the Theology Faculty. The reason given for this step was that "Theology students should not have to be in the situation of taking sacred oaths from a non-Catholic rector." [26]

This decree, by reducing the German rector's authority over the Theology Faculty, not only further weakened the German position in Prague, but put Mach, formally a Catholic and actually an atheist, in a very difficult position.[27] The decree could encourage an investigation into his opinions on Christianity and religion, which conceivably could result in a scandal and his being pressured out of his job. A close reader of Mach's books could hardly be in much doubt concerning his atheism, but we still do not know who the "close reader" was or who "informed" on Mach to the authorities in Vienna, though we have a private suspicion.

Mach's words that night at the gala banquet were not cautionary as on the Carolina occasion more than three years before. He did not conceal his emotional state. In reply to a student toast, Mach, who identified Czech nationalism with political backwardness, urged the whole student body "to oppose reactionary forces with the same determination as their professors had done before them and were doing now as long as their manly strength held out, and not to darken the old age of those who had struggled so hard in their youth to banish the specter of reaction forever." [28]

Herr Wolf, head of the student *Lesehalle,* continued the evening by toasting the German people. Professor Philip Knoll praised the contributions of German culture in Prague. And Herr Schmenkel spoke for German parliamentarians in hoping that the students "would carry the necessary work even further for the holy interests of the Germans in the fight for justified national goals." [29]

After a period of reflection Mach wrote a letter on December 10, 1883, to the Minister of Education in Vienna. He stated that he did not agree with the minister's decision concerning the Theology Faculty and that unless the privileges of the rector over that faculty were restored he would resign.

Mach's mood was evident in a December 30 letter to Popper-Lynkeus: "The Rectorate embarrasses me ["geniert mich"] a great deal. I cannot reflect in peace and must always defend myself from becoming occupied with mere trifles. I deeply want to write the *Analysis of Sensations."*

Mach finally announced his decision two weeks later on January 13, 1884. His letter was read before the Academic Senate.[30] He alleged that his health had been so shaken by events during his time as rector, especially by the pressure that theologians had exercised upon him during the "immatriculation conflict," that he simply could no longer carry out the work.[31] The Academic Senate accepted the resignation with deep regret and sent the prorector, Hering, and the four deans as a special deputation to express their feelings and also to give thanks for his manly intercession for the rights of the University.

The German students planned to show their loyalty and admiration for Mach with a torch parade through the city to Mach's house. The police, however, refused to allow it.[32] Nonetheless, on January 17, 1884, students from several nationalistic organizations did gather before Mach's house to praise him. We have only a brief snatch of his personal reply to them in his garden which a newspaper reporter recalled from many years later: "Should perhaps the German University choose a rector whom our opponents were satisfied with? I don't even need to answer the question. You yourself will not say yes. So let us stop this moralistic St. Vitus's Dance and not give them the honor of having us thrown out. . . ." [33]

The extent of Mach's support among the students was perhaps best indicated by their crowded presence in his lecture hall four days later. "Mach's entrance into the lecturehall . . . brought stormy applause from the students." [34] But the gesture of resignation changed nothing. Mach's act had no effect. The Theology Faculty was no longer under the German rector and in the 1890s the last of the undivided faculties was split between the German and Czech Universities.

On the face of it, Mach merely carried out his threat to resign, and that is "why" he resigned, but causal explanations are rarely that simple. Mach publicly stated that his health was the cause. Was it? Or was it a concern for the rights of the University concerning Vienna "intervention"? Or was it to protest the Czech rector receiving a Landtag seat, as one Czech writer alleges? Or was it merely that he was tired of the job and wanted to get back to his writing so that almost any plausible excuse for resigning would suffice? Or was it a combination of factors? Alas, we do not know. There is even the outside possibility that the resignation of the University of Vienna rector only shortly before (November 27, 1883) helped plant the idea in Mach's mind. [35] Lest we give the wrong impression, though, rector resignations were not common. Mach's was the only one at Prague from 1848 to 1900. But Mach went beyond this. He was truly upset. In April 1884 he also resigned from the Union of Czech Mathematicians and Physicists of which he had been a founding member. [36]

v

Almost all of Mach's best friends were Jews: Kulke, Popper-Lynkeus, and later, Wilhelm Jerusalem, and both Theodor and Heinrich Gomperz. Hence, it became hard to remain neutral when anti-Semitism began to take a serious hold on the Prague Burschenschaften and on his colleagues.

At first, the University of Prague seemed an exception. Many Jews, including the Jewish professor Horaz Krasnopolski, had vigorously defended the German position in Prague against the Czechs. [37] As equally threatened minorities it seemed foolish for Germans and Jews (who were largely German speaking) to fight among themselves. Both were needed to resist Taaffe's "reactionary" measures. Long after student groups in Vienna and Graz had become strongly anti-Semitic, Prague with its peculiar German-Czech confrontation had been able to avoid organized student prejudice against Jews.

General objections against Jews included lack of German patriotism, financial opportunism, and the belief that they were largely responsible for many of the economic dislocations resulting from the Industrial Revolution. Private enterprise is largely admired in America, but in Austria it was often understood to mean Jewish shady speculation which undermined traditional or stable manufacture and commerce, and led to low wages, bad working conditions, and job insecurity. Particular objections came to the fore in a series of sensational newspaper reports during the early 1880s on murders which were attributed to Jews and their supposed need for using Christian blood for ritual purposes. These so-called "blood accusations" were widely believed at the time.

The change in Prague came in 1883 with the arrival of the notorious anti-Semite, Professor August Rohling, to take over a theology chair in Hebrew Antiquities and the controversy that immediately erupted. Unfortunately, there are major gaps in the story, and the most important of these concern the relationship between Mach and Rohling. Nonetheless, there is enough information to indicate how seriously Rohling and anti-Semitism affected the University and disturbed Mach's peace of Mind.

First of all, why was Rohling so important concerning anti-Semitism? The answer is that he gave academic and a measure of University support to the newspaper allegations about the Jewish need for "blood sacrifices." In the words of L. Strack and the *Encyclopedia of Ethics:* "The most dangerous of these means [arguments against the Jews] since the 13th Century has been the 'blood accusation'. . . . The most influential propagator of this accusation was the canon August Rohling in Prague in the years 1883–1892." [38]

The Austrian Government greeted Rohling's arrival from Germany with a prohibition against him publishing any more anti-Semitic material. Ernst Mach followed this up a few days later on the night of his inaugural speech on assuming his second rectorate (October 18, 1883) with a comment that deeply offended August Rohling. Regrettably, we do not know what the comment was. Later evidence suggests that Rohling misunderstood Mach. Apparently, the new professor thought Mach was either attacking him, his anti-Semitism, or was openly supporting the prohibition. In any case, the grievance persisted within Rohling for several years only to explode into a quite mysterious academic scandal in the late 1880s. [39] Whether intentionally or not, Mach had made an enemy—and a dangerous one.

In spite of Mach's alleged criticism, however, Rohling quickly gained new allies. The Academic Senate of the German University, which presumably had invited him in the first place, resented Vienna interference and strongly defended their man. They argued that he had the right of academic free speech; that his most outspoken anti-Semitic "research" had been written before he came to Austria; and that in his last published article he was merely defending himself.[40]

The suspicion is that Rohling sought to undermine Mach's position by helping to spread the word in Vienna about Mach's atheism and by trying to detach the Theology Faculty from Mach's control, but mere suspicion is far from conclusive evidence. Two facts stand out. First, Mach was strongly opposed to anti-Semitism; and second, Rohling had found support among both the professors and the student body. Furthermore, Rohling continued to publish anti-Semitic articles and books in Germany which were then easily smuggled into Austria.

The first clear evidence that anti-Semitism was on the rise among German-speaking Prague students came about a year after Rohling's arrival when in June 1884 the student organization *Lesehalle* voted down two Jewish candidates for their governing board.[41] Shortly afterward, students from the Burschenschaft Teutonia pressured a number of Jews from the staff of the influential student magazine *Deutsche Hochschule*. The Burschenschaft Carolina from 1885 on apparently accepted no more new Jewish members, and by 1890 even removed old ones from the rolls.[42] Other Prague Burschenschaften soon fell into line.

The ostensible reason why the Burschenschaften excluded Jews was that they were considered *Satisfactionsunfähig,* that is, incapable of giving satisfaction by means of a duel using sabers or other weapons. The grounds for this odd opinion are not self-evident.[43] At first, no professors were willing to be openly associated with the new anti-Semitic student groups, but by the middle 1890s, that is, about the time Mach decided to leave Prague, a great many professors including Mach's successor, Ernst Lecher (1856–1926), openly opted for anti-Semitism.[44] The 1897 Prague riots between Czechs and Germans had as a side effect enough increased persecution of the Jews to complete the story. Organized prejudice against the Jewish part of the student body had become the prevailing force among both professors and the student body as a whole at the German University of Prague.

Anti-Semitism is not a pleasant subject, but no biography of an Austrian university professor during the last two decades of the nineteenth century would be complete without describing the development of this phenomenon and the reaction of that professor to it. All Austrian professors lived in this atmosphere of increasing race hatred and student turmoil. To omit this background would be to falsify history.

Ernst Mach never compromised with anti-Semitism. He never joined any anti-Jewish organization. Instead, he was a conspicuous member of a society to defend the rights of Jews.[45] He openly repudiated race prejudice. According to a Prague police report: "Open opponents of the anti-Semitic student movement include professors Ewald Hering the elder, Ernst Mach, Dominick Ullmann, and the Jew Horaz Krasnopolski; supporters include Hans Chiari, Karl Rabl, Richard von Wettstein and the privatdozent Adolf Hauffen." [46]

If the thought occurs that Mach could or should have done more to oppose Rohling and anti-Semitism in Prague, it is probably wise to stress these facts: first, Mach's primary interests were in science and philosophy and not in day-to-day local politics; second, it is extremely doubtful whether he could have significantly helped reverse the anti-Semitic tide in any case; third, we are still ignorant of relevant information; and fourth, with the threat of being accused of "atheism" always standing over him he was not in the best position to make an all-out fight against anti-Semitism. In this sense, Professor Rohling had Mach at a disadvantage, and he probably knew it.

In 1895, Ernst Mach left a beautiful but triply divided city of Germans, Jews, and Czechs. The torment of the situation was best summed up in the life of a young, sensitive Jewish child of the period—Franz Kafka.

CHAPTER 7

Theoretical Physics

I

We often use the terms "mathematical physics" and "theoretical physics" interchangeably, but Mach did not, and in terms of his understanding of the distinction there was a sense in which he did not believe in theoretical physics at all. If the purpose of science (the "internal" purpose) was merely to describe and relate the appearances in the simplest way possible, which for Mach was by means of mathematical functions, then "theories" would seem to have at best merely "provisional value."[1] Eventually, the discovery of the most suitable mathematical functions would make all theories superfluous and presumably theoretical physics as well. Mach was an experimental physicist who wished to redirect mathematical physics from the description of theories to the direct description of nature, but in order to show the inadequacies of theoretical physics, he found it neceessary to read through the subject in detail. Out of this effort came a number of books on the history of different branches of physics and a number of contributions to theoretical physics. But we should not mislead ourselves with respect to his primary motivation. He aimed to make all physics experimental in method and mathematical (sans theory) in end result.[2]

Robert Mayer formulated his version of the law of the conservation of energy in 1842. James Joule, Von Helmholtz, and Lord Kelvin each contributed an essential part to the general acceptance of this major addition to theoretical physics. Rudolf Clausius put forward the second law of thermodynamics in 1850 and later refined it with the notion that the amount of "entropy" in the universe (the amount of heat divided by its absolute temperature) increased in irreversible transformations. Mach did not so much oppose these laws, provided that they could be put in strict mathematical form, as reject the attempt of Helmholtz and Clausius to understand them as mechanical theories or as mathematical formulas requiring mechanistic explanation in terms of atoms and molecules.

Mach argued in his *Conservation of Energy* (1872) that the first law of thermodynamics had two forms: a mathematical form and the verbal notion that "It is impossible to create work out of nothing, or to construct a *perpetuum mobile.*" He further argued that this second or nonmathematical version of the "law of the conservation of work," as he preferred to call it, first, had been known from the earliest times; second, was merely a form of the law of causality (i.e., when understood in terms of "functional relations"); third, had been known before the development of mechanics; and fourth, was logically more fundamental than mechanics. Mach believed that mechanics was no more basic to physics than optics, acoustics, electricity, magnetism, or heat theory, that its historical priority was only accidental, and that because the atomic theory seemed to have some transient value in mechanics was no evidence that either mechanics or the atomic theory had necessary relevance or value in the other branches of physics, particularly in thermodynamics.

Mach ended his book with a final rather poetical attack on theoretical physics. "The object of natural science is the connexion of phenomena, but theories are like dry leaves which fall away when they have ceased to be the lungs of the tree of science." [3]

But while Mach's division of physics resembled that of the nature-philosopher Friedrich Schelling in his attempt to have each branch study a different type of sensory object, nonetheless, there were ambiguities that mirrored the influence of practical considerations. When Mach was philosophically consistent he denied that "electricity" was a separate field, and argued that it was a mere inclusive label that covered quite diverse "thermal," "optical," and "chemical" phenomena. But in other more practical moments he allowed that it was a separate field. Also, he sometimes treated "mechanics" merely as "the study of motion," as if other branches of physics were not concerned with motion, but needless to say, he found it hard to follow consistently such a point of view. Also, when in this particular phenomenalistic or

Schelling mood he defined "chemistry" as primarily the study of color and changes in color phenomena.[4]

Mach's *Conservation of Energy* (1872) anticipated almost all his major ideas in the rest of his books. Here are a few quotations reflecting some of his more radical views:

If then, we are astonished at the discovery that heat is motion, we are astonished at something which has never been discovered.[5]

To us investigators, the concept "soul" is irrelevant and a matter for laughter, but matter is an abstraction of exactly the same kind, just as good and just as bad as it is. We know as much about the soul as we do of matter.[6]

We say, now, that water *consists* of oxygen and hydrogen, but this oxygen and this hydrogen are merely thoughts or names which, at the sight of water, we keep ready, to describe phenomena which are not present but which will appear again whenever, as we say, we decompose water.[7]

What we represent to ourselves behind the appearances exists *only* in our understanding, and has for us only the value of a *memoria technica* or formula, whose form, because it is arbitrary and irrelevant, varies very easily with the standpoint of our culture.[8]

Thus the law of causality is sufficiently characterized by saying that it is the presupposition of the mutual dependence of phenomena. Certain idle questions, for example, whether the cause precedes or is simultaneous with the effect, then vanish by themselves.[9]

II

In light of Mach's aggressive philosophical point of view and his rather speculative and negative approach to theoretical physics it should not be surprising that most German and Austrian physicists during the 1860s and 1870s ignored his criticism and continued their efforts to base thermodynamics on the atomic theory. This brings us back to Vienna physics and to the work of Stefan, Loschmidt, and Boltzmann. While Mach was in Graz and Prague what had they been doing?

Josef Stefan became the permanent chief of Von Ettinghausen's physical institute in 1866, helped Josef Loschmidt to become a privat-dozent in the same year, and in 1867 made Ludwig Boltzmann his assistant.[10] All three men were hard working and productive and almost overnight the reputation of what was soon known as the Vienna Physical School was established.

Josef Loschmidt (1821–1895), while a middle-aged grade school teacher, made a famous calculation (1865) which caught Stefan's attention and soon resulted in an honorary doctorate (1868) and a regular teaching position at the University of Vienna (1872). Loschmidt was the first person to work out a reliable estimate of the size and number of molecules in a given volume of gas. He estimated that a cubic centimeter of nitrogen at zero degrees centigrade under normal barometric pressure contained about 100 trillion molecules and that the gaseous molecules were spheres with diameters of the order of 10^{-8} cm.[11] The Loschmidt number, as it was called, which seemed proportional to the Avogardo number, attracted the attention of numerous scientists who soon began using it in their own work.

Ludwig Boltzmann (1844–1906) was born in Vienna, the oldest son of a revenue official (*Steuerbeamter*). Both his sister Hedwig and his younger brother Albert died at an early age.[12] When Ludwig was fifteen his father died. His widowed mother augmented her small pension with the remainder of her dowry, which ran out just when Ludwig began to earn money as Stefan's assistant.[13]

Boltzmann studied under Petzval, Von Ettinghausen, and Stefan. He may even have attended some of Mach's classes, that is, before Mach left Vienna in 1864.[14] Stefan seems to have introduced Boltzmann both to the work of Maxwell and to his own law on heat radiation, which later became known as the Stefan-Boltzmann law.

In 1866 Boltzmann received his doctorate and published his first article on the second law of thermodynamics, the "entropy" law. The following year he wrote an article on molecular behavior in gases. Boltzmann was a talented mathematician, and building on the work of Stefan, Loschmidt, Clausius, and James Clerk Maxwell, was to devote the rest of his life to statistical mechanics and in particular to the kinetic theory of gases. He worked long and hard over the next thirty years to make the atomic theory indispensable to modern physics, until he became known as the most outstanding theoretical physicist in all of Central Europe.

But the more progress Boltzmann made in applying the atomic theory to help understand the structure and behavior of gases the more opposition he encountered from men such as Robert Mayer, Ernst Mach, and Wilhelm Ostwald.

Robert Mayer, considered by Mach as the founder of the mechanical theory of heat, rejected the reality of atoms and molecules and reduced "mechanical" explanation to a mere affair of sensations, ideas, and numbers. Both Mach and Popper-Lynkeus were strongly influenced by Mayer's ideas on thermodynamics.[15] Mayer, like Mach, opposed inference beyond the appearances: "the attempt to penetrate by hypotheses to the inner recesses of the world order is of a piece with the efforts of the alchemists." [16]

Since the efficiency of steam engines working between the same temperature levels had been presumed to be the same (i.e., since Sadi Carnot), "irrespective of their mode of operation or the material used to transport the heat and do work," many phenomenalistically and idealistically inclined physicists supposed that theory of heat, that is, thermodynamics, could be developed without any reference at all to material particles or mechanistic "force" explanation. Thermodynamics had no need of "atomistic hypotheses." It was a "pure" science based only on observation, experiment, and general laws. It was a true "positivistic" science. Indeed, there are still physicists today who retain and advocate ideals of this sort.

A most telling argument against the kinetic theory of gases as developed up to that time came from Boltzmann's friend, Loschmidt (1876, 1877), who suggested that since all mechanical motion was supposed to be reversible and entropy was not reversible, therefore, neither heat nor entropy consisted of mechanical motion. This reasoning supported Mach's attempt to restrict the scope of mechanics and to "free" heat and optical theory from the notions of "atoms" and "molecules." Also, if every real process contained irreversible components and all mechanical motion were reversible, then mechanics was confined to indirect description of nature, and hence, should be considered less scientific than direct phenomenalistic thermodynamics. Mach speculated further that the second law of thermodynamics, far from measuring time, was itself a definition of time.

Ludwig Boltzmann was not prepared to meet speculative and philosophical objections at this time, but in 1877, through mathematical and statistical reasoning, he appeared to meet the objections of Loschmidt. Boltzmann argued that the irreversibility of entropy flow was merely a statistical probability of what was to be expected of a huge number of particles. The entropy of individual particles of the group, however, might very well decrease rather than increase, and hence, heat might indeed consist of the mechanical motions of atoms and molecules.

But Boltzmann was plowing a field of dragon's teeth with scientific and philosophical opponents sprouting up everywhere. Mach in 1872, Gustav Kirchhoff in 1874, and Richard Avenarius in 1876 all voiced a major philosophical objection. They argued that science should describe and relate the appearances in the simplest way possible, and Mach kept hammering home the point that the atomic theory was not the simplest way to describe and relate the appearances, and that a simpler approach was needed.

Wilhelm Ostwald seemed to find that approach in the early 1890s with his philosophy of energeticism. He attempted to substitute the notion of "energy" for that of discrete "ultimate" particles such as atoms and molecules. Many physicists accepted this philosophy as introducing a genuine simplification.[17]

Boltzmann was now up against the wall. It had become obvious that if he was to refute his opponents and successfully defend his kinetic theory of gases he would have to learn enough philosophy to meet and vanquish his opponents on their own grounds. Could a middle-aged physicist who disliked philosophy turn the trick? It was quite a challenge. But was he simply too late?

How Mach's situation had changed! As a refugee from "atomistic Vienna" in 1864 with few if any physicist allies he had now twenty years later found numerous fellow "antiatomists." Opposition to atomism was once again coming into fashion, at least within physics. But why? Was it the disappointingly slow progress of the atom-based physics of Helmholtz and Du Bois-Reymond? Was it the revival of neo-Kantianism under Friedrich Lange which merely condescendingly accepted a watered version of atomism within the scope of his form of "scientific" phenomenalism? Was it the result of a camouflaged return to *Naturphilosophie?* Or was it the search for a new approach in the face of frustrating complexities?

We do not know the answer, but if there was a single turning point in physics which symbolized this fin-de-siècle opposition to atomism it was the publication of Ernst Mach's *The Science of Mechanics* in 1883. Henceforth, the tide increasingly seemed to run against Boltzmann. There is every evidence, however, in spite of the growing seriousness of the philosophical confrontation between Mach and the harassed atomist, that both men continued to remain on good personal terms. Nonetheless, Boltzmann had an expression for Mach; he called him "the nutcracker." Mach's followers in turn called Boltzmann "the last pillar." [18] But the pillar had not yet even cracked, let alone fallen. The climax was still to come.

III

In spite of Mach's efforts to criticize the most fundamental aspects of the Galileo-Newton tradition in physics primarily on physical grounds, there can be little doubt that his primary objections were philosophical or had philosophical roots. Given Mach's epistemological and ontological phenomenalism and the "common sense" philosophy of Galileo and Newton, that is, their causal, representational realism and mind-matter dualism, Mach could not have other than strongly opposed their most basic assumptions in machanics.

Mach's *Science of Mechanics* was primarily an attempt to show how the historical development of mechanics necessitated the correction of major aspects of the so-called Newtonian Synthesis in terms of Newton's own ideals and philosophy of science. Mach chose Newton's famous scholia to different parts of his *Principia Mathematica* as best indicating the Englishman's point of view, and then interpreted these scholia in terms of Mach's own phenomenalism. An examination of the rest of this book and of Newton's *Optics,* however, has suggested to E. A. Burtt and those scholars capable of distinguishing between presentational and representational philosophy that Newton held an epistemology and ontology very different from that of Mach and very different from what Mach imagined Newton to hold. In short, Newton was not a phenomenalist, even in the scholia to his *Principia Mathematica.*[19] In passing, I should also mention that Newton was not a Platonist either. Unlike Plato, Newton held that represented physical objects could move and change, that physical causes were efficient causes, and that qualities such as *vis insita* or inertial mass, while indirectly measurable by means of mathematics, were not mathematical or geometrical themselves.

Newton's work on optics, which firmly established the representative theory of perception, amply demonstrated that he identified physical objects with represented external causes of perception and not with the presented sensations or sensory impressions themselves.[20] Mach, on the other hand, denied the representative theory of perception and insisted on identifying physical objects with sensations, that is, with referents that common sense considered mental. This was a big difference. When Newton talked about physical reality he meant what lay entirely beyond experience (i.e., consciously noticeable experience). When Mach talked about physical reality he meant what lay entirely within experience (consciously noticeable experience). In other words, when they were consistent with their philosophical assumptions neither man was talking about the same thing when referring to physical objects or the "external" world. This must be taken into account when dealing with Mach's criticisms of Newton's ideas.

Newton wrote: "In philosophical disquisitions we ought to abstract from our senses and consider things themselves, distinct from what are only sensible measures of them." [21]

Mach wrote: "The assertion, then, is correct that the world consists only of our sensations." [22]

Hopefully, but not probably, these quotations should settle the matter once and for all. Newton's philosophy was substantially, and not merely "linguistically," different from Mach's philosophy, as well as from the contemporary presentationalist thought of our own day.

For Newton, to be "empirical" meant, first, to be interested in studying sensory impressions; second, to believe that sensory impressions could give a reliable indication of many aspects of physical objects; third, to use sensory data as evidence to help determine the probable truth or falsity of statements about physical objects; and fourth, not to frame hypotheses that could not be supported by relevant sensory data.

In other words, unlike Mach's understanding of "empirical," Newton held that the empirical world was not the external world, that inference beyond empirical data could be legitimate if supported by that data, and that the physical world could be reliably understood by man but only through mathematics and analogy with experience, and never with absolute certainty.

Mach thought that Newton used the word "empirical" in the same way that he himself did. He compounded this error by failing to distinguish between an empirical methodology in science and a phenomenalistic epistemology and ontology. This confusion was at the root not only of his failure to properly understand Newton's philosophical assumptions, but also, for his difficulties in later life in understanding the ideas of his critics and opponents. All experimental scientists are empirically minded and follow an empirical methodology, but what they mean by the word "empirical" necessarily shifts according to their epistemological and ontological assumptions. People assuming different theories of knowledge and reality cannot mean the same thing by the words they use.

For Mach, physical objects contained both primary and secondary qualities, but for Newton they possessed neither, but merely had qualities closely resembling the experienceable primary qualities of size, shape, extension, density, number, and weight. Since it was possible, however, to imagine objects with indistinguishably similar qualities, say two rubber balls, except one bounced higher or responded to pressure differently, then clearly an additional quality had to be attributed to physical objects.[23] Newton called this quality *vis insita,* i.e., "resident force," which might best be translated as a combination of textural and structural resistance or what we now call "inertial mass." [24]

Newton was very reluctant to speculate on the nature of this "resident force." In terms of his philosophy he would have had to frame an "hypothesis," that is, make an inference that he could not properly support with empirical data. Most of the other qualities of physical objects he presumed were quite similar to experienceable primary qualities, but resident force seemed to have no empirical analogue at all. Our "feeling" of force might historically have first suggested the physical notion of force to prehistoric man, but in a reliable fashion such an "analogy" could hardly more than merely symbolize what Newton was driving at without in any sense being descriptively accurate.

The problem was not the reality of "resident force" but the obscurity of its nature. If an object had all of the other qualities similar to observable primary ones but lacked resident force, then presumably anything could penetrate it without opposition and it could not affect anything else. In other words, from a common sense point of view it would remain a mere geometrical configuration, a spatial phantom, a referent without causal significance, and hence, in effect, nothing. In ontological terms, resident force transformed a mere geometrical particle into a physical cause and hence into a physical reality. In dynamic terms, Newton anticipated the qualitative aspects of Einstein's mass-energy law.

Newton, besides wanting to be empirical, was also a mathematician. He distinguished between "mathematical causes," which could be reliably measured by an analogous empirical measurement of selected sensations, and "physical causes" such as resident force, which did not seem to be measurable even by analogous or other indirect means.[25] The closest he could come to measuring resident force was to hope that measurement of the size and density of particles would give a reliable indication of the relative strength of that force, as if that force varied directly with size and density. Needless to say, this was whistling in the dark, but it did give a kind of justification for his mathematical definition of mass.

Newton's "empiricism" meant that he thought that the mathematical aspects of objects which lay outside of experience, that is, physical objects, but which were reliably represented in consciousness by the primary qualities of sensations, could be understood in a scientific way. These mathematical aspects, that is, in the physical object outside of experience, he called "mathematical causes." The nonmathematical (and nongeometrical) aspects of physical objects such as resident force he called "physical causes," and apparently, he did not believe that they could be understood in a scientific way because they did not even seem to have experienceable analogues of any kind.

Newton defined "mass" as quantity of matter. This was a mathematical definition, and mass was supposed to be a mathematical cause. If his hope that resident force varied directly with the size and density of particles were true, then for practical purposes there should be no harm in treating mass as though it were not only a mathematical but also a physical cause, in Newton's use of those two terms.

The advantage of Newton's definition of "mass" was that it made particular masses measurable. The formal disadvantage was the one that threatened all mathematical definitions, especially when the author was not extremely careful, namely, that someone would discover a circularity. And of course in this particular case that someone was Mach. The factual disadvantage was that by formulating a mathematical instead of a physical definition (nonontological *vs.* ontological, kinematic *vs.* dynamic) Newton avoided the whole issue as to the real efficient cause or causes of physical motion and change. In his laws of motion Newton presupposed mass as resident force, but in his explicit definition he retreated to mass as quantity of matter.

Before studying Mach's criticisms in detail it is necessary to present and clarify some of Newton's other definitions that Mach opposed. This is not an easy task, and it requires making distinctions that Newton merely assumed, but did not clearly express.

Newton's most basic distinction with respect to space rested on his ontological mind-matter dualism. *Apparent space* was mental and relative.[26] *Physical space* was of two kinds, absolute and relative, neither of which was mental or in any way experienceable (i.e., consciously noticeable). Our understanding of physical space came from inference based on sensory and ideational evidence.

Absolute physical space had the qualities of extension, duration, and penetrability. It was immovable and apparently unbounded.[27] It was also unchanging except that its penetrability varied with respect to the strength of gravitational and magnetic forces exercised through it by physical objects.

Relative physical space was a part of absolute physical space as determined by physical coordinates. If the physical coordinates moved in absolute space while retaining their positions relative to one another, then one could speak of a relative physical space moving along with them or changing its position with respect to absolute space as a whole.[28]

Absolute physical place was merely that part of absolute physical space which a material body or particle occupied.[29]

Relative physical place was the same part within the context of one or more relative physical spaces.[30]

Absolute physical time was another name for equally flowing, undisturbable duration, which was neither defined by or contingent on any particular means of measurement.[31] Indeed, it should continue unaffected even if there were no material objects in the universe, much less measuring instruments or people to use them.

Relative physical time was a measure of duration as determined by some means of motion like the hands of a clock.[32]

Absolute physical rest was the continuance of a body in the same absolute physical place.[33] Both this kind of rest and absolute physical place tacitly assumed measurement from the borders of the universe, if the universe had borders, and if the universe had no borders then from the limits of the detectable universe treated as if those limits constituted an inclusive border.

Relative physical rest was the continuance of a body in the same relative physical place.[34]

Absolute physical motion was defined in two different ways: first, as "the translation of a body from one absolute place into another";

and second, as what was "neither generated nor altered but by some force impressed upon the body moved." [35]

Relative physical motion was also defined in two different ways: first, as the translation of a body from one relative place into another; and second, as a kind of motion which may be "generated or altered without any force impressed upon the body." [36]

Let me attempt to clarify what Newton most likely meant by the terms "relative" and "absolute."

1. "Relative" meant measurable from a local perspective in physical space and time, and "merely relative" meant uncaused and/or not measureable from the "fixed stars" or the borders of the universe.

2. "Absolute" meant: first, what something had to be "in itself" to satisfy all measurements from all perspectives; second, what something was as measurable from the most distant stars or from the borders of the universe; and third, what something was as made by God or as moved or changed by physical agents possessing inertial mass, gravitational mass, or some other kind of efficient force.[37]

3. Everything "absolute" had numerous "relative" characteristics, but not vice versa. Neither "absolute" nor "relative" physical referents could literally be sensed or noticed. Things "in themselves" had both internal and external relations. Physical relations were not observable. All relations were not causal relations. Exact measurement did not imply observability, and neither implied the causal dependence of physical objects on measurement or sensory observation.[38]

IV

George Berkeley anticipated a number of Mach's criticisms of Newton's ideas. Mach admitted that he read Berkeley, but Mach, who was usually very conscientious in giving sources for his ideas, did not mention Berkeley in connection with these particular criticisms. Hence, it might be both unfair and wrong to assert that Mach took or developed his criticisms from Berkeley. Nonetheless, the similarity in many of these criticisms does seem to justify relabeling some of our expressions. We should probably speak about the "Berkeley-Mach criticism of mass" and the "Berkeley-Mach Principle."

The analyses of Karl Popper and John Myhill into the similarities between the ideas of Berkeley and Mach probably deserve to be pursued more than they have been.[39] Berkeley's opposition to many of Newton's ideas and definitions can be found in his *An Essay Towards a New Theory of Vision* (1709) and in *De Motu* (1721).

v

If Mach had understood Newton's philosophy in terms of what it actually was, that is, an ontological dualism that identified physical reality with what lay entirely outside experience, Mach logically would have had to reject all of Newton's ideas on physics as "metaphysical" and "unscientific." Mach, however, did not so understand it, and a blanket rejection of Newton's contributions to physics would not have been likely to influence his colleagues or young students in a favorable way. Instead, he tried to understand and accept Newton's ideas in terms of his own phenomenalism, and when he was simply unable to do this, he accused Newton of being "unfaithful" to Newton's own "empirical" ideals as expressed in the scholia to his *Principia Mathematica*.[40] It is within this curious context of misunderstanding that Mach launched his epoch-changing criticisms.

Mach praised Newton for his resolution to deal only with "actual facts" and for his rejection of "hypotheses." [41] But for Mach, only sensations were facts, while Newton meant all happenings, both "mental" experienceable ones and "physical" nonexperienceable ones. Similarly, Mach used the word "hypothesis" in a different way than Newton. For Mach all inferences beyond the appearances were "hypothetical," and at best provisional, but for Newton since the entire physical world was outside the appearances careful inference beyond sensations was not only legitimate, but was required by science.[42] Only those inferences beyond the appearances which were not supported by relevant empirical analogues deserved to be considered "hypotheses" and hence from Newton's point of view, "illegitimate." [43] In other words, Mach's praise of Newton's attitude toward "facts" and "hypotheses" was misleading since Mach misunderstood what Newton meant by the terms.

Mach's basic opposition to Newton's understanding of mass was that it only made sense if we assumed the reality of physical qualities outside experience, that is, resident force. Mach's best known opposition referred to a logical flaw in the written form of Newton's definition.

In his 1868 and 1872 criticism Mach still allowed for an alternative to circularity. "[Newton's definition] . . . is either a very repugnant circle, or it is necessary for one to conceive of force as 'pressure.' . . . But pressure looks very strange at the head of the quite phoronomical [kinematic] mechanics of today." [44] Mach's 1883 *Science of Mechanics*, however, left room for no alternative. Here is a quotation from a later edition (1912): "With regard to the concept of 'mass', it is to be observed that the formulation of Newton, which defines mass to be the quantity of matter of a body as measured by the product of its volume and density, is unfortunate. As we can only define density as the mass of unit of volume, the circle is manifest." [45]

The advantage of this logical criticism was that it seemed to be valid even when understood within the context of widely differing philosophies and points of view. Even philosophical opponents like Boltzmann were impressed by it. [46] Openly phenomenalistic objections to Newton's definition of "mass" would have had a much more limited appeal. But once pointed out, the circularity in Newton's definition was simply too manifest to be easily argued away. What form could or should be used to replace it?

Two solutions were evident; first "mass" could be redefined as resident force, that is, as a nonmathematical quality best in accord with Newton's epistemological and ontological philosophy, and quite consistent with common sense; or second, "mass" could be redefined in strictly phenomenalistic terms, but in a way less consistent with common sense. Mach chose the latter alternative. We do not know to what extent Mach developed his own preferred definition of "mass" himself or to what extent it was suggested by his reading of Berkeley or by an analysis of Newton's third law of motion. To the extent that it seemed to follow from the third law Mach could argue that he was merely correcting Newton in accordance with Newton's own intention to be "empirical." On the other hand, as already mentioned, Newton did not mean the same thing as Mach by the term "empirical," and he surely did not intend his laws of motion to be understood in a phenomenalistic way. Newton's physical definition of mass as "resident force" treated mass as a quality of an object. Mach, following Hume, defined mass as merely a relation.

Mach first introduced his own definition of "mass," a phenomenalistic description of the effects of mass in an 1868 article. He repeated his kinematic—but dynamic seeming—definition in his 1872 book *On the Conservation of Energy.* He wrote: "Definition—bodies which com-municate to each other equal and opposite accelerations are said to be of equal mass. We get the mass-value of a body by dividing the accelera-tion which it gives the body with which we compare others, and choose as the unit, by the acceleration which it gets itself." [47]

In a late edition of his *Science of Mechanics* (1912) he defined "mass" in somewhat stronger fashion: "it is possible to give only one rational definition of mass, and that a purely dynamical definition. It is not at all, in my judgment, a matter of taste. The concept of force and the principle of action and reaction follow of themselves." [48]

Many scientists accepted Mach's redefinition of "mass" in terms of the observable accelerations of observable physical objects on what they thought were purely scientific grounds. This acceptance, however, meant the beginning of a profound philosophical revolution within physics in the direction of Mach's ultimate positive goal, namely, the establishment of physics and all of the sciences on a strict phenme-nalistic foundation, and in particular, reunderstanding the distinction between "kinematics" and "dynamics" within a "describe and relate the appearances" context such that dynamics would be deprived of all ontological significance and could especially be "freed" from represen-tationalist ontology, that is, from resident force as a transexperiential "reality." [49]

From the point of view of Newton's causal realism Mach's definition of "mass" was no definition at all, but merely a description of one of the behavioral consequences of mass. Almost everyone would probably admit that "bodies which communicate to each other equal and op-posite accelerations were of equal mass," but for most people until the why and how of the accelerations were understood "mass" was not satisfactorily understood. Mach thought that discovering the mathe-matical "constant relations" between the appearances of accelerating bodies both defined "mass" and gave all the "causal explanation" pos-sible. But from Newton's point of view; first, appearances of accelerat-ing bodies were not those bodies; second, the accelerations of bodies were causal effects of forces impressed on the particular masses of bodies and did not define or describe the masses; and third, mathe-matical "constant relations" did not constitute physical causes and hence could not fully explain the nature or behavior of masses.

Newton's mathematical definition of "mass" needed correction, but the fact that the correction came from a phenomenalistic point of view and not from within the framework of Newton's own "common sense" philosophy has led to such changes and confusions within physics as to constitute a true historical landmark. The criticism of Newton's definition of "mass" was by no means the only influential attack that Mach launched against his ideas. Equally influential was his criticism of Newton's distinction between "relative" and "absolute" as applied to space, time, motion, place, and rest. But influential or not, there is no evidence that Mach correctly understood the philosophical context in which Newton made the distinction or the distinction itself.

Mach, like Berkeley before him, supposed that Newton meant "relative" for apparent and "absolute" for outside of experience or unrelated to experience. While Newton's use of critical terms was often inconsistent and confusing, nonetheless, the understandings of both Mach and Berkeley were mistaken. If Newton had attempted to distinguish between relative apparent space and absolute apparent space, then the criticisms of Mach and Berkeley would have held. It is hard to speak coherently about an apparent space whose characteristics are independent of how it could or does appear to people. But of course when Newton was talking about relative or absolute space, he did not mean apparent space, that is, the noticeable space of perception, observation, or experience. Both "relative" and "absolute" pertained to referents outside conscious experience; though both could often be "related" to what lay within such experience as well. For Newton, apparent space was merely an empirical analogue that provided evidence from which inferences could be drawn to help understand the nature of relative and absolute space. From Newton's point of view both Mach and Berkeley were concerned merely with mental and not with physical space at all. Their criticisms had no relevance for physics or understanding physical reality, which lay entirely outside all conscious impressions.

Mach objected to "absolute space" on the grounds: first, that it was unobservable; and second, that it could not be related to an observable frame of reference. The first objection was of course true, but since all physical reality, both "relative" and "absolute," was unobservable for Newton, the criticism was inconsequential. The second objection was not true, if we accept Newton's mind-matter dualism and insist that neither relations nor the things related need be observable to be real.[50] For Newton "absolute space" was "related" to an observable frame of references in that all such frames were in people's minds, all such minds were located in living brains, and all such brains existed in "absolute space." Mach's objections to other "absolutes," such as time, motion, place, and rest, were basically the same as those against absolute space, but should seem plausible only to people who think that relations or what are related have to be consciously noticeable to be real or "scientific."

Here are some quotations reflecting Mach's opposition to Newton's understanding of space, time, and motion:

It would appear as though Newton in the remarks here cited still stood under the influence of the medieval philosophy, as though he had grown unfaithful to his resolve to investigate only actual facts.[51]

A motion may, with respect to another motion, be uniform. But the question whether a motion is *in itself* uniform, is senseless. With just as little justice, also, may we speak of an "absolute time"—*of a time independent of change.* This absolute time can be measured by comparison with no motion, it has therefore neither a practical nor a scientific value; and no one is justified in saying that he knows aught about it. It is a metaphysical conception.[52]

It is utterly beyond our power to *measure* the changes of things by time. Quite the contrary, time is an abstraction, at which we arrive by means of the changes of things, made because we are not restricted to any one *definite* measure, all being interconnected.[53]

No one is competent to predicate things about absolute space and absolute motion; they are pure things of thought, pure mental constructs, that cannot be produced in experience. All our principles of mechanics are, as we have shown in detail, experimental knowledge concerning the relative positions and motions of bodies.[54]

No one is warranted in extending these principles [of mechanics] beyond the boundaries of experience. In fact, such an extension is meaningless, no one possesses the requisite knowledge to make use of it.[55]

It is scarcely necessary to remark that in the reflections here presented Newton has again acted contrary to his expressed intention only to investigate *actual facts.*[56]

A thing that is beyond the ken of knowledge, a thing that cannot be exhibited to the senses, has no meaning in natural science.[57]

All *physical* determinations are *relative.* Consequently, likewise all *geometrical* determinations possess validity only relatively to the measure. The concept of measurement is a concept of relation, which contains nothing not contained in the measure.[58]

Mach also opposed other "absolutes" such as "absolute zero" and "the absolute speed of light." [59] It is possible he opposed other scientific constants as well. The only "absolutes" he seems to have favored were the "absolute certainty" that sensations were "immediately given," that in and of themselves they could not be deceptive, and that depending on the way in which they were related they constituted the external world.

VI

Newton attempted to support his argument for the reality of absolute motion by appealing to what has been called "the bucket experiment":

If a vessel hung by a long cord is so often turned about that the cord is strongly twisted, then filled with water and held at rest together with the water, thereupon by the sudden action of another force it is whirled about the contrary way, and while the cord is untwisting itself the vessel continues for some time in this motion, the surface of the water will at first be plain, as before the vessel began to move; but after the vessel, by gradually communicating its motion to the water, will make it begin sensibly to revolve and recede by little and little from the middle, and ascend to the sides of the vessel, forming itself into a concave figure (as I have experienced); and the swifter the motion becomes, the higher will the water rise, till at last, performing its revolutions in the same times with the vessel, it becomes relatively at rest in it. This ascent of the water shows its endeavor to recede from the axis of its motion; and the true and absolute motion of the water, which is here directly contrary to the relative, becomes known and may be measured by this endeavor.[60]

The effects which distinguish absolute from relative motion are the forces of receding from the axis of circular motion. For there are no such forces in a circular motion purely relative, but in a true and absolute circular motion they are greater or less according to the quantity of the motion.[61]

There is only one real circular motion of any one revolving body, corresponding to only one power of endeavoring to recede from its axis of motion, as its proper and adequate effect; but relative motions, in one and the same body, are innumerable, according to the various relations it bears to external bodies, and, like other relations, are altogether destitute of any real effect, any otherwise than they may perhaps partake of that one only true motion.[62]

Mach responded ingeniously to the challenge: first by inquiring whether Newton's water results would follow if the bucket were several leagues thick; second, by suggesting that the stars could as easily be interpreted as revolving around the stationary bucket as the bucket spinning under fixed or relatively fixed stars; and third, by returning to the arguments of Cardinal Bellarmine against Galileo's defense of the Copernican theory as a theory of reality.[63] In Mach's own words:

When quite modern authors let themselves be led astray by the Newtonian arguments which are derived from the bucket of water, to distinguish between relative and absolute motion, they do not reflect that the system of the world is only given *once* to us, and the Ptolemaic or Copernican view is *our* interpretation, but both are equally actual. Try to fix Newton's bucket and rotate the heaven of fixed stars and then prove the absence of centrifugal forces.[64]

Newton's experiment with the rotating vessel of water simply informs us that the relative rotation of the water with respect to the sides of the vessel produces *no* noticeable centrifugal forces, but that such forces *are* produced by its relative rotation with respect to the mass of the earth and the other celestial bodies. No one is competent to say how the experiment would turn out if the sides of the vessel increased in thickness and mass till they were ultimately several leagues thick. The one experiment only lies before us, and our business is, to bring it into accord with the other facts known to us, and not with the arbitrary fictions of our imagination.[65]

Relatively, not considering the unknown and neglected medium of space, the motions of the universe are the same whether we adopt the Ptolemaic or the Copernican mode of view. Both views are, indeed, equally *correct*, only the latter is more simple and more *practical*.[66]

Newton's bucket experiment and Mach's criticisms of it have remained of interest to physicists today. There have also been a number of attacks on Mach's stand. His defense, for example, of the Ptolemaic approach as "equally correct" has run afoul of the fact that the stars would have to exceed the speed of light if under our present understanding they would be construed as revolving around the earth. Equally telling in this age of space travel is the likelihood that observation from other planets would much more easily fit the Copernican theory than the Ptolemaic one.[67]

The plausibility of Mach's criticism was contingent on accepting his phenomenalism, his definition of physical space and time as "relations," and on overlooking defects in his causal theory and failure to define what he meant by "relations."

Even if we allow that the stars revolve around a stationary bucket, and not the opposite, it is still not clear how the stars can exercise any causal influence on the behavior of the bucket or the water inside it. The stars are too far away to act as either a contact or as a gravitational or magnetic cause. Mach's solution of course was to reduce what he meant by a cause to a mere observable relational constancy. For most people there are many "constant relations" which in no sense are causes and which at best are merely "incidentally co-present," but

Mach's phenomenalism made no allowance for noncausal constant relations.[68] When Mach claimed that all sensations were "relative" he meant that some kind of relation could be found between all sensations such that no sensation was entirely "unrelated" or "absolute." The only "constant relation" he was able to find between the water swirling in the bucket and an outside appearance was with the stars. Hence, he suggested that they were responsible for the strange water concavity in the bucket.[69]

Newton, of course, would have admitted that the concave circular water motion in the bucket was "relative" in that it could be causally "related" to the untwisting of the bucket cord and speculatively "related" to the stars. The same motion was also "absolute," however, in that it was caused by a particular force (the untwisting of the cord), and hence, was not merely relative (i.e., uncaused) and because observation and measurement from the most distant stars would record the motion and thus prove that it was not *merely relative* (i.e., local). In other words, Newton held that the terms "relative" and "absolute" were not mutually exclusive and that "absolute" meant a particular type rather than the absence of relation. To be sure, Newton used the word "absolute" in different ways; nonetheless, these uses seem to be remarkably compatible with each other. On the other hand, it would be hard to argue that Mach either correctly understood Newton's various definitions of "relative" and "absolute" or successfully refuted Newton's bucket argument. But we should not overlook or forget the basic point. Mach and Newton were arguing over apples and oranges. Mach identified the physical world with sensations, and Newton identified it with what lay beyond or outside of sensations. The two men were simply not referring to the same things.

"Progress" is strange, however. Mach misunderstood Newton's ideas and rejected theoretical physics, and a brilliant theoretical physicist, who was even less philosophically sophisticated than either Newton or Mach, was so stimulated by Mach's phenomenalistic criticisms as to develop a revolutionary physical theory that legitimately refuted many of Newton's physical ideas or reduced them to special case application, but which, philosophically, was closer to the views of Newton than Mach, even though the author of the theory for many years did not realize it.

Newton's theory of causal explanation with its distinctions between "physical" and "mathematical" causes, and causal "agents" and "laws," was never clearly expressed, and, while an extension of common sense, practical, and informative, was a rather complex, matter. Mach's theory, on the other hand, while in many ways impractical and uninformative, was the essence of simplicity. Causes did not exist, except insofar as one chose to call constant relations and mathematical functions "causes." Mach's interest in relational constancies, however, led him into a further development of his appeal to the stars. "I [Mach] have remained to the present day [1912] the only one who insists upon referring the law of inertia to the earth and in the case of motions of great spatial and temporal extent, to the fixed stars." [70]

But Mach was not quite alone. At almost exactly the time he wrote this, Albert Einstein introduced a variation of Mach's star speculation, which he called "Mach's principle," into his developing general theory of relativity. I am, however, getting ahead of the story. Suffice it to say here that the plausibility of trying to explain the law of inertia by relating it to the earth and stars rests nowadays on the conceivability that the totality of all stars and matter in the universe may exert some kind of supergravitational influence on local motion. The extent, however, to which Einstein and later physicists have understood what might best be called "The Berkeley-Mach principle" within the context of Mach's phenomenalism is perhaps no greater than Mach's similar attempts to understand Newton's ideas within the framework of Newton's philosophy. We might mention in passing that Boltzmann, who read Mach's books closely, could not resist calling Mach's star speculations "transcendent" (i.e., "metaphysical"). He thereby successfully played turnabout with one of Mach's favorite abusive tools.[71] Not only did Mach have no idea how the stars could affect local motion, but in referring to the stars as a vague whole, he was referring to many unobserved entities, perhaps many unobservable entities, and quite likely numerous heavenly bodies with characteristics incompatible with his explanation of inertia. On the other hand, Mach rarely grieved over the fate of "mere theories," even his own. New "simpler" theories with more value for science or for satisfying human "biological needs" might always appear. In any case, all theories would eventually be replaced by "mathematical functions" referring directly to experienceable sensations.

CHAPTER 8

Mach Shock Waves

I

One day in 1881 while Ernst Mach was visiting the First International Electrical Exhibition in Paris, where he was also a delegate to the First Electro-Technical Congress, he happened to hear a lecture by the Belgian artillerist, Louis Melsens.[1] Mach was so struck by one of Melsens's theories about the explosive impact of compressed air as a cause for the crater-like wounds in victims shot by gunfire during the Franco-Prussian War that, on returning to Prague, he decided that when he could find the opportunity, he would set up an experiment to test the theory.[2]

Dr. Merzkirch of the Ernst-Mach-Institut in Freiburg in Germany gives two reasons for Mach's interest:

One reason was the well-know observation of artillerymen that one perceives usually two bangs while a fast projectile is flying by. One of them had to be the bang originating at the muzzle of the gun. The second, however, found no appropriate explanation; it did not appear when the speed of the projectile was rather low. The second reason traces back to the German-French war of 1870/71. It had then been noticed that the French Chassepôt-bullets caused big, crater-shaped injuries; the French had been charged therefore with using explosive projectiles violating the International Treaty of St. Petersburg of 1868, which prohibited the use of such projectiles. These charges had been . . . [disputed] by the Belgian physicist M. Melsens, who reported on his investigations in 1872 at the Royal Academy of Sciences in Brussels. He made the following suppositions: (1.) A spherical projectile is able to carry a considerable amount of compressed air which depends on its velocity; (2.) The compressed air precedes the projectile and may cause mechanical, explosion-like effects. The reported injuries have to be explained in this way.[3]

Mach wanted to check the reliability of Melsens's conclusions. Mach's own background in ballistic experimentation was extensive, especially concerning the speed of projectiles and trying to photograph them in motion.[4] He had also learned a great deal from other experiments on rapid motion, such as those concerned with the Doppler theory (1860, 1878), blood pressure measuring instruments (1862), liquid pressure in pipes (1862), acoustic waves in the human ear (1863), the effects of sound waves on glass and quartz (1872), and soot, electric spark, and explosion experiments (1875).[5] Equally valuable was the experience he had gained from constructing (together with his laboratory helper Franz Hajek) laboratory equipment that could measure rapid motion.

II

We normally think of electric sparks as flashes of light, but with care they can often be heard as well. In a sense they are miniature explosions that give off audible waves which Mach naturally supposed could not exceed the speed of sound. In 1875, Mach's assistant Čeněk Dvořák brought to his attention an article by K. Antolik. The article "Acoustic Phenomena of Electric Spark Discharges" stimulated Mach to make a series of curious experiments. Since we know the speed of sound, the measured distance that these spark waves travel should give us an exact measurement of time. Mach went to work to build a suitable "time machine," or rather, time-measuring apparatus. But something went decidedly wrong.

Mach had devised a technique whereby spark waves would blow soot across a glass plate. If there were two sparks separated at a distance from each other then the waves would cancel each other out and a soot line would be formed. If the sparks were discharged at the same time then the line should presumably be halfway between them.

In one experiment he used a flying bullet to discharge both sparks, with a ballistic pendulum to measure the exact speed of the projectile. This gave an exact delay time, but unfortunately, the soot line did not form the expected pattern. Two unanticipated "V" *angles* appeared (see diagram 4). On close examination it was discovered that the spark wave had gone faster than the speed of sound! Hence, it could not be an acoustical wave in any normal sense, even if it was audible. It was, in fact, a shock wave. The discovery ruined Mach's "time machine," but it excited his imagination to proceed further.

Another peculiarity soon turned up. Spark (i.e., shock) waves bounced off a perpendicular wall in expected fashion, that is, as normal sound waves do, but when the wall was tilted beyond a certain angle a strange effect took place. A three-front or Y soot pattern resulted with a primary front, a reflected front, and a doubly reflected front (see diagram 5). Mach published these results in an 1878 article.[6] Dr. Merzkirch has described Mach's new discovery as follows:

According to Mach the intersection of the two waves of finite amplitude becomes the origin of a new wave which travels along the primary wave front with a certain velocity ω. When the velocity component of the secondary wave parallel to the direction of motion of the primary wave, $\omega \cos (\zeta/2)$, exceeds the speed W if the primary wave, then the Y-shaped separation is supposed to start, and the irregular reflection begins. It is possible to determine for given W and ω a limiting angle ζ_0 below which the regular reflection cannot exist. W, ω and hence also ζ_0 are functions of the shock strength. The phenomenon is the same when the axis is replaced by a solid wall, at which the blast wave originating from one spark gap is now reflected." [7]

Mach's name gradually became associated with a number of soot wave and angled wall phenomena.[8]

Mach's soot experiments were important both in themselves and in preparing him for his later major shock wave discoveries.[9] With respect to Mach labels, Raymond J. Seeger during World War II seems to have been the first to give published reference to the expressions "Mach effect" and "Mach reflection." [10] The term "Mach stem" has gained a measure

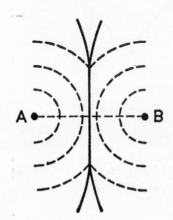

DIAGRAM 4.
Double "V" Diagram.
The two soot line angles (Mach effects)
are joined by a soot line
(Mach bridge) halfway between *A* and *B*.
The letters represent simultaneous
explosion points.

of notoriety from atomic bomb explosions where it is often used to refer to the resulting ground-level shock waves. On the whole, the notions of Mach effect and Mach reflection have become important in gas dynamics, even though they set in at angles somewhat less than those predicted by theory.[11]

In 1878 Mach attempted to follow up the success of his soot experiments by using the so-called Toepler striation method to get a clear photograph of what shock waves looked like. But their extreme speed, beyond the speed of sound, made this a very formidable undertaking. It was one thing to infer the waves from soot formations and quite another to get a sharp photograph picture of them.

Mach was extremely busy during the next six years with two rectorates, the writing and publication of two books, scattered explosion experiments, and work in electricity. The latter field had suddenly become very popular at least among physicists, but Mach's contributions in it were not very important and stood in depressing contrast to those of his old Vienna rival Josef Stefan, now president of both the Austrian Electro-Technical Union and the Vienna International Electric Fair (1883). In addition, Stefan had also become known as the director of the best-run physical institute on the Continent.

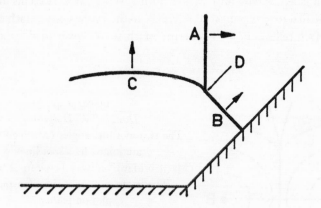

DIAGRAM 5. "Y" *Diagram.* Irregular or Mach reflection of
a direct shockwave on an angled wall:
(*A*) primary shock wave, (*B*) Mach stem,
(*C*) part of the regular reflected wave, and (*D*) triplepoint.

III

Mach's first serious attempt to test Melsens's hypotheses on the nature of shock waves in front of projectiles took place in 1884. He started by trying to take exact photographs of four different kinds of speeding phenomena: flying projectiles, sound waves, spark waves, and projectile shock waves.

Reasonably successful attempts to photograph moving projectiles had been made as early as 1866 in Woolwich, England, and again in 1882 by Marey in France, but Mach's 1884 pictures represented a substantial improvement in clarity and distinctness. Mach was also successful in taking good pictures of sound and spark waves in 1884. With respect to projectile shock waves a Frenchman, Captain Journée, claimed that he had seen one by using a telescope down a projectile's line of flight, and on that basis he claimed precedence.[12]

In this same year, 1884, Mach began his major effort to photograph projectile shock waves. By this time Mach had learned how to circum-

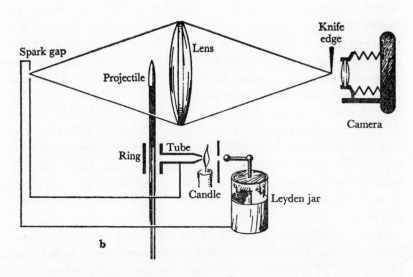

DIAGRAM 6.

Toepler's *Schlierenmethode.* An apparatus reconstructed by Ludwig Mach to photograph the shock wave in front of a projectile without also having to photograph a trip wire.

(Courtesy of Holden-Day Incorporated)

vent a major obstacle. Besides being fast and small, shock waves were normally invisible, that is, since they consisted of air they were transparent. Mach's solution was to use an illuminated magnifying lens which would make the water condensation within the shock wave visible as a shadow contrast.[13]

Professor Floyd Ratliff has described how the arrangement (see diagram 6) worked:

Mach designed an improved version of the [Toepler] apparatus in which the projectile, passing through a ring, forced air through a small tube; the escaping air caused a candle flame at the end of the tube to waver. The flame in turn shorted a circuit, causing a leyden jar to discharge and produce a brief spark for illumination of the projectile. By an adjustment in the length of the tube, the discharge could be set off at the moment the projectile reached the center of the field covered by the camera.[14]

Mach first tried a target pistol and soon obtained excellent photographs of the hurrying bullets, but without any accompanying shock waves! Where were they? Had he done something wrong? Mach soon rightly suspected that the velocity of the pistol bullets had not exceeded the speed of sound. Their speed was only about 240 meters per second whereas the speed of sound at that altitude was about 340 meters per second. Another experiment had failed. The shock waves remained elusive. About two years later after finishing his book on psychology and having completed a number of additional experiments on spark and explosion waves, he returned to the problem. This time he was determined that the projectiles would move faster than the normal speed of sound. Mach wrote to Professor P. Salcher of the Austrian Naval Academy in Fiume on the Adriatic in early 1886. He was able to persuade him and a Professor Riegler to conduct ballistic experiments under closely written instructions from Mach. Over a hundred letters from each side were exchanged during the next year, as advice, analysis, corrections, and reports were communicated back and forth.

Success finally came, and on June 10, 1886, Mach deposited a short notice with the Austrian Academy of Science along with the first two photographs of projectile shock waves ever successfully taken.[15]

The small but respected Austrian Navy (undefeated in its only fleet action using armored ships, i.e., against Italy in 1866) was pleased with Mach's and Salcher's results and soon made a large cannon available to the latter at Pola on the Adriatic. Not to be outdone, Prussia, an ally of Austria-Hungary, through Herr Krupp of the famous steel-and munitions-producing family, offered Mach himself a location at Meppen in Hannover to continue his experiments. Mach and his son Ludwig, then a student of medicine, accepted the offer. Mach's photographs were well publicized at the time, even in popular magazines and newspapers.

In spite of public recognition and the generosity of the Naval Department and Krupp, Mach soon came to a rather practical conclusion: "All these experiments [at Pola and Meppen] furnished tolerably good and complete pictures; some little progress, too, was made. The outcome of our experience on both artillery ranges, however, was the settled conviction that really good results could be obtained only by the most careful conduct of the experiments in a laboratory especially adapted to the purpose." [16]

With his first projectile shock wave photos Mach could now confirm the suspicions of artillery officers as to why two reports were often heard after a gun was fired. The first report was from the accompanying head shock wave which was faster than the speed of sound, and the second report was from slower but normal sound waves coming from the exploding powder. If only one report was heard then presumably the projectile must have been traveling slower than the speed of sound.

Mach also discovered that the head waves resembled the front or bow waves of ships and could largely be explained as Christian Huygens had done with acoustic waves some two hundred years before.

Mach now felt competent enough to refute two of Melsens's hypotheses. First, projectiles did not carry air masses along with them, either in front as with Melsens or behind as with Aristotle, but rather, consecutive dynamic air disturbances of relatively stationary air gave the impression of a continuing motion of the same air. Second, the projectile head waves were so thin as to have negligible velocity against objects, certainly not enough to be responsible for significant aspects of battle wounds. In Mach's own words:

A forward-moving sound [i.e., shock] wave is not a forward-moving mass of matter, but a forward-moving form of motion, just as a water-wave or the waves of a field of wheat are only forward-moving forms of motion and not movements of masses of water or masses of wheat. . . . it was found that the bell-shaped headwave in question is an extremely thin shell and that the condensations of the same are quite moderate, scarcely exceeding two-tenths of an atmosphere. There can be no question, therefore, of explosive effects in the body struck by the projectile through so slight a degree of atmospheric compression. The phenomena attending wounds from rifle balls, for example, are not to be explained as Melsens and Busch explain them, but are due as Kocher and Reger maintain, to the effects of the impact of the projectile itself.[17]

In a sense, Mach's experimental discovery supported the original accusation, namely, that the French Chassepôt bullets caused illegal "crater-like wounds." But since it was not true that they included an explosive charge, the probable explanation lay in their high velocity, and of course, in the shape of the projectile.

IV

Mach published a most significant paper in 1885 in which for the first time he presented what we now call Mach number, that is, a ratio in which we divide the flow velocity by the speed of sound.[18] This ratio was soon picked up and used by many other physicists and scientists, but apparently the first man to explicitly label it *Mach number* was Professor J. Ackeret in his *Habilitationschrift* in 1928. In the following year he made the first published reference to it in an article.[19] To help confuse matters, the French lexicon *Grande Larousse* (Paris, 1962) has claimed that the ratio is also sometimes called "Nombre de Sarrau" after the French scientist Emile Sarrau, who like Mach experimented on explosion and pressure waves in the 1870s and in 1880s.[20]

The expressions Mach 1, Mach 2, and so forth, which gave numerical value to the above ratio, became important during the 1940s with the increased possibility of supersonic jet aircraft. Especially after Charles "Chuck" Yeager broke the sound barrier in 1947 and numerous other pilots and airplanes quickly followed suit, the terms have become so popular that they are now widely used and understood by non-scientists around the world. Some related neologisms used in aeronautics include: Machmeter, Mach hold, and critical Mach number.

Mach formulated the equation $\sin a = \dfrac{\text{speed of sound}}{\text{flow velocity}}$ in December 1886 for what we now call Mach angle (see diagram 7). According to Professor Ackeret, Mach probably received the suggestion for this equation from Doppler who had written something similar in 1847.[21] We do not know who first coined the expression Mach angle, or when, but presumably it was common before the late 1920s. It is possible that Ludwig Prandtl was responsible for introducing or at least for popularizing the term.

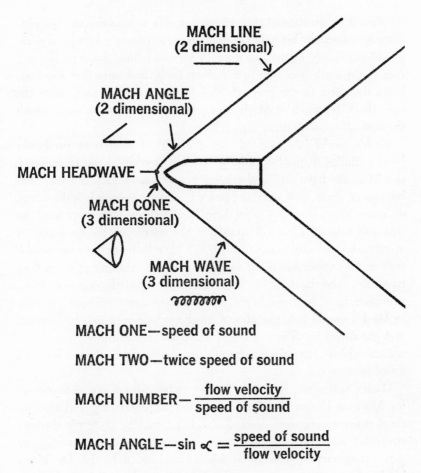

MACH ONE—speed of sound

MACH TWO—twice speed of sound

MACH NUMBER— $\dfrac{\text{flow velocity}}{\text{speed of sound}}$

MACH ANGLE—$\sin \alpha = \dfrac{\text{speed of sound}}{\text{flow velocity}}$

DIAGRAM 7.
Mach Shock Wave Terminology
(Courtesy of Miss Nancy Martsch)

v

Some by-products of Mach's work included an explanation of meteor reports, a so-called model law, Salcher's idea of a wind tunnel, and Ludwig Mach's design and construction of an improved interferometer. Dr. Merzkirch discusses Mach's article on meteors (1887) as follows:

"It should be mentioned that Mach was able to explain another phenomena related to his ballistic findings which some scientists had reported previously in the literature. A meteor falling down to the surface of the earth produces first a sharp bang, and only thereafter one hears the noise of the impact! This bang is nothing more than the bow shock reported by Mach, since the meteor comes down through the atmosphere with supersonic velocity." [22]

Mach's model law asserted that geometrical models of projectiles having similar shapes but different sizes, if moving at the same speed, should ideally have similar shock waves and cone angles. But there has been some doubt how reliable Mach's kinematic approach and reliance on mere visual geometry were here. If the shock wave was small in size and velocity it would seem that the nature of the medium, its atomic and molecular structure, would have to be taken into consideration. Of course, Mach did not believe in the existence of atoms and molecules, and he tried to avoid having to use the atomic theory whenever possible. Nonetheless, the objection seems relevant not only to Mach's model law, but also to Mach's whole approach to ballistics and gas dynamics. There are limitations to an ostensibly physical approach which relies almost entirely on macroscopic observation and visual geometry.

Mach's colleague, Professor Salcher, who carried out experiments for Mach at Fiume and Pola, attempted an interesting variation on shock-wave experiments. Instead of firing a moving projectile through stationary air, why not reverse the situation and force moving air past a stationary projectile, and this is exactly what he did. Dr. Merzkirch relates: "The experiments were again performed by Salcher in a torpedo factory in Fiume; these experiments are interesting in so far as this was certainly the first time that the idea of a supersonic blow-down wind-tunnel had been expressed." [23]

By the late 1880s Ludwig Mach was devoting more time to improving his father's laboratory equipment than on his own medical studies. In short, Ernst Mach was already beginning to lean on the talented laboratory and practical skills of his eldest son, and in this respect he was quite fortunate. No father ever had a more dutiful child or useful assistant.

Ludwig Mach worked to improve an instrument, called Jamin's Interferometer, which Ernst Mach had been employing to obtain linear graph readings of the sizes and presumed strength of shock waves.

The twenty-three-year old Ludwig later wrote: "Concerning the apparatus I am describing here, I had already finished putting its parts together by July 1891, but could not completely put it in functioning order until November 1891 because of a delay in the arrival of a needed machine tool." [24] The instrument soon became called the Mach-Zehnder Interferometer and is still used today.[25] With this machine Ernst Mach was able to determine "that the relative density at the shock front is about 50 times what had been measured for regular sound waves." [26] In other words, since Mach had already experimented with the power of acoustic waves to break glass, the suspicion may finally have occurred to him that perhaps shock waves were not necessarily so harmless after all. If large enough and with sufficient velocity, then we have that product of the jet age, a sonic boom.

CHAPTER 9

Early Philosophical Influence

I

Mach used various means to help spread his philosophical ideas. He was an excellent lecturer; he wrote many articles, he had a wide correspondence; and starting in 1886 he wrote a number of textbooks for middle school and university science students. In this chapter I concentrate on the influence of three of his best-known books on a few prominent scientists and philosophers during the last quarter of the nineteenth century.

Mach's *Conservation of Energy* (1872) did not pass entirely unnoticed. Wilhelm Tobias in his *Frontiers of Philosophy* (1875) criticized Mach's notion of mathematical multidimensionality from, strangely enough, a phenomenalistic point of view.[1] Anton Leclair, a Prague "Immanentist" philosopher and gymnasium teacher, in his *The Realism of Modern Natural Science in Light of the Epistemological Critique of Berkeley and Kant* (1879), enthusiastically praised Mach's book, even calling it "revolutionary."[2] Leclair, known as an excellent teacher, was a close friend of Wilhelm Jerusalem. In his writings Mach never mentioned Leclair at all; but they both lived in Prague, they did correspond, and Mach had at least one of Leclair's books in his library.[3] It is not impossible that Leclair may even have influenced Mach, especially in the criticisms of Newton's ideas in Mach's *Science of Mechanics*. In any case, immediately after the appearance of Leclair's book Mach started to work on his *Mechanics* (i.e., in 1880).

Max Planck, whose doctoral dissertation was concerned with the conservation of energy (1879), presumably read Mach's book on the same subject at that time. Later, during the Mach-Planck confrontation (1909–1911), Mach questioned Planck's knowledge of it: "When M. Planck wrote 15 years after I did on the 'conservation of energy' he only brought one general observation against one of my detailed points, without which one would have had to assume that he had not even seen my book at all." [4]

II

Mach's *Science of Mechanics* (1883) was immediately influential among scientists around the world. Ostwald, Hertz, Boltzmann, and later Einstein all read it and were deeply influenced by it.

Wilhelm Ostwald (1853–1932) was born in Riga, graduated from the University of Dorpat, and taught chemistry in the Technical University of Riga from 1881 to 1887. His early scientific work led to the cofounding of a new science, physical chemistry. His long professorship at the University of Leipzig (1887–1906) allowed him to build up a large and highly successful laboratory in this new field which attracted students from all over the world. He also wrote the first major treatise and founded the first journal in physical chemistry.

Ostwald claimed that Mach among the living, and Robert Meyer among the dead, were the men who had influenced his thinking the most.[5] He was especially attracted to Mach's notions of economy, substance, and hypothesis. Mach defined "substance" as that which persisted through all changes and transformations and doubted that any referent could qualify. Ostwald was more optimistic. But what reality could possibly meet this standard?

W. J. M. Rankine first suggested the answer in his "Outlines of the Science of Energetics" in 1855. Mach's friend Popper-Lynkeus was even more explicit in his "The Fundamentals of Electric Power Transmission" in 1883. Georg Helm (1851–1923) made Popper's finding the basis for his *Theory of Energy* (Leipzig, 1887). But Helm's elaboration did not attract much attention until Ostwald incorporated the "factorization of energy" into the second edition of his own treatise on physical chemistry, *A Textbook of General Chemistry,* in 1892. In short, both Helm and Ostwald adopted the opinion that the only "substance" that persisted through all changes and transformations was *energy*. Energy was the only genuine reality, the substrate of all appearances, and we never perceive anything but energy, or rather, differences in energy. "We never perceive a material substance itself, but only its energetic interaction with our own organism." [6]

Mach defined a "hypothesis" as any inference beyond the appearances, but Ostwald attempted to reconcile this definition with Mach's belief in the incompleteness of science by stressing that in order to penetrate into new areas of knowledge it was necessary to start by making provisional assumptions or hypotheses of a second sort. In Ostwald's own words: "I distinguish hypotheses as arbitrary ["metaphysical"] assumptions, which one cannot prove, from prototheses as provisional assumptions, which one makes for the purpose of being able to establish proofs in previously unknown fields." [7]

Ostwald's distinction between two types of hypotheses has fitted in well with contemporary views of our own day and has helped to bury Newton's (and Mach's) misleading claim that they "make no hypotheses."

Mach's own reaction to Ostwald's "Energeticism" did not fully satisfy the Leipzig professor. Mach claimed: "The fundamentals of a general energeticism were very briefly included in my 1872 book [*Conservation of Energy*], and hardly differed from Ostwald's at all except for his chosen label." [8] Ostwald, however, was very suspicious of Mach's claim of *virtual* agreement. "He [Mach] was one of the first to recognize and promote the general significance of the laws of energy, but he would not associate himself with Energeticism." [9] "Very characteristically Mach introduces this [his "antimetaphysical" tendency] into his attitude toward Energeticism, which he has not explicitly rejected, but towards which he is much more critical than sympathetic." [10]

In spite of Mach's claims to priority and occasional support, Ostwald's doubts were well grounded. Mach needed Ostwald as an ally against atomism, but basically, Mach opposed both "Atomism" and "Energeticism."

Ostwald believed in Energeticism as an explanatory theory to describe the appearances and in energy as a reality. Mach as an ontological phenomenalist denied the reality of everything that could not be a sensation, and held that *all* theories whether "atomistic," "energetical," or whatever were merely historical stages, of at best provisional value, which science might pass through on its way to the end goal of scientific simplicity in the form of mathematical functions. On the basis of the available evidence it seems, contrary to what one might expect and contrary to what some of his followers seem to have taken for granted, that Mach preferred some varieties of atomic theory to energetical theory in making provisional explanations in physics.[11] But in the larger context this "preference" meant virtually nothing. In gist, Mach opposed both atomism and energeticism on two counts: first, with respect to their alleged necessity as scientific theories; and second, with respect to the reality of atoms and energy as referents outside the appearances.

III

Heinrich Hertz (1857–1894) was born in Hamburg, the son of a lawyer and senator of the old Hanseatic seaport. He studied engineering, and later, turned to physics under Helmholtz in Berlin. He subsequently taught at Kiel (1883), Karlsruhe (1885), and Bonn (1889). Hertz became famous during the late 1880s for his experimental demonstration of the existence of electromagnetic waves.

According to Hertz's diary he first read Mach's *Mechanics* on March 4, 1884.[12] Ten years later, shortly before his premature death, Hertz finished an influential book describing alternative approaches to physical theory, couched within Kant's epistemology and Mach's philosophy of science.[13] In Mach's own words: "[Hertz's ideas] coincide as exactly as is possible with my own, considering that Hertz was a supporter of the mechanical and atomic physics and a follower of Kant." [14]

The most important consequence of Hertz's book was to impress physicists with alleged differences between "classical" and "modern" physics. The expressions themselves were apparently not used by Hertz himself, but Poincaré in 1897 and Boltzmann in 1899 used them in referring to Hertz's book, thereby helping to popularize both the distinction and the labels.[15] What is especially to be noted is that the terms were in use before the discoveries of both Planck and Einstein, that is, before the discoveries that are currently supposed to have caused and justified the distinction and labels in the first place! The most reasonable explanation would be that Hertz noticed difficulties in Newtonian mechanics and anticipated major experimental and theoretical discoveries. Nevertheless, the significance of his distinction was that he based "modern physics" largely on Mach's philosophy of science so that when the genuine modern physics of Planck and Einstein appeared, the new results became understood to a major extent within the context of epistemological phenomenalism and Mach's ideas on the methodology and purpose of science.

In detail, Hertz attempted to describe sensations in terms of mechanical laws based on only three fundamental notions: space, time, and mass. He agreed with Mach in rejecting "force" as a basic physical concept, but whereas Mach tried to retain a phenomenalistic equivalent, derivative from his definition of "mass," Hertz wanted to eliminate the notion from physics altogether. Hertz also held that mechanical laws could be properly developed into a tight deductive system only if perceived mass, motion, and time were supplemented by assumptions about unperceived mass and motion. Mach criticized this "metaphysical" addition, but in fact, even Mach normally allowed for the existence of unconscious sensations.

IV

Ludwig Boltzmann, who wanted to understand more about philosophical attacks on "classical" physics in general and on his own contributions to the kinetic theory of gases in particular, opened a correspondence with Ostwald in 1890 and with Mach in 1892.[16] He also encouraged both men to publish articles and books clarifying their criticisms. Boltzmann read all of Mach's major books and many of his articles as well. He made a genuine and remarkably successful effort to understand what Mach was driving at.

During the 1890s, Boltzmann came to the conclusion, even allowing for Mach's phenomenalistic epistemology and purpose of science, that the most "economical" way to "describe and relate the physical appearances" was to use the atomic theory as an indispensable aid.[17]

V

Ernst Mach published *Contributions to the Analysis of Sensations* in 1886, an important book in epistemology and psychology, but it received immediate and heavy criticism from two leading psychologist-philosophers, Carl Stumpf and Theodor Lipps, mostly because of its psychophysical parallelism and treatment of space and time as sensations.[18] Years later Mach sadly recalled: "In the great majority of cases it was points of detail that found acceptance, in so far as the reception was favorable, while the fundamental views which had led to the details were for the most part rejected." [19] "I believed that I could interest philosophers more than scientists in it, but I was profoundly deceived in this." [20]

One writer even claimed that "a philosopher gave such an unfavorable opinion on the book . . . that Mach had to give back half of the not exactly princely honorarium just to pacify the publisher." [21] The story seems more than a bit doubtful, but it is a fact that the next printing of the work took place over ten years later and in a foreign language. The next German edition of the book appeared in 1900 and included numerous additional chapters with one specifically added to meet previous criticisms.[22]

But if Mach was not happy with the book's initial reception, nonetheless, it was during this period that he first began to feel that his philosophy was in tune with the times after all. "Until the 80's of the last century I had the feeling that I was alone swimming against the current, even though this had not been the case for a long time." [23]

Who, then, were some of Mach's nonphysicist allies? Which German philosophers held views similar to those of Mach?

VI

I have already briefly mentioned allies such as Popper-Lynkeus and Richard Avenarius and the fact that Friedrich Lange's "neo-Kantian" movement advocated a philosophy of science which had important resemblances to that of Mach, but it is now necessary to point out that during the 1880s there were also two other closely related movements and philosophies in Germany.

Ernst Laas openly advocated positivism in his book *Idealism and Positivism* (3 vols., 1884–1886). This movement, however, never prospered in Germany under its correct title. Mach's "Elementism" and "Universal Phenomenology" and Avenarius's "Empirio-Criticism" probably came closest to traditional epistemological positivism of any other movements in Germany and Austria, but since the differences between their views and those of Comte were still considerable the fact that they avoided Comte's label, though this action probably misled at least a few students of philosophy at the time, should on the whole, not be regretted. "Positivism" about this time acquired a bad connotation almost everywhere because of its supposed connection with atheism. Nor has this charge, inspite of its irrelevance where philosophy and science are concerned, ever been entirely lived down.

The second closely related movement was called "Immanentism," which lingered in Germany for about fifty years (1870–1920). Wilhelm Schuppe was normally recognized as its leader. Other "Immanentists" included Hans Cornelius, R. von Schubert-Solden, Anton Leclair, and to an extent Theodor Ziehen.

Wilhelm Schuppe (1836–1913) was born in Brieg Silesia, studied at Breslau, Bonn, and Berlin, and taught at the University of Greifswald on the Baltic Sea from 1873 to 1910. He wrote three important books *Human Thinking* (1870), *Epistemological Logic* (1878), and *Outline of Epistemology and Logic* (1894). The second of these books impressed Mach with the similarities in their ways of thinking.[24]

Both Mach and Schuppe were epistemological and ontological phenomenalists and sometimes referential phenomenalists, that is, both men held that we can only know sensations (in the inclusive sense), that only sensations exist, and that we can only refer to what is or could be presented to consciousness. Schuppe went beyond Mach, however, to argue that only what is conscious now is real, hence, the reason for labeling his philosophy as "Immanentism" or "Immanent Idealism."

But this slight extension in his phenomenalism entailed some rather extraordinary conclusions. Though he tried to widen his definition of consciousness, to avoid seeming to take the position, almost all critics have agreed that his philosophy was pure vintage solipsism. Mach claimed to know the existence of other people and their conscious life by means of an "irresistible analogy," but Schuppe by being more logically consistent than Mach and denying that analogy was knowledge chose to deny the psychic aspects of the reality of other people. Nonetheless, Schuppe's philosophy has had its influence on German thinkers, especially on Edmund Husserl and his "phenomenological" disciples.

Mach corresponded with Schuppe and several other members of his philosophical entourage and, unlike Avenarius, always seems to have remained on good terms with them.[25] Mach dedicated his 1905 book *Knowledge and Error* to Wilhelm Schuppe.

VII

Even though Ernst Mach and Friedrich Nietzsche were contemporaries and fellow German-speaking professors the suggestion that there were close similarities in many of their ideas and that Mach may have influenced Nietzsche could come as something of a shock to a number of readers; hence, a measure of clarification and quotations are in order. The basic facts are that both men were epistemological phenomenalists, advocated the subordination of science and truth to satisfying human "biological needs," and had similar ontological views of "matter," "ego," and "God." [26] The primary differences were: first, Mach treated sensations as facts and Nietzsche suspected they were only interpretations; and second, Mach saw the satisfaction of "biological needs" in a preexisting moral and social context which included respect for the rights of others, whereas Nietzsche suggested that each "superior" individual should interpret this preexisting context in that way most likely to bring about biological satisfaction for himself, even if that meant the rejection of traditional Judeo-Christian values.[27]

Here is part of a letter from Hans Kleinpeter to Mach, dated November 9, 1912: "I received the news from Weimar, that Nietzsche read one of your essays in a scientific journal in 1885 and spoke very favorably about it."

Philipp Frank wrote: "In this opinion I am strengthened also by the striking agreement of his [Mach's] views with those of a thinker for whom he cannot have had any great sympathy, Friedrich Nietzsche. This agreement was first pointed out by Kleinpeter. The more one delves into the posthumous works of Nietzsche, the more clearly one observes the agreement, particularly in the basic ideas related to the theory of knowledge." [28]

Leszek Kolakowski has added: "And yet, though it is hard to define, there is a real affinity between, on the one hand, Nietzschean biologism and the 'philosophy of life' or 'vitalism' to which it gave rise, and . . . the variety of positivism that flourished at the turn of the century, on the other." [29]

But lest we be carried away by these similarities and possibilities of influence let us recall Mach's own stated rejection: "The ethical ideal founded on this [my] view of life will be equally far removed from the ideal of the ascetic which is not biologically tenable for whoever practices it, and vanishes at once with his disappearance and from the ideal of an overweening Nietzschean 'superman', who cannot and I hope will not be tolerated by his fellow men." [30]

VIII

Ernst Mach's philosophical ideas penetrated the English-speaking world very quickly and well before his books were translated into English. A few English and American thinkers who could read German and a surprising number of German immigrants to America helped give Mach a second philosophical home. Indeed, in the long run his basic ideas at least with respect to philosophy of science were to find a more widespread and congenial reception in America than anywhere in Europe.

William Kingdon Clifford (1845-1879) was a precocious and brilliant mathematician who died before he could finish his most important and influential book *The Common Sense of the Exact Sciences* (London, 1885). He venerated Berkeley and Hume and considered "mind" the only reality. Anthony Quinton has claimed that Mach's theory of economy was evident in Clifford's *Lectures and Essays* (1879).[31] Mach also noted this, but suggested that Clifford may have developed the idea independently.[32]

Karl Pearson (1857-1936) was born in London, studied at King's College, Berlin, and Heidelberg, was called to the bar in 1881 (but did not practice), and in 1884 took over Olaus Henrici's chair in applied mathematics and mechanics at University College in London which he held until 1911. Pearson seems to have been strongly influenced by Clifford's ideas and took it upon himself to finish his last book. Pearson related to Mach how he first became acquainted with Mach's ideas: "If William Kingdon Clifford's *Common Sense of the Exact Sciences* (International Scientific Series) is in your university library you might possibly care to read the chapters on *Position* and *Motion* which I wrote for that work in 1883, when the perusal of your *Mechanik* had been a great support to me. You will find a reference to the matter in the preface." [33]

Pearson was especially impressed by Mach's phenomenalistic approach to mass and force and his attempt to reduce dynamics to kinematics. Making extensive use of Mach's 1886 *Contributions to the*

Analysis of Sensations Pearson published in 1892 his *Grammar of Science,* a popular classic in the philosophy of science which has continued to be widely read in England and America to the present.

Pearson's phenomenalism was enthusiastic and guileless to the point of openly admitting its idealistic foundations and being almost entirely oblivious of philosophical difficulties. Mach's caution and understatement were absent, but otherwise Pearson might be called the complete Machian. Almost as soon as Pearson finished the book his interests permanently shifted away from philosophy to "Biometrics" and "Eugenics."

The rest of Pearson's life was almost entirely spent in trying to introduce statistical methods and Francis Galton's ideas on heredity into modern genetics and biology. Pearson was certainly right on the importance of mathematics and statistics in biology, and he must be given credit for his long fight to persuade biologists of their importance, but for a short period between 1900 and 1910 he, Galton, and Weldon, the leaders of the "Biometric" movement, seem to have stood in the way of the acceptance of a most important theory in genetics and biology.

Just as Mach opposed the atomic theory, so Pearson fought Mendelism. Both men tended to frown on all "theories" as mere "provisional aids" and "uneconomical" vis-à-vis "functional relations." In light of the philosophical ideas he had picked up from Clifford and Mach, Pearson for a long time was simply unable to give Mendelian theory its due. Galton's statistical results, generalized to apply to specific cases, seemed much more scientific to him.

L. C. Dunn in his *A Short History of Genetics* (New York, 1965), has given the following account of the controversy:

Biometry founded by Galton in the 1880's, was vigorously developed during this period by Pearson. But the failure of both men to appreciate the essential features of Mendelian heredity led their school into opposition to Mendelism and hindered rather than helped the testing and extension of Mendel's principles.[34]

The fact was that a mechanism of particulate heredity based on genes could not be deduced from correlations between relatives, whereas the correlations between relatives found by biometricians were necessary consequences of Mendelian heredity.[35]

Josiah Royce was familiar with Mach's *Mechanics* and theory of economy as early as 1892, and Charles Peirce wrote a savage review of that
same book in the following year, but when one begins to speak of
Mach's influence on American philosophy, the proper place to start
is, of course, with William James himself, probably America's most
colorful thinker, and with John Dewey, her best known and most
influential.[36] William James (1842–1910), son of an idealistic philosopher and Swedenborgian mystic, and brother of a cosmopolitan novelist almost as famous as himself, made significant contributions, like
Mach, to both psychology and philosophy. James, the psychologist, was
one of the few Americans ever to read Mach's psychological and physiological articles of the early 1860s. A reason for this was that James,
like Mach and Wundt, had been attracted to Fechner's "psychophysics" and attempts to measure human sensation times in an exact
and scientific way. James in his well-known *Principles of Psychology*
(1890) made extensive use of Mach's experimental data, both agreeing
and disagreeing with particular results.

The William James we want to compare with Ernst Mach, however,
was not the technical psychologist, nor the long-time Harvard professor with his many responsibilities, but the enthusiastic champion of
experience, change, and pragmatism, a man to whom all categories
and stability were repugnant.

James eagerly awaited the publication of Mach's 1886 *Contributions
to the Analysis of Sensations.* He wrote to Carl Stumpf: "His [Mach's]
book . . . is about to appear. I am thirsty to read it. . . ."[37] James's
public opinion of it, however, was delayed until it appeared in English
in 1897 when he was quoted as saying: "A wonderfully original little
book. Like everything he writes a work of genius."[38] It seems very
possible that Mach's phenomenalism and theory of "biological needs"
encouraged James to develop his theory of experience and, with Peirce
helped lead him to his notorious special philosophy, Pragmatism.

According to R. B. Perry:

There were three German philosophers of his time to whom James was
especially indebted, G. T. Fechner, Hermann Lotze, and Ernst Mach.[39]

James reckoned among his allies the experimental scientists who offered
a pragmatic interpretation of their own technique. Among these he frequently named Ernst Mach, Karl Pearson, Wilhelm Ostwald, and Henri

Poincaré. From Mach James had learned something of what he knew about the history of science, and he had readily accepted his view of the biological and economic function of scientific concepts.[40]

James accepted Mach's view of functional relations in science: "The clearness and elegance of your way of writing, the subtlety of your thought and above all the truth (as I firmly believe) of your general conception of the relation of our formulas to facts, put you into an entirely unique position among writers on the philosophy of science." [41]

James shared with Mach the belief that consciousness was merely a relation and the "nativistic" view that physiological space was immediately given in consciousness.[42] James expressed his particular form of phenomenalism as follows: "Everything real must be experienceable somewhere and every kind of thing experienced must somewhere be real." [43] Both men, together with Bertrand Russell, accepted "neutral monism," the belief that ontological phenomenalism was as distant from idealism as it was from materialism or representational realism. In short, in order to make their point of view more acceptable to people who might have a prejudice against the label "idealism," they deliberately played down the close historical and logical relation of their philosophy to Berkeley, Hume, and Kant, thinkers normally considered to be in the idealistic tradition in philosophy.

James's phenomenalism, however, overflowed in all directions well beyond what he might have learned from Mach. Contrary to Mach, James held: first, sensations could be doubted; second, experience was in no way limited to "elements" or what could be scientifically tested; third, moods, values, interests, and mental experience were different in quality from physical experience and interact with physical experience (i.e., no psychophysical parallelism); and fourth, to understand change (rather than mere scientific constant relations) was to understand reality.

Mach's theory of "biological needs" was compatible with James's Pragmatism, and, as we have already mentioned, probably helped develop it, but again, as with phenomenalism, James exploded his views so far beyond Mach, that eventually the resemblance seemed feeble to the point of virtual disappearance. In spite of the fact that Mach justified scientific investigation and his philosophy of science in terms of how well they satisfied human "biological needs," in practice, he tended to ignore this ultimate goal almost entirely and concentrated on the "internal" goal of science, to describe the appearances in the simplest way possible, as if that were an end in itself. James, on the other hand, took "biological needs" seriously and insisted that there were other ways to satisfy them than by following a narrow scientific methodology. Both men defined truth and error in terms of how well consequences matched intended or desired consequences, but Mach, again in practice, stuck closely to what most non-Pragmatists accepted as true. For example, James violated Mach's atheism and bitter opposition to organized religion by blithely reasoning that Christianity satisfied the "biological needs" of a great many people, and hence, in a Pragmatic sense, was "true," at least for those people. The basic point was that James drew some of the logical consequences from Mach's philosophy, something Mach himself in his dislike of speculation, and in his belief that he was not really a philosopher anyhow, was reluctant even to attempt.

x

Edward C. Hegeler studied under Professor Julius Weisbach at the Freiberg mining academy in Saxony, married the latter's daughter, emigrated to America, and founded a flourishing zinc manufacturing company. He read Mach's *Mechanics* in 1883 and established *The Open Court* magazine in La Salle, Illinois, in 1887 to help spread his own philosophical and religious ideas. He soon hired as editor a well-educated German immigrant, Dr. Paul Carus, who held compatible views on science, philosophy, and religion. Hegeler wanted Mach's articles and especially his *Mechanics* translated into English and published as soon as possible.[44]

Paul Carus (1852–1919) was born in Ilsenburg in the Harz region in Germany, studied philosophy and classical philology at Strassburg, Greifswald, and Tübingen, and taught at various schools in Dresden, but his unusual religious views brought him into conflict with local authorities. He emigrated first to England in 1881 and three years later to America where he married Edward Hegeler's daughter on March 29, 1888.

After a false start, Carus found in his able and much-worked assistant, Thomas J. McCormack, the right translator for Mach's *Mechanics*. The book appeared in English in 1893. Meanwhile, however, Mach and Carus got into a friendly philosophical dispute in which Mach had somewhat the better of it. The disagreement had special value in helping Carus to think through his philosophical position more carefully.[45]

The Open Court, joined by *The Monist* in 1890, became sounding boards for different religious, philosophical, and scientific ideas in the hope of developing a truly scientific religion. Hegeler and Carus felt that Mach's phenomenalistic monism provided an almost ideal philosophy to reconcile science and religion. Carus disagreed with Mach on the following two points: Unlike Mach, he chose to retain Fechner's mind-matter parallelism, and while accepting Mach's substitution of functional relations for causes as forces the German-American editor went further by identifying these relations with "eternal laws," dependent on a single law, "the principle of form," which he called "God."

Carus soon discovered what he thought was a scientific religion in Buddhism. According to Carl Jackson:

Carus's conversion to an active personal interest in Oriental thought can be traced to the Parliament of Religions held in September 1893, in conjunction with the Chicago Columbian Exposition.[46]

Buddha is, so far as we know, the first positivist, the first humanitarian, the first radical free-thinker, the first iconoclast, and the first prophet of the religion of science. Buddhism, he asserted, was "but another word for Religion of Science." Buddha, he declared, "anticipated even in important details the results of a scientific world-conception." [47]

Mach enjoyed reading Carus's numerous books on Buddhism, and he increasingly began to notice Buddhist parallels with his own philosophy. While Mach was slow to make public mention of his new sympathy, he was openly and immediately appreciative of Hegeler, Carus, and McCormack for their desire to publish anything and everything Mach wanted to have published.

XI

Jacques Loeb (1859–1924), a German-American physiologist who studied at Munich and Strassburg before emigrating to America in 1890 and who became famous as the discoverer of tropism in animals, claimed to have been strongly influenced by Mach, but Loeb's reputation as a leader of turn-of-the-century scientific materialism and mechanistic explanation has thrown the extent of Mach's influence in considerable doubt. In philosophical terms, was Jacques Loeb a genuine mind-matter dualist verging on a monistic materialism or was he merely a Machian phenomenalist hiding behind a "physical object" language in the fashion of Rudolph Carnap a generation later? In spite of the involved and in some respects leading nature of the question, the answer is still very much in doubt. A monograph on this question is very definitely needed.

W. J. V. Osterhout has claimed that Loeb "seems to have conceived a distaste for metaphysics (ca. 1880 under Paulsen at Berlin) and in his subsequent career the only philosopher who influenced him appears to have been Mach." [48] Loeb wrote to Mach from the physiological institute in Würzburg in 1887 "Your *Analysis of Sensations* and *Mechanics* are the sources from which I draw inspiration and energy to work. . . . Your ideas are scientifically and ethically the basis upon which I stand and upon which I think the natural scientist has to stand." [49]

"About 12 years ago [1888] while Alexander von Koranyi, currently professor in Budapest, and I worked in the physiological institute in Strassburg we discussed your *Analysis of Sensations*. We finally came to the conclusion that we would have to make a pilgrimage to you." [50]

We do not know if they ever physically went, or if so, how they were received at the shrine, but with respect to Mach's influence on Loeb's subsequent thinking there were at least a few clear indications. First, Loeb adopted a theory of economy, presumably from Mach, and second, he dedicated much of the rest of his life to realizing Mach's notion of reducing psychology to physiology. The suspicion is, however, that he may have misunderstood what Mach meant by "physiology"; for what a phenomenalist means by it bears almost no resemblance to what a materialist means. And furthermore, not all phenomenalists would be likely to mean what Mach meant by it, since his understanding of it tended to be unique by any standards.

Jacques Loeb was quite successful in his scientific work in explaining animal behavior by means of "physicochemical" factors, indeed so successful that he wrote a number of books urging a "physicochemical" approach as the only truly scientific method possible in biology and physiology. He accepted the atomic theory, violently opposed "vitalism," and even doubted Darwin's theory, preferring the ideas of Mendel, De Vries, and Pavlov, since he believed that they could be conclusively tested and proved. Readers of Loeb's physiology books, unaware of his correspondence and early philosophical contacts, would probably suppose that his epistemology and ontology were closer to those of Du Bois-Reymond and even Vogt, Büchner, and Moleschott than Mach. To be sure, we can interpret a "physicochemical" approach in phenomenalistic terms, but Loeb's stress on this method was so overwhelming and unquestioned. It seems difficult to believe that he could have made such a point of it, even attempting to explain all "psychic" happenings by it, had he not literally believed not only in the usefulness of the atomic theory but in the real existence of atoms and molecules as entities outside the "appearances."

The easiest way to distinguish among mind-matter dualism, monistic materialism, and ontological phenomenalism is normally to look for the kind of causal explanation used or assumed. If the appeal is to physical agents or forces as causes, then dualism or materialism is the logical choice, and if the appeal is merely to relational constancies or regularities, then phenomenalism is the logical ontology to hold. Jacques Loeb, however, was inconsistent even on this issue.

Both Loeb and his biographer, Osterhout, believed that he accepted Mach's identification of causes with "functional relations." According to Loeb: "All 'explanation' consists solely in the presentation of a phenomenon as an unequivocal function of the variables by which it is determined." [51] And Osterhout: "[Loeb's] notion of biological research was simple: all the observed phenomena should be expressed in the form of equations containing no arbitrary constants." [52]

But how well can the following quotations be reconciled with a phenomenalistic point of view?

Nobody doubts that the durable chemical elements are only the product of blind forces. [53]

We eat, drink, and reproduce not because mankind has reached an agreement that this is desirable, but because, machine-like, we are compelled to do so. [54]

. . . for the metaphysical term "will" we may in these instances safely substitute the chemical term "photochemical action of light." [55]

Let us bear in mind that "ideas" also can act, much as acids do for the heliotropism of certain animals. [56]

An image consists of a number of points of different intensity of light. [57]

The possibility that vision is based on the formation of an image in the brain is supported by a group of facts which to my knowledge have never received any consideration in this connection. [58]

All life phenomena are determined by chemical processes. [59]

CHAPTER 10

Educational Theory and Textbooks

I

Ernst Mach gradually developed ideas about education, teaching, and children to complement and help popularize his phenomenalism and philosophy of science. He also took an active part in educational politics from the middle 1880s into the twentieth century. He coedited an educational journal, wrote textbooks for secondary school students, and helped lead the gymnasium reform movement of the period. His only speech while a member of the Austrian House of Peers was to advocate spending more money on popular adult education.

II

Mach did not develop a comprehensive philosophy of education nor write a book exclusively on the subject, but his articles, "On Instruction in the Classics and the Mathematico-Physical Sciences" (1886), "On Instruction in Heat Theory" (1887), and "On the Psychological and Logical Moment in Scientific Instruction" (1890), and scattered comments in his other writtings, give a coherent picture of his basic educational assumptions and views.[1]

The primary purpose of education, like that of science and all human activity, according to Mach, was to help satisfy human "biological needs" in the most "economical" way possible. Mach understood "biological needs" in the collective sense of what best aided the survival and progress of the human species on a moral and civilized level.

The special purpose of education "was simply the saving of experience."[2] That is, education provided a quick and efficient way of learning what many people know now and what ages of people learned in the past, so that we do not have to rely solely on learning by means of limited and time-consuming personal experience and trial and error.

But while Mach held that the purpose of education was "economical" (in the two senses mentioned above), he insisted that the most "economical" way of imparting education was quite indirect. Instead of teaching the most "economical" end results of science directly, that is, mathematical equations and functions, he believed that it was more "economical" from a pedagogical point of view to begin instruction with visual examples and imaginative demonstration, slowly evolving into a historical presentation of the subject.[3] Only when the student mastered the problem in its concrete and historical development was he capable of adequately understanding general and abstract solutions to the problem. In other words, the most economical way of learning started with uneconomical understanding (i.e., "images" and "history") and culminated after a gradual process in the learning of the most "economical" and valuable knowledge possible, the use of mathematical functions to describe sensations.

One product of Mach's multifaceted "economical" approach to education was his emphasis on always learning for an extrinsic purpose. The only value of understanding was what else it helped to sustain or bring about. Mach rejected learning for its own sake, for personal pleasure, and for the mere information gained. He scorned both curiosity and wonder.[4] He associated them with an attraction toward the odd and exceptional, whereas, as one might expect from a physicist, Mach put more importance on learning similarities and constancies. Mach both recommended the value of history and was an influential historian himself, but his aversion to the odd and singular should indicate that he was a historian from need rather than love, and that he found it uncongenial to work as a serious research or archive historian.

When Mach advocated teaching science in a historical way, especially to beginners in science, he meant teaching the ideas of earlier scientists to show the logical development of modern theories. He did not mean that the particular actions or thoughts of particular scientists should be taught or the historical factors that influenced why they thought as they did. Nor was he overly interested in the actual historical development of theories. Mach's primary purpose in recommending a historical approach was to make contemporary science more understandable, not to make past science more understandable.[5]

Drawing on his own childhood experience, and reasoning from his belief in "unconscious memory," Mach opposed early education for children. In fact, he thought it could be harmful.[6] Either the child's lack of success might turn him against certain types of learning, as Mach was turned against learning Greek and Latin, or what he did learn might destroy or confuse what he knew by "instinct" (i.e., from inherited "unconscious memory").

Mach also opposed toys for children, especially elaborate commercial toys. He believed that they were decadent and slowed a child's development toward adulthood. Toys kept the child awkward and tentative in constructing things; they helped to prevent self-reliance, and like fairy tales, they led to daydreams, confusion of fantasy with reality, and interfered with the development of a reliable approach toward causal understanding.[7]

Ernst Mach believed that the main purpose in elementary scientific instruction should not be "the acquisition of a sum of positive knowledge, but rather a certain education in observation and especially in scientific thinking, an adjustment to a more delineating logical approach. . . ." [8] He accompanied this emphasis with the opinion that pupils should have more free time to learn on their own. He especially disliked "overfeeding" children details and memory work.

How can the mind thrive when matter is heaped on matter, and new materials piled constantly on old, undigested materials? [9]

Furthermore, thoughts cannot be accumulated beyond a certain limit in a single head, any more than the produce of a field can be increased beyond certain limits.

I believe that the amount of matter necessary for a useful education, such as should be offered to *all* pupils of a preparatory school, is very small. . . . I should cut down considerably the number of school hours and the work done outside the school.[10]

I know nothing more terrible than the poor creatures who have learned too much. Instead of that powerful judgment which would probably have grown up if they had learned nothing, their thoughts creep timidly after words, principles, and formulae, constantly by the same paths. What they have acquired is a spider's web of thoughts too weak to furnish supports, but complicated enough to produce confusion.[11]

III

The Industrial Revolution and the rise of democratic ideas in the middle of the nineteenth century encouraged widespread demands for educational reform throughout Europe and America. Many people wanted less Greek and Latin and more practical and science-oriented education. Professional educators, however, defended "humanistic" education largely on the basis of its moral and civilizing value. Let us now consider an important educator, Friedrich Paulsen (1846–1908), philosopher, historian of education, and leader of gymnasium reform in Germany who began to challenge this argument, and who has given the following account of his own metamorphosis:

When I first lectured on pedagogics, I had endeavored to show, as best I could, that the classical languages must always remain the foundation of higher education. It was not long, however, before my convictions underwent a change, brought about by my historical studies. It appeared that the orthodox view just referred to was really of quite recent origin, being hardly older than the new *Gymnasium* itself, which was the creation of the Nineteenth Century. The old grammar school (*Lateinschule*) had been entirely innocent of such ideals. The languages taught there were not taught for the sake of any "formalistic" and "humanistic" education, but solely for the purpose of acquiring the necessary facility of expression in the language concerned which also explains why Latin predominated to such a degree.[12]

Paulsen's discovery of the recent origin of the "humanistic argument" with respect to instruction in Greek and Latin appeared in print in his *History of Learned Instruction* (Vol. I), published in 1885.[13] This book gave backbone to the reform movement and made Paulsen its best-known champion. The reform movement in Germany and Austria wanted to redress the balance among the *Gymnasium, Realgymnasium,* and *Realschule.* The *Gymnasium* emphasized Greek and Latin; the *Realgymnasium* stressed Latin, science, and modern languages; and the *Realschule* concentrated on science and modern languages. The trouble was that even as late as 1900 over 80 percent of all secondary school graduates (at least in Prussia) came from the Latin- and Greek-oriented gymnasiums.

Paulsen advocated more realgymnasiums and realschules, fewer hours for students in all schools, and, especially, fewer hours in Latin. He also wanted Greek and upper division mathematics made optional

135

subjects. Of equal importance was the need to allow realgymnasium and realschule graduates entry into and equal rights in German universities.

Ernst Mach independently developed a point of view very similar to that of Friedrich Paulsen. Mach's first speech on educational reform was canceled in 1881 because of his trip to Paris at the time.[14] He gave his major reform speech on April 16, 1886, before the Union of Realschule Men in Dortmund. Why did Mach speak out in Germany rather than in Austria? Presumably, because Taaffe's "clerical-reactionary" regime was still in control in Vienna and blocked reform, whereas in Germany there was at least a chance for major alterations in the educational system.

Mach's Dortmund speech, "On Instruction in the Classics and the the Mathematico-Physical Sciences," was not indiscriminate propaganda for science at the expense of Greek and Latin. Mach, no more than Paulsen, wanted to eliminate all instruction in the ancient languages; nor did either man accept Friedrich Lange's approach of a single secondary school for all students of the type we have now had in America for many years. Mach did stress the importance of teaching science in a scientific age, but like Paulsen he saw no advantage in forcing advanced science or mathematics on all students.[15] Above all, he recommended fewer instructional hours and more optional courses. Mach sought to reduce school regimentation and "oppression" to a minimum.[16] The speech received attention in newspapers and journals all over Germany and Austria and even in France.[17] Science realschule teachers were encouraged, and "humanists" wrote bitter criticisms.[18] Mach was joined in his campaign by Du Bois-Reymond and Wilhelm Ostwald. Nor did he let the iron cool.

In the same year Mach published the first of his many science textbooks for secondary school students (*Textbook of Natural Science for Middle-School Lower Classes* [Prague, 1886]).[19] In the following year Friedrich Poske (1852–1925) founded a new educational magazine (*Journal for Physical and Chemical Instruction*) with Mach and Bernhard Schwalbe as coeditors.[20] Mach followed this up by publishing several articles outlining his educational philosophy.

By 1890 the gymnasium reform movement had become so powerful that a conference was finally called in Berlin to settle the problem. Representatives from all significant points of view were to have been invited, but in fact Lange's "single school" advocates were not, and the conference was weighted in favor of gymnasium men. Little would probably have been accomplished had not Wilhelm II, the young and only recently crowned Kaiser, attended the meeting in person.[21] This historical figure informed his elders and educational betters that reform was the only answer since "We should bring up young Germans and not young Greeks and Romans."[22] That settled the issue, and two years later "humanistic" gymnasiums were reformed with more German, less Greek and Latin, and fewer hours overall.

The long-range consequences were the construction of more realgymnasiums and realschules and a gradual increase in students receiving degrees from other than classical gymnasiums. However, even as late as World War I, 60 percent of all Prussian secondary school graduates came from "humanistic" schools. By 1914 Austria and most of the other German states had adopted gymnasium reform.[23] Compared with changes in American education (which to an extent were influenced by Paulsen and by German experience), the "reform" was comparatively slight. Greek and Latin by no means disappeared from secondary schools, and the "single" or "united school" approach has never replaced the complex *Volkschule, Gymnasium, Realgymnasium, Realschule* arrangement.

IV

Mach contributed a dozen articles to Poske's journal during his eleven years as an active coeditor (1887–1898).[24] The articles were evenly divided in content: a third on educational theory pertaining to physics; a third on physical experiments and laboratory equipment; and a third on so-called thought experiments.

Mach's phenomenalism came out strongly in his articles on how to teach physics. He especially ridiculed the notion that heat could be the cause of the sensation of heat.[25] According to what has become common sense, heat is a motion of particles and the sensation or feeling of heat is merely a type of conscious experience. The two things are different, and if we accept the representative theory of perception with respect to touch, it makes good sense to argue that heat in an object we touch can be a contributing cause to the sensation of heat in our brain. Mach, however, rejected the representative theory of perception, rejected all attempts to localize sensations in the brain, and tried to reduce heat as the motion of particles to an idea. For Mach, it was absurd to argue that a mere concept, such as the motion of hypothetical particles, could be the cause of a fact, such as the sensation or feeling of heat.

Mach's advice to physics teachers was to avoid confusing ideas with facts, or to think that the former could be the "cause" of the latter. Teachers should be wary of reifying such hypothetical entities as atoms or molecules. Mach dismissed the common sense view of heat in a typically positivistic way, by associating it with the Middle Ages and "prescientific" thought. "Such things are the natural residue of the scholastic methods of our ancestors whose understanding with all of its sharpness always started with dogma and ended again with dogma. These things will disappear as soon as they are examined with greater care." [26]

Some of Mach's other advice to science teachers included the suggestion that logic should be subordinated to psychology in the sense that the teacher should always wait for the right psychological moment before giving a logical explanation of a detailed matter. Even the most impeccable logic would be misunderstood if the audience was not sufficiently attentive and knowledgeable.

Mach believed that verbal disagreement and even bitter argument could be profitable from a learning point of view. "I don't even consider contradiction tragic. It often illuminates like a flame in the dark, even the most inward parts of the understanding." [27] "I was never persuaded of my own infallibility [with respect to other than sensations] and have many a polemical attack to thank for it." [28]

Mach often pointed to Euclid's *Geometry* as precisely how not to present mathematics and physics.

Great inquirers, even in recent times, have been misled into following Euclid's example in the presentation of the results of their inquiries, and so into actually concealing their methods of investigation to the great detriment of science. But science is not a feat of legal casuistry. Scientific presentation aims to expound all the grounds of an idea so that it can at any time be thoroughly examined as to its tenability and power. The learner is not to be led half-blindfolded. There therefore arose in Germany among philosophers and educationalists a healthy reaction, which proceeded mainly from Herbart, Schopenhauer, and Trendelenburg. The effort was made to introduce greater perspicuity, more genetic methods, and logically more lucid demonstrations into geometry. [29]

Besides concentrating on sensations and a historical approach Mach also believed that university teachers should alert their students to relevant philosophical literature.

I led [during doctoral examinations in Vienna, 1895–1898] candidates into a conversation on general and even the most general questions of their special field. I recommended to philologists that they study the writings of philosophers of speech, to historians cultural history and prehistory, and mathematicians and natural scientists normally Mill and Jevons. It often became evident that the candidates did not know the philosophical writings of their own special fields. They were usually very thankful for my suggestions about future study.[30]

Mach's paralysis in 1898 forced him to give up active work as a coeditor for Poske's journal. He recommended that the Austrian philosopher and educator, Alois Höfler (1853–1922), be offered the post.[31] Höfler, a former student of Brentano, accepted Poske's offer and remembered Mach's thoughtfulness with personal respect and admiration: "[The philosophical differences between us] had so little damaged our pedagogical and personal relations, that Mach . . . recommended me as his successor as coeditor of [Poske's] magazine, which post I still hold today." [32] Mach's recommendation may well have followed from his desire that physics students learn more about philosophy and from his realization that Höfler felt the same way. Paulsen commented: "A special service of Höfler was that he understood how to bring instruction in introductory philosophy in close relation with physics and the exact sciences. . . ." [33]

v

Apart from numerous revised editions with a variety of titles, Mach basically wrote three textbooks: *A Compendium of Physics for Medical Students* (Vienna, 1863); *A Textbook of Natural Science for Middle-School Lower Classes* (Prague, 1886); and *A Textbook of Physics for Students* (Prague and Vienna, 1891).[34] I have already discussed the first book at length. Only the last two concern us here.

Mach's 1886 textbook was coauthored by Johann Odstrčil for use in gymnasiums and a second edition was reworked by K. Habart for realschules. The books did not please the education ministry of the Taaffe government; neither version was quick to receive a license for Austrian schools and neither became widely employed by Austrian teachers until after the fall of that regime in 1893. On the other hand, stimulated by Mach's Dortmund speech, the books were widely introduced into German secondary schools. After 1893 Mach's textbooks in both Germany and Austria were frequently reprinted and revised. The variety of preparations required for different types of secondary schools, and often listed under different titles or under the reviser's name, has made it impossible to pin down all the different editions of "Mach's" 1886 work, but twenty editions have been traced, dating from 1886 to 1919.

Mach's 1891 textbook had 372 pages of which 203 were by Mach himself, with chapters on chemistry and astronomy by Mach's assistant, Gustav Jaumann, and a Mr. C. Brunner. The basic difference between the 1886 and 1891 textbooks was that the first was used for lower classes in secondary schools and the other for upper classes. The latter book, too, had difficulties receiving permission for use in Austrian schools. Both books came to be published in increasingly truncated and revised forms during the next three decades. The 1891 book went through fourteen editions between 1891 and 1917. Ferdinand Harbordt and Max Fischer reworked both books for German schools in 1893 and were responsible for most of the more radical revisions.

The important questions are: first, to what extent were Mach's phenomenalism and philosophy of science represented in these textbooks? And second, which important physicists or philosophers were significantly influenced by Mach's ideas as given in them?

In answer to the first query, here are some quotations from his 1891 textbook and from an 1894 version of it:

The essence of everything which we perceive through the senses (colors, tones . . . etc.) we call the sense world or nature.[35]

Changes in the qualities of matter which are always represented by particular connectd conditions, we call appearances (*Erscheinungen*).[36]

Physics (in the wider sense) is the science of the simpler appearances of inorganic nature.[37]

Mach was very discreet in his treatment of atoms and molecules.

The relations between heat and work become more vivid if one thinks of bodies as consisting of ultimate parts (molecules and atoms) and thinks of all physical processes as mechanical events. One should not forget, however, that these representations are hypotheses.[38]

In short, Mach's phenomenalism was well represented in his textbooks but his philosophy of science only moderately so. His criticisms of Newton's ideas seem to have been omitted altogether.

In answer to the second query, one can safely speculate that many well-known physicists were exposed to Mach's phenomenalism and physical ideas during their school days. Albert Einstein, Werner Heisenberg, Erwin Schrödinger, Philipp Frank, and most members of the "Vienna Circle" were in secondary schools in Germany and Austria during the period in which Mach's textbooks were available for use in physics classes, and virtually all have testified to the pervasiveness of Mach's influence during their school days. But it is not clear to what extent Mach's textbooks contributed to that pervasiveness; nor is it evident which, if any, particular scientists or philosophers were philosophically "seduced" by them. Nonetheless, Mach's textbooks were widely distributed in Central Europe and presumably did influence a number of intelligent minds, whether his name was remembered as the author of those books or not. Einstein at least hinted at that influence when he wrote in 1916: "I even believe, that those who consider themselves opponents of Mach, scarcely know how much they have taken from his way of looking at things, so to say along with their mother's milk." [39]

PART II 1895–1916

CHAPTER 11

Return to Vienna

I

Serious problems developed in Mach's laboratory in Prague during the late 1880s and early 1890s. First, the total number of students in the philosophical faculty in the German University fell to under a hundred with only a fraction of this meager number interested in physics.[1] Second, Education Ministry financial support for Mach's experimental work declined accordingly.[2] And third, Mach's laboratory staff slowly degenerated into an insubordinate, inefficient, and disputatious group.

Franz Hajek, who had worked in Mach's laboratory since 1868, became a drunkard. Out of respect for Hajek's earlier accomplishments in constructing useful laboratory equipment and because of Hajek's large family, Mach retained him.[3] Gustav Jaumann (1863–1924) served as Mach's laboratory *Aushilfsassistent* from 1886 to 1891 and as *Assistent* from 1891 to 1893.[4] Two of his responsibilities were to put together and prepare equipment for lectures and student use and to manage correspondence with companies that provided equipment and other laboratory material. He soon considered these tasks onerous and neglected them.[5]

During the late 1880s Mach's eldest son, Ludwig, took over most of the laboratory responsibilities of both Jaumann and Hajek.[6] Indeed, he gradually became the most active person in Mach's institute during the last years of his father's residence in Prague. Jaumann reacted to Ludwig Mach's laboratory work by "insulting and slandering him." [7] Ludwig's intervention was surely an attempt to correct a bad situation, but it may also have helped to make the situation worse by aggravating already strained personal relations. In any case, Ernst Mach welcomed the assistance and defended his son's behavior.

Two undated stories, referring to events in Mach's institute during the early 1890s, have suggested an evolution toward confrontation and violence. Georg Alexander Pick (1859–1929), who had earlier been Mach's *Aushilfsassistent* and was now an *Extraordinarius* professor in Prague, became involved in a bitter personal conflict with Hajek.[8] Perhaps the old instrument-maker, who had won prizes for his work at the Prague World Exhibition twenty years before, resented the former student and assistant who had now become so important. Mach, however, refused to admonish either Pick or Jaumann openly, probably because both were philosophical allies.

The second incident had a humorous side. In a letter to an unknown *Hochgeehrter Herr Doctor* in his institute, Mach refused to allow a sword duel between laboratory personnel.[9] He even threatened punishment if it took place. Clearly, Mach's laboratory had become a painful place to work. In retrospect, Mach had shown by his actions, or rather reluctance to act, that he could be kind and indulgent to his employees. It is possible he had become too lenient.

II

Josef Stefan, founder of the Vienna school of physical atomism and a long-time opponent of Mach's philosophical ideas, suffered a heart attack on December 18, 1892, and died on January 7, 1893. One week later, Eduard Krischek wrote to Mach: "Because of the slight warmth of your reciprocal relations you scarcely need to reproach yourself [for not attending the funeral]."[10] Stefan had stood in the way of Mach's possible return to Vienna in the same fashion as Brücke, the old friend of Helmholtz, had blocked Hering's return.[11] But as things turned out, Stefan's death did not change anything.

Vienna physicists were agreed that Ludwig Boltzmann should occupy Stefan's chair at the University of Vienna. Mach had advocates in the faculty, especially Gustav Tschermak (1836–1927), a prominent Vienna mineralogist, but Mach did not encourage his supporters and they were outvoted.[12] The negotiations with Boltzmann, who was then teaching at Munich, dragged on for a year. The peripatetic atomist took the post in 1894 and was soon given the Imperial title of *Hofrath*, or court councillor. Boltzmann's latest triumph left Mach more depressed than ever.

In the winter of 1893/1894 Mach was seriously ill with influenza.

He also declined to employ any laboratory assistants for that university semester. Most likely it was during this bleak period that he wrote his unhappy "last testament" remarks about his former employees. We have already discussed his criticisms of Wosyka, Hajek, and Jaumann (see chap. 4). Here are some additional comments by Mach about the last gentleman:

I wish, in case of my death, that the Institute *not* be given to Jaumann, at least not immediately. I wish, that beforehand, *someone else* become acquainted with it. Jaumann has for the last ten years, so to say, worked as a guest, that is, for himself, and for that drawn a salary. During the first few years I requested very little of him as an assistant, and then nothing at all. On the contrary, I was continually having to defend myself against his tendency toward extravagant behavior and disorder. . . .

How irresponsible Jaumann's behavior was can best be judged by those who know how hard I have tried to promote his welfare.[13]

III

Eighteen ninety-four was a transition year, a time of expectation and stunning surprises. First, the great luminaries of physics dimmed or blinked out, one by one. Heinrich Hertz died; Hermann Helmholtz died; Josef Loschmidt had retired and would die the following year; and aging Emil du Bois-Reymond died the year after that. These events were difficult for Mach but tragic for Boltzmann. Stefan and Loschmidt had been his close friends, and together with Helmholtz and Du Bois-Reymond had all supported Boltzmann's stand in favor of the atomic theory in physics.

The carnage shifted the balance of power in German and Austrian physics. Four pillars supporting the temple of atomism had fallen or were in the process of falling. Ernst Mach and Wilhelm Ostwald, the two leading anti-atomists, were now the most respected living Central European physical scientists, except of course for Boltzmann—the last pillar.[14]

Second, Mach's publishing situation saw an upswing. Several new books and translations were being prepared for publication. He worked hardest in 1894 on his new book on thermodynamics. It was time to drive the final nail into the coffin of atomism and Boltzmann's "kinetic theory of gases."

Third, Mach's university and personal life underwent several un-

147

expected changes, of which a few were quite drastic. Gustav Jaumann wrote Mach a friendly letter in July 1894 when he withdrew his books and equipment from Mach's Institute. Jaumann properly thanked Mach for his patience and assistance, and apologized for his earlier conduct. "At the same time, I take the occasion of my departure from the Institute to express my sincere thanks for the good times which I have had and for the many indulgences which you have shown toward my less agreeable qualities. I have left my Institute room in as good order as possible. . . ." [15]

Three of Mach's children were on the verge of adulthood and a future career. Ludwig, the oldest at twenty-five, took up his medical studies again and declared that "the doctorate was merely a question of time." [16] Caroline, the next oldest at twenty-one, married Anton Lederer on April 16, 1894, and later emigrated to America.

Mach's third child, Heinrich Mach, was brilliant and hardworking. At fifteen he studied chemistry as a private student under Professor Maly in Prague. At seventeen he entered the German University there, and two years later published his first scientific article. Unlike his father, he used the atomic theory in his work.[17] We do not know if he accepted the reality of atoms and molecules as particles existing outside the appearances. In 1893 Heinrich Mach transferred to the University of Göttingen where he studied under Otto Wallach, Walther Nernst, and others. Heinrich passed his examinations for the doctor's degree on July 30, 1894. That night he sent a postcard from Gebhard's Hotel in Göttingen.

Dear Mama:
This evening I passed my examinations and have received my doctor's degree. More later.

Greetings to everyone
Schrupp

His dissertation was titled *Contributions to the Knowledge of Abietic Acid—Treatise #2*. The inscription read: "To his dear parents, dedicated in gratitude, by the author."

Heinrich Mach had successfully received his doctor's degree before his older brother. His diploma was dated precisely on his twentieth birthday, September 4, 1894. Seven days later he took an overdose of sleeping powder and died.[18]

Ernst Mach took the blow of his son's death without illusion or evasion. He accepted as a fact that it was suicide and blamed himself for errors and omissions in raising his child. He could have denied all responsibility by simply falling back on "functional explanation" and refusing to admit that particular "agents" could be genuine causes. But in this instance he took the manlier course, even though it meant favoring common sense over his own philosophy.

One of my sons, who was considered a gifted chemist, took his own life in Göttingen shortly after a brilliant graduation. Mindful of my own youth I did not wish him to suffer want. If he had had to earn his own bread, he would not have found time for such a thing.[19]

I believe today, that my younger son Heinrich, whom I sent to Göttingen during the critical period of his puberty, was also psychopathic and that by the careful help which I bestowed upon him, I drove him to suicide.[20]

Heinrich's death affected Mach's family life, future place of work, and his attitude toward biographical publicity. Anyone who has had a suicide in his immediate family knows how much it resembles a mass murder in that all members of the family tend to torment themselves with lingering feelings of guilt and depression. Mach lost all pleasure in the intellectual growth and ambition of his children and ceased to encourage his two younger sons, Felix and Victor, to try for a university education. He refused ever again to allow a Christmas tree in his house. Mach insisted on leaving Prague for Vienna, and in a letter to Professor Tschermak even offered to teach there as an "honorary" professor without salary.[21] And he became extremely reluctant to allow personal information about himself or his family to appear in print. This reluctance was primarily responsible for the fact that no book-length biography was ever written during his life or for many years afterward. One result has been that while his accomplishments and influence have gradually been recognized, Ernst Mach, as a person, has never become as widely known as his intellectual and philosophical peers. In short, Heinrich Mach's death and manner of death contributed to more than a half century of unnecessary mystery concerning the character and life of Ernst Mach.

IV

Mach's siege of Vienna lasted eight months. The key to success was timing and strategically placed allies. According to intelligence reports the two main points of resistance, the Vienna philosophy faculty and the Austrian Ministry of Education, were particularly vulnerable at this time. Ludwig Boltzmann thought that the addition of Mach would increase the prestige of the university; it would also give Boltzmann more opportunity to talk with and learn from a man whose intelligence he respected.[22] Also, the Taaffe regime had finally fallen and had been replaced by the so-called United Left, a coalition including the liberal and progressive parties, a group of German conservatives, and the Poles. The new minister of education was himself a Pole. Church influence was less strong in the new ministry. If Mach was to succeed it was now or not at all.

Mach knew that there were no physics chairs open in Vienna, but that all three chairs in philosophy might be available. "Brentano's chair" had long been left open in the hope that the controversial "old" Catholic might reclaim it. Brentano's fiery *Last Wishes for Austria* and departure for Italy ended that idea. The second chair had also remained unoccupied for a long time, but in early 1894 a teaching contract as an *extraordinarius* professor had been given to Franz Hillebrand thereby filling it in a provisional manner.[23] The third philosophy chair had been occupied by Robert Zimmermann since 1861, who was about to retire.

Two weeks after Heinrich's death, Mach made a brief visit to Vienna where he gave a special lecture before the General Session of the German Association of Naturalists and Physicians. It was titled "On the Principle of Comparison in Physics."[24] He must have been eloquent that night as his speech was long remembered by many listeners, in spite of the fact that he seems not to have finished it.[25] Apparently, he was overcome by emotion or by the incongruity of attacking traditional causal theory while at the very same time using it to punish himself with guilt and remorse. Four months later, Alois Höfler read and discussed a continuation (*Fortsetzung*) of Mach's lecture to the Philosophical Society of the University of Vienna.[26]

Theodor Gomperz, the distinguished historian of Greek philosophy, writer on John Stuart Mill, and friend of positivism, heard Mach's speech against the notion of cause and effect and took a printed copy of it home with him. Shortly afterward, he encouraged his son, Heinrich Gomperz, to read it. The young philosophy student was so enthusiastic about it that he woke his father in the middle of the night and said: "Excuse me if I disturb you! I only wanted to say: Why do you find it so hard to find a philosopher [to fill one of the empty chairs]? If one has Mach in the country one would think that the search shouldn't take long." Theodor Gomperz replied: "Mach? Why that's an idea!" He then thought the matter over.[27]

Meanwhile, Professor Tschermak replied favorably (October 11, 1894) to Mach's idea of coming to Vienna to teach as an "honorary" professor.[28] He later stated that all three University physicists approved.[29] He warned, however, that Mach would make less money teaching on a private basis and eventually would regret no longer having a laboratory of his own available.

Mach's friend, Eduard Krischek (letter, October 2, 1894), and Tschermak (letter, October 11, 1894), also discovered that Herr Kleemann, a government adviser (*Referent*), was willing to recommend Mach's transfer to Vienna not merely as an "honorary" professor but on an official basis to fill one of the open philosophy professorships. The wheels were now turning more quickly. The Education Ministry (*Das Ministerium für Cultus und Unterricht*) on November 4, 1894, unexpectedly asked the philosophy faculty for new proposals to fill one of the empty philosophy chairs.[30] Theodor Gomperz put forward Mach's name before the faculty selection commission and for the rest of November did his utmost to bring the rest of the commission and philosophical faculty around to his way of thinking. He also communicated with Mach himself in order to check his availability and interest.[31]

Mach, however, was of two minds. He wanted to come to Vienna, and was willing to accept a professorship in philosophy, but he still preferred to think of himself as a scientist and wanted other people to think of himself in that way too. Professor Gomperz sought to ease Mach's fears on this point and was apparently rather successful.

Heinrich Gomperz later described how the only "professional philosopher" on the committee withdrew his opposition to Mach's nomination.

Robert Zimmermann, the follower of Herbart, saw a disrespect to philosophy in calling a physicist to fill a chair in philosophy. Should a majority support such a proposal, he would register a minority vote in the faculty. But it now happened (indeed, mainly from reasons of that kind which generally tend to favor the success of "outsiders"), that finally all [ten] other members of the commission united in support of Mach. Zimmermann then declared that since the other members of the commission were unanimous, he [as head of the commission] was ready to write a report supporting their point of view. This report of Zimmermann—as my father often remembered with laughter!—began roughly as follows: "The Stoics already divided philosophy into logic, physics, and ethics. It is therefore desirable that the three philosophy chairs in Vienna be occupied by a logician, an ethicist, and the third chair by a physicist." [32]

Heinrich Gomperz further related: "Above all there were some reservations to be overcome about Mach's 'radical' views. To help persuade those members of the faculty who were novelty-shy it was hinted that Mach's ideas displayed a close relationship with those of Bishop Berkeley."

Five days after Zimmermann's report, on December 15, 1894, the issue came to a vote before the entire philosophical faculty. To make the vote as near unanimous as possible a bone was thrown to the "humanistic" wing of the faculty in the form of an accompanying recommendation to fill the second philosophy chair with Dr. Benno Erdmann as *primo loco* and Dr. Rudolf Eucken, the future Nobel Prize winner, as *secundo loco*. The double recommendation was approved by the faculty forty-three to two with two abstentions.[33] The Ministry rejected the second proposal out of hand, claiming that there was only one actual vacancy.[34] The first proposal also ran into serious opposition. On January 26, 1895, Theodor Gomperz wrote to Mach that J. von Karabaček, dean of the philosophy faculty, had promised to see the Education Minister soon and argue energetically for the faculty's recommendation.[35]

The decisive breakthrough, however, came through the efforts of the classical philologist, Wilhelm von Hartel, a close friend and confidant of the Education Minister, who was also a member of the selection commission. He discovered the real reason for the Ministry's silence and procrastination. Von Hartel communicated his findings to Mach, and encouraged the would-be Prague émigré to reply to the charges against him. Here are a few quotations from some of the scrawled notes that the classical scholar sent to Mach:

February 11, 1895:

Today for the first time I was offered the long-sought opportunity to inquire in the ministry about your transfer and about the different rumors concerning the real state of affairs. What I had not believed [possible] is now clear. You are under attack from the side of the clericals. . . . Our opponents have ferreted out [*aufgestöbert*] two places in your writings which are directed against religion.[36]

February 12, 1895:

Since I cannot believe that your moderate statements could form an obstacle in themselves in the eyes of responsible people, I will speak without further delay with the minister himself, which will take place tomorrow or in a day or two. You shall then hear from me at once.

February 14, 1895:

I called on the minister today who named with great frankness both the accusers and the accusations.

February 22, 1895:

In all haste I will disclose to you, that finally the ice is broken. . . . I only wish now that the negotiations will take a fast and smooth course. My advice is, if it is at all possible, to come here and conduct the matter in person.

A few weeks later Mach wrote to Popper-Lynkeus (March 14, 1895):

The situation stands so, a gentleman who the Minister has named as an intermediary [Herr Rittner] has designated several places in my writings as directed against religion, belief in immortality, etc. I have gathered my writings together, underlined the places in red, and sent the whole business to Vienna; at the same time the intermediary has offered to tell the Minister that indeed I do not agitate in my lectures, but on the contrary am very careful; but should it be demanded that I take the position in my writings 'epistolae obscurum virorum,' then it would be better to forget the whole thing, because I refuse to accept that condition. I then considered that the whole matter as concerned me was as good as lost. To my surprise, a few days afterward the intermediary wrote saying that everything was going well, and that the Minister had only still to ask the governor [*Statthalter*] of Bohemia about me, because it was customary in such cases. Since then, three weeks have passed, without having heard any more news. He can indeed do what he pleases. For the present say nothing about this. I will see this matter through to the end.

The governor of Bohemia had already written the Education Minister, however, about Mach (March 5, 1895):

Allow me . . . to make it known, that no objection on moral or civic grounds has been raised here against . . . Professor Dr. Ernst Mach; he concentrates exclusively on science and on his work and stands quite apart from political life.[37]

We do not know the reason for the governor's generous remarks, since in fact, there were many reports through the years on file on Mach's political activities in Prague. Nonetheless, one may still appreciate the governor's kindness, and in an overall sense, his fairness and good judgment.

Franz Josef, Emperor of Austria and King of Hungary, on May 5, 1895, signed a document making Ernst Mach a professor of philosophy at the University of Vienna. The following month the government of Prince Alfred Windischgrätz was overthrown. This was the last Habsburg government in which the Austrian Liberals exercised a decisive influence. Mach believed that only the fear of arousing another "Brentano Affair" inclined the Education Ministry to overlook his religious deficiencies.[38]

Most people in Vienna seem to have thought that Mach intended to follow in the footsteps of Brentano and fight for the establishment of a psychology laboratory. Mach had other ideas, however; in his own way he intended to realize the full implications of his new position. According to his new title he was appointed an *ordinarius* professor of philosophy "especially for the history and theory of the inductive sciences." [39]

v

Mach's return to Vienna became a prodigal triumph. From an obscure name he flashed overnight into prominence as Vienna's leading philosopher. The years from 1895 to 1898 must be considered the most intellectually successful and satisfying of the burdened thinker's entire life. His lectures, new publications, and previously little-known republications mesmerized the Danube metropolis. Mach truly became the toast of the Ring city. There were ominous portents of future struggles such as Boltzmann's defeat of Ostwald in the Lübeck debate in 1895 and Carl Stumpf's oblique ridicule of Mach's philosophy in the International Psychology Congress in 1896, but such distant rumbling could not mar the majesty of the present. His tribulations had not been in vain. Mach had found a large and appreciative audience. Could a philosopher ever reasonably expect more? According to a Viennese journalist of the time:

[Prior to Mach's return] who knew anything of him? In any case we in Austria did not. The name Mach was only familiar to his colleagues in physics. Otherwise one scarcely knew more of him than that in the National conflicts over the Prague University he had been in the forefront of the German professors. The first weak glimmer for the population as a whole of the significance of this man was a lecture which he gave at the start of the 1890s before the Conference of German Natural Scientists and Medical Doctors.[40]

Hermann Bahr, a leading Viennese critic and dramatist of the period, attributed the sudden popularity of Mach's philosophy to his denial of the "self" or "ego."

Mach's effect, especially on the youth, was very great at that time, and indeed, it was actually based only on a single sentence. Mach had asserted that *Das Ich ist unrettbar* [literally, "the I is unsavable," i.e., "unreal"]. With that even the ego was overthrown and the last of the idols seemed to be smashed, the last refuge fallen, the highest freedom won, the work of annihilation completed. There really remained nothing else left.[41]

Bahr's account was confirmed by the example of W. Fred, a Vienna gymnasium student, who even skipped classes in order to hear Mach's "horizon-opening" lectures. Fred, who was later a literary figure in his own right, remained impressed—unlike Bahr—with Mach's "egoless" philosophy. "Mach uttered and proved the magnificent and pregnant saying *Das Ich ist unrettbar,* which has understandably become a popular catchphrase." [42]

Besides his evanescent and unexpected influence on the general population Mach also had a permanent influence on the thinking of many intellectually promising Viennese students and privatdozents.

Mach's inaugural lecture, "The Part Played By Accident in Invention and Discovery," was given on October 21, 1895, in the largest lecture hall in the University of Vienna before a huge audience.[43] Mach reminded his listeners that he was still a scientist and not a philosopher and that he would build no speculative systems for them. He stressed the frequency of accidental discoveries in science and the fact that only alert, well-trained observers adept at seeing relationships were likely to take proper notice and advantage of them.

Lecture hall #38 which at that time was the largest in the University could hardly hold the number of listeners, and one had the impression of an extraordinary occurrence. . . . My [Lieutenant Viktor Niesiolowski's] reaction was uncommonly favorable . . . natural speech, free from all emotionalism . . . thoughts presented with the greatest clarity, expressed in an unforced, skillful way. Every listener had to feel what heights of knowledge had arisen here through long, fundamental, beloved investigation.[44]

Viktor Niesiolowski, the future Austrian general and longtime lecturer at the Austrian Imperial War College, was so captivated by

Mach's lecture and philosophy that he audited as an extension student all of Mach's courses for the next four years. The military officer, who was to establish his own physical laboratory a few years later, remembered walks and conversations with his pacifist professor.

After his lectures I often found occasion to make remarks or ask questions. Mach was always willing to go into them with me. Meanwhile, I would normally accompany him through the portico of the magnificent University arcade to his office. He even went so far as to have the goodness to make books and articles available to me from his well-stocked library for more exact study of the questions which had been raised. Returning the books would then give the opportunity to have another conversation with him. In this way I received an education in a manner similar to Plato's disciples in the "Academy." [45]

Niesiolowski recalled that Mach gave the following lecture courses:

1895/1896 Winter Semester
Development of Mechanics and the Mechanical Sciences (3 hours)
The Psychology and Logic of Scientific Investigation (2 hours)
1896 Summer Semester
History of Acoustics and Optics (3 hours)
Theory of Sense Perception (2 hours)
1896/1897 Winter Semester
History of Heat and Energy Theory (3 hours)
Critical Discussions on Physical Instruction (2 hours)
1897 Summer Semester
History of Electrical Theory (3 hours)
On Some Questions of Natural Science (2 hours)
1898 Summer Semester
Main Epochs in the Development of Natural Science (4 hours)
On Some Special Questions of Psychology (1 hour)

What a contrast with Prague! For the previous two decades Mach had confined his academic teaching to the same five-hour course in experimental physics given every semester with few changes or additions plus laboratory exercises. But now, every course was different and many were in completely different fields. Mach taught courses in philosophy, history, psychology, physics, and education. Nor could this sate Mach's appetite for work and new lecture preparations. His demon drove him into giving additional special lectures.

Mach spoke "On the Sensations of Orientation" on February 24,

1897, and on "Some Phenomena Attending the Flight of Projectiles" on November 10, 1897. Both speeches summarized the results of Mach's own scientific investigations in two particular fields.[46] He especially enjoyed giving lectures before adult education groups such as the Vienna Union for the Spread of Scientific Knowledge.[47]

Mach's lectures had now become so popular that publication was obviously in order, which brings us to the major vehicle of Mach's influence, his books and more books.

VI

Mach published two new books in 1896, the German edition of his *Popular Scientific Lectures* (the American edition had come out the previous year) and his *Principles of Heat Theory*. Both books found a ready audience and were republished at regular intervals well into the 1920s.

The German edition of the former started with fifteen "popular lectures" and 335 pages and gradually ballooned by 1923 into thirty-three lectures and 628 pages.[48] It was normal for orators to sound better than their speeches read, but in Mach's case he was equally effective as a speaker and as an author. He had learned what was vital for a philosopher and unusual for a scientist—the art of communicating with an interested but unprofessional audience. Few of Mach's published lectures were ostensibly philosophical, but virtually all of them conveyed a philosophical message, which for all of its inconspicuousness, nonetheless, often affected the philosophical beliefs of the half-lay, half-youthful audience he had in mind. It is doubtful if Mach was unaware of the fact that a pleasant literary style can aid persuasion. We may add that Mach's *Popular Scientific Lectures* is still a readable book.

His *Principles of Heat Theory* was a different story. It was probably the only book ever written on thermodynamics with over a dozen chapters overtly on philosophy. Boltzmann's counteroffensive against Ostwald and "Energeticism" had forced Mach into publishing this strange work before it was truly ready for publication. The chapters on philosophy seem to have been included to persuade, if possible, Boltzmann himself! Critics, on the whole, were not kind to the book. J. E. Trevor, who thought well of Mach's other books, gave his opinion as follows (1897):

Mach's treatment of the early history of the theory [of heat], say of the period preceding Gibbs, arouses only admiration, but the remainder of the book has by far neither the same completeness nor the same finish. Horstmann's practical application of thermodynamic method to chemical action is neglected, Massieu's characteristic functions, Helmholtz's theory of free energy and its application, V. Oettingen's antithetic developments and the magnificent work of Gibbs are all but little more than cited. This is indefensible, especially since the author brings his treatment so far down into the present as to touch upon the recent discussion on "energetics." Then again, the assemblage of both new and reprinted philosophical sketches at the close, instructive as they are, is very disconnected; the book as a whole is neither a collection of scientific papers nor a well-rounded critical treatise on its subject,—we get the impression that a splendid work, partially finished has been dumped upon the market in company with the materials for its completion.[49]

In spite of hostile reviews, however, Mach and his philosophy were in fashion, and the several new editions of the book over a period of almost thirty years indicated not only that the book continued to be read but that phenomenalistic or "pure" thermodynamics continued to have its friends and advocates over an extended period of time, even after Mach's point of view dropped out of fashion.

Mach had four major books published or republished in 1897. The German edition of his *Mechanics* was republished for the first time in nine years, and his *Contributions to the Analysis of Sensations* was published for the first time in English. All in all, things were going quite well.

VII

Mach's initial success on his return to Vienna temporarily obscured the formidable nature of his opposition. Karl Lueger was elected mayor of the city for the first time in 1895. He was an extremely popular social reformer, federalist, strong Roman Catholic, and vitriolic anti-Semite who took pleasure in baiting "atheistic" professors. Carl Toldt, noted professor of medicine, German nationalist, and anti-Semite, became Rector of the University in 1897. The student body was dominated by a strong pro-German and anti-Jewish faction. Philosophically, Mach's ideas were challenged from several directions. First, Franz Brentano's influence as exemplified by Alois Höfler was strong in Vienna, and Brentano's former pupil, Husserl, was to exercise from a distance an even greater influence in later years. Also, the rise of

Lueger's Christian Socialist Party helped revive the Catholic Church in Austria which soon became a central political issue with its persistent efforts to establish a Catholic university. Catholic philosophy, both Thomism and Modernism, were prominent at the time. In addition, Ludwig Boltzmann, who had returned to Vienna a year before Mach, was lecturing and writing articles such as "On the Indispensability of Atomism in Natural Science" (1897), that is, he was fighting back against the influence of Mach and Ostwald over the younger generation of physicists and physical chemists.[50]

Ernst Mach found three privatdozents, or unsalaried lecturers, to help root his philosophy deep into the intellectual soil of the University of Vienna. The arrival of Mach in the Habsburg capital also gave great encouragement to them.

Anton Lampa (1868–1938) became a privatdozent in experimental physics in 1891. He was inclined toward Mach's phenomenalism and became noted for his efficient handling of laboratory exercises and his attempt to introduce Mach's "economical" approach into physical experimentation.[51] His presence at the University of Vienna acted as a partial counterweight to Boltzmann's influence, that is, among the more philosophically inclined physics students. Lampa was also attracted to Mach's ideas on education, pacifism, and eventually even to Mach's sympathy with Buddhism.[52]

Wilhelm Jerusalem (1854–1923) and Heinrich Gomperz (1873–1942) had a good deal in common. Both were Jewish, both were strongly opposed to Brentano's philosophy and his "dogmatism," both had long waits before becoming salaried professors, both taught at the University of Vienna for over thirty years, and both, especially Gomperz, helped form a philosophical bridge between Mach's ideas and those of the "Vienna Circle and "Logical Positivism."

Wilhelm Jerusalem was originally educated as a classical philologist at the University of Prague during the middle 1870s. Immediately after his graduation he married and began teaching in a gymnasium. Anton Leclair, his Prague "Immanentist" colleague, gradually interested him in philosophy.[53]

He became a privatdozent in philosophy in 1891 and combined university with gymnasium teaching for many years. Jerusalem was a prolific writer and had wide interests. He was especially remembered for his studies on the blind-deaf Laura Bridgman and Helen Keller, for his efforts to found a sociological society in Austria, and for his books on William James and pragmatism. During the last twenty years of his life he became the leading exponent of American pragmatism in Austria.

He was attracted more to Mach's biological ideas and comparative lack of dogmatism than to his sensationalistic phenomenalism.[54] Like James he refused to abandon belief in an individual "ego" and in the "interaction" of different types of experience.[55] His belief that formal logic should be understood in a psychological and historical context provoked strong opposition from Brentano and Husserl. Jerusalem's polemical replies seem to have helped delay his academic advancement to a regular professorship.[56] He later told about his personal contact with Mach:

> I had already become accidentally acquainted with [Mach] during a train trip before he transferred to Vienna and soon got to know him much better.
>
> Mach had two rooms set up underneath the University where he could carry out experiments undisturbed. He named them "the hole." Their location was rather out of the way and not easy to find. In spite of that the number of visitors soon increased so much, that he became annoyed, especially since he was almost always there alone and had to open the door himself. One day he told me that I should always ring three times, otherwise he would not open the door. He had arranged this signal with all his close acquaintances in order to avoid being disturbed too often. So in this manner I often came to "the hole" and spent many stimulating hours there.
>
> On February 18 in the year 1898 I came in and congratulated him on his sixtieth birthday, but added at the same time that I hadn't told anyone else about it. "For that I am especially thankful," answered Mach, and that this was his real opinion I discovered to my deep sorrow ten years later. I had made all the arrangements in union with some of his friends and admirers for a special publication [*Festschrift*] honoring his seventieth birthday, which would have an international character. The publisher had been found, contributions from William James, from Harold Höffding and others had been promised, then Mach heard about the plans and protested so vigorously that we had to abandon the whole thing.[57]

Heinrich Gomperz studied in Berlin and Vienna, received his doctor's degree in 1896, became a privatdozent in 1900, and, like Wilhelm Jerusalem, had to wait for a Social Democratic government after World War I before becoming an *extraordinarius* and then an *ordinarius* professor.[58]

Gomperz became an undogmatic, but nonetheless, thoroughgoing phenomenalist whose inability to grasp how ontology could be other than experience oriented inclined him to minimize the differences between rival theories of reality.[59] In this respect, he may well have influenced his friend Rudolf Carnap and the latter's attempt to reduce all "metaphysical" systems to mere linguistic variations of one another.

Heinrich Gomperz was interested in epistemology, Oriental religion, and in the history of philosophy. He wrote numerous books and articles, but never developed a systematic philosophy. He was witty and intelligent, but seems to have lacked the ambition and determination to realize his full intellectual potential. Most members of the "Vienna Circle" of the 1920s enjoyed his conversation but considered him a skeptic.[60] His last major work was a three-volume biography of his father, the last two volumes, though completed, have never been published. Heinrich Gomperz remembered three of his teachers well.

I had in Berlin, thoroughly enjoyed the mild and mature wisdom of Friedrich Paulsen for whom philosophy was still a guide through life and, who, though he had long since shifted from theology to philosophy, had yet remained a true pastor of souls.

I had been indignant at the brilliant sophism of Franz Brentano who was soon penalized for his dogmatism by seeing men like A. Meinong and E. Husserl, definitely inferior to him in ability and who had been his disciples, but whom he now regarded as apostates, rise to a degree of fame and influence surpassing his own.

But it was only in the oral examinations for the Ph.D. that I first met the man whom I consider to have been the most original and the most penetrating thinker with whom it has been my privilege to associate: the great Austrian physicist and epistemologist, Ernst Mach. And he was in his modest way, a great personality as well as a great thinker. In a sense, one might style him the Buddha of science, for like the great Hindu prophet he held "no one and nothing dear in this world"—except insight, and the facts and arguments on which it is based. Universally kind and friendly to all, he yet never seemed interested in one person more than another. A man for him was a being that had something to say and the only thing important about him was whether what he had to say was wise or foolish, true or false. He appeared to me as the incarnation of the scientific spirit.[61]

VIII

Mach had written books on the history of two branches of physics, mechanics and heat theory. He now wanted to write a similar book on another branch, optics. He had been collecting data and carrying out confirmatory experiments for some time when a new discovery aroused the interest of physicists all over Europe.

On November 8, 1895, Wilhelm Röntgen, a professor at the University of Würzburg in Bavaria, discovered what non-Germans now call X rays. He submitted a paper on the subject to a local physico-medical society on December 28. It was immediately published and offprints were sent to well-known physicists and medical men.

Franz Exner in Vienna received a letter from Röntgen within the week and on January 4, 1896, reported the findings to a group of Vienna professors.[62] Ernst Mach, with his skill in optics, stereoscopy, and photography, almost immediately proposed a way for an observer to "see" the X-rayed object as if it were three-dimensional. A month later in February 1896 J. M. Eder and Eduard Valenta, using Mach's stereoscopic approach, published the first X-ray atlas. Though Mach's work in this area has never been widely recognized, he was in fact the earliest contributor to X-ray stereoscopy.[63]

Encouraged by this latest success Mach looked forward to more optical experiments and finally finishing his book on light, which in German was first called *Lichtlehre* and was intended to companion his work on heat, *Wärmelehre,* but events gradually overtook him so that only the first part was ever finished (1913) and even that was published only after his death and with a longer and less felicitous title.

IX

Ernst Mach's only daughter, Carolina Lederer, once recalled: "Travel was my father's passion. He visited Paris, Berlin, and London. In his short summer holidays he normally went up the Semmering [a mountain pass south of Vienna] to Abbazio or Brioni." [64] Mach's wanderlust was especially pronounced in 1898. At the beginning of the year, during his first and only sabbatical, he visited Italy. During the summer he laid plans to visit his son, Ludwig, who had finally received his degree in medicine and was now employed in the Zeiss Optical Works in Jena. Ernst Mach remembered the tragic journey in detail:

I was in a railway train [July 1898] when I suddenly observed, with no consciousness of anything else being wrong, that my right arm and leg were completely paralysed; the paralysis was intermittent, so that from time to time I was able to move again in an apparently quite normal way. After some hours it became continuous and permanent, and there also set in an affection of the right facial muscle, which prevented me from speaking except in a low tone and with some difficulty.[65]

Mach had suffered a stroke which permanently paralyzed the right half of his body. His son accompanied him back to Vienna where Mach endured a long and largely unsuccessful convalescence. His traveling days were over. His memory had suffered and he could no longer write.[66] His son would have to conduct all future experimentation. Lecturing was a torture for both Mach and his audience and it had to be curtailed. The flood of publications ran dry. Thiele has listed four Mach books and three articles in 1897, one book and two articles in 1898, and nothing in 1899.[67] The new century brought hope and promise around the world, but not in the heart of Ernst Mach. He made his will and prepared for the next stroke and death.

CHAPTER 12

Philosophy of Science

I

Ernst Mach has often been thought of as a halfway figure between the positivism of Auguste Comte and the logical positivism of the mid-twentieth century. To understand and evaluate this impression in proper fashion we must first clarify what we mean by "positivism." Mach himself rejected the label, never identified his philosophy with that of Comte, except in mnior aspects, and died before logical positivism came into existence as a conspicuous movement. On the other hand, Mach's verbal reticence should not obscure factual similarities.

Mach and Comte were both presentationalists in identifying the physical world with what could be immediately sensed, and were phenomenalists in rejecting causes as agents or forces in favor of describing conscious referents in terms of mathematical functions or equations. They also were both "scientistic" in believing in human progress and in the indispensable role of science in helping to realize that progress. Epistemologically, their types of phenomenalism were somewhat different. Mach was sensation-oriented, while Comte, the originator of the term "sociology," disdained introspective psychology in favor of holistic theorizing about vague, cross-causal conceptual conglomerates which more recent sociologists following Émile Durkheim have labeled "social facts." Mach obviously was not a positivist in this sociological or Durkheimian sense, but in at least one or more of the other common uses of the term he clearly was. Let us then examine some of these other definitions.

1. *Narrow definition:* Positivism was the philosophy of Auguste Comte.
2. *Broad definition:* Positivism was the philosophy that combined epistemological phenomenalism with "scientism," that is, with the belief in the desirability of scientific and technological progress.
3. *Hostile "definitions":*
   a. Positivism was a materialistic and atheistic philosophy (religious objection).
   b. Positivism was a philosophy that exaggerated the importance of an empirical approach to science (rationalistic objection).
   c. Positivism was a philosophy that concentrated on mere details at the expense of a more general and profound understanding (Hegelian or holistic objection).
   d. Positivism was a philosophy that attempted to impose a mathematical, formalistic, or idealized method on subject matter often unsuited to this kind of approach (humanistic objection).
4. *Most common self-definition:* Positivism was a scientific *methodology,* which not only was not a philosophy, but which aimed to make all philosophy superfluous, at least as concerned science.

Ernst Mach was a self-definition positivist, a religious objection positivist (which included confusing presentationalist phenomenalism with representationalist materialism), shared enough of Auguste Comte's basic views on the philosophy of science to be considered at least partially a narrow definition positivist, and was also a complete broad definition positivist. In addition, he augmented both narrow and broad definition positivism with his theories of "economy" and "biological needs" and by accepting ontological as well as epistemological phenomenalism.

Mach as a broad definition positivist was of course merely part of a huge and in many respects dominant nineteenth-century movement. Many followers of Hume and Kant have as much right to be called positivists in this sense as the express disciples of Auguste Comte. John Stuart Mill, Herbert Spencer, Claude Bernard, Theodor Gomperz, and many others contributed to the hopes and efforts of this influential ideology.

Like Comte, Mach denied that he was a philosopher, that he had a philosophy, or that science did or should rely on philosophy or on any particular type or system of philosophy. Both men flattered the specialist by denying the need for scientists to study philosophy, but they did urge them to study the historical development of science and try to follow a positivistic methodology of science.

Ernst Mach defined "philosophy" in two different ways. When he opposed philosophy he identified it with "metaphysics." [1] When he favored it he usually meant epistemology or a "critical uniting of the results of the special sciences." [2]

Mach had many reasons for adopting Comte's approach to the question of philosophy. There was Comte's own argument, that a positivistic methodology represented an advance beyond the metaphysical or philosophical stage and justified the rejection of all philosophy. Also, many sciences around the turn of the century were attempting to prove how "scientific" they were by deliberately disowning everything to do with philosophy. Furthermore, Mach hoped to avoid damaging attacks from "professional philosophers" such as Brentano and his numerous academic followers by making clear that he had no intention of competing with them. And last, by denying that he was a philosopher or had a philosophy, Mach hoped to make his books and opinions more attractive to the vast number of scientists, both those with a positivistic bent and not, who disliked philosophy and who would not read further if they realized that what they were reading was philosophy. Here is Mach's version of his position:

I am a scientist and not a philosopher. [3]

Above all there is *no* Machian philosophy, but at most a scientific methodology and psychology of knowledge [*Erkenntnispsychologie*], and both are, like all scientific theories provisional, incomplete attempts. [4]

But:

I have already alluded to points at which the views here advocated are in touch with those of various philosophers and philosophically inclined scientists. A full enumeration of these points of contact would require me to begin with Spinoza. That my starting point is not essentially different from that of Hume is of course obvious. I differ from Comte in holding that the psychological facts are as sources of knowledge, at least as important as the physical facts. My position, moreover, borders closely on that of the representatives of the philosophy of immanence. This is especially true in the case of Schuppe. . . . [5]

Mach's claim not to have a philosophy, a point of view first conspicuously put forward in his introductory lecture at the University of Vienna in 1895, was a major step toward accomplishing Auguste

Comte's goal of persuading scientists to accept a positivistic philosophy while at the same time honestly believing that they held no philosophy at all, and that science—in particular their own special field—had successfully "advanced" beyond philosophy and the need to consider philosophical questions.

Broad definition positivism has normally appealed to religious opposites. Believers have supplemented positivism's epistemological phenomenalism with a nonphenomenalistic "transcendent" ontology which allowed for the existence of God. These people, such as Cardinal Bellarmine long before Comte and more recently Pierre Duhem, saw that by restricting the scope of science to the study of the "appearances," the world of "nonappearances," that is, the religious world, was kept free from scientific attack. Broad definition positivism was an ally of religion in this sense.[6]

Nonbelievers on the other hand, who have supplemented their epistemological phenomenalism with an ontological phenomenalism, have defined God out of existence except as a "sensation," "appearance," or Spinozistic pantheistic totality. Many people who have failed to grasp how epistemological phenomalism has prevented positivists as positivists from taking a position on religion have tended to regard all positivists as "atheists," which was not true. Furthermore, they have made false accusations of "materialism," a strange charge given the opposition of most nineteenth-century positivists to hedonism, atoms and molecules, and to representationalism, the only epistemology in which materialism made sense.

Both narrow and broad definition positivists have long used the expression "metaphysics" to refer to the study of what lay outside the appearances, but many people have been misled by the term into rejecting all ontology or theory of reality, even that which would apply to sensations or the appearances. How there could be a theory of knowledge without what is known being real apparently did not occur to a number of people.

Mach had both an ontology and a "world picture," but somehow they became lost in his campaign against "metaphysics," at least for most of his followers. Perhaps the following siren call was responsible:

I should like the scientists to realize that my view eliminates all metaphysical questions indifferently, whether they be only regarded as insoluble at the present moment, or whether they be regarded as meaningless for all time. I should like then, further, to reflect that everything that we can know about the world is necessarily expressed in the sensations, which can be set free from the individual influence of the observer in a precisely definable manner. . . . Everything that we can want to know is given by the solution of a problem in mathematical form, by the ascertainment of the functional dependency of the sensational elements on one another. This knowledge exhausts the knowledge of "reality." [7]

Atheists such as Mach seem to have been attracted to positivism largely from the belief that epistemological phenomenalism could provide an absolutely certain foundation for science.[8] Mach was undogmatic with respect to scientific theories and the incomplete nature of scientific accomplishments, but if "dogmatism" were understood in its normal sense, as the belief that we could be absolutely or infallibly certain of something, then Mach was a dogmatist, at least with respect to sensations. Furthermore, he compounded this dogmatism by restricting the scope of science to the analysis of sensations, as if there could be no other legitimate definition or understanding of science.

Science has always required self-evident propositions as a safe foundation upon which to build.[9]

For me every scientific work is lost which is not *solidly grounded* [*festhält*] in the immediately given.[10]

We are immediately certain of that which we are perceiving, less of that which we attentively observed and now remember, still less of that which we have experienced by analogy and construe as possible, and not at all the unexperienced which has no conceivable sense. . . .[11]

Mach did not *want* to be dogmatic, hence, he tried very hard to believe that it was possible to be both infallibly certain of sensations and a fallible human being who always could be deceived or mistaken. "But in general the assumption of constancies does not include the assumption of infallibility in individual cases. On the contrary the scientist must always allow for deception." [12]

Ernst Mach thought that a positivistic approach could be applied advantageously to all the sciences and in such a way as to unite the sciences together. This has been the dream of positivists from Auguste Comte to Philipp Frank and the latter's Institute for the Unity of Science at Harvard University and more recently at the University of Minnesota.[13] Unfortunately, particular sciences have not only differed from one another in terms of subject matter, but historically, they have developed different philosophical assumptions and methodologies, and while attempts have been made repeatedly to turn all of them into "positivistic" sciences, the results have amounted to little more than lip service, wasted time, vast frustration, and a lot of formalistic, jargon-ridden textbooks.

In point of fact, contrary to the views of Comte and Mach, both narrow and broad definition positivism were philosophies, resting on particular epistemological foundations, and most scientists have either rejected both forms of positivism, failed to understand them, or applied them in ways injurious to the development of science. We have already given two examples of the detrimental effect of positivistic thinking, one was the nineteenth-century positivistic opposition to the atomic theory and to the reality of atoms and molecules, and another was the anti-Mendelism of Karl Pearson and other English "biometricians" at the turn of the century. A third and very fundamental example from a period long before positivism became an organized "methodology" was Cardinal Bellarmine's phenomenalistic opposition to Galileo's defense of the Copernican theory as a representationalist theory of reality.

II

Ernst Mach developed several different purposes of science, but even though he expressed them at different times and each had a quite separate origin (i.e., his "internal" purpose resembled that of Bellarmine, his "intermediate" purpose suggested the influence of Heinrich Hertz, and his "external" purpose the ideas of Lamarck and Darwin), nonetheless, they were sufficiently consistent with one another to suggest the outlines of a philosophical system, as follows:

A. Mach's "Internal" Purpose of Science

(The description and relation of sensations)

The adaptation of thoughts to facts accordingly is the aim of all scientific research.[14]

For the investigator of nature there is nothing else to find out but the dependence of phenomena on one another.[15]

(Theory of economy)

The goal which (science) has set itself is the *simplest* and *most economical* abstract expression of facts.[16]

The aim of research is the discovery of the equations which subsist be-tween the elements of phenomena.[17]

B. Mach's "Intermediate" Purpose of Science

The goal of scientific economy is the most complete, consistent, cohesive . . . world picture, a world picture of the greatest possible *stability*. The closer science comes to this goal, the more capable it becomes of limiting the disturbances of practical life. . . .[18]

C. Mach's "External" Purpose of Science

The biological task of science is to provide the fully developed human individual with as perfect a means of orienting himself as possible.[19]

All this abundantly shows that the scientist and scholar have also the battle of existence to fight, that the ways even of science itself lead to the mouth. . . .[20]

Ernst Mach's "intermediate" purpose of science with its stress on a stable "world picture" anticipated and probably influenced the similar view of Max Planck, and Mach's "external" purpose of science fitted in well with pragmatic theories of the time, but it was Mach's "internal" purpose that helped revolutionize twentieth-century philosophy of science.

Describing the appearances in the simplest way possible as a method was overtaken and superseded by Ludwig Boltzmann's emphasis on the indispensability of theories, but as an end goal, understood in log-ical as opposed to psychological terms, Mach's "internal" purpose of science, his theory of economy, has become popular to the point of being taken so for granted that it has swallowed up and subordinated to it the notorious hypothesis-deduction-verification methodology so often referred to by contemporary philosphers of science.

Mach's greatest success as a philosopher was to persuade several gen-erations of philosophically inclined scientists to abandon Galileo's understand-reality science for an updated version of Bellarmine's de-scribe-and-relate-the-appearances science. This triumph has been iden-tified by many recent positivists with the spectacular scientific advances manifested in relativity and quantum physics, as if the philosophical revolution (or more accurately, "counterrevolution," if one may plagiarize from F. A. von Hayek) made the scientific revolution possible, and indeed, on a logical basis was presupposed within the scientific theories themselves, as if the theories were intrinsically phenomenalistic or at least presentationalist in epistemology.[21]

Historically, Mach's philosophical ideas did influence the thinking of Albert Einstein and Max Planck, the founders of relativity and quantum theory, but in light of the fact that both men later repudiated Mach's phenomenalism and returned to Galileo's understand-reality science, and the abundant evidence that both the relativity and quantum theories were more compatible with epistemologies other than Mach's phenomenalism, then in all fairness one must challenge this still popular positivistic thesis.[22]

Mach's philosophy of science was and remains influential, but the extent to which it was presupposed or necessary in recent scientific advances was considerably less than phenomenalists and positivists have been inclined to believe. Or to put the matter another way, all basic scientific advances have been compatible with Galileo's understand-reality philosophy of science, but they have not all been compatible with the approach of Berkeley, Hume, and Mach, that is, with the most recent revival of Cardinal Bellarmine's "describe-and-relate-the-appearances" reductionism.[23] Kant spoke of his own "Copernican Revolution" in philosophy, but in fact, he and his presentationalist cohorts have been chiefly responsible for reviving Bellarmine's anti-Copernican approach, in both science and philosophy.

III

Mach deepened the wedge between common sense and presentationalist philosophy of science by developing a justification for the abstract nature of science. He argued that all men were mortal creatures with overriding biological needs, who had to "economize" their efforts if they were to survive and prosper. He felt that human beings could not afford the luxury of a curiosity-oriented, learning for mere pleasure, particularistic science. In light of the need to be as "economical" as possible, it was his conclusion that this required the utmost in abstract understanding, which he believed only mathematical functions could provide. Most scientists did not believe that the abstract nature of science needed a defense, but Mach provided one should the occasion arise where a defense might be useful. Practical people and those men in academic disciplines such as history who thought their work was or could be reliable and who resented that such work was not generally considered "scientific," however, had already begun to question the restriction of science to abstract science.

As a good teacher and skillful writer Mach appreciated the value of historical or particularistic understanding in arousing interest and enthusiasm for learning, but as a physicist he denied it any place in "end science." It was simply not economical enough. Along this line we should mention that when Mach spoke about a "complete" understanding, he normally meant a complete abstract or mathematical understanding. Similarly, his positivistic goal of "the unity of science" was understood merely as a mathematical, or idealized unity.

Mach's defense of abstract science could seem strange to those readers who have thought of him as an "empiricist." But the explanation was simple. Mach held that all science should be grounded in observation and experiment, but that all genuine science was necessarily mathematical in character. He did not oppose mathematical physics, but rather "uneconomical" use of formalism, mathematical theory, and mathematical equations whose physical meaning was not clear. It was true that his interests were more empirical and experimental than mathematical, but that was another question.

Mach was well aware of the three major objections that could be raised against his theory of abstract, idealized description as the only legitimate end science. Indeed, his frequent attacks on mathematical "dogmatism" and formalistic speculation strongly suggested that he sympathized at least in part with these objections. Nonetheless, as Mach's increasing, Hume-like references to common sense and particularistic understanding as "vulgar" demonstrated, he had no intention of compromising on the matter. Only science could provide knowledge, and only mathematical science was true science.[24]

The three principal objections were: Abstract, idealized description was not reliable enough with respect to particular objects and happenings. It was not informative enough for either practical or curiosity purposes; and it was not interesting enough to attract the numbers of students into the pursuit of understanding which could occur were end science to include both abstract, idealized description and non-idealized, particularistic, historical understanding.

IV

Ernst Mach developed a number of methodological aids which he hoped would prove useful in actual scientific work. Many of these suggestions were first worked out in his lectures on the philosophy of science between 1895 and 1898.[25] He recognized the first need as methodological freedom. Scientists would be handicapped either if they could not introduce promising aids or if they insisted upon using inappropriate aids. Freedom of choice and fitting the right method to the right problem were both necessary.

Mach's "theory of economy" was a major, even if controversial, contribution to the methodology of science. He, himself, emphasized economy of thought (*Denkökonomie*), but it was economy in logic and mathematics which has attracted the most attention since his time. For the sake of clarity I have singled out a few of the different ways in which Mach employed his theory of economy.

1. Economy of thought

No knowledge worthy of the name can be gathered up in a single human mind limited to the span of a human life and gifted only with finite powers, except by the most exquisite economy of thought and by the careful amassment of the economically ordered experience of thousands of co-workers.[26]

2. Economy of energy

This fundamental view . . . [epistemological phenomenalism] is consequently the one that accommodates itself with the least expenditure of energy, that is, more economically than any other, to the present temporary collective state of knowledge.[27]

3. Economy of work and time

The scientist sets himself the task of gaining the greatest possible amount of . . . truth with the least possible labor, in the shortest possible time, and with the least possible thought.[28]

4. Methodological economy

The *methods* by which knowledge is gained are of an economical nature.[29]

5. Economy as mathematical simplicity

The requirement of *simplicity* is of course to the expert a different matter from what it is to a novice. For the first, description by a system of differential equations is sufficient; for the second, a gradual construction out of elementary laws is required.[30]

6. Economy as abbreviation

In the economical schematization of science lies both its strength and its weakness. Facts are always represented at a sacrifice of completeness and never with greater precision than fits the needs of the moment.[31]

7. Economy as abstraction

Our reproductions [of facts into thoughts] are invariably abstractions. Here again is an economical tendency.[32]

8. Logic as incomplete economy

The demands of economy go further than those of logic, which serves, so to speak, only as a negative rule [*Regulativ*].[33]

9. Ontological economy

The main thing is the abolition of an unnecessary doubled existence [i.e., "appearance" and "reality"].[34]

10. No economy in nature

Therefore, in this sense there can be nothing said about an economy in physical processes, since between *factual* occurrences there can be no choice. Therefore in this field I have not applied the concept of economy in any way.[35]

11. Linguistic economy

Language, the instrument of this communication, is itself an economical contrivance.[36]

Ernst Mach attempted to understand formal logic and mathematics in terms of sensory elements and an evolutionary-historical approach. For his pains he received the charge of "psychologism" from Edmund Husserl.[37] No aspect of Mach's philosophy has been more severely criticized than his refusal to exempt logic and mathematics from a phenomenalistic reduction. Mathematical "intuitionists," "a priorists," and "Platonists" all felt deeply wounded by Mach's attempt to relate pure, timeless verities to mere grubby experience. Here are two of Mach's more provocative observations:

Unbiased psychological observation informs us, however, that the formation of the concept of number is just as much initiated by experience as the formation of geometric concepts.[38]

The mathematician who pursues his studies without clear views of this matter [Mach's theory of economy] must often have the uncomfortable feeling that his paper and pencil surpass him in intelligence. Mathematics thus pursued as an object of instruction is scarcely of more educational value than busying oneself with the Cabala. On the contrary, it induces a tendency toward mysticism, which is pretty sure to bear fruits.[39]

Mach not only subordinated the use of formal logic to his phenomenalism and theory of economy, but in a sense the latter was his theory of logic. Wilhelm Jerusalem pointed this out:

If we should decide to regard logic simply as the doctrine of the methods of thought, and would consistently apply the concept of the "economy of thought" introduced by *Ernst Mach,* the possibility of extension in this direction would become much greater. Logic would then be nothing more than a universal economy of thought, and its task would consist in discovering how thought-instruments have always tended towards economic adjustment and how these adjustments may be still further advanced.[40]

Mach's stand on logic and mathematics closely resembled the approach of William James, John Dewey, and other Pragmatists of the period. To understand the plausibility in their point of view it may be necessary to emphasize the close relation between both their ideas on logic and mathematics and Mach's theory of economy with what might best be called: *common sense "means-end" logic.*

In everyday life an end or goal is "logical" to the extent it corresponds with more important goals or with primary values, and a means or action is "logical" the more it satisfies a particular purpose or purposes with a minimum of unfortunate side or after effects. Formal logic is "logical" only insofar as it serves as an efficient means or aid to reach a desirable goal.

Practical people have long insisted on subordinating formal logic to common sense "means-end" logic, and many logicians, scientists, and philosophers just as adamantly have insisted either that such a subordination cannot or should not take place. Mach was probably closer to common sense on this particular issue than anywhere else in his philosophy, and yet, it was precisely on this matter, the relation of logic and mathematics to experience and practical life, that Mach's views were most decisively rejected by the more prominent German and Austrian philosophers of his day. Historically, Husserl had more influence than Mach on this issue, and German and Austrian chairs of philosophy are occupied today much more by friends of Husserl than by friends of Mach. Nor did Mach fare better with the "Vienna Circle" or with "logical positivism." The development of mathematical logic and the concern with abstract formalism has brushed aside this aspect of Mach's philosophy and methodology of science.

Mach attributed more "certainty" to sensations than to the rules and assumptions of formal logic or mathematics. Many if not most of his critics treated logic and mathematics as more, or at least equally, "certain." This was probably the root of their opposition. Mach never treated "analytic truth" as the sacred cow it has since become in England and America, nor had he much sympathy with Husserl's infallibilistic non-sensory "intuition."

Mach had influential methodological ideas on hypotheses and theories. He pretended to follow Newton's rejection of hypotheses. In fact, however, as previously related, Newton and Mach did not mean the same thing by them, and both men did use what we now call "hypotheses." Mach opposed them as inferences beyond the appearances and as speculation. He did, however, grant them a place in *becoming science (werdenden Wissenschaft)* as sometimes useful "guesses" or "hunches." [41]

Ernst Mach was strongly opposed to what he called "fictive-hypothetical" science, in particular to the "as if" pragmatic approach of Hans Vaihinger.[42] If Mach's biological and economic purposes of science had truly been a first consideration with him, he presumably would have rejected his belief in the "certainty" of sensations as "uneconomical" and would have followed the undogmatic approach of William James, Jerusalem, Vaihinger and other pragmatists, but instead, he preferred to have the best of both worlds. The ultimate justification for Mach's phenomenalism was presumably its biological value, but in point of fact, Mach regarded sensory phenomena as absolutely certain and in this sense as their own justification. In other words, while Mach often made biological and economical defenses of his philosophy and methodology of science, both were based on his phenomenalism in large part, and had he to choose between keeping his phenomenalism or his biologicoeconomical approach all the evidence has suggested that he would have retained his phenomenalism. James saw that his own version of phenomenalism, his so-called radical empiricism, was logically independent of his philosophy of Pragmatism. Mach, however, not only did not see the disparateness in the two wings of his philosophy, but deliberately tried to justify each in terms of the other, an approach that critics have not been slow to expose as illegitimate.[43]

Mach's objection to "fictive-hypothetical" science was precisely that it would cast doubt on the certainty of sensations, and by doing that, presumably leave all science "up in the air." Mach failed to notice that a consistent subordination of science to something as vague—and he never defined the notion—as "biological needs" could hardly result in other than a "fictive-hypothetical" science. Mach wanted both the "certainty" of appearances and the absolute priority of "biological needs," but there was no rational way to base a consistent philosophy on both these notions. One had to be plausibly and unequivocably subordinated to the other.

Mach's attitude toward theories has already been discussed. He granted that they often had "provisional value," even the atomic theory, but he denied them all place in end science. They were simply not as economical as mathematical functions.

Mach's positivistic approach to scientific laws, his attempt "to cut them down to size," was quite influential. He was sharply critical of the belief in their "causal power" or "aesthetic beauty," and denied them existence "outside," "prior to," or as "intrinsic" within nature.

Natural laws are a product of our psychological needs, according to our view.[44]

The grand universal laws of physics . . . are not essentially different from descriptions.[45]

Laws cannot be ascribed to nature. We find only as much "lawfulness" [*Gesetzmässigkeit*] in nature as we ourselves have assumed in simplified external experience.[46]

Some laws were expressed in words and some in terms of mathematical equations. Only those in terms of mathematical functions, which could not be simplified further, were genuine "laws" in the sense of belonging in end science, for Mach. His belief in the idealized nature of scientific constancies was especially influential on the thinking of Henri Poincaré and Hugo Dingler, and on their well-known "conventionalism."

Mach rarely discussed the question of evidence as a methodological factor in science, and when he did his ideas tended to be negative. According to common sense, both scientists and historians gather relevant information, which they call "evidence," infer "hypotheses" from that "evidence," test them in terms of "evidence," and draw conclusions compatible with the preponderance of "evidence," and uncontradicted by any unquestionably reliable "evidence." Mach, like most phenomenalists, however, had little use for the notion of "evidence" at all. Theories were to help understand the appearances; appearances were not "evidence" for theories. Or to put the matter another way, the "evidence" has suggested that Mach blandly believed that all "evidence" equally supported all theories. "The forcible reduction of all appearances to what is mechanical seems unnecessary since the same degree of evidence can be found for what is nonmechanical. That there are masses, contact series, chemical equivalents are insights with the same degree of evidence." [47]

Mach's stand with respect to the use of models in science was not as hostile as subsequent philosophers of science have supposed. He himself freely used both mathematical and mechanical models in his own experimental work. His doubts with respect to mathematical models, especially those concerning four-dimensional space, related to their deviation from what could be observed and their lack of simplicity. His second thoughts about mechanical models were closely associated with his low opinion of the atomic theory and mechanistic explanation in general.

Ludwig Boltzmann in his article on "Models" in the eleventh edition of the *Encyclopedia Britannica* presented Mach's views on suiting the type of model to the particular branch of physics and on the provisional nature of models:

Another phenomenology in the widest sense of the term, maintained especially by E. Mach, gives less prominence to mathematics, but considers the view that the phenomena of motion are essentially more fundamental than all the others to have been too hastily taken. It rather emphasizes the prime importance of description in the most general terms of the various spheres of phenomena, and holds that in each sphere its own fundamental law and the notions derived from this must be employed. Analogies and elucidations of one sphere by another—e.g., heat, electricity, etc.—by mechanical conceptions, this theory regards as mere ephemeral aids to perception, which are necessitated by historical development, but which in course of time either give place to others or entirely vanish from the domain of science. [48]

Mach developed and named several methodological principles; their titles clearly indicated what most of them were about: (1) principle of the adjustment of thoughts to facts, (2) principle of the adjustment of thoughts to each other, (3) principle of continuity, (4) principle of compensation, (5) principle of permanence, (6) principle of variation, and (7) principle of sufficient differentiation.[49] It would be unfair to assert that these principles have lacked influence on scientists or philosophers of science. It would be more accurate to say that they have generally lacked influence under the titles that Mach gave them. Some of them, indeed, went back to Francis Bacon and Galileo, and others were narrowly tied to Mach's phenomenalism. His best remembered one was probably his principle of continuity, which he also called "the principle of broadest possible generalization":

When once the inquiring intellect has formed through adaptation, the habit of connecting two things, A & B, in thought, it tries to retain this habit as far as possible, even where the circumstances are slightly altered. Wherever A appears, B is added in thought. The principle thus expressed, which has its root in an effort for economy, and is particularly noticeable in the work of the great investigators may be termed the *principle of continuity*.[50]

Last and perhaps least, Mach gave a name to a particular type of experimentation. That name and the type of experimentation have since become quite popular.

The thought experiment is a necessary *precondition* of physical experiment. Every experimenter, every discoverer must have in his head the arrangement which is to be carried out, before he translates the same into action.[51]

It can scarcely be doubted, that thought experiments are of importance not only in physics but in all fields. . . .[52]

CHAPTER 13

World Influence: Philosophy

I

In July 1898, a few days after Mach's stroke, which paralyzed the right side of his body, he began to use a typewriter with his left hand.[1] Age, immobility, deafness, slurred speech, rheumatism (1903), neuralgia (1906), and prostate infection (1912) failed to prevent a most remarkable willed comeback.[2] He could not dress, so his wife clothed him.[3] He could not write, so he typed. He could not experiment, so his son Ludwig experimented for him. He could not walk, so he used a cane and even an ambulance when necessary.[4] Mach was a prolific writer before his paralysis and with effort and prolonged determination he gradually returned to being a prolific writer. He deprecated his own production, but for a normal person it was still immense. He started slowly, but after his official retirement from the University of Vienna in 1901 he took up his challenges again, met them head on, and mastered most of them.

Mach thought about spending his last years in Florence where he could converse with Franz Brentano and John Bernard Stallo.[5] He had only recently (1897) become acquainted with Stallo's ideas, but was impressed by the closeness in their points of view and by the fact that this then obscure German-American philosopher had anticipated many of Mach's own ideas.[6] Shortly after Stallo's death in 1900, Mach canceled his Italian retirement plans.

In early 1901, after having refused a title of nobility, Mach accepted an appointment from the Emperor to the Austrian Upper House.[7] He rarely attended sessions and made only one recorded speech, but he

did come to vote on major social and economic issues when the outcome was in doubt.[8]

From 1900 to 1913 Mach revised his *Analysis of Sensations* (dou-
bling it in size), deleted and added chapters to his *Science of Mechanics,* added eleven chapters to the German edition of his *Popular Scientific Lectures* (1910), put his philosophy of science lectures together
into a new book, *Knowledge and Error* (1905), finished the first half
of his *Principles of Physical Optics* (1913), the only part to be published, and gathered materials for his last book, *Culture and Mechanics*
(1915).[9]

He also published more than a dozen new articles on philosophy,
popular science, and on his experimental work. His two most important philosophical articles were both lengthy and were published together in book form in 1919.[10]

In addition to all this autumnal energy and accomplishment, Mach
wrote forewords to more than a dozen books, kept up a large correspondence, and defended his ideas in special chapters appended to
new editions of older works.

The first decade of the twentieth century witnessed a simultaneous
rise both in Mach's world influence and in the extent and ferocity of
published opposition to his phenomenalism and philosophy of science.
The most important attacks are covered in the next two chapters. Below is a list (using abbreviated titles) relevant to understanding the
spread and high period of Mach's direct philosophical influence.

New editions and translations

1900 *PW* (2d ed.), *Analyse* (2d ed.)

1901 *Mechanik* (4th ed.), *PSL* (Russian, 1st ed.)

1902 *Analyse* (3d ed.), *SOM* (American, 2d ed.)

1903 *Analyse* (4th ed.), *PWV* (3d ed.), *AOS* (Italian, 1st ed.)

1904 *Mechanik* (5th ed.), *SOM* (French, 1st ed.), *AOS* (Russian,
1st ed.)

1905 *E & I* (1st ed.)

1906 *E & I* (2d ed.), *Analyse* (5th ed.), *S & G* (American, 1st ed.)

1907 *SOM* (American, 3d ed.), *AOS* (Russian, 2d ed.)

1908 *Mechanik* (6th ed.), *E & I* (French, 1st ed.), *SOM* (Italian,
1st ed.), *AOS* (Russian, 3d ed.), *SOM* (Russian, 1st ed.)

1909 *EDA* (2d ed.), *COE* (Russian, 1st ed.), *SOM* (Russian, 2d
ed.), *PSL* (Russian, 2d ed.), *E & I* (Russian, 1st ed.)

1910 *PWV* (4th ed.), *PSL* (English and American, 3d ed.), *AOS* (Hungarian, 1st ed.), *Leitgedanken* (in article form), *Sinnliche Elemente* (in article form)
1911 *Analyse* (6th ed.), *COE* (American, 1st ed.)
1912 *Mechanik* (7th ed.)
1913 none [11]

II

Mach's influence in Vienna at the turn of the century was most prominent with young people, scientists, Jews, nondogmatic socialists, and literary and artistic figures. He was the philosopher of what remained of civilized, humanitarian, non-Catholic, Austrian "liberalism." In the Empire as a whole, the political situation was bleak and tended toward chaos. The proliferation of nationalistic and class-oriented political parties had destroyed any realistic hope of any government having a parliamentary majority. Hungary went her own domestic way, and Austria survived by decree and those rare occasions when a majority vote could be had in favor of a government measure. By the first decade of the new century it was clear that national differences were irreconcilable. The best that could be done was to accept the fact and try to preserve public peace and order by not emphasizing differences or introducing controversial policies. Austria survived until 1914 in suspended animation on a "don't rock the boat" policy. Should heavy waves come the Empire must founder. Loyalty to one's "nationality" had long taken precedence over "Austrian" or "Habsburg" allegiance. Even Austrian socialists were split along "national" lines.

Amidst such gloomy prospects, the remnants of "liberal" Vienna created a cultural renaissance unbelievable in its brilliance in light of the eroding influence of an increasingly hostile philistine majority which demonstrably had the future on its side. Mach's role as an intellectual leader during this immortal sunset had magnetic qualities.

Two students, Viktor Kraft and Othmar Spann, helped form a reading group (*Studentenkreis*) in Vienna between 1900 and 1903.[12] The members would meet in the "drying" room of Spann's father who was a bookbinder. With wet pages hanging from lines around them the group would discuss the ideas of leading philosophers of the day. Avenarius made a strong impression upon them, but they soon turned to Mach's much more readable books. Viktor Kraft later became a member of the "Vienna Circle" and its most dedicated historian. Unlike most of his colleagues, he remained in Vienna where he has continued to represent the best in that tradition. Othmar Spann eventually became a professor of law and developed a "holistic" social philosophy.

Hans Thirring, the noted physicist, whose father and son were also physicists, first began to read Mach's books about 1907 when he found one in his father's library.[13] Thirring became so interested in Mach's criticism of Newton's bucket experiment that during World War I he set up an elaborate experiment to prove Mach's "relativistic" thesis. Unfortunately, material shortages caused by the war and his own lack of financial resources hampered his attempt.[14] Nonetheless, he felt encouraged by the results, though they failed to give conclusive support either to "Mach's principle" or his epistemological "refutation" of Newton's "absolute" space, time, and motion. Through the years, Thirring gradually came closer to the philosophical and methodological views of Ludwig Boltzmann.[15]

Philipp Frank (1884–1966), the mathematical physicist, biographer of Einstein, friend of the "Vienna Circle," philosopher of science, and one of the more skillful writers at attempting to place Ernst Mach in the van of recent scientific progress, recalled the development of another Vienna student group which became enthusiastic about Mach's ideas.

At the time when the first chapter of this book [*Modern Science and its Philosophy*] was written (1907) I had just graduated from the University of Vienna as a doctor of philosophy in physics. But the domain of my most intensive interest was the philosophy of science. I used to associate with a group of students who assembled every Thursday night in one of the old Viennese coffee houses. We stayed until midnight and even later, discussing problems of science and philosophy.[16]

Philipp Frank wrote two books on Einstein's theory of relativity (1909–1910). Ernst Mach sent Frank two letters in 1910 at least partly in the hope that Frank could help clarify the ideas of Einstein and Minkowski for him. This correspondence helped seal Frank's lifelong loyalty to most aspects of Mach's philosophy of science. Frank wrote further: "About 1910 there began in Vienna a movement which regarded Mach's positivistic philosophy of science as having great importance for general intellectual life. . . . To this group belonged the mathematician H. Hahn, the political economist Otto Neurath, and the author of this book, at that time an instructor in theoretical physics in Vienna." [17]

Hahn and Neurath became major figures in the "Vienna Circle" of the 1920s and helped to shape the form that "logical positivism" assumed during the 1930s. Rudolf Carnap elucidated on the former as follows: "Hahn was strongly influenced by Ernst Mach's phenomenalism, and therefore recognized the importance of the reduction of scientific concepts to a phenomenalistic basis." [18]

Ludwig Wittgenstein (1889–1951) was the son of a wealthy Viennese industrialist of Jewish descent. He had four brothers and three sisters. Two brothers were skilled musicians and one sister was a gifted painter. Ludwig's schooling was irregular, his behavior erratic, his emotions unstable, and his father indulged him with money. But if he was spoiled, he tried to resist it by living humbly and giving money away. The suicide of two brothers, the war death of a third, the war crippling of a fourth, and the early death of his father complicated his already neurotic personality.[19]

On the one hand, he was attracted to extremely abbreviated writing and mathematical description. On the other, he enjoyed detective stories and emotional novelists such as Tolstoy and Dostoevsky. According to Rudolf Carnap Wittgenstein's basic problem "was a strong inner conflict . . . between his emotional life and his intellectual thinking." [20]

Wittgenstein originally intended to study physics under Boltzmann, but before that could take place Boltzmann died. Wittgenstein then wandered first to Berlin and later to England where he impressed some rather important people with his understanding of modern logic. He failed, however, to receive a degree.

Wittgenstein wrote his notorious *Tractatus* at the end of World War I. It was published in 1921 and appeared as a book in the following year with a controversial preface by Bertrand Russell. The book attempted to set limits to "meaningful" discussion. Its extreme abbreviation, however, tended to conceal as much as clarify his basic philosophy. The *Tractatus* had a powerful influence in both Austria and England, and more recently, in America.

It would be hard to determine how much reading Wittgenstein did in the history of philosophy. He was clearly not impressed by its importance, but he may have done more serious reading than he is normally given credit for. Wittgenstein was especially contemptuous of

Mach: "Mach writes such a horrid style that it makes me nearly sick to read him; however, I am glad you [Bertrand Russell] think so much of a countryman of mine." [21]

F. A. von Hayek, the respected economist-philosopher, who is also a family relation of Wittgenstein, has elaborated on the connection. "Others with whose ideas he [Wittgenstein] was very familiar though he disliked their manner were Ernst Mach and the psychologist Otto Weininger." [22] In point of fact, Wittgenstein's intellectual debt to Mach, whether acquired directly or indirectly, was massive and fundamental, as more than one well-known scholar has suspected:

Mach and the early logical positivists (Wittgenstein, Carnap) also postulated protocol and atomic propositions as absolute beginnings. [23]

The atomic viewpoint was in a sense fundamental to his [Mach's] system, as he conceived of the world of the scientist as a stream of unit observed facts, or atomic perceptions. One of his followers, Ludwig Wittgenstein, stated explicitly, "the totality of existent atomic facts is the world." [24]

The sense-impressions spoken of by Pearson and the sensations spoken of by Mach, Avenarius, and Petzoldt as neutral elements that constitute all the facts of the world, both physical and psychical, correspond exactly to the objects (Gegenstände) spoken of by Ludwig Wittgenstein in his *Tractatus Logico-Philosophicus* as the constituents of atomic facts and to the elementary experiences (Elementarerlebnisse) spoken of by Rudolf Carnap in *Der logische Aufbau der Welt.* [25]

Wittgenstein also held Mach's distinction between becoming and end science and in a way similar to that of Fritz Mauthner even borrowed Mach's analogy of a disposable "ladder": "My [Wittgenstein's] propositions are elucidatory in this way: he who understands me finally recognizes them as senseless, when he has climbed out through them, on them, over them. (He must so to speak throw away the ladder, after he has climbed upon it)." [26]

In addition, Wittgenstein adopted Mach's idea that nothing could be said about the world as a whole, a strange notion in common sense terms, but understandable if one looks from the perspective of epistemological "relativism." [27] Mach also had a significant indirect influence on Wittgenstein's ideas. Wittgenstein read one or more books by the speech philosopher, Fritz Mauthner, a former student of Mach. Wittgenstein referred to Mauthner in the *Tractatus* (p. 63) and there is also evidence that some of his ideas on language had an effect on Wittgenstein's posthumous *Philosophical Investigations* as well. "Wittgenstein's later concern with ordinary language and his conception of it as a game played according to rules echoes Mauthner, but there remain many implicit differences in their outlooks." [28]

Fritz Mauthner (1849–1923), as a young man, attended Mach's Prague lectures (1871–1873). He was especially impressed by a lecture that became the basis of Mach's *Conservation of Energy* (1872).[29] Mauthner later corresponded with Mach (1895–1906) and admitted that Mach persuaded him to base his philosophy of speech on an epistemological (presumably presentationalist) foundation.[30]

Wittgenstein was also attracted to scientific authors who owed a great deal to Mach with respect to epistemology and philosophy of science. But it is not clear what Wittgenstein learned from them. Von Hayek has stated: "It was also to a large extent their language which made Maxwell, Heinrich Hertz, and Boltzmann his [Wittgenstein's] favorite scientific authors." [31]

Ernst Mach long stood in close relation with the Adler family in Vienna. Viktor Adler (1852–1918) became a Social Democrat in the 1880s, founded the party newspaper in Vienna, and for thirty years until 1918 was the recognized head of the Austrian socialist movement. His major talent was in reconciling divergent wings of the party. But nationalistic differences finally won out. The heaviest blow was when the Czech Social Democrats formed their own separate organization in 1911. Mach's daughter remembered that her father was on good personal terms with Viktor Adler.[32] Our concern, however, is more with the relations between Adler's son Friedrich and Mach.

Friedrich Adler (1879–1960) studied chemistry before switching to physics and philosophy at the University of Zürich where he taught as a privatdozent from 1907 to 1911. He attempted to apply the reconciliationist approach of his father to the solution of theoretical and philosophical differences. He first tried to reconcile the materialism used in physical science with Marxist "dialectical" materialism. In order to do this he made a special effort to refute Mach's "antimaterialistic" theory of mass. He started by reading Mach's *Conservation of Energy,* but instead of refuting it was persuaded by it.[33] From this time on, Friedrich Adler's chief purpose in life was to persuade both scientists and Marxists to base their philosophy of science on the ideas of Ernst Mach. The tragedy in Friedrich Adler's life was not merely his failure to distinguish between presentationalist and representationalist materialism, a failure shared by Jacques Loeb, John Watson, Otto

Neurath, and many better-known "philosophers" than himself, but it was the basic hopelessness of his task. How could he possibly persuade philosophically sophisticated Marxists and scientists to accept Mach's presentationalist epistemology when both "dialectical materialism" and most Newtonian and post-Newtonian physical science rested on representationalist epistemology? Nor was Adler even able to persuade "unsophisticated" readers with claims such as the following: "The designations 'materialism' and 'dialectic' as used by Marx and Engels completely coincide [*decken*] with the concepts 'experience' and 'development' as used in modern [i.e., Machian] science." [34]

Scientists and philosophers of science normally have little impact on literary and artistic people. Mach, however, was an exception:

> At the turn of the century, Schnitzler, together with Hermann Bahr, Richard Beer-Hoffman, and Hugo von Hofmannsthal, formed the center of a literary movement known as "Young Vienna," a movement that stood in violent opposition to the naturalism of Berlin and Munich as well as to the pseudo-classicism of Grillparzer and his epigones. This group dominated Austrian letters until the outbreak of the World War and the rise of expressionism. [35]

Mach influenced Schnitzler, Bahr, and Hofmannsthal. Arthur Schnitzler (1862–1931) practiced as a medical doctor and developed an interest in science before turning to literature. He was a gifted playwright and short story writer. According to Mach's daughter-in-law, Mach was a good friend of Schnitzler and together they tried to compose an opera. [36]

Hermann Bahr (1863–1934) prided himself on being the first to take up new fashions and the first to abandon old ones. He led Vienna taste with his avant garde enthusiasms as expressed in the *Neues Wiener Tageblatt* from 1898 to 1904. Like Schnitzler he wrote many successful plays which were probably of high enough quality to deserve revival. Bahr passed through his "Mach phase" early in the century. In 1903 he even wrote a skit on Mach's "egoless" philosophy called *The Unsavable I.* [37] Bahr later became a strong Catholic with a conspicuous aversion to Mach's phenomenalism. As a critic he was one of the first to point out the resemblance between Mach's ontology and that of Buddhism. [38]

Hugo von Hofmannsthal (1874–1929) attended Mach's classes in Vienna and referred to his ideas in his doctoral dissertation. [39] Like Bahr and Schnitzler he was an interesting and popular dramatist. He is best known today, however, merely for his librettos to Richard Strauss's operas *Elektra* (1903), *Der Rosenkavalier* (1911), and *Ariadne auf Naxos* (1912).

Mach's most significant influence on a literary figure was probably on the still fashionable Austrian novelist Robert Musil (1880–1942). This unhappy man was born in Klagenfurt, Austria, successively left three promising careers as a military officer, an engineer, and as a scientist-philosopher, and spent the last third of his life in financial difficulty writing a long, fictional account of Viennese society which he never finished. In select circles this book, *The Man Without Qualities* in three volumes (1930, 1933, 1943), has been esteemed a classic. An admirer has written:

This monumental novel is an ironic analysis of the ills of the age, an unmasking of false attitudes of mind and an attempt to apply scientific precision of thought to social and spiritual experiences; Musil also explores a way of life for his hero who seeks to live without pretence. His style is translucent and often resembles a scientific mode of writing, but leaves room for expression of emotion.[40]

Robert Musil read Mach's *Popular Scientific Lectures* in 1902 and wrote in his diary that the book fell into his hands at the right time "in order to prove to me the presence of a largely understandable [external] reality of nonetheless high significance." [41]

Musil wrote his doctoral dissertation on Mach's philosophy: *A Contribution to the Understanding of Mach's Ideas* (1908). He largely took Mach's phenomenalism for granted but was critical of the latter's philosophy of science. Musil had hoped that positivism would provide a point of view which the practicing scientist could easily and beneficially follow in his work. But he found out that this was not possible. "All attempts to reconcile the contradiction [between theory and practice] failed to be persuasive. The personal result for the young doctoral graduate was therefore disappointment. Science and philosophy remained different things. *The most dazzling and attractive* promise of positivism had not fulfilled itself." [42]

Robert Musil received his degree from the University of Berlin. His main field was philosophy. Secondary fields were mathematics and physics. His foremost professor was the irascible Carl Stumpf, who as one might expect, was not entirely satisfied with the dissertation, presumably because of the narrowness of Musil's approach, his weakness in the history of philosophy, and his uncritical acceptance of basic aspects of Mach's epistemology.

Musil from time to time considered trying for his *Habilitation;* a *Dozentur* was even available for him in Graz, but his desire for a literary career prevented the idea from bearing fruit.

The young Austrian wrote several short novels and plays before attempting his masterpiece: *Young Törless* (1906), *The Enthusiast* (1921), *Vinzenz or the Friend of Significant Men* (1924), and *Three Women* (1924).

The title of Musil's novel *The Man Without Qualities* mirrored the influence of Mach's "egoless" point of view, but even more important, the *way* in which the book was written, and it was largely its style which has made it reasonably well known, strongly suggested Mach's experimental approach, his "shadowless" description of sensations. Musil's "unpathetic" treatment of his characters and "objectivity" might have drawn appreciation from Mach the scientist, but the novelist's pessimism and seeming lack of humanity probably would have repelled him.

III

Zürich, Switzerland, became a "Machist" stronghold around the turn of the century. Mach's philosophical ally, Richard Avenarius, had taught in the city from 1877 to 1896, and after his death many of his followers, such as Rudolf Holzapfel, Joseph Petzoldt, and Rudolf Wlassak, switched allegiance to Mach. Furthermore, Mach's ideas on "mechanics" proved influential with many students in the Zürich Technical University. In addition, many of the students from Russia, who were numerous in Switzerland at that time, either brought a version of Mach's philosophy with them or picked it up from other students or from the so-called Mach colony which had recently developed there.

Bruno Altmann recalled (1922):

More than 18 years ago a small colony of students and graduated ex-students was formed in Zürich. They were quite unique. Several Austrians, several Germans, two Swiss, a Russian, a Bulgarian, and a Turk. Albert Einstein also participated. But it cannot be said that the whole circle revolved around Einstein. . . . The Russian Ivan Ossipitsch Stoitscheff for his part awakened greater hopes.

In the Zürich circle everyone had his own ideas. But outside of that, one person thought for all of us: Ernst Mach. The great Vienna physicist and natural philosopher was the central sun for us. In his name we had collectively founded a quasi organized society. We had made it our task to spread the teachings of the master inside and outside of the academic professions and in so far as possible to employ their fruitfulness in our own investigations.[43]

The Mach colony was strongly impressed by Mach's criticisms of "classical mechanics." The members also took the Michaelson-Morley experiments seriously, and were perplexed by them.

Altmann suggested that a discussion between Stoitscheff and Einstein on a winter evening in 1904 was significant for Einstein's special theory of relativity which appeared the following year.[44] Altmann's account, however, is still lacking in confirmation from other sources.

Zürich books favorable to Mach's point of view included Rudolf Willy's *The Crisis in Psychology* (1899), Edmund Abb's *Critique of Kantian Apriorism* (1906), and Rudolf Wlassak's *Ernst Mach* (1917). Mach in turn provided forewords to books by the Zürich authors Rudolf Holzapfel and Rudolf Laemmel.[45]

IV

Even though Mach acquired serious philosophical opponents in Berlin such as Carl Stumpf and Max Planck, his influence finally broke through on the eve of World War I. The Mach-oriented Society for Positivistic Philosophy was founded in 1912 and their journal *Zeitschrift für positivistische Philosophie* appeared the following year.

The Berlin movement was carefully planned and started with a successful public manifesto (1911) which was signed by Albert Einstein, David Hilbert, Felix Klein, Georg Helm, Sigmund Freud, and many other prominent people not normally associated with positivism.[46]

Joseph Petzoldt and Hugo Dingler were the prime movers behind the manifesto, the formation of the positivistic society, and, along with Hans Kleinpeter, of the positivistic journal.

Joseph Petzoldt (1862–1929) was born in Altenburg in northern Germany. His parents were strongly religious, and he remained a convinced Lutheran until shaken by Darwin's theory of evolution. He read widely and was especially attracted to Kant's *Prolegomena*. Petzoldt studied physics and mathematics at the University of Jena, read

Mach's *Mechanics* in 1883, and was immediately impressed by it.[47] Following up a footnote reference in Mach's book, he then turned to the more systematic writings of Richard Avenarius, whose approach was more agreeable to his rigorous and well-disciplined mind. After the death of Avenarius in 1896 Petzoldt remained on friendly terms with his family and attempted to popularize Avenarius's philosophy with his own articles and books.

Petzoldt taught physics and mathematics at the Kant-Gymnasium in Spandau near Berlin. He wanted to become a privatdozent and professor so that he could teach philosophy in a university. He hoped that his two-volume *Introduction into the Philosophy of Pure Experience* (1900–1904) would open the right doors. Unfortunately, his radical positivism aroused powerful opposition. Petzoldt appealed to Mach for a strong recommendation. One Berlin professor, however, replied: "Yes, but Mach is even more of a complete atheist."[48] Nonetheless, Mach was a world figure by this time, at least in physics and philosophy, and his recommendation together with Petzoldt's threat of a lawsuit did accomplish the desired purpose. Petzoldt remained permanently grateful to Mach for his assistance.

Joseph Petzoldt may best be remembered as an organizer and synthesizer. He tried to bring the followers of Avernarius and Mach together under the banner of "positivism" and the advocates of philosophical and scientific "relativism" into one group under the slogan of "relativistic positivism." Nor were his efforts without influence, controversy, and serious misunderstanding.

Mach successfully remained on good terms with Petzoldt by not mentioning their many differences. The most important one concerned Einstein's theory of relativity. A second difference concerned "positivism" itself. Mach wanted to be known as a *methodologist* of science, not as a philosopher, and least of all as a "positivistic philosopher." Mach wanted his point of view to be persuasive and not tied to a label such as "positivism" which had acquired a bad connotation with a great many people. Petzoldt long remained in the dark with respect to Mach's ideas about Einstein and "positivism." But he should have suspected something when Mach went out of his way to compliment the least "positivistic"—and also the most original—member of the Berlin group.

This man, Hugo Dingler (1881–1954), was born in Munich, attended a Gymnasium in Aschaffenburg, studied physics and mathematics at Erlangen, Munich, and Göttingen, and received his doctor's degree in 1906. When he was fifteen, he read J. S. Mill's *Logic* which inspired him to attempt to develop a mathematical philosophy. In 1902 he rejected F. Klein's notion that geometric axioms stemmed from experience and in the same year read Mach's *Mechanics*.[49] Dingler's book, *The Limits and Aims of Science* (1910), helped him to become a privatdozent at Munich in 1912 and strongly impressed Ernst Mach, who wrote in the same year: "I myself, seventy-four years old, and struck down by a grave malady—shall not cause any more revolutions. But I hope for important progress from a young mathematician, Dr. Hugo Dingler, who, judging from his publications has proved that he has attained to a free and unprejudiced survey of *both* [i.e., "empirical" and "rational"] sides of science." [50]

Professor Alf Nyman has revealed that Mach was by no means alone in expecting important things from the Munich dozent:

The name of Hugo Dingler was first mentioned to me in the circle which had been formed around Joseph Petzoldt, Berlin-Spandau, H. Boruttau, Berlin, and Surgeongeneral Dr. Berthold von Kern, Berlin, and which had its publishing outlet in the *Zeitschrift für positivistische Philosophie*. . . . This circle, which frequently met in Petzoldt's house, but also elsewhere, considered Dr. Dingler the "Young Siegfried" of the neo-positivist movement and their most promising thinker, in spite of his strong tendency toward conventionalism at that time.[51]

Mach respected Dingler's opinions largely because he seemed to have an understanding both of Mach's methodology of science and Husserl's attempt to make the foundations of science absolutely certain. Mach shared Dingler's opposition to speculative mathematical systems which claimed to describe or explain physical nature in a reliable way. Both men considered scientific laws to be idealizations. Dingler eventually subordinated "uncertain" science to "certain" philosophy, an "unpositivistic" step which Mach never accepted. Nor did Mach ever accept Dingler's "a priorism." Was Dingler responsible for turning Mach against Einstein's theory of relativity? My attempt to answer this question is in chapter 17.

Ernst Mach had a number of prominent "negative" allies in Germany, men who opposed that which Mach opposed, but who held different "positive" doctrines.

Wilhelm Ostwald, who has already been discussed, was a major "negative" ally. Both Mach and Ostwald opposed "mechanicism" as

a methodological approach in science. But Mach refused to accept Ostwald's "positive" solution, that is, his "energeticism." Hans Driesch
(1867–1941), a well-known biologist, acquired a reputation of sorts
with his revival of "vitalism." Mach welcomed his attacks on "mechanistic" explanation and its "inadequacy," but in spite of his own Fechnerian past, Mach could not bring himself to support Driesch's "answer." Ernst Haeckel (1834–1919) was largely responsible for the early
acceptance of Darwin's ideas in Germany. He also made significant
contributions to biology himself. Relatively late in life he published a
book on his philosophy of nature. This book *The Riddle of the Universe* (1899) with its emphasis on evolution, matter, and atheism became a popular sensation around the world. This success spawned a
flood of philosophical and religious "refutations," such that in spite of
his contributions to science his old age was largely spent in controversy
and in warding off bitter pamphlets and diatribes. Mach attempted to
ease his last years by writing to him and stressing their points of agreement. First, both rejected mind-matter dualism, and second, Haeckel's
presentationalist "materialism" was only verbally different from Mach's
ontological phenomenalism.[52] Mach did not allude to their differences,
that is, to Haeckel's use of the atomic theory and his curious attribution of psychic reality to living cells.

Mach's large correspondence with "negative" allies in order to help
make them more conscious of the beliefs they held in common succeeded well beyond Mach's original intentions. Shortly after the turn
of the century, Ernst Haeckel and Wilhelm Ostwald, men who held
quite different theories of reality, joined together to lead what was
called the Monistic Movement. Everyone who believed that there
was only one kind of reality was invited to participate. The response
was remarkable. Many scientists advocated monism to exclude "metaphysics" from science and to emphasize their atheism. Many pantheists
and Buddhists were attracted to the movement because of its emphasis
on undivided nature and the one. "Professional philosophers," however, even those who were in fact ontological monists, largely refused
to associate themselves with it at all. Apparently, they were disturbed
by the philosophical naïveté of most of the leaders and their followers.

The German Monistic Society (*Monistenbund*) was founded in 1906
with Ernst Haeckel as president. The first International Monistic Congress was held in Hamburg in 1911 with Wilhelm Ostwald in charge.
The latter grandiloquently ended the conference with the remark: "I

close the first Monistic Congress and open the monistic century."[53]

The following year, 1912, Ostwald took the logical step and offered Mach the honorary presidency of the Monistic Society.[54] Caesar, however, waved away the crown. Or, to be more exact, Dr. Mach refused to be swallowed by his own monster.

There are as many different monisms as there are people in it. Monism is provisionally a *goal,* after which we all strive, but is scarcely anything fixed or sufficient. . . . It seems to me, as I remarked in my previous letter, ludicrous to found a kind of religious sect, while refusing to consider philosophical questions [as to its nature]. But this is not so terribly important in so far as the movement is limited to a small circle of intellectuals. But if it expands more widely, then it will probably let loose a kind of *counterreformation* for which *I* definitely have *no sympathy.*[55]

V

If we consider Ernst Mach's influence on French philosophy of science in isolation we see one picture, but if we consider that influence in terms of the development of French philosophy as a whole we notice a very different situation.

In the hands of Henri Poincaré, Pierre Duhem, Edouard Le Roy, Abel Rey, and Louis Couturat, French philosophy of science flourished from 1900 to 1914. Methodology of science became richer and more flexible. The understanding of science became more realistic and profound. But precisely while this "renaissance" was occurring and in intimate relation with it, French philosophy as a whole, led by Henri Bergson, Edouard Le Roy for "modernist" Catholics, and Pierre Duhem for Bellarmine-Aristotelian Catholics, was successfully attacking many aspects of "positivism," (indirectly including Machian positivism), and the importance and influence of philosophy of science itself.

Their aim was not destruction, but subordination. The argument was that mere "flexible," "conventionalistic" science could not reveal genuine reality and therefore must be subordinated to "intuitive" philosophy and/or religion. In other words, the very arguments of Poincaré in favor of "hypotheses" and "conventions" in science were used by Duhem, Le Roy, and others to belittle science vis-à-vis their chosen form of "higher" truth. In this manner a two hundred and fifty year old tradition was terminated. From Descartes to Comte French philosophy was philosophy of science. But from the beginning of the twentieth century to the "existentialist" present, science and philosophy of science have been minimized in importance. Nonscientific understanding and "knowledge" have revived in esteem. From the point of view of Descartes and Comte French philosophy has degenerated. In spite of careful thinkers such as Alexandre Koyré and Bertrand de Jouvenel it has become overwhelmingly irrational.

Henri Poincaré (1854–1912) was born in Nancy, attended the École Polytechnique, taught mathematics at Caen in 1879 and at the University of Paris from 1881. E. T. Bell has labeled him the last universalist, "the last man to take practically all mathematics, both pure and applied, as his province." [56] Poincaré became famous for his mathematical discoveries before he turned to philosophy of science. He also anticipated aspects of Einstein's special theory of relativity.[57]

Poincaré shared Mach's preference for "functional" over "causal" explanation, and both men rejected the reality of atoms as entities existing outside the appearances. Mach's most conspicuous influence on Poincaré's ideas was his theory of economy, which, when combined with Poincaré's acceptance of Mach's understanding of scientific laws and that of Émile Boutroux, prepared the way for Poincaré's "conventionalism." [58] "They [geometrical axioms] are in fact *conventions* or disguised definitions. Our choice of convention is guided by the necessity of avoiding contradictions. Some conventions are more useful than others, but questions about their truth are meaningless." [59]

Even though Ernst Mach frowned on Vaihinger's "hypotheticofictive" approach, his so-called philosophy of "as if," Mach was surprisingly receptive to Poincaré's not unrelated "conventionalism." Mach wrote: "Poincaré in his *La science et l'hypothèse,* is, then, right in calling the fundamental propositions of mechanics conventions which might very well have proven otherwise." [60]

Poincaré's theory of "hypotheses" helped to liberate scientific inquiry by incorporating within it a fundamental tool of common sense. Mach and Newton feared "hypotheses" because of their speculative nature. Poincaré, however, wisely insisted that there were many different kinds of hypotheses, of which many could hardly be called "speculative," that scientific investigation, especially in its early stages could often benefit from a measure of speculation, and that the proper identification and qualification of hypothetical knowledge should seriously reduce its capacity to deceive or mislead, which was the real question at issue.[61]

The most important difference between Mach and Poincaré with respect to philosophy of science was over the "external" purpose of science. Galileo accepted an ontological purpose, that is, to understand reality. Mach accepted a biological purpose, to preserve and benefit the human species. And Poincaré declared for an aesthetic purpose. "The scientist does not study nature because it is useful to do so. He studies it because he takes pleasure in it, and he takes pleasure in it because it is beautiful." [62]

Pierre Duhem (1861–1916) was born in Paris but remained a "provincial" professor. He taught mathematics and physics at Lille and Rennes and from 1895 at Bordeaux. Duhem made significant contributions to thermodynamics, philosophy of science, and history of science. His interest in thermodynamics and opposition to "atomism" made him receptive to Ostwald's "energeticism." He also marveled at the resemblance of "pure" thermodynamics to basic aspects of Aristotelian physics, and hoped that future physics would demonstrate more of these "remarkable" similarities.[63] He especially disliked the use of pictorial models in science. He felt they gave the false impression that they could accurately represent a physical reality behind the appearances, which he believed only religion could reliably determine.

Pierre Duhem was an open follower of Cardinal Bellarmine in his defense of methodological phenomenalism against the views of Galileo.[64] Only the church could determine reality, and the purpose of science was merely "to describe and relate the appearances in the simplest way possible."

Duhem had a much better understanding of history than Mach. He fully realized that a presentationalist epistemology and purpose of science, such as Mach, Hertz, Poincaré, and he himself held, represented a *return* to a pre-Galilean, Scholastic point of view. Furthermore, while Comte and Mach tended to misunderstand and undervalue medieval contributions to science, Duhem helped pioneer historical research into the science of that period. Indeed, this is probably what he is best known for today. Duhem's affinity for Scholastic philosophy of science is conspicuous in the following quotation:

Bellarmine maintained the distinction familiar to the Scholastics, between the physical method and the metaphysical method, a distinction which to Galileo was no more than a subterfuge.

The one who contributed most to break down the barrier between physical method and metaphysical method, and to confound their domains, so clearly distinguished in the Aristotelian philosophy, was surely Descartes.[65]

Ernst Mach influenced Pierre Duhem with respect to theory of economy, becoming science, arguments against atomism and mechanistic explanation, and possibly with respect to the value of historical investigation in science.[66]

Duhem, however, was not averse to making some rather severe alterations. For example, he drastically transformed the relation between "theories" and their "economical use." For Mach, theories were "provisional aids" to help determine and relate mathematical laws, equations, and functions. For Duhem: "The reduction of physical laws to theories thus contributes to that 'intellectual economy' in which Ernst Mach sees the goal and directing principle of science." [67]

On the other hand, Duhem very courteously acknowledged his considerable intellectual debt to Mach: "Believe, I beg you, in my profound respect and permit me to call myself your disciple." [68]

Duhem made no secret of which he placed more confidence and certainty in, science or religion:

For us the principle of the conservation of energy is by no means a certain and general affirmation involving really existent objects.[69]

Of course, I believe with all my soul in the truths that God has revealed to us and that He has taught us through His Church. . . .[70]

Henri Bergson (1859–1941) brought the "positivistic" phase of French intellectual history to a close with his book *Creative Evolution* (1907). His neo-Lamarckian *élan vital* caught popular attention, but philosophically, his theory of "intuition" was more important. The *word* "intuition" could be used in harmless or pretentious ways. Bergson pretended that a judicious combination of intelligence and "intuition" was able to reach truths and enlightenment beyond mere science. Duhem and Le Roy subordinated science to religion. Bergson subordinated it to philosophy as well.

Both Mach and Bergson held generally presentationalist views, but the Frenchman firmly rejected Mach's psychophysical parallelism. Both men were curious about the ideas of the other, but their contrary attitudes on the scope and value of science were unbridgeable.[71]

VI

How strange that just as the dominant trend in British and American philosophy was escaping from speculative idealism in the direction of "positivism" and becoming more "scientific," so French and Italian philosophy was rejecting "positivism" and retreating into "intuitionism" and speculative idealism. To be sure, these movements in opposite directions all continued to be presentationalist, and hence, within the epistemological tradition of Berkeley, Hume, and Kant, nonetheless, this shift, especially with respect to the importance and value of science, is worth noting.

Mach's influence in Italy was real, but as in France, it was overwhelmed by the philosophical reaction against the ideas of Auguste Comte and his followers and the "overvaluing" of science and philosophy of science. Mach's *Popular Scientific Lectures* appeared in Italian in 1900, his *Analysis of Sensations* in 1903, and his *Science of Mechanics* in 1908, but the big news in Italian philosophy was Benedetto Croce and the publication of his four-volume work *The Philosophy of the Spirit* with the first volume coming out in 1902. Mach's books were never republished in Italy.

Benedetto Croce (1866–1952) was born in Pescasseroli in southern Italy. His parents were killed in an earthquake when he was seventeen. He then lived with his paternal uncle in Rome where he also attended the University, but did not graduate. He went through a Marxist phase between 1896 and 1900, but his debt to Hegel lasted his entire life. As an independently wealthy heir he founded the periodical *La Critica* in 1903 in whose pages most of his ideas first appeared.

Croce was as much an epistemological and ontological phenomenalist as Mach. Both men were atheists and rejected "metaphysics." The primary differences in their points of view were that Croce had a low opinion of "empirical" science and was more interested in emotions, purposes, values, ideals, and especially in history. Croce emphasized what he called "becoming" and "spirit." The former he identified with both reality and history, and the latter, he believed, was always present in becoming and first manifests itself as art. Croce is perhaps best known for his identification of philosophy with history. His major international influence has been on the fields of aesthetics and philosophy of history. Neither Croce nor Mach held anything resembling a common sense understanding of causal explanation.

Mach's only conspicuous influence on Croce's philosophy was his theory of economy.

He [Croce] adopted the so-called economic theory of science which had been originally developed by scientists like Mach and Poincaré and which considers scientific concepts to be logical fictions produced for practical convenience. So according to Croce the sciences of nature deal with fictions and abstractions, while concrete reality can only be reached through perception of the individual fact, or historical knowldge. Only history provides us with true knowledge, and philosophy is its foundation. Croce was well aware that the originators of the "economic theory" did not favor philosophic idealism, but he attached more weight to their ideas on the method of the sciences than to their opinions on philosophy, in which he did not consider them competent.[72]

VII

Ernst Mach had a major, if largely indirect, influence on twentieth-century English philosophy and in particular on Bertrand Russell's understanding of physics and on one of the epistemological stages through which he passed. Russell later reminisced:

> To some extent, they [Russell's doubts] were laid to rest by a book which greatly delighted me: W. K. Clifford's *Common Sense of the Exact Sciences.*[73]

> I studied Hertz's *Principles of Mechanics,* and I was delighted when Hertz succeeded in manufacturing electro-magnetic waves.[74]

It is possible Russell never noticed the extent to which the above books were influenced by Mach's understanding of mass, force, and functional relations. Bertrand Russell entered Cambridge in 1890, became a fellow at Trinity College in 1895, left in 1901, and returned as a lecturer from 1910 to 1916. Philosophically he passed through four major periods: Bradleyan Idealism (1894–1898), Platonic "realism" (1898–1914), "Logical Atomism" (1918–1940?), and representative realism and mind-matter dualism (1940?–1969).

Bertrand Russell's most important contribution to philosophy has normally been considered to be his three-volume *Principia Mathematica* (1910, 1912, 1913), which he coauthored with Alfred Whitehead. But apart from his work on symbolic logic, the logical atomism of his third period has probably drawn more attention from the philosophic public than other "periods" and aspects of his thought. Bertrand Russell became interested in the "neutral monism" of William James before World War I, but while he knew that Mach had developed a similar doctrine, he nevertheless, was more attracted by the approach of James and American "New Realists" such as Ralph Barton Perry.[75] He also believed that James had developed his theory independently of Mach.[76]

At first, Russell opposed "neutral monism." He wrote: (1914):

I conclude that neutral monism, though largely right in its polemic against previous theories, cannot be regarded as able to deal with all the facts, and must be replaced by a theory in which the difference between what is experienced and what is not experienced by a given subject at a given moment is made simpler and more prominent than it can be in a theory which wholly denies the existence of specifically mental entities.[77]

Ludwig Wittgenstein, Mach's peripatetic and unwilling disciple, was a primary catalyst in helping to change Russell's mind. Wittgenstein studied and worked in England from 1908 to 1913, and became personally acquainted with both G. E. Moore and Bertrand Russell at Cambridge. He was argumentative and extremely critical of the ideas of both men. He struck directly at Russell's Platonic "realism" by claiming that all mathematical truths were merely "tautological" and said nothing about the world. His epistemological and ontological attacks along with the ideas of James and Perry also undermined Russell's confidence in the reality of the "subject" or "ego" and in the distinction between "sense data" and "sensations."

During 1918 my view as to mental events underwent an important change. I had originally accepted Brentano's view that in sensation there are three elements: act, content, and object.[78]

American realists induced me to abandon the distinction between a sensation and sense-datum.[79]

In 1921 Russell saw that the rejection of the "subject" naturally led to "neutral monism." [80]

Russell's new positive philosophy was called "Logical Atomism" and in its mature form was *directly* based on Wittgenstein's "atomic facts" and *indirectly* on Mach's theory of elements. Russell now openly accepted "neutral monism." He wrote (1927):

The view which I have suggested is that both mind and matter are structures composed of more primitive stuff which is neither mental nor material. This view, called "neutral monism" is suggested in Mach's *Analysis of Sensations,* developed in William James' Essays in *Radical Empiricism,* and advocated by John Dewey, as well as by Professor R. B. Perry and other American realists. The use of the word "neutral" in this way is due to Dr. H. M. Sheffer of Harvard, who is one of the ablest logicians of our time.[81]

During the 1920s Wittgenstein made as strong an impression on Moritz Schlick, the leader of the "Vienna Circle," as he previously had on Moore and Russell in England. As a result, a successful effort was made to give Wittgenstein a belated doctor's degree at Cambridge

(1929) so as to encourage him to give philosophy lectures there. Wittgenstein gradually developed a new philosophy at Cambridge which contrasted sharply with many aspects of his *Tractatus* (1921). In many ways he became a kind of avant-garde philosophical Pied Piper, or Rasputin, who attracted a coterie of presentationalist devotees from around the world—especially from America.

Meanwhile, Russell, who felt himself no longer "in fashion," developed second thoughts about Wittgenstein and both "logical atomism" and "neutral monism."

He [Wittgenstein] made it [the theory of "atomic facts"] the basis of a curious kind of logical mysticism.[82]

This was connected with his mysticism. . . .[83]

He, himself, as usual, is oracular and emits his opinion as if it were a Czar's Ukase, but humbler folk can hardly content themselves with this procedure.[84]

Russell began to question the compatibility of presentationalism with science. His defense of the representative theory of preception soon led to the adoption of more aspects of representative realism and mind-matter dualism. "I have been surprised to find the causal theory of perception treated as something that could be questioned. I can well understand Hume's questioning of causality in general, but if causality in general is admitted, I do not see on what grounds perception should be exempted from its scope." [85]

VIII

Edward Bradford Titchener (1867–1927) was an Englishman who tried to implant Wilhelm Wundt's "Experimental Psychology" into American universities. He directed the psychological laboratory at Cornell University from 1892 to 1927.[86] He was strongly influenced by Mach's psychological and philosophical ideas, but was opposed by most of his "behaviorist" colleagues as immersed in old-fashioned "introspectionism." Edwin G. Boring wrote:

Titchener never became a part of American psychology. . . . [His] interests lay in the generalized, normal, human, adult mind that had also been Wundt's main concern. He did not desire to initiate research in animal psychology, which in its experimental phase, really began in America, nor in abnormal and child psychology, nor—and this is perhaps the most important point of all—in individual psychology. He wanted to work on the *mind;* Americans were beginning to be concerned with *minds.*

He gave fifty-four doctorates in psychology during his thirty-five years at Cornell, a great personal achievement because most of these dissertations bore the stamp of his own thought.[87]

Professor Boring also mentioned Mach's influence:

The teaching of Mach and Avenarius seems to have been ingrained even into Titchener's everyday thinking.[88]

This underlying "epistemology" of Titchener was, of course, not philosophically sophisticated. Ever since Locke, philosophers have concentrated upon this problem and Mach and Avenarius are regarded today as naive. Titchener, however, refused to admit that he was philosophizing; he held that he was forming a practical scientific distinction, and it is undoubtedly true that, if his position had been fruitful of scientific progress, the philosophers would have had to interpret it in their own terms.[89]

The "main stream" of American psychology followed the path opened up by William James into "functionalism" and "behaviorism." But William James and many of his followers, as we have already noted, were also influenced by Mach. "With philosophers too, his influence has been considerable, and through William James, who stood in close contact with him, both the new Amercian doctrines of neo-realism and pragmatism can be traced to him." [90]

Mach's influence became a critical factor in the establishment of "New Realism" in 1910. Ralph Barton Perry, Edwin Bissell Holt, and four other American philosophers issued a joint manifesto in that year, "The Program and First Platform of Six Realists," in which they attempted to create a new epistemological position, presentationalist in character, but more satisfactory than either naïve realism or phenomenalism.[91]

Their solution was to adopt the "neutral monism" of Mach and James and Mach's theory of "functional relations." [92] In point of fact their "realism" scarcely differed from epistemological and ontological phenomenalism, except in their quite compatible use of a "physical object" language and opposition to immanent phenomenalism, the notion that sensations had to be conscious to be real. On the other hand, they did reject Mach's theory of "biological needs" and his "psychologistic" handling of logic and mathematics.

The first wave of Mach's influence in America, led by William James and the "New Realists," was partly checked during the 1920s by "Critical Realists" such as Arthur Lovejoy and George Santayana. These men argued that physical reality should be identified neither with sen-

Populäre Vorlesungen

für

Herren und Damen

über

Akustik als physikalische Grundlage der Musiktheorie.

Diese Vorlesungen haben den Zweck, die reichen und interessanten Resultate der Forschungen **Helmholtz's** einem weiteren Kreise zugänglich und nützlich zu machen; sie behandeln eine Reihe von Fragen, über welche die bisherige Musiktheorie keine Auskunft zu geben wusste. Der Gefertigte wird das Vorgetragene durch Experimente erläutern.

Der Gegenstand wird einen Cyclus von 8—10 Vorlesungen ausfüllen, welche im Universitätsgebäude, 2. Stock, Hörsaal Nr. 4, von 7—8 Uhr Abends an folgenden Tagen abgehalten werden: Montag 14. Dezember, Freitag 18. Dezember, Montag 21. Dezember, Montag 28. Dezember, Samstag 2. Jänner, Montag 4. Jänner, Freitag 8. Jänner, Dienstag 12. Jänner.

Der Stoff der Vorträge vertheilt sich folgendermassen:

1. Einleitung. Gesetze der Schallbewegung in der Luft und in festen Körpern.
2. Wechselwirkung der Schallwellen. Schwebungen. Combinationstöne.
3. Gesetze des Mitschwingens. Erklärung der Resonanz.
4. Einrichtung des Ohres. Entstehung der Tonreihe. Erklärung der Klangfarbe.
5. Physik der musikalischen Instrumente.
6. Erklärung des Consonirens und Dissonirens. Begründung der Octavenperiode.
7. Entstehung der Tonleitern und Tonarten. Psychologische und historische Begründung.
8. Hauptgesetze der Musiklehre auf physikalischer Grundlage.

Karten à 5 fl. öst. Währ. für den ganzen Cyclus werden in der Musikalien-Handlung Spina (Graben) ausgegeben.

Dr. Ernst Mach,

Privatdocent der Wiener Universität.

Druck von Alex. Eurich in Wien

Z. N. St G.

Handbill advertising a series of lectures by Ernst Mach (1863)
(Courtesy of the
Austrian National Library)

Ernst Mach at Graz (1864-1867)
(Courtesy of Friedrich Herneck)

Left: Joseph Petzval.
Mathematician, early
photographer, and opponent of
Ernst Mach and of
the Doppler theory

Above: Cenĕk Dvořák. Mach's
favorite student and long-time
professor of physics at the
University of Zagreb
(Courtesy of the Physics Library
at the University of Zagreb)

Čenĕk Strouhal. Mach student
(1869) and later Rector
of the Czech
University of Prague
(Courtesy of the Strouhal Family)

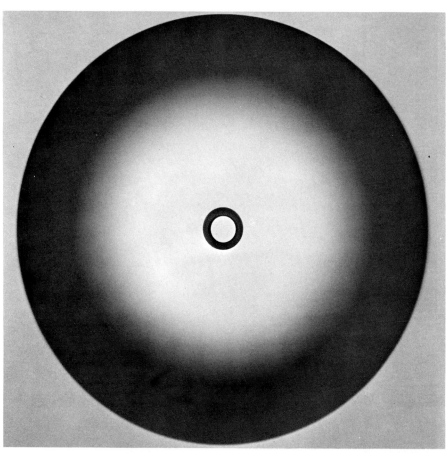

Black-white color disk in motion.
The blackest-black ring and the
whitest-white ring are the "subjective"
phenomena called Mach bands.
(Courtesy of the German Museum in Munich)

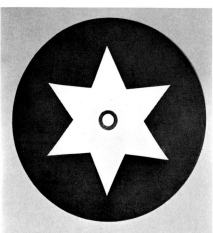

Black-white color disk at rest
(Courtesy of the German Museum in Munich)

Mach's laboratory office in Prague
(Courtesy of Frau Anna Karma Mach)

The "Carolinum." The oldest, most historic, and central building of the University
of Prague as it appeared at the end of the nineteenth century
(Courtesy of the Austrian National Library)

Ernst Mach at Prague
(Courtesy of the Ernst Mach Institute)

First two photographs of Mach
shock waves (1886) enlarged
from the originals which
were only a half inch square.
(Courtesy of the Ernst Mach Institute)

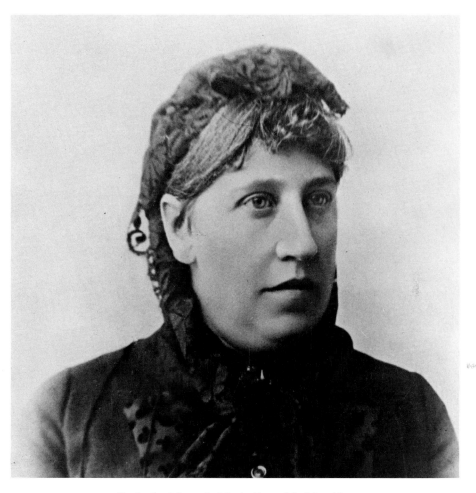

Ludovica Marussig Mach. Ernst Mach's wife

Carolina Mach Lederer
Ernst Mach's daughter

Ludwig Mach
Ernst Mach's first son

Heinrich Mach
Ernst Mach's second son

(Courtesy of Frau Anna Karma Mach)

The University of Vienna. "The New Building" (1897)
(Courtesy of the Austrian National Library)

Left:
Ludwig Boltzmann. Prime developer of the kinetic theory of gases which helped make the revolutionary work of — Planck and Einstein possible. His tenacious defense of the atomic theory earned him the label "The Last Pillar" from Mach's followers.
(Courtesy of the Ernst Mach Institute)

Right:
Joseph Petzoldt. Philosophical follower of Richard Avenarius and Ernst Mach whose attempt to connect Ernst Mach's epistemological theory with Albert Einstein's physical theory of relativity has helped lead to so much contemporary controversy and confusion.
(Courtesy of the Library Archive of the Technical University of Berlin)

Ernst Mach at Vaterstetten. The last years (1913-1916)
(Courtesy of Frau Anna Karma Mach)

sations (phenomenalism), sensed objects (naïve realism), nor with any immediately experienceable or conscious referents, but with material forces in a space and time outside all possible or actual conscious immediacy.

This dispute between "New" and "Critical" Realism shifted the battle away from "naïve" *vs.* "causal realism" to one simply between *presentationalist* and *representationalist realism.* The former is sometimes understood as naïve realism with "functional" instead of "causal" explanation and minus some of the traditionally objectionable features of naïve realism. Another identification of presentationalist "realism" is indistinguishable from phenomenalism except for its language.[93]

The tragedy is that when most contemporary philosophers oppose "realism" to either "positivism" or "phenomenalism," they normally mean presentationalist realism, when in fact, most practical people are representationalist in their epistemology (which they also call "realism") and oppose presentationalist "realism" just as strongly as they oppose other presentationalist views such as "positivism" and "phenomenalism." No aspect of modern philosophical usage is more misleading and regrettable than identifying the word "realism" with views based on a presentationalist or idealistic (in eighteenth-century terms) epistemology.

The second wave of Mach's influence in the new world came with the emigration of the "Vienna Circle" during the 1930s. All "logical positivists," as members of this movement were soon called, held a number of Mach's ideas. Under the influence of the linguistic ideas of Wittgenstein and Carnap they came to believe that they had shifted from Mach's "phenomenalism" to "realism," by which they meant a "physical object" language. During the 1940s and 1950s some of the older members of this movement genuinely tried to shift from Mach's epistemology and not merely from a "phenomenalistic language," but again, to the extent they succeeded it was merely to another form of presentationalist realism, usually one closer to "New" Realism.[94] There is no evidence that members of the "Vienna Circle" any more than their American counterparts of the 1910 manifesto ever comprehended what representationalists meant by "realism," much less ever came close to adopting such a position. Only in the last decade, in a move resembling Bertrand Russell's last philosophical metamorphosis, have a few elderly survivors of the "Vienna Circle" begun to appreciate representationalist, that is, "common sense" realism.[95]

CHAPTER 14

Mach vs. Boltzmann, Planck, Stumpf, and Külpe

I

Ludwig Boltzmann visited England shortly before Mach's return to Vienna in 1895 and was very pleasantly surprised by the favorable reaction to his atomistic views. R. H. Bryan remembered Boltzmann's visit: "In 1894 the British Association meeting at Oxford, with its memorable field-day on the kinetic theory, came simultaneously with Lord Rayleigh and Sir William Ramsay's announcement of the discovery of argon. The part which Prof. Boltzmann took in these discussions will long be remembered." [1]

The success of his English visit encouraged Boltzmann to attempt to set up a similar type of "discussion" in Germany with his opponent, the "energeticist," Wilhelm Ostwald. He wrote to the latter on June 1, 1895: "Professor Helm will referee the scientific meeting over Energeticism at Lübeck. I would like, if possible, to provoke a debate à la British Association, mainly in order to instruct myself. For this, it is above all necessary, that the main representative of that orientation —— be present. I need not be the first to tell you how much your presence would please me." [2]

Preparation for the debate was no problem for Boltzmann. He had already made his objections to "energeticism" known in private correspondence with Ostwald (1892–1893), that is, shortly after the Leipzig professor had shocked the scientific world by publishing a chemistry book with no reference to atoms or molecules (1892).

The Lübeck Scientific Conference (*Naturforscherversammlung*) took place September 16-20, 1895, shortly after Mach's arrival in Vienna, but a month before his brilliantly successful inaugural lecture. The famous debate took place on September 17 between 9 and 12 A.M. Arnold Sommerfeld remembered the occasion:

Helm spoke for energeticism; Wilhelm Ostwald stood behind him, behind both stood the nature philosophy of Ernst Mach, who was not present. The opponent was Boltzmann, seconded by Felix Klein. The fight between Boltzmann and Ostwald resembled, both externally and internally, the struggle between a bull and a supple fencer. But the bull defeated the matador in spite of all of the latter's fencing skill. The arguments of Boltzmann broke through. We, who were then young mathematicians, all supported Boltzmann. It was quite obvious to us that it was impossible to derive the motion equations of a single mass point from an energy equation, to say nothing of optional degrees of freedom.[3]

Professor Erwin Hiebert has described the immediate consequences:

The discussion at the Conference of 1895 initiated reverberations which penetrated deeply into and beyond European and American scientific circles. . . . Within 6 weeks Boltzmann had submitted a detailed criticism of the energetic views of Helm and Ostwald.

Boltzmann [in his article] censured Helm and Ostwald for their confused and erroneous derivations in dynamics and heat theory, their mathematical errors and curious inconsistencies, and above all for their ambiguous limitations of the entropy function to the dissipation of radiant energy. He also criticized them for their simplistic *ad hoc* assumptions concerning energetics as a panacea for all the unsolved problems in science.[4]

Helm and Ostwald quickly wrote articles defending "energeticism," and Mach hurried his book on thermodynamics into publication (1896) to point out that imperfect as "energeticism" might be, Boltzmann's "mechanicism" was certainly not the final answer, but the damage had been done. Many young fashion-riders continued to favor "energetical" and/or "phenomenalistic" approaches to thermodynamics, but more thoughtful physicists, such as Robert Millikan, the future Nobel prizewinner, were impressed:

The penetrating and devastating attack upon Ostwald's school of the "energetikers" which the foremost German physicists, Planck and Boltzmann, published in the *Annalen der Physik* in the spring of 1896 . . . pointed out definite errors in reasoning which Ostwald had made in his *Allgemeine Chemie,* to which Ostwald replied in the next issue of the *Annalen* altogether disarmingly, that his friends Planck and Boltzmann had pointed out some errors but that he knew of others which they had not discovered.[5]

Encouraged by his polemical victory for "mechanicism" over "energeticism" as a methodological approach in physics, Boltzmann next turned his attention to Mach, and in two articles ("On the Indispensability of Atomism in Science" [1897] and "Once Again on Atomism" [1897]) he attacked Mach's *methodological* phenomenalism and his rejection of the atomic theory.[6] This attack, by identifying "phenomenalism" with a *methodology* and *language* rather than with an *epistemology* or *ontology,* anticipated the later somewhat deceptive attacks of "new realism" and the "Vienna circle" (deceptive because both movements presupposed essential features of both epistemological and ontological phenomenalism). Nor did Boltzmann stop his counteroffensive here. Scarcely halting to regroup, he then argued in favor of representationalist materialism, for the real existence of atoms as particles in a space and time outside possible conscious experience. Indeed, he even used some of Mach's own terminological expressions for covering fire. Boltzmann later recalled, if not the *casus belli,* at least a relevant proximate occasion:

I have only written a single article on philosophy [i.e., ontology] and that was caused by an accident. I once [1897?] engaged in a lively debate on the value of atomic theories with a group of academicians, including Hofrat Professor Mach, right on the floor of the academy [of science] itself. . . . Suddenly Mach spoke out from the group and laconically said: "I don't believe that atoms exist." This sentence went round and round in my head.[7]

Boltzmann thought the matter over and then wrote an article in reply: "On the Question of the Objective Existence of Happenings in Inanimate Nature" (1897). Boltzmann insisted that if Mach had the right to argue for the existence of the thoughts and feelings of other people on the basis of *analogy* then he, Boltzmann, had the same right to argue for the existence of atoms outside possible or actual conscious experience also on the basis of *analogy,* and that there was just as much evidence to support his own as Mach's conjecture.[8]

Mach, however, did not respect Boltzmann's ideas on philosophy and casually dismissed his entire argument with the remark: "I never had it in mind to replace the language of the vulgar or even the everyday speech of scientists. Also, I hope I will be credited with having long been familiar with the simple considerations which Boltzmann has raised. . . ."[9]

Three "clever" Mach disciples, F. Wald, H. Cornelius, and G. Jaumann, attempted at this time to refute Boltzmann's kinetic theory of gases by proposing substitutes for the atomic theory.

František Wald (1861–1930), former Mach student and chief metallurgist at Kladno in Bohemia, supported Ostwald against Boltzmann in his book *Energy and Its Dissipation* (1889). Wald corresponded with Mach and in 1897 announced a phenomenalistic theory of multiple proportions to replace the atomic theory in chemistry.

Hans Cornelius (1863–1947) received his doctor's degree in chemistry at Munich in 1886. He "habilitated" in philosophy, however, and published *Psychology as the Science of Experience* in 1897, a book that confined science to laws and the study of the "immediately given." Chemistry was now a branch of psychology and no longer needed the atomic theory. Ernst Mach was pleased with Cornelius's book and tried to interest other people in it.[10]

Gustav Jaumann, Mach's wayward, longtime assistant, carried out extensive work on cathode rays. In his opinion it was "barbarous" to try to explain them by means of "electrons." He was rewarded for his alternative method of explanation with an *ordinarius* professorship at the Technical University of Brünn in 1901. Three years later he published *The Foundations of Motion Theory Presented from a Modern Point of View* in which he advocated a theory of continuous matter to replace both the atomic theory and the notion of "force."

Ludwig Boltzmann was deeply depressed by this latest surge of opposition to the atomic theory nor was he happier in Leipzig where he taught for two years (1900–1902). In a foreword to the second part of his classic work *Lectures on Gas Theory* (1898) Boltzmann openly admitted his dismay:

> In my opinion it would be a great tragedy for science if the theory of gases were temporarily thrown into oblivion because of a momentary hostile attitude toward it, as was for example the wave theory because of Newton's authority.
>
> I am conscious of being only an individual struggling weakly against the stream of time. But it still remains in my power to contribute in such a way that, when the theory of gases is again revived, not too much will have to be rediscovered. Thus in this book I will now include the parts that are the most difficult and most subject to misunderstanding.[11]

The situation changed, however, with Mach's official retirement in 1901. In order to recapture Boltzmann, the University of Vienna offered the homesick Austrian both his former chair in theoretical physics, which had not been filled during his two-year absence in Leipzig, and Mach's professorship in the philosophy of science as well. Boltzmann eagerly accepted, and his pessimism vanished in the tumultuous applause from the overflowing audience which greeted his reappearance at the University of Vienna. His initial physics lecture in 1902 started with his characteristic, partly unintentional, humor. He said that there was no need to pay the usual compliments to his predecessor since he was his own predecessor. His inaugural philosophy lecture in 1903 became a public event attended by several professors. Alois Höfler wrote: "I was . . . one of the 600 listeners of both first lectures of Boltzmann on 'nature philosophy' [October 26 and 27, 1903]. An unchained storm of laughter greeted his opening words: 'How have I come to teach philosophy?' And the laughter re-erupted from sentence to sentence." [12] Ludwig Flamm remembered: "The lectures of Boltzmann on nature philosophy were immensely popular, but his lectures on theoretical physics were also well attended." [13]

Lise Meitner recalled:

I was able to hear his lectures from 1902 until his death in 1906. . . . Boltzmann had no inhibitions whatever about showing his enthusiasm while he spoke, and this naturally carried his listeners along. He was also very fond of introducing remarks of an entirely personal character into his lectures—I particularly remember how in describing the kinetic theory of gases, he told us how much difficulty and opposition he had encountered because he had been convinced of the real existence of atoms, and how he had been attacked from the philosophical side, without always understanding what the philosophers had against him. [14]

Some of Boltzmann's students, however, were confused or offended by his "personal" remarks. Gabriele Rabel, for example, was so upset that she even sent a letter to Mach to find out if what Boltzmann was saying was true. "From the side of a prominent university teacher [i.e., Boltzmann] I have heard you repeatedly characterized—and today once again—as a sensualist or even a psychomonist, as one, for whom the world exists only as perceptions, and who views the psyche as the only reality." [15]

Mach tried to placate her by mentioning that words can be used and understood in different ways. That she remained disturbed, however, is clear enough from the fact that she published her letter and that of Mach almost twenty years later to illustrate how important people could "misunderstand" Mach's ideas.

If "professional philosophers" were irritated by Mach occupying "Brentano's chair," and they were, imagine their reaction when Boltzmann sat in it. *"Boltzmann?"* Even Mach's supporters were aghast at this newest joke.[16] Surely this meant the end of philosophy.

Nor were science students any the less divided and upset over Boltzmann's tenacious defense of the "outmoded" atomic "hypothesis." Those who disliked philosophy generally supported Boltzmann and those with an interest in philosophy, Mach; other students were simply confused or tried to believe that the ideas of Mach and Boltzmann were basically compatible with each other. Who was "modern" and who "old-fashioned" was also a matter of dispute, or rather of perspective. Here are some diverse quotations from scientists who were Vienna students shortly before or after the turn of the century.

Lise Meitner preferred Boltzmann:

Lampa was an excellent experimentalist, but as an enthusiastic follower of Mach, was rather sceptical of the modern developments of physics.[17]

A pro-Mach student declared (1906):

It was well known, that the whole atomic theory was only a picture, but he [Boltzmann] held on to it as a convenient hypothesis. He thereby found himself in opposition to Ostwald, Ernst Mach and most other physicists, who for the most part are energeticists, which means that they make no special assumptions with respect to type of matter [*Stoff*], but try to understand all physical processes merely with the help of concepts of pure energy. Boltzmann is the last great representative of the atomic theory in the physical world.[18]

Ludwig Flamm recalled:

H. Mache confesses that he suffered at that time and for many years afterwards because he had had two teachers with such different scientific views as *Boltzmann* and *Mach*. He thinks that if Mach himself had not taught that the experimental physicist need not trouble himself too much about epistemological matters, that he would have suffered even more from this [intellectual] discord.[19]

Philipp Frank reminisced:

Also, strange as it was, in Vienna the physicists were all followers of Mach *and* followers of Boltzmann. It wasn't the case that people would hold any antipathy against Boltzmann's theory of atoms because of Mach. And I don't even think that Mach had any antipathy. At least it did not play as important a role as is often thought. I was always interested in the problem, but it never occurred to me that because of the theories of Mach one shouldn't pursue the theories of Boltzmann.[20]

The year 1904 was an exciting one for Boltzmann. He was sixty years old, and on his birthday he received many honors. A *Festschrift* was prepared for him with over thirty articles from his colleagues, and he was also honored within his own lecturehall: "Paul Ehrenfest, who had come from Göttingen to Vienna, asked the audience to remain standing after the professor had come in as he wished to pay tribute to Boltzmann's great accomplishments in a short ceremonial address."[21] Shortly afterward, a son and daughter of Boltzmann both received doctor's degrees on the same day in Vienna.

Boltzmann also attended the St. Louis World Exposition in 1904 where at a scientific congress he once again defended the atomic theory. According to R. A. Millikan:

Ostwald came over from Leipzig to defend the negative of the proposition, while Van't Hoff came from Berlin to take the other side of the debate. Boltzmann was also there to support Van't Hoff. The amazing thing is that this question could be debated at all at that time, and that outstanding men like Ostwald and Helm, and even the brilliant philosopher Ernst Mach, could at that epoch be proponents of the continuum theory. By 1912 all this had changed. . . .[22]

Philosophically, 1904 meant the hundredth anniversary of Kant's death, an event that Boltzmann celebrated by making a violent attack on the old Pietist's theory of antinomies.[23] Of equal interest, he bested Wilhelm Ostwald once again, this time on the question of "psychic energy." Ostwald gave a lecture before the Vienna Philosophical Society in the fall of 1904 titled "The Energetical Theory of Happiness." He argued that a happy life depended upon an excess of well-applied over misapplied psychic energy and that the amount of happiness can be expressed by the formula: $E^2 - W^2 = (E + W)(E - W)$ with E meaning energy applied with purpose and success (i.e., economically), and W meaning energy applied with aversion or reluctance (i.e., uneconomically).[24]

As soon as the lecture was over, Boltzmann accused Ostwald of confusing psychic with physical energy. Physical energy is measurable but not psychic energy, hence, no scientist as a scientist should place significant confidence in a theoretical structure based on so-called psychic energy. Boltzmann, as was his habit, immediately wrote down and published his objections, indeed, as he afterward humorously remarked, they appeared in print before Ostwald's original speech. In his article Boltzmann poked especial fun at Ostwald's use of mathematics: "That next to the difference $E - W$ the sum $E + W$ also contributes to happiness is the persuasion of an action-loving West European. A Buddhist, whose ideal is the annihilation of the will, would perhaps write: $\dfrac{E - W}{E + W}$." [25]

Boltzmann completed his victory by using Mach's ideas against Ostwald:

Herr Geheimrat Ostwald pays the highest acknowledgment to Mach in all of his writings and certainly with justice, nor do I honor Mach any the less when I do not completely agree with him in everything. But as concerns Ostwald's energeticism, I believe that it simply rests on a misunderstanding of Mach's ideas. . . . [Sense perceptions and representations] are therefore the only existent things; the physical concepts are merely added by us in thought. Ostwald only understood half of this sentence, that atoms do not exist; he at once inquired: "But what then does exist?" and gave the answer that energy is real. In my opinion, this answer is entirely contrary to Mach's view, that energy, no less than matter, should be considered merely a symbolic expression of certain relations between perceptions, of certain equations between given psychical appearances. [26]

Ernst Mach, while agreeing with Boltzmann that "psychic energy" was an unscientific notion (though not as conspicuously as to arouse Ostwald), redirected the argument into an attack on mind-matter dualism and into a defense of his "neutral monism" and "psychophysical parallelism." In other words, while Boltzmann used Mach's ideas in an effort to refute Ostwald's theories of "psychic energy" and "energeticism" itself, Mach used Boltzmann's argument to show not only that "psychic energy" was unscientific but that it did not exist and that no other kind of peculiarly mental entities existed either. [27] Alas, such are the ways in which old men try to outflank each other.

Boltzmann, the philosopher-critic, perhaps went too far three months later when he gave a lecture on Schopenhauer before the Vienna Philosophical Society. The original title was: "Proof that Schopenhauer Was a Degenerate, Unthinking, Unknowing, Nonsense Scribbling Philosopher, Whose Understanding Consisted Solely of Empty, Verbal Trash." [28] He was persuaded, however, to use a different title in the published article.

Boltzmann's interest in philosophy had developed to such an extent by 1905 that he attended sessions of the Vienna Philosophical Society more frequently than he visited physical laboratories or even his own university institute.[29]

II

We have now come to the point where we must discuss the factors that led to Ludwig Boltzmann's tragic death. This discussion has become necessary because of the occasional charges leveled against Ernst Mach to the effect that he or his ideas were responsible for what eventually happened.[30] The best answer to these suspicions would be a thorough understanding of the last months of Boltzmann's life as remembered by his immediate family and friends and as given in newspaper accounts of the time. Mach believed that overwork was a contributing factor, and Karl Przibram has suspected angina pectoris, a very painful heart disease. Here are some quotations introducing other considerations and detailing aspects of his last days:

> Those who knew Boltzmann will remember the pair of heavy highly-powerful spectacles resting on a deep groove in his nose. For many years his eyesight had been failing, and he found it increasingly difficult to complete the many researches which were on his mind.[31]

> At the end Boltzmann had almost completely lost his sight. He had a lady read scientific articles to him during the last years.[32]

> In the fall of last year [1905] the scholar [Boltzmann] decided to visit a mental hospital near Munich, but he left the asylum a short time later and returned to Vienna.[33]

> I, myself [Ludwig Flamm], as a student was able to hear the last lecture which Boltzmann held on theoretical physics; it was in the winter semester 1905/1906. A nervous complaint [headaches] prevented him from continuing his teaching activity. Together with another student I took and passed my oral examination in his Villa in Währing. On leaving after the examination was over we heard from the front hall his heartrending groans.[34]

> His headaches and failing eyesight finally convinced him that he could never work again.[35]

> When I [Alois Höfler] visited him during the Easter holidays [1906] for the last time, he expressed his physical and mental suffering thus: "I never would have believed that such an end was possible." [36]

> Boltzmann had announced lectures for the summer semester [1906], but had to cancel them, because of his nervous condition. In informed circles one knew that Boltzmann would most probably never be able to exercise his professorship again. One spoke of how necessary it was to keep him

under constant medical surveillance, for he had already made earlier attempts at suicide.[37]

(And finally three quotations relating to events on September 5, 1906)

He had brought his family to Duino, a small, beautiful seaside resort near Gradicka [on the Adriatic Sea] to go swimming, yet he was also upset and nervous because he was anxious to return to Vienna. His condition otherwise seemed better. On the day of his death Boltzmann showed himself to be particularly excited [*erregt*]. While his wife and daughter went swimming, he carried out the deed.[38]

He was very melancholy for a long time and did not want to send his suit to be cleaned because it would mean a further delay in returning to Vienna. After his wife left, taking the suit with her, he hanged himself.[39]

He used a short cord from the crossbars of a window casement. His daughter was the first to discover the suicide.[40]

III

In order to understand the relation between the influence of Mach's philosophy of science and that of Boltzmann it is necessary to be as clear as possible on the philosophical similarities and differences in the ideas of the two men. Let me start by quoting two prominent scholars and then give a fundamental outline of the basic approaches of Mach and Boltzmann.

Philipp Frank wrote:

It is said that Boltzmann was so desperate about the rejection of atomic theory by physicists, resulting from Mach's attacks on it, that he took his life. As a matter of fact this could hardly be true, since Boltzmann was himself philosophically speaking, rather a follower of Mach. Boltzmann once said to me, "You see, it doesn't make any difference to me if I say that the atomic model is only a picture. I don't mind this. I don't require that they have absolute, real existence. I don't say this. 'An economic description,' Mach said. Maybe the atoms are an economic description. This doesn't hurt me very much. From the viewpoint of the physicist this doesn't make a difference." Boltzmann had a philosophical viewpoint [in science] which did not require that you believe in the real existence of atoms. And there wasn't, I would say, any opposition to Boltzmann's physics from the veiwpoint of Mach. This opposition existed only, so to speak, in the philosophical realm [i.e., in philosophy of nature, not in philosophy of science].[41]

Paul K. Feyerabend has added (1967):

It is unfortunate that Boltzmann's general philosophy, which is intimately connected with his physics, is practically unknown, for his ideas are still relevant to contemporary discussions and present a promising field for further study.[42]

Few people, including philosophers, are consistent in all their assumptions and opinions all the time. But given a measure of fluctuation and occasional inconsistency, the outline on the facing page lists how Mach and Boltzmann understood nature and science.

Ernst Mach was much more influential with respect to philosophy of science than Boltzmann, or to be more exact, he exercised a more conspicuous influence. On the other hand, more physicists today probably hold views nearer to Boltzmann with respect to philosophy of science. This paradox may best be explained by pointing out that philosophically unsophisticated physicists have had a tendency to react to the positivistic ideas of Mach and his followers in much the same way that Boltzmann did, hence, by a form of causal parallelism their philosophical views on science have more closely resembled those of Boltzmann. Also, developments within physics, especially quantum and relativity theory, have probably been more compatible with the latter's overall approach.

Boltzmann's methodology of science emphasized that mechanistic physics contained fewer arbitrary assumptions than continuum or energetical physics; that it was doubtful whether a physics without hypotheses was either possible or desirable; that there were no a priori, intuitive, or absolutely certain truths in physics; that lack of clarity in the principles of physics came from their origin in induction and from attempts to conceal hypothetical aspects and assumptions; and that the hypothetical character of our knowledge made criticism the most important method of investigation.[43]

If we may define "pure Machism" as a phenomenalism hostile to atomism and theoretical physics, and "Boltzmannized Machism" as one friendly to atomism and theoretical physics, then we would have to conclude that Philipp Frank and many modern physicists may best be labeled as "Boltzmannized Machists." As the next few chapters show, "pure Machism" was crushed in physics from about 1910 to 1920. The philosophical conflicts from that time on, such as those concerning the so-called "Copenhagen interpretation of quantum theory," have tended to be between different groups of "Boltzmannized Machists," namely between those physicists who augmented their philosophy of science with a philosophy of nature which allowed for the trans-

	MACH'S PHILOSOPHY OF NATURE *and* SCIENCE	BOLTZMANN'S PHILOSOPHY OF *science*	BOLTZMANN'S PHILOSOPHY OF *nature* (AND EARLIER VIEW OF SCIENCE)
Epistemology	*Phenomenalism* (Machian variation: We can only know sensations.)	*Phenomenalism* (Same as Mach's view.)	*Representational realism* (The physical world exists entirely outside conscious appearances.)
Ontology	*Phenomenalism* (Machian variation: Only sensations are real.)	*Phenomenalism* (Same as Mach's view.)	*Mind-matter dualism* (but verging on a representationalist matter monism.)
Goal of Science (internal)	*Bellarminian phenomenalism* (To describe and relate the appearances in the simplest way possible.)	*Amended Bellarminian phenomenalism* (To describe and relate the appearances in the simplest, *least arbitrary way possible*.)	*Galilean universalism* (To understand all reality in as reliable and informative a way as possible.)
Ideal End-Science	*Mathematical functions* (Machian variation: Direct description of sensations.)	*Mechanical Laws* (directly or indirectly describing sensations.)	*Mechanical laws* (directly or indirectly explaining physical reality.)
Ideal Becoming-Science (methodology)	*Direct measurement of sensations*	*Hypothesis-deduction-verification*	(Same as on left.)
Attitude on Theories	*Avoid theories* (Machian variation: If unavoidable, theories may be used as "provisional aids" in becoming-science. They should never be used in end-science.)	*Theories are indispensable in both becoming- and end-science*	(Same as on left.)

experiential reality of atoms and those physicists who refused to so augment their philosophy of science.

Positivists have often stereotyped Boltzmann as a defender of Newtonian and "mechanistic" physics when both were in the process of being superseded or substantially altered. In point of fact, Boltzmann was sympathetic with most of the revolutionary discoveries of his time but felt obligated to make sure that sound discoveries of the past would not be disregarded in the wild scramble for new ideas.[44] Also, "mechanistic physics" was not and has not been refuted; rather, particle and radiation discoveries were in the process of strengthening it, though also gradually reducing its scope to the "macroworld" in between gravitation-explained "cosmic events" and electromagnetic theorizing about "micro or quantum happenings." Furthermore, "mechanistic" explanation remains indispensable in everyday, practical life.

Who, then, won the "thirty years' war" between Mach and Boltzmann? On a methodological level for all his "mechanicism" Boltzmann was clearly the winner. On an epistemological and ontological level Mach not only won (at least within philosophy of science), but he even transformed Boltzmann into one of his own disciples. Philosophically, Mach won his greatest victory when Boltzmann abandoned understand-reality-physics for describe-and-relate-the-appearance-physics. That triumph philosophically trivialized all of Boltzmann's methodological success in gaining more respect for the atomic theory. From a philosophical point of view Boltzmann's long struggle for the atomic theory in physics has merely served to grace and strengthen Mach's revival of Cardinal Bellarmine's "describe-and-relate-the-appearances" philosophy of science.

IV

Shortly after Boltzmann's death, new support for his kinetic theory of gases and for the atomic theory first became influential. A major turning point was Albert Einstein's article on "Brownian Motion" (1905) and its effect on Wilhelm Ostwald (1908). Philipp Frank described Einstein's contribution:

In 1902 Einstein restated Boltzmann's theory of random motion in a simplified form. He now [1905] treated the Brownian motion [the movement of microscopically visible particles suspended in a fluid of approximately the same density] with this method and arrived at a surprisingly simple result. He showed that the results of the kinetic theory of molecules should also hold for particles visible by microscope. . . .

The actual observations were later made by the French physicist Jean Perrin, who completely verified Einstein's theory. The phenomenon of Brownian motion has subsequently always been included among the best "direct" proofs of the existence of the molecule.[45]

Arnold Sommerfeld remembered the effect of Einstein's theory on Ostwald: "It is a pity that he [Boltzmann] was no longer able to put together the final proof of atomism by a theoretical explanation of Brownian motion [something] which was done shortly before his death and which also persuaded Ostwald, as he has told me from time to time, to accept atomism." [46]

Ostwald publicly admitted his conversion to atomism in the fourth edition of his *Outline of General Chemistry* (1908). He also acknowledged Boltzmann's genius as a theoretical physicist: "A man who was superior to us all in intelligence, and in the clarity of his science." [47]

The real story of Ostwald's "conversion" was of course, much more complicated. Like Boltzmann, Ostwald distinguished between philosophy of nature and philosophy of sicence. In the former energy was the ultimate reality, and in the latter energeticism as a theory was used to describe and relate the appearances. When he "abandoned" energeticism for atomism he merely made a methodological alteration in his philosophy of science; he did not abandon his ontological "energeticism," his belief in energy as the ultimate reality in nature. Indeed, Einstein's famous equation $E = mc^2$ helped to strengthen that view. Ostwald attempted to make the purely methodological nature of his long struggle with Boltzmann clear in the following quotation: "My opposition was therefore not against the real existence of atoms and molecules, which on both sides were acknowledged as hypothetical, but against the scientific utility of the hypotheses." [48]

▼

Max Planck, who owed a great deal to Ludwig Boltzmann, and who felt that at least in a spiritual sense he was his successor decided in his Leiden speech (1908) to destroy the influence of Ernst Mach, the last great anti-atomist. Planck's speech was a bombshell which split the ranks of physicists around the world. Einstein, who may not have fully understood the philosophical issues at stake at this time, sided with Mach.[49] But before becoming consumed in the heat of the Mach-Planck polemics of 1908–1910 let us backtrack and look for causes. What had happened in Planck's earlier life to fuel this most unprofessional outburst against a respected, elderly, physically half-crippled, colleague?

Max Planck was born in Kiel in northern Germany in 1858. He studied at Berlin and Munich and received his doctor's degree in physics in the Bavarian capital in 1879. His doctoral dissertation, *On the Second Law of Thermodynamics,* indicated the area of his most intense concern for the remainder of the nineteenth century. Like Boltzmann, Planck wanted to relate the irreversible spread of entropy with the reversible motion of mechanics, but whereas Boltzmann relied on a probabilistic approach, Planck wanted an absolute foundation. He tried for years to interest other physicists, including Boltzmann, in his work on the subject, but got nowhere. His mathematical and experimental competence in other areas, however, first won him an *extraordinarius* professorship at Kiel in 1885 and, in conjunction with Boltzmann's refusal to accept Kirchhoff's chair, helped him to attain the latter post in Berlin in 1889. Planck became an *ordinarius* professor in the Prussian capital in 1892. As a young physicist he was much taken with Mach's ideas: "I counted myself while I was at Kiel (1885–1889) as one of the most confirmed followers of Mach's philosophy, which, as I gladly acknowledge, had a strong effect on my physical thinking."[50]

Professor Erwin Hiebert has expanded on Mach's influence:

> Max Planck stood under the strongest influence of Ernst Mach's ideas between the time of the completion of his doctoral dissertation at Munich in 1879 and the early years of his professorship in theoretical physics in Berlin beginning in 1889. His earliest reactions to Mach's views appeared in 1887 in an essay which merited the second prize of the philosophical faculty of Göttingen. . . .[51]

Planck was especially impressed by Mach's theories of economy and unity of science and by his rejection of "metaphysics" and the atomic theory. He wrote about the latter: "Under the influence of Ernst Mach I tended at that time to reject atomism and to my sorrow thereby brought upon myself the enmity of Ludwig Boltzmann. He was almost the only one in Germany who was devoting his main efforts to the construction of the kinetic theory of gases."[52]

Planck's continued failure during the 1890s to influence fellow physicists into accepting his "absolute" interpretation of the second law of thermodynamics was accompanied by increasing disillusion concerning many of Mach's ideas.

"As concerns Mach, I must confess [1891], that much as I acknowledge his acute and independent mind, I do not consider him competent with respect to the second law." [53]

I later turned away from him, mainly because I arrived at the insight, that Mach's nature philosophy with its brilliant promise which had attracted most of his supporters to it in the first place: the elimination of all metaphysical elements from physical theory of knowledge, could in no way be realized.[54]

I am forced to clearly state at this point, that the study of this aforementioned book [Mach's *Principles of Heat Theory*] can in all cases only lead to a superficial grasp of the principles of thermodynamics. . . . All of this [Clausius's law] and a great deal else of no less importance is not even mentioned in Mach's book, although, as I especially stress, at the time of its composition [1896] these things . . . had been made completely clear for 40 years.[55]

Planck, like Boltzmann, opposed Ostwald's energeticism and shortly after the 1895 Lübeck debate the Berlin professor wrote a savage attack on Ostwald's ideas. The article was frankly titled "Against the New Energeticism." [56]

In 1897 Planck made still another effort to show that entropy spread should be understood in an absolute and not in a probabilistic sense. He chose to illustrate this point by investigating what was called the black-body problem. The astonishing results of this investigation have of course become world famous today. It was through this study that Max Planck formulated his quantum theory (1900).

The turning point in Planck's work was the discovery of energy "quanta." The significant point was that Planck "seeing no other way out" reluctantly applied Boltzmann's probabilistic approach and discovered that it was indispensable to a satisfactory explanation of quantum behavior.[57] The irony, of course, was twofold. Planck became famous for a theory which was made possible by adopting the leading ideas of a longtime opponent; and second, Planck's theory, by adopting Boltzmann's approach, refuted Planck's own efforts over the previous twenty years (to establish an "absolute" theory of entropy).

Planck graciously acknowledged that he had been wrong and Boltzmann right, that the entropy law was a statistical law, and that the atomic theory was a necessity in physical science. Indeed, Planck's switch, his integrity in admitting past errors and in praising Boltzmann, has clearly revealed that people could be surprisingly rational (at least if gifted with a strong character), and that his own pessimistic assessment of how science advances was an exaggeration: "A new scientific truth does not become accepted by persuading its opponents . . . but rather by the opponents gradually dying out and a new generation arising which happens to take the new truth for granted." [58]

On the other hand, we should not attribute superhuman powers to Max Planck. His own conversion also took time.

According to Erwin Hiebert:

Planck did not pledge his support for the atomic-molecular interpretation of nature until after his own results with the quantum theory forced him in that direction—reluctantly. Rather, it was Einstein who suggested in June of 1905 the revolutionary idea that light itself might be looked upon as quanta—particles of energy. The light quantum hypothesis was much too radical a departure for Planck, and he did not come around to accepting Einstein's views until about a decade later—certainly not before 1913. [59]

Planck's quantum discovery affected his thinking in three grimly emotional ways: first, he became a strong admirer and sword-bearer of Ludwig Boltzmann as a man and physicist; second, he considered himself in large measure a failure, and third, he looked for and found a scapegoat who he thought was the primary cause for the unjust isolation and disdain which had been forced on Boltzmann's ideas for so many years by so many of his physical colleagues and which in large part had been responsible for his own fruitless investigations and wasted years. That scapegoat and primary cause in his opinion narrowed down to one man—*Ernst Mach*.

Max Planck gave his Leiden address, "The Unity of the Physical World Picture," on December 9, 1908. The speech was divided into four parts with only the last one specifically referring to Mach. But it was that part which Planck's audience remembered.

Planck accepted Mach's goal of "the unity of science" and even Mach's "intermediate scientific purpose," the creation of a unified world picture, but he argued that a system of ideational constants and physical laws, freed from all anthropomorphic and sensory elements, could better describe and relate the appearances and achieve that unified world picture, than could Mach's "economical," sensationalistic approach. In particular, he pointed out that while Boltzmann's statistical theory had helped to unite thermodynamics and mechanics and thereby helped to develop a unified world picture, Mach's opposition by keeping the two branches of physics apart hindered the development of that picture and the unity of science.[60]

Like Heinrich Hertz, Max Planck attempted to understand his Mach-influenced philosophy of science within a Kantian context. To many Englishmen and Americans Kant's ideas often seem idealistic and contrary to common sense, but when a German wants to adopt a practical and realistic philosophical position he normally falls back on Kant, who on the whole comes the closest to common sense of any widely known, reputable thinker within the German philosophical tradition.

Planck came to believe in the reality of atoms and of a physical world distinct from that of sensations or sensory objects, but while his view sufficiently resembled representative realism and mind-matter dualism to be safely confused with it in practical life, nonetheless, he did not mean reality in common sense terms. For Planck, atoms, matter, and natural laws were real not because they existed in a transphenomenal space and time, but because they had constant features which participated in the "unified world picture which physics and science were developing and which would continually be enlarged in the future." [61]

Constancy, independent of all human and intellectual individuality, is what we call reality.[62]

The fixed unity of the world picture is, however, as I have endeavored to show, the fixed goal which true science approaches through all its changes.[63]

As the great masters of exact research threw out ideas in science—as Copernicus removed the center of the universe from the center of the earth, as Kepler propounded the laws named after him, as Newton discovered general gravitation, as Huyghens set forth the undulatory theory of light, as Faraday created the foundations of electrodynamics—very many more can be listed—the economic point of view was the very last with which these men armed themselves in the war against inherited opinions and commanding authority. No—they were moved by their fixed belief in the reality of their picture. . . . We can even go a step further. These men did not speak of their world picture, but only of the world or nature. Is there any recognizable difference between their "world" and our "world picture of the future"? Certainly not. For it is known—after Immanuel Kant—that there is no method of proving the existence of such a difference. The expression "world picture" has only become common for the sake of caution, in order that certain illusions are excluded from the start. Applying the necessary foresight, and knowing exactly that we mean by "world" nothing but the ideal picture of the future, we can, if we wish, institute the single word and obtain a more realistic expression. This expression evidently recommends itself far more from the economical standpoint than Mach's positivism, which is fundamentally very complicated and difficult to grasp, and it is actually used now by scientists when they talk about science.[64]

Until the last paragraph in his speech Planck's first attack on Mach's philosophy of science could be considered restrained, but in that last paragraph, indeed, in the very last sentence, in Planck's parting words, he questioned the entirety of Mach's point of view with the phrase: "A lasting confidence . . . has given us an ultimate infallible test for distinguishing false prophets from true—"By their fruits ye shall know them!"[65]

Planck asked the scientific world to consider the consequences of Mach's ideas on science, both directly and through the contributions of Mach's followers. Had Mach's teaching produced healthy fruit? Or was it all as spoiled as Ostwald's "energeticism," Wald's "phenomenalistic chemistry," Jaumann's "continuum physics," or the anti-atomism of Georg Pick, Friedrich Adler, or of Ernst Mach himself? Boltzmann could number the Nobel prizewinners Walther Nernst and Svante Arrhenius among his students as well as Lise Meitner, Friedrich Hasenöhrl, Paul Ehrenfest, and many other outstanding physicists, but who could Mach name? Had any of Mach's students ever really made any truly significant contributions to physics or science? Planck did not stop to answer the questions which his attack had suggested. Perhaps he would have thought them "rhetorical"—as if the answers were obvious.

VI

Friedrich Adler, Joseph Petzoldt, and Philipp Frank all wrote articles defending Mach.[66] Adler and Petzoldt insisted that Planck misunderstood Mach, and that actually, both men were in close agreement. Philipp Frank in a skillful article denigrated Planck's fears that Mach's philosophy might have an injurious effect on science:

[Planck thinks that] if the Mach principle of economy were really to be put at the center of the theory of knowledge, the trains of thought of such leading spirits (as Copernicus, Kepler, and Newton) would be disturbed, the flight of their imagination crippled, and consequently the progress of science perhaps fatefully hindered.

That these fears are groundless can be readily seen if one recalls the views of one of the greatest theoretical physicists of the nineteenth century, James Clerk Maxwell, on the nature of physical theories. One need only read the introduction to his essay on Faraday's lines of force (1855) to be convinced that he was completely an adherent of the phenomenalistic standpoint.[67]

Private letters of support came from Paul Jensen, Albert Einstein, and Carl Cranz. Jensen wrote:

I can scarcely ever remember having read anything which has made me so upset. Such a frivolous judgment and condemnation by such a mature scientist who had previously shown such character—is utterly unheard of.[68]

Einstein added:

You have had such an influence on the epistemological conceptions of the younger physical generation, that even your current opponents, such as Herr Planck for example, would be considered "Machists" by physicists holding the views of most physicists of some decades ago.[69]

Cranz continued:

Planck's attack was very painful and disagreeable for me. . . . The name of Mach could scarcely find more honor and acknowledgment anywhere, than in the ballistic laboratory of Charlottenburg and in those military circles, where your electric instant photography has *repeatedly* been applied to practical weapon and firing tests.[70]

VII

The months after Boltzmann's suicide in September 1906 were difficult ones for Mach. He suffered severely from headaches and neuralgia. His wife was also in bad health. Another worry concerned the lack of education of his two youngest sons. Felix Mach attended an art academy in Munich and became an "academic painter." He was frequently in bad health, traveled from town to town, and was only moderately successful in his profession. He did, however, contribute a number of drawings to Mach's articles and especially to his last book, *Culture and Mechanics* (1915). Victor Mach, the youngest son, struggled in machine work for several years until he set up a small company of his own in 1912. The company produced screws and bolts.

Ernst Mach took a facetious attitude toward Max Planck's 1908 attack. He could no more take Planck's philosophizing seriously than that of Boltzmann. Both men were competent physicists, but Mach believed that philosophy was beyond them. He first replied to Planck's speech with a few comments in the 1909 German edition of his *Conservation of Energy*. After Planck published his address Mach came back with a hefty article which both clarified his philosophy and attempted to answer Planck's criticisms. Mach's article "The Leading Thoughts of My Scientific Theory of Knowledge and Their Reception by My Contemporaries" (1910) was by far the most carefully argued and pithy presentation of Mach's philosophy of science and has deserved to survive its reputation as a mere polemical document.

Mach was amused by two aspects of Planck's philosophy: his uncritical faith in the absolute validity of a future, constant "world picture," and his curious definition of "reality" as *constancy*. Mach, as a philosophical "relativist," did not believe in absolutes or constancies if that meant they were independent of sensations. Furthermore, if atomic or molecular particles changed in space and time, then they were not "real" in Planck's sense. Planck, himself, saw the problem, however, and reacted by attributing an unknowable Kantian "noumenal" existence to atoms, a "solution" which a presentationalist like Mach could only take even less seriously. Here are some of Mach's more irreverent comments on Planck as a philosopher and theologian of physics:

> The concern for a physics valid for all times and peoples even for the inhabitants of Mars, while there are still quite pressing everyday physical problems, seems very premature, indeed almost comical.[71]

> If Planck had ended his lecture with page 32, there would have been no reason for me to concern myself with it. But at this point he starts his polemic which is especially directed at me. . . . In particular his polemical last remarks, their unusual form, complete ignorance of the matters in dispute, and their highly singular conclusion have compelled me to utter a few words in reply.[72]

> The essential difference between us concerns belief in the reality of atoms. . . . Planck admonishes . . . with Christian mildness, but finally brands me with the well-known Bible phrase as a false prophet. One sees, that physicists are on the best way to becoming a church. . . . My answer is simple: If belief in the reality of atoms is so crucial, then I renounce the physical way of thinking, I will not be a professional physicist, and I hand back my scientific reputation. In short, thank you so much for the community of believers, but for me freedom of thought comes first.[73]

In retrospect, one should probably admire the analogy imagined by Stephen Brush: "Mach gives the impression of being a sinner on his deathbed, refusing to be converted by Father Planck to the faith which all of his colleagues have accepted. . . ." The trouble with this picture, however, is that it ignores the terrible nature of Planck's second attack which little reflected either a desire to persuade Mach out of error or to save his soul in either a literal or figurative sense.[74] Max Planck was deeply offended by Mach's condescending humor and contemptuous treatment of his ideas. As a result, he wrote a second article devoted entirely to criticizing Mach's philosophical and scientific ideas in such a way as to force Mach into recognizing and respecting the type of person he was dealing with. Planck aimed to break Mach. The article was titled: "On Mach's Theory of Physical Knowledge—A Reply" and appeared in 1910. Here are some quotations:

While my ideas have found a certain interest and occasional agreement from professional representatives of transcendental philosophy they have experienced, as might have been expected, a more or less sharp rejection from followers of Mach's orientation.

Until recently I had no intention of returning to these matters. . . . Mach not only claims that his epistemology stands unrefuted, but he is not serious with my objections and even thinks I am entirely incapable of contributing anything to the epistemology of physics.

Since Mach, strangely, seems unable to find a stronger opponent . . . I feel obliged to represent my objections to Mach's theory of knowledge somewhat more clearly than before. . . .[75]

[Mach] confuses perpetuum mobile of the first type (production of work from nothing) with perpetuum mobile of the second type (uncompensated production of work from heat).[76]

Concerning absolute zero Mach remarks: "One has assumed that it is inconceivable to cool a body under -273 C., and that such a body contains no heat. I believe, however, that this conclusion rests on an inadmissibly bold extrapolation." Alas, one can as little compel as forbid belief in a scientific law.[77]

Let us now consider Mach's tenaciously fought for but physically useless notion that the relativity of circular motion corresponds to the relativity of translation motion, that one cannot decide in principle whether the fixed stars rotate around the earth at rest, or whether the earth rotates around the fixed stars at rest. . . . To depict more closely the physical conceptual errors which this inadmissible transfer of the law of the relativity of rotary motion from kinematics into dynamics has already caused would carry us too far afield.[78]

Up to now Mach's "fruits" have not been worth much. But perhaps in the future? I am ready at any time to be taught better by the facts. Mach doubts that the second law [of thermodynamics] can be carried through on the basis of probability; he does not believe in atoms. Well then, perhaps he or one of his disciples will develop another theory which will accomplish more than these. Let us wait and keep our eyes open.[79]

With Mach's slippery notion of economy naturally everything is possible, or rather, nothing is definite.[80]

But doesn't his physical view follow strictly from his theory of knowledge? Far from it. As I have already stressed above, such a formalistic view is incapable of producing any determinate physical result, neither anything correct nor anything false. Indeed, I wouldn't be surprised at all if a member of Mach's school won't one day come up with the great discovery that the probability hypothesis or the reality of atoms exactly fits the requirements of scientific economy! [81]

Ernst Mach prepared to enter the lists again, but on seeing his eager squires take and keep up the challenge, he decided to shift his attention elsewhere. He finally chose to match his anti-Planck article with a less polemical, but equally acute, anti-Stumpf essay. But before turning to this new subject, let me attempt an evaluation of the significance of the Mach-Planck confrontation.

Max Planck failed to halt the spread of Mach's philosophy of science, indeed, he may well have interested more young scientists in it; also, the violence of Planck's attacks against an elderly man did not enhance his professional reputation, and finally, Planck's criticisms of Mach's atomism probably did help influence some scientists, such as Anton Lampa, to attempt to see the atomic hypothesis in a more favorable light.

The primary reason for the comparative ineffectiveness of Planck's attacks was that it did not strike at Mach's basic epistemological and ontological assumptions, but instead, concentrated on mere methodology of science and what to leading physicists had already become ancient history. Or to put the matter another way, Planck's Kantian epistemology shared too many assumptions with Mach's epistemology for a truly "radical" criticism to take place.

But if the Mach-Planck war has failed to exercise a major influence on subsequent scientific thought and practice, at least it has served to demonstrate once again that positivism is primarily a young man's philosophy and that violent denunciations of it may always be expected from disappointed, middle-aged, would-be, or actual defectors. The conflict also illustrates the danger of adopting any philosophy of science which contains features inconsistent with the rest of one's philosophical beliefs or assumptions. First, it is very likely that the latter, as with Planck, will "infiltrate" one's philosophy of science, and second, sooner or later, one may have to make a very painful choice between "contradictory" views.

VIII

After Carl Stumpf and Theodor Lipps had made such a conspicuous effort to carve up Mach's *Contributions to the Analysis of Sensations* by means of reviews in 1886, Mach tended to be leery of the behavior of his "colleagues" in psychology. Ten years later Mach was invited to attend the 3d International Congress of Psychology at Munich. He was even offered the chairmanship of one of the general sittings.[82] On discovering the exact situation, however, he declined to attend. It turned out that Stumpf and Lipps were copresidents and that the special guest speaker was Franz Brentano himself. Stumpf opened the Congress on August 4, 1896, with a speech on the relation of mind and body in which he defended his interaction theory against the argument of the conservation of energy and attacked Ostwald's "energeticism" and Mach's psychophysical parallelism. But neither running away nor silence could save Mach. Stumpf kept after him. Whether speaking before professional bodies or lecturing to Berlin students Stumpf kept criticizing Mach's ideas. Eventually, students started writing directly to Mach asking if he "really" held such an old-fashioned notion as psychophysical parallelism.[83]

Mach patiently replied that his theory was very different from the dualisms of both Descartes and Fechner and depended merely on differentiating *types* of functional relations. At first, Mach answered Stumpf in a very brief and passing way, namely, by adding short remarks to consecutive editions of his *Analysis of Sensations*. But by 1910 and a third edition of Stumpf's 1896 speech, Mach finally put his foot down. Enough was really enough. He wrote "Sensory Elements and Scientific Concepts" specifically to answer Stumpf's charges and to clarify his stand on "psychological atomism." Unfortunately the article was whipsawed by the almost simultaneous discovery in Oswald Külpe's Würzburg laboratory of so-called imageless thoughts, entities that were neither sensations nor necessarily conscious. But before continuing with this, let me first present a little more background information on both Stumpf and Külpe and position them better within the constellation of psychological writers.

Carl Stumpf (1846–1936) was born in Wiesenthied, Bavaria, became a child prodigy in music, and attended the local University of Würzburg, where he fell under the sway of Franz Brentano's personality and insight. Stumpf wrote on musical tones and sense physiology and developed an eclectic philosophical position which influenced his students Edmund Husserl and the Gestalt psychologists Wolfgang Köhler and Kurt Koffka.

Formally, then, Stumpf took his stand with the act school [of Brentano], ruling the sensationistic phenomena out of psychology into phenomenology. Actually, however, what he did was the opposite of what he said: he brought phenomenology [not the same doctrine as that of his pupil Husserl] into psychology. In the first place he legitimized it as an alternative to the act as a subject-matter for study. In the second place, he never got rid of it, for the reason that he was too much interested in it himself.[84]

In 1894 Stumpf became an *ordinarius* professor at the University of Berlin:

Stumpf . . . had the most distinguished appointment that Germany could offer. As the world sees things, Wundt was undoubtedly then the foremost, as well as the senior, psychologist. His writings were already enormous; he had founded the first and leading laboratory. . . . It has been said that the great and influential Helmholtz opposed Wundt's appointment at Berlin. However this may be, the chair fell to Stumpf, and he now had a small laboratory and a large future.[85]

Stumpf never produced a scientific masterpiece to justify his academic preeminence, but his acid tongue and polemical manner silenced most of his critics. He was best known for a stormy University of Berlin rectorate and a personal dispute with Wilhelm Wundt. Compared with the heat and fury of these battles his persistent sniping at Wundt's fellow "elementist," Ernst Mach, was a small matter indeed, at least to him.

The published and republished criticism that most offended Mach was short and blunt: "So, if I see correctly, this sensationalistic monism [of Mach] dissolves into nothing. The real direction of science has contradicted his assertions about the physical world, and about the psychological has not confirmed him in the least." [86]

Ernst Mach in his 1910 anti-Stumpf article defended his phenomenalistic monism by arguing that since only sensations could be accurately measured it was futile to discuss on a scientific basis the reality or characteristics of "nonsensations."

Mach also repeated his argument that phenomenalistic monism and sensory "elementism" facilitated the unity of science by making physics and psychology more compatible with each other.[87] He concluded with the remark that "Physicists have nothing to seek 'beyond the sensory appearances' but that philosophers [such as Stumpf] may find it necessary to maintain the existence of realities independent of consciousness, which do not exist in themselves at all, but only in the abstract form of equations. . . ."[88]

IX

Oswald Külpe (1862–1915), Mach's most dangerous philosophical opponent was born in Candau in Courland, Latvia. He attended secondary school at Libau on the Baltic coast and studied under Wilhelm Wundt at Leipzig in 1881. Undecided between history and psychology he switched from university to university finally returning to Leipzig and Wundt in 1886 where he received his degree in the following year.

Külpe became a talented experimentalist, published *An Ouline of Psychology* in 1893, and became an *ordinarius* professor at Würzburg in 1894. Wundt's stress on measurable sensations had ignored thinking as a subject for laboratory analysis. Külpe tried to make good the omission and in the process he firmly established the reputation of what became known as the "Würzburg school."

Külpe, like Planck, had been strongly attracted to Mach's "rigorous" positivism while a young man, but, like so many other scientists turned against Mach's views during his middle years.[89] Külpe, however, unlike Planck, was able to cut beneath mere methodological questions and strike directly at fundamental epistemological and ontological assumptions, though again without cutting enough roots to kill Mach's philosophy as a whole. Nonetheless, Külpe's stiletto thrusts went deep, and all in all, had they been sufficiently publicized, Külpe's criticisms might well have mortally wounded if not Mach's philosophy at least his influence and much of his reputation among those scientists with an interest in philosophy.

Külpe's first attack on Mach's ideas came in his *The Philosophy of the Present in Germany* in 1902. Külpe made many criticisms, but the most penetrating one concentrated on Mach's attribution of certainty to sensations. First, he questioned how directly and completely sensations were apprehended, and second, he pointed out that while sensations surely were what they were, and hence, in a tautological sense might be "certain," all statements and claims about sensations were fallible and subject to error.[90] In other words, Külpe rejected what logical positivists would later call "protocol" or "incorrigible" statements.

Külpe's second major thrust resulted from his own experimental work and that of his students. Mach was aware of Külpe's opposition to many of his ideas, but both Külpe (1915) and Mach (1916) died before the devastating results of those experiments had been fully put together and applied to philosophical problems. Patrick J. Capretta has written:

Külpe and his associates (Ach, Marbe, Mayer, Orth, and Watt) undertook a research program involving a direct introspective assault upon thinking, which yielded surprising, if not embarrassing, results for the content psychologists. Unlike the Wundtians [and followers of Mach], who asserted that all thought could be reduced to sensory, and consequently imaginal elements, the psychologists at Würzburg found that some thoughts occur without any noticeable sensory or imaginal content.[91]

Edwin G. Boring continued:

Watt discovered that the thought-process would run itself off at the presentation of the stimulus-word, provided the task or *Aufgabe* had been adequately accepted by the observer in the preparatory period. This was really a remarkable result. So far as consciousness goes, one does one's thinking before one knows what he is to think about; that is to say, with the proper preparation the thought runs off automatically, when released with very little content.[92]

What had happened? In the first place, the work of the school seemed to have failed of its positive purpose. It had yielded determining tendencies and imageless thought. . . . For many years the discovery of imageless thoughts was regarded as a purely negative discovery.[93]

If there were "imageless thoughts," that is, nonsensory realities, then Mach's ontological phenomenalism, monism, and psychophysical parallelism were undermined along with his theory of elements and his purpose of science. If other than sensations existed and could be scientifically determined to exist, then no "describe-and-relate-the-appearances" purpose of science could be a satisfactorily inclusive purpose of science, unless "appearances" were understood to include other than sensations or "elements."

There was a lag of from ten to twenty years before Mach's disciples and most fellow philosophers reacted to the discovery of "imageless thoughts." Bertrand Russell, Rudolf Carnap, and Ludwig Wittgenstein all wrote books in the tradition of Mach's theory of elements. "Logical atomism," "atomic facts," and also Victor Lenzen's "aspects" all seem to have been based on ignorance of "imageless thoughts." By the 1930s, however, at least verbal corrections had been made. Philosophers came to agree that "phenomenalism" had been refuted, but their definition of this term tended to be somewhat singular. In effect, they rejected immanent and elementist phenomenalism, but retained Gestaltist experience phenomenalism, that is, continued to hold a presentationalist epistemology which included vague psychic referents in addition to sensations. Furthermore, they redefined "phenomenalism" as if it were a mere methodology or linguistic approach, thereby obfuscating the extent to which they retained the essentials of epistemological and/or ontological phenomenalism.

In short, while Mach, himself, died before he could make adjustments in his philosophy to accommodate the discovery of "imageless thoughts," the adjustments that most later philosophers have made have tended to be more linguistic than substantive. Most "professional" philosophers remain presentationalist in their identification of the physical world, while most practical people and many scientists continue to accept a representationalist approach. "Imageless thoughts" have undone elementist phenomenalism, but it is possible that one day they may also be understood to refute the entire Humean tradition and physical presentationalism as well, including all philosophy based on trying to reduce different epistemologies and ontologies to mere linguistic variations of each other.

CHAPTER 15

Politics, Russia, and Vladimir Lenin

I

Ernst Mach developed a number of abstract ethical, social, economic, and political opinions which he expressed from time to time before and during his membership in the Austrian *Herrenhaus* or Chamber of Peers (1901–1913). A cornerstone of Mach's social philosophy was his belief in the moral progress of mankind. He was persuaded that ethical individuals and a moral world order were becoming more manifest on the planet as a whole (1897):

> Very, very gradually, however, as civilization progresses, the intercourse of men takes on gentler forms. . . . In the intercourse of nations, however, the old club law still reigns supreme. But since its rule is taxing the intellectual, the moral, and the material resources of the nations to the utmost and constitutes scarcely less a yoke for the victor than for the vanquished, it must necessarily grow more and more unendurable. . . . [But] here as elsewhere, the evil itself will awaken the intellectual and ethical forces which are destined to mitigate it. Let the hate of races and nationalities run riot as it may, the intercourse of nations will still increase and grow more intimate.[1]

Mach altered Hegel's optimism by arguing that if the rational was not always the real at least it would normally become the real (1912): "However far the distance is from theoretical understanding to practical conduct, still the latter cannot in the long run resist the former."[2]

Mach shared much of the "half-individualism" and "half-socialism" of his friend Josef Popper-Lynkeus. In the individualistic "half" Mach supported personal freedom and a carefully circumscribed "state" authority; in the socialist "half" he favored social and economic reforms which would lead to a redistribution of wealth but which would require a large measure of "state" intervention in order to help bring the reforms about. The following quotations indicate the first "half" of his position, Mach's love of freedom and fear of the "state":

But how does it come, we must ask, that institutions so antiquated as the German gymnasiums could subsist so long in opposition to public opinion? The answer is simple. The schools were first organized by the church; and since the Reformation they have been in the hands of the state. [3]

It is to be hoped that the Americans will jealously guard their schools and universities against the influence of the state.[4]

On the other hand, slavery in a worker's state could be even more *general* and *oppressive* than under a monarchy or oligarchy.[5]

[One] must entertain grave doubts as to the rightness of our method of exercising justice, which consists in making good one misery by a second, the second being added to the first by means of a process that is revolting because deliberate, cruel, and solemn.[6]

[The same absurdity] is committed by the statesman who regards the individual as existing solely for the sake of the state.[7]

Nowadays it is difficult for a free-thinking German to feel brotherly affection for clerical, Christian Socialist, or anti-Semitic Germans. For what has a blank, empty Germandom to offer him devoid of German culture, or even hostile to it? . . . Already numerous free-thinking Germans stand closer to free-thinking Czechs, Jews, Frenchmen, and Italians than to numerous other "Germans". The result of the current war of ideas will not favor this or that race or folk but all peoples.[8]

Mach's humanitarian concern for "the working class," and his adoption of popular left-wing slogans of the day brought aspects of his thinking very near social holism and Marxist ideology.

The two classes that virtually hold the reigns of power in the state [are] the jurists and theologians. . . .[9]

Today in Europe and America the name and traditional form of slavery has ceased, but its essence, the robbery of the many by the few, persists.[10]

It therefore cannot fail that one day this part of mankind, in just recognition of the situation, will consolidate against these lords and masters and demand a more purposeful and mutually satisfactory use and division of our common wealth.[11]

The "colonial", i.e., profit-bringing, "activity" of the Dutch, Spanish, Portuguese, but especially the English, will constitute, like the religious and modern greed wars [*Geldkriege*], the most distasteful chapter of history for coming generations.[12]

While Mach shared Marxist indignation with existing economic and industrial conditions in the "capitalist" world he rejected their obsession with economic causes in favor of individual human "egoism" as the primary villain.

We have already touched on Mach's denial that either the human "ego" or "force" exist in nature. His *social* philosophy, however, not only allowed their existence, but made their *use* primary archenemies.

In a sense Mach tried to return to an Eastern or mystical attitude, which was also a common Christian position in the Early Middle Ages before the crusades of the eleventh and later centuries, namely, that it was not the misuse of force that was evil but force itself. The Crusades encouraged many Christians to believe that force could be justified when used in the service of a Christian or just cause. Mach wanted to change this belief and renew the earlier "forceless" tradition.

Mach did not want "egoists" to prevail in human society, but he felt that the only way to prevent this without using force would be through the gradual reorganization of society by educating present and future generations to believe that neither the "ego" nor "force" exists, (as if ignorance could deter people from learning how to become "egoists" or from becoming able to manipulate "force.") The person with common sense would reply that only force can defeat force, that the more people abandon force the more opportunistic those who retain it will become, and that while "egoism" may be concealed or directed into less conspicuously antisocial channels, nonetheless, it cannot be eliminated without destroying all human ambition and spirit. Mach, of course, rejected this common sense point of view. He was basically not a competitive personality, therefore many of the pleasures and virtues associated with sport, business, and military competition were beyond his understanding. To Mach, the successful industrial tycoon was not a heroic champion to be admired, but a hateful egoist who could not have "won" had he not used force or fraudulent means. Indeed, Mach opposed the very goal of personal "triumph." To be first meant that other people had to be second. Or to put the matter another way, it is likely that Mach would have opposed any dominant person, group, or "ten thousand" whether of "aristocratic," "bourgeois," or "proletarian" orientation to the extent that they seemed to behave in a "forceful" or authoritarian manner. In other words, had Mach worked out a detailed and consistent social philosophy (as it seems he never did), then the result would probably have been neither liberalism nor socialism but a pacifistic, socially conscious form of *anarchism*.

Ernst Mach publicly displayed his sentiments in favor of "oppressed" social classes by a number of conspicuous political actions. In 1896 side by side with Social Democratic laborers he chaired a protest assembly against the allegedly negative attitude of the ruling Christian Socialist Party concerning adult education in Vienna.[13] In 1899 he made known that in his will he planned to leave large sums of money to both the Adult Education Union and the Social Democratic newspaper the *Arbeiter-Zeitung*.[14] In 1901 with the aid of an ambulance he insisted on attending the Austrian Upper House in person and voting in favor of a bill limiting the working day for Austrian coal miners to nine hours.[15] In 1902 he spoke bluntly and successfully against the Christian Socialist idea of setting up an exclusively Catholic university in Salzburg.[16] In 1906 Mach became attracted to the ideas of the socialist theoretician Josef Dietzgen (1828–1888) and urged Karl Leistner and presumably other "Machists" with socialist inclinations to study his works with care.[17]

Mach's political activity reached a peak in 1907. He made a point of being present in the Austrian House of Peers to vote in favor of an election reform bill, and he wrote several newspaper articles, one against race prejudice, one against the Pope's new syllabus on Catholic dogma, and two defending the University of Vienna and its unruly students against Karl Lueger and the Christian Socialist city government.[18]

By this time Mach had become good friends with Viktor Adler, the respected head of the Austrian Social Democratic Party, and with his son, Friedrich Adler, the physicist-philosopher, but Mach's flirtation with socialism seems to have cooled rather quickly. It became clear that Dietzgen's ideas were saturated with Hegelian speculation, and a little-known Russian socialist devoted a whole book to attacking Mach, Avenarius, phenomenalism, and their entire philosophy of science.

Mach had been aware of the influence of his own philosophical ideas in Russia for some time and even of some of the controversies they aroused.[19] But Friedrich Adler seems to have been the first person to inform him how seriously his philosophy was splitting the Russian socialist movement and how the very extent of his influence was responsible for the hostile book. Adler further advised Mach in this same letter (July 23, 1909) not to worry about the Russian attack since the author was a philosophical amateur and obviously did not know what he was talking about. Mach took the advice, lost interest in socialism, and allowed V. I. Lenin's book, *Materialism and Empirio-Criticism* (1909), to circulate unchallenged. Mach died before this mistake could be corrected, and even Lenin probably never anticipated at that time how much his book would eventually contribute to the uprooting of Mach's philosophical influence from Eastern Europe and other countries which have since come under Communist control.

II

Ernst Mach's influence in Russia started early with an appreciation for his scientific work and middle school textbooks but reached its zenith with the bitter philosophical controversies of 1909 and 1910 (see chap. 10).

G. V. Osnobschin came from Moscow to work and learn in Mach's Prague laboratory in 1875. He collaborated with Mach on a number of experiments concerning spark shock waves and soot dispersion patterns.[20] Eight years later he wrote a letter describing his appreciation for Mach's friendly assistance and for all that he had learned in Prague.[21]

Bruno Kolbe wrote from St. Anne's School in St. Petersburg in 1891 that he had introduced Mach's textbook *An Outline of Natural Science* into his classes with great success.[22] Other Russian teachers were equally enthusiastic. In 1892 Colonel Zindeberg wrote from Simbirsk that he had been strongly impressed by Mach's *Textbook for Physics Students* and would he be kind enough to recommend an equally excellent textbook on cosmology for the upper classes of the Russian Corps of Cadets.[23] Three years later work was in progress on a pirate translation of at least one of Mach's textbooks.[24]

In 1895 the Russian scientist and postal official, Sergei von Koschliakov, appealed to Mach for information on how to improve Russian photographic technique since Russian photographs commonly seemed to be underexposed.[25]

At this time Mach began his long correspondence with the remarkable Russian engineer-philosopher, Peter Klementich von Engelmeyer. The correspondence began from Paris where the Russian informed Mach of his influence in France, shifted to Prague where Engelmeyer's wife was an opera singer, and continued for another fifteen years from

Moscow where the Russian owned a factory, wrote philosophy books, and published manuals on automobiles and automobile repair. Engelmeyer was sufficiently multilingual, to write and publish articles in French, German, and Russian. He was also a prominent delegate at the Bologna World Philosophical Congress in 1911. Engelmeyer described Mach's influence on Russian scientists and intellectuals in a letter dated March 28, 1900:

I have become acquainted with a number of your admirers in Moscow and Petersburg. The philosopher *Filippov* [Petersburg] is giving a series of articles on your epistemology in the Russian magazine *Scientific Review*. Professor *Umov* [Moscow] is interested in your spark-photography and a short time ago demonstrated before his students and the general public Ludwig's continuation of your work. Professor *Zhukovsky* studies wind resistance, which is my weakness, and at the moment possesses all of the material from both "Machs" [Ernst and Ludwig] which I received from you. Also, it was he who first directed my attention to your book on mechanics. Professor *Von Stein,* director of the ear clinic here, has made your centrifuge into a diagnostic tool.

Engelmeyer was also responsible for editing and arranging for publication the first Russian translation of Mach's philosophical ideas. The book was a collection of chapters of a primarily philosophical content taken from two of Mach's works.[26] But in spite of this unusual approach it stimulated Russian interest and soon led to the translation into Russian and publication of all of Mach's philosophy books.[27]

Engelmeyer saw hopeful prospects both for Russia and Mach's philosophy in a letter written to Mach on March 2, 1906:

The intellectual situation in Russia is very favorable for the acceptance of your views—naturally not at the *immediate* moment when politics is everything—On the other hand, I consider myself fortunate to be a part of this historical period [i.e., of the short-lived Russian revolution of 1905–1906]. Yet, I merely behave as a spectator; first, because I am a bad politician, and second, because I cannot find the time.

Engelmeyer did find the time, however, in 1910 to organize a Moscow-based Society for Positivism which included ten to twenty leading professors and Moscow intelligentsia among its members.[28] He even established Mach as a kind of spiritual patron. We do not know the eventual fate of the society, but Engelmeyer himself became involved in a conflict between narrow and broad definition positivism and left the organization in 1912:

I must tell you with regret that our new philosophical society has taken a comical direction: aggressive orthodox-positivism one could call it. Freedom of thought has been excluded, I walked out. The gentlemen could not conceive that positive science and philosophical positivism are two different things, that the first has never been so strong and the second never so weak. Hence, I am once again completely alone, like an island. . . .[29]

By this time, however, Mach's philosophical influence had become if not really well entrenched, at least widely circulated. Mach had several highly enthusiastic Russian correspondents. Dr. W. Sharwin wrote exuberant letters from Moscow (1906).[30] Alexander Jollos eagerly adopted Mach's philosophy at Heidelberg and after his return to Moscow (1908) vigorously helped spread Mach's ideas.[31] Mach's point of view also had numerous supporters in the Ukraine. Levintov, an Odessa student, was especially attracted (1901) to Mach's rejection of Du Bois-Reymond's philosophy of science.[32] Gottesmann in Kiev even as late at 1911 was impressed by the continuing increase of Mach's philosophical influence.[33] Engelmeyer in 1912 spoke of Mach's impact in Kharkov.[34]

Mach had an especially interesting correspondence with the Ukrainian Vladimir Nochotowich (1908–1911) who was first a student at Yekaterinoslav (Dnepropetrovsk) and later—following Mach's advice—at the Technical University of Zürich. Nochotowich has given an interesting glimpse from a non-Marxist point of view of Mach's controversial impact on Russian socialist ideology. (Between 1905 and 1917 there was a measure of press freedom in Russia.) The letter was dated February 26, 1910:

It is probably not unknown to you that at present many circles in Russia have directed their attention to your ideas. But even beyond this (which I think will surprise you a great deal) violent newspaper battles are being fought around your name. There is even a special expression "Machism." You may ask, what have you done to cause this. And in fact you are only a passive originator of this conflict.

You are known here more as an Empirio-Criticist than studied as a scientist, with the result being the above-mentioned battles in the Marxist camp.[35]

III

In order to understand Mach's influence on prominent Russian socialists let me start by mentioning that few socialists had a reliable understanding of the epistemological and ontological assumptions of Marx and Engels, and that all socialists had not yet concluded that the recently dead Marx (1883) and Engels (1895) had provided the final answer to all philosophical as well as all social and economic problems. Many socialists believed that Marx's "scientific socialism" could be strengthened and popularized by linking it with the most modern philosophy of science held by a large number of practicing scientists themselves. For the large number of Russians who had studied at Zürich, or who had been taught by professors who had studied there, this could only mean that Marxism should be updated by the "Empirio-Criticism" of Mach and Avenarius. Many socialists honestly believed, as did many Central Europeans, that Mach's philosophy of science had swept away the "metaphysical" past and that it represented not only the ideology of current science but of future science as well.[36]

The most important Bolshevik follower of Ernst Mach was Alexander Bogdanov (1873–1928). He was influenced toward phenomenalism by the Russian author V. V. Lesevich, a former student of Avenarius.[37] Bogdanov has been accused of passing through several different philosophical positions in the course of less than a decade (1899–1908) with Ostwald's "Energeticism" immediately preceding his switch to Mach's "Elementism," but whether these shifts have been exaggerated by critics or not, his *major* philosophical work, *Empirio-Monism* (3 vols.; 1904–1906), was clearly in the presentationalist spirit of Mach and Avenarius. Bogdanov became the most conspicuous Russian "Machist" with his preface to the first Russian edition of Mach's *Analysis of Sensations* (1907). This preface, "What Should the Russian Reader Look for in Mach?," became extremely controversial. Non-Marxists were annoyed by its political orientation, and many socialists opposed its philosophical "idealism." Dr. Scharwin, an anti-Marxist, protested in the following letter to Mach, dated October 4, 1907:

It is very definitely to be regretted that Mr. Bogdanov has taken so much trouble to write such a completely unsuitable preface to your work. This juxtaposition clashes so disharmoniously, as if someone wanted to play Offenbach as an introduction to Beethoven's Fifth Symphony. Why this agitation handbill? Why does "comrade" Bogdanov polemicize against "comrade" Plekhanov? What has Carl Marx and "the revolutionary proletariat" to do with your *Analysis?* This preface can only have a very damaging effect, naturally not for your majestic work, but for the unknowing people who will lay your book aside because of Bogdanov's work, without ever becoming acquainted with the beauty of your ideas.

Other leading Russian socialists who published articles or books favoring Mach's ideas included V. Bazarov, Anatoly Lunacharsky, and V. Valentinov. Bazarov, cotranslator of Marx into Russian, prepared the way by rejecting much of Engel's philosophy of science as old-fashioned and in need of revision. A. V. Lunacharsky in his article, "The Future of Religion" (1908), used his presentationalist philosophy to help reconcile socialism with the spirit of religion.[38] And Valentinov, in his book *Ernst Mach and Marxism* (1908), made perhaps the most determined Russian effort to ally socialism and science by means of Mach's philosophy.

Revising Marxism was one thing, but redefining it in Machian terms was quite another, yet Bazarov, Bogdanov, Lunacharsky, and Valentinov tried to do just that in two books, the first coauthored by the first three men and titled *The Philosophy of Marxism* (1908) and the second book written by Valentinov in the same year, *The Philosophical Constructions of Marxism*. Needless to say, such radical daring provoked a storm from the more "traditional" followers of Marx and Engels, and especially from the leader of the majority faction of the "Russian Social Democratic Worker's Party" himself, Vladimir Lenin. The question was no longer one of "modernizing" socialist doctrine, but of determining just what Marxism was so that one could distinguish Marxists from non-Marxists and force the latter either to change their opinions or to leave the party or at least the Bolshevik wing of it.

IV

George Plekhanov (1857–1918) had long been the leading Russian philosophical interpreter of Marxism. In 1904 at the time of the Bolshevik-Menshevik split he sided briefly with Lenin and then took a more independent position. Leszek Kolakowski has described his criticisms:

Plekhanov's writings at the time stressed the fact that a revolution cannot be successful unless the economic and historical conditions are ripe for it (the proletariat cannot seize power before capitalism has reached a certain stage of development). Together with Trotsky, he accused Lenin of "Blanquism," belief in an arbitrary, "conspiratorial" attempt to speed up social development. At the time, he saw a connection between the Bolsheviks' political position and the popularity of this philosophy among them. The Russian followers of Mach were unaware of any incompatibility between their own position and Marxism; they pointed to the *Theses on Feuerbach,* which they interpreted in a subjectivist spirit.[39]

Lenin had deep admiration for Plekhanov despite their differences and hoped to bring him back into the Bolshevik fraction. Lenin believed that a tightly disciplined party could win power in Russia by means of a violent revolution without necessarily having to wait until an advanced capitalist economy provided the right opportunity for success. He agreed with Plekhanov that Bogdanov and his Machist followers were taking a "subjectivist" philosophical course, but he denied that his own so-called Blanquism necessarily implied Bogdanov's philosophy.[40]

Lenin at this time (1904) did not publish a philosophical attack against Bogdanov, but he did support much of Plekhanov's attack against the latter, and specifically requested Lyubov Akselrod to write an article against Bolshevik Machism ("A New Variation of Revisionism").[41] Neither Plekhanov nor Akselrod, however, were able to silence Bogdanov and his followers. Indeed, their philosophical influence both inside and outside the fraction seemed to grow by leaps and bounds.

Lenin also tried a personal approach: "I made his [Bogdanov's] acquaintance in 1904 when I presented him with my "Steps," and he presented me with his philosophical work of that time (*Empirio-Monism,* Vol. I). I immediately wrote him from Geneva to Paris that his writings firmly persuaded me of the incorrectness of his views and convinced me of the correctness of Plekhanov's views." [42]

Bogdanov finished the last two volumes of his opus in 1906 and once again Lenin expressed his dismay, this time in a letter to Gorky: "I have become unusually annoyed and angry; Bogdanov is taking an exceedingly wrong non-Marxist line." [43]

The situation was by now well out of hand. Bogdanov had combined his philosophical deviation with a political heresy, labeled "Otzovism": Bogdanov wanted socialist deputies to boycott the Russian Duma; Lenin opposed this policy. Perhaps the last straw came when Bogdanov and his Machist followers won Maxim Gorky himself as a philosophical ally.[44]

By this time Alexander Bogdanov was widely recognized as the second most important figure in the Bolshevik wing, in spite of his schismatic influence. Lenin's final personal attempt to change Bogdanov's independent course took place in the spring of 1908, that is, a few months after Lenin had begun collecting material for a book against "Machism." [45]

In mid-March Lenin again put off his trip to Capri: "There is no money, no time, and I cannot leave the [party] paper." . . . The philosophers, notably Bogdanov, Bazarov, and Lunacharsky, were living with or near Gorky on Capri. In April finally Lenin went to Capri—alone. . . . Once Lenin said: "Explain in two or three phrases what your 'position' gives to the working class and why Machism is more revolutionary than Marxism." Bogdanov began, but before he got far Lenin interrupted: "Drop it." [46]

In Capri, Gorky reports, Lenin, confronting A. A. Bogdanov, said, "If you write a novel on the subject of how the sharks of capitalism robbed the workers of the earth and wasted the oil, iron, lumber, and coal—that would be a useful book, Signor Machist." [47]

By 1908 Bogdanov had altered his philosophy once again, this time specifically to slip the charge of "Machism," so he saw no reason to confess doctrinal error, but Lenin had no intention of letting his prey go. The war was now on in earnest. From Lenin's point of view the issue was simple. The Bolshevik fraction had to decide: Marxism or Machism? There was no third alternative, and Bogdanov represented "Machism" whether he liked the designation or not.

v

Lenin carried out research in Geneva, Zürich, and London and completed his philosophy book, *Materialism and Empirio-Criticism,* in September 1908. It was published in May 1909. (Lenin used the terms "Machism" and "Empirio-Criticism" interchangeably. The former he normally preferred for polemical and the latter for more formal occasions.) [48]

Lenin accepted what he believed were the true philosophical opinions of Marx and Engels. All reality was material but moved and changed according to eternally valid laws. Most of these laws came from science but some of them were selected from the philosopher Hegel. The most important Hegelian carry over was the notion that all reality contained "internal contradictions" which were resolved through a "dialectical process" in history. Everything in nature was determined, and there was an inevitable course in history.

Lenin supported a "copy" theory of epistemology which must be clearly understood to comprehend why he so strongly opposed "Machism." According to the Communist leader, physical objects had both the primary and secondary characteristics that phenomenalism and naïve realism agreed they had, but instead of being directly presented to consciousness those objects, while exactly copying experienceable characteristics, existed entirely outside all possible experience, and were merely represented by conscious experience. Galilean or common sense realism agreed with the "copy" theory on its representationalist approach to "external" physical reality, but denied Lenin's claim that both primary *and secondary* qualities existed in physical objects. Granting physical status to secondary qualities meant that mechanical explanation would not suffice to understand the behavior of physical reality. Marxists answered this objection by appealing to "dialectical" interpretation. The common sense rebuttal would be that the Marxist stand on secondary qualities has simply created unnecessary problems.

Many people have considered Marxist epistemology to be a form of "naïve realism," but this is not correct. Naïve realism is presentationalist while "dialectical materialism" is representationalist. The confusion arises from the fact that most people, including Marxists, do not fully grasp the distinction between the two fundamental forms of epistemology. Nor does the problem end there. One must also distinguish between presentationalist materialism and representationalist materialism, between matter monism and mind-matter dualism, and in Marxist terminology between dialectical materialism and mechanistic or "metaphysical" materialism.

Lenin was not a profound philosopher, but he did come to understand the basic difference between presentationalist and representationalist philosophy, and that "Machism" supported the former and "Marxism" the latter. Many "Marxists," who failed to understand the difference, supported presentationalist materialism, which was only verbally different from Mach's point of view. Lenin's task was to point out that genuine "dialectical materialism" was representationalist and that all Machists and presentational materialists were merely "idealists" in the eighteenth-century sense, where "ideas" included both sensations and thoughts. Unfortunately, Lenin could not rely merely on "reason" to persuade his opponents. Even today there are many "professional philosophers" who still seem unable to understand the fundamental nature of the distinction between presentationalism and representationalism, hence, he could hardly expect less philosophically sophisticated members of the communist movement to grasp the difference.

A consequence of this difficulty was Lenin's decision to use extremely abusive and personal language against his philosophical opponents. If he could not persuade them at least he could insult their intelligence, frighten them, or somehow intimidate them. Though the means were somewhat brutal, he was as we know, successful. On the other hand, he also gained a number of intentional philosophical allies, who thought they accepted Lenin's understanding of the philosophical assumptions of "dialectical maternalism," but who actually did not, mostly again, because of lack of clarity over the differences between representationalist and presentationalist epistemology.

Lenin took especial exception to Bogdanov's tricky "renunciation" of most aspects of Mach's philosophy while retaining epistemological presentationalism (along with Mach's "neutral monism," "elementism," theory of "functional relations," and other theories):

> Bogdanov, arguing against Plekhanov in 1906, wrote: "I cannot own myself a Machian in philosophy. In the general philosophical conception there is only one thing I borrowed from Mach—the idea of the neutrality of the elements of experience in relation to the 'physical' and 'psychical,' and the dependence of these characteristics solely on the *connection* of experience." This is as though a religious man were to say—I cannot own myself a believer in religion, for there is "only one thing" I have borrowed from the believers—the belief in God. This "one thing" which Bogdanov borrowed from Mach is the *basic error* of Machism, the basic falsity of its entire philosophy.[49]

Besides clarifying the philosophical assumptions of what has subsequently been labeled "Marxism-Leninism," the leader of the Bolshevik wing also challenged Bogdanov's contention that Machism was the philosophy of science held by most up-to-date scientists themselves. Lenin argued that most scientists were materialists in practice regardless of their philosophical opinions or those of most philosophers of science, and that Machism or Empirio-Criticism far from being "modern" was derived from and closely resembled the idealistic views of Bishop Berkeley, who had lived almost two centuries before.[50] Furthermore, as the bishop himself gladly admitted, his views were adopted not to aid science but to protect the Christian religion from attacks emanating from "atheistic" discoveries made by science.

Lenin probably could have strengthened his case against presentationalist philosophy of science had he introduced more examples of its unfortunate effect on the development of science, particularly the presentationalist opposition of Cardinal Bellarmine to Galileo and to the Copernican theory, of Mach to the atomic theory, and of Pearson to Mendel's theory. Lenin's timing, however, was excellent. His book, *Materialism and Empirio-Criticism,* perfectly "crossed the 'T'" of four books by Mach in Russian translation, all launched in 1909.[51] Even more important—and fortuitous—Max Planck's bitter criticisms of Mach's philosophy, and increased evidence for the reality of atoms and molecules, coincided almost exactly with the publication of Lenin's book so that one of Lenin's major purposes, to prove that Mach's philosophy was not identical with the views of most up-to-date scientists, was accomplished, even if not primarily by means of his own book.

Lenin did not express, but clearly believed in, a second line of argument against all Machist and presentationalist philosophy. Lenin realized that causal representationalist philosophy, was compatible with understanding action in terms of particular forces located at particular places and times and that presentationalist philosophy with its reliance on "mathematical functions" was not. "Forceless" explanation might have value in kinematics or in understanding ideal types of problems, but where the problems were particular and real as in politics, and Bolshevism was a political movement, a reliable understanding of force in general and of historical forces in particular was a necessity for political survival, let alone victory. Given the need to understand and use force in a practical and effective way, Bolshevism had to be based on a representationalist, and hence "anti-Machian," philosophy.

Lenin had originally welcomed Bogdanov and his Machist followers into the Bolshevik wing of the party. Indeed, immediately after the Bolshevik-Menshevik split Lenin needed all the supporters he could muster, but with his own increasing emphasis on violent revolution as a means of taking power, on the need for a more disciplined fraction, and on his desire to place more members of "the working class" in positions of authority in a worker's party, it became more and more evident that "intellectuals" with no practical grasp of force in either causal understanding or political action had no place in the upper echelons of the fraction or perhaps even in the party.

Bogdanov, himself, gave some details on his own decline and fall: "In the summer of 1909 Krasin and myself were expelled as left Bolsheviks from the Bolshevik 'Zentrum' . . . and in January 1910 with the merging of the Bolshevik and Menshevik fractions I was finally removed from the central committee of the party itself."[52]

The 1917 October Revolution found posts for many socialist "ex-" Machians. Bazarov became an economist and state planning expert, Lunacharsky a minister of education, and Bogdanov founded and directed the Moscow Institute of Blood Transfusion, but Lenin remained distrustful.[53] Robert Payne in his *The Life and Death of Lenin* (1964) has written as follows:

> When he [Lenin] came to power it [*Materialism and Empirio-Criticism*] was reprinted in Moscow with an introduction in which once more he bitterly assailed Alexander Bogdanov. This time Bogdanov was not accused of misinterpreting philosophy so much as being one of the leaders of the Proletcult movement, celebrating a purely proletarian culture. Under Mayerhold the Proletcult theater became one of the major glories of the revolution, but Lenin was suspicious of the movement and did everything possible to thwart it.[54]

Louis Fischer in his own book on Lenin continues: "He objected . . . to an independent cultural organization outside the party and considered the quest for autonomy an effort to elude party control . . . Lunacharsky and Bukharin continued to resist Lenin and assist the Proletcult as late as September 27, 1922. . . ."[55]

The abolition of the movement in 1923 discouraged Bogdanov into writing the following pessimistic statement: "In the old days one called me 'Machist'. . . . But now I observe with satisfaction that I am no longer so designated, because since then, a more accurate term of abuse has been found: 'Bogdanovism'."[56]

In 1928 Bogdanov conducted a medical experiment on himself and died. According to rumor it was suicide.[57]

CHAPTER 16

Mach and Einstein

I

This and the next chapter deal with the Mach-Einstein relationship, the focus in this chapter being on Einstein and in the next on Mach. I start with a limited-information analysis to suggest Einstein's understanding of the relationship, and then in the next chapter, while trying to settle or at least clarify a lingering dispute among scholars, go over the same period again with information available to Mach but incompletely known, if at all, to the younger physicist.

II

Albert Einstein (1879–1955) was born in Ulm, lived there several months, and spent the next fourteen years in Munich where he attended grade school and from 1890 to 1894 the Luitpold Gymnasium. We do not know if Mach's science textbooks were used in his classes, but Mach's name and that of Boltzmann, who was then teaching physics in Munich, were certainly familiar to his science teachers and were probably at least occasionally referred to in classroom discourse.

Einstein's interest in science was stimulated by his reading of Ludwig Büchner's *Force and Matter,* a popular approach to science from a believer in matter monism.[1] The book was first published in 1855, became extremely controversial, and continued to be reprinted until the end of the century.[2] "Professional philosophers" rejected it as "crude" and "naïve," and Marxists scorned it as "metaphysical" (because Büchner would not incorporate "the dialectic" and other Hegelisms), but young Einstein was enthralled by it.[3] Another significant event took place three years later:

The line of reasoning which led to [the special theory of relativity] . . . began when Einstein was sixteen years old. He was "wondering," wondering about motion and light. The speed of light had been clocked; in a vacuum it travels approximately 186,000 miles every second. . . . What would happen . . . if an observer could travel as fast as he liked, even as fast as light? Suppose I were running almost that fast and I chased a light beam? Its speed in relation to me would be much less than 186,000 miles per second. And at the same instant that light moved slowly for me, another person who was standing still and measuring the speed of the beam would clock it at 186,000 miles per second.

This conclusion seemed wrong to him somehow, but there was nothing in physics which denied it. He carried the reasoning a step further; suppose, he thought, that I was running at the *same* speed as light. Suppose I were riding on the beam. Then for me, light would be at rest. A beam of light at rest? How could there be such a thing? Light was defined in terms of its frequency of *motion;* light at rest was a contradition in its own terms —a paradox.[4]

In short, even at this early age Einstein already had the essential insight of light constancy in mind.

III

After numerous family and personal misadventures, Einstein entered the Zurich Technical University in 1896. He did not enjoy attending lectures and seems to have done a good deal of reading on his own.[5] He became especially familiar with the scientific work of Helmholtz, Kirchhoff, Maxwell, Hertz, and Boltzmann.[6]

Einstein became interested in Mach's ideas shortly after his arrival in Zürich. "My attention was drawn to Ernst Mach's *History of Mechanics* by my friend Besso while a student, around the year 1897. The book exerted a deep and persisting influence upon me . . . owing to its physical orientation toward fundamental concepts and fundamental laws." [7]

Mach revolutionized Einstein's epistemological views, broadened his physical understanding, and tended to obscure his ontological beliefs. Einstein adopted Mach's "internal" purpose of science, namely, that the goal of science was to describe and relate the appearances in the simplest possible way.[8] He questioned Newton's definition of mass and adopted to the best of his understanding Mach's "relativistic" views on space, time, motion, place, and rest. Einstein became temporarily interested in laboratory physics and began to disdain mathematical elegance as a formalistic, scholastic trap.[9] He maximized the value of direct observation and logical economy, and finally, he adopted a Machist "sense data" terminology which never entirely left him.[10]

Mach's criticism of Newton's mechanics allowed Einstein to introduce his own view on the constancy of light in such a way that the physical relativizing of space and time would seem to be within the tradition of Mach's epistemological relativism such that there should be less opposition from Mach's numerous sympathizers when Einstein finally reached the point of publication. But I am getting ahead of the story.

Albert Einstein received his university diploma in 1900 and looked for a job. His attempt to become an assistant to Wilhelm Ostwald highlighted his numerous unsuccessful efforts. In spite of a plea from Einstein's father that his son held Ostwald "most highly among all currently active scholars in physics" the Leipzig portals remained closed.[11]

Einstein began amending some of his "Machist" ideas early in the new century. In particular, he shifted his interests away from experimental and back toward theoretical physics and mathematics.

Reflections of this type made it clear to me as long ago as shortly after 1900, i.e., shortly after Planck's trail-blazing work, that neither mechanics nor thermodynamics could (except in limiting cases) claim exact validity. By and by I despaired of the possibility . . . of discovering the true laws by means of constructive efforts *based on known facts*. The longer and the more despairingly I tried . . . the more I came to the conviction that only the discovery of a universal formal principle could lead us to assured results.[12]

A second non-Machian philosophical notion popped up, this time concerning causality: "Einstein always believed that the ultimate laws are essentially causal and deterministic and that it is only our inability to deal with large numbers of particles in any other way that compels us to use statistical methods." [13]

Einstein found reasonably satisfactory employment in 1902, namely, in a patent office in Bern, the capital of Switzerland. He held this post for seven years, and it was during this time he wrote his famous papers on the special theory of relativity, the mass-energy law, Brownian motion, and photons.

Gerald Holton has described Mach's conspicuous influence on Einstein's special relativity paper of 1905:

> The Machist component of the 1905 papers shows up prominently in two respects: First, by Einstein's insistence from the beginning that the fundamental problems of physics cannot be understood until an epistemological analysis is carried out, most particularly with respect to the meaning of the conceptions of space and time. And secondly, Einstein's first relativity paper clearly has a Machist component because he equates reality with the givens, the "events", and does not, as later, place reality on a plane beyond or behind sense experience.

> To be sure, reading Einstein's (1905) paper with the wisdom of hindsight, we can find in it also very different trends that indicate the possibility that "reality" in the end is not going to be left identical with "events", i.e. that sensory experiences will in Einstein's later work not be regarded as the chief building blocks of the world.

> . . . But taking the early papers as a whole, and remembering the setting of the time, we realize that Einstein's pilgrimage *did* start on this historic ground of positivism.[14]

IV

Those physicists who readily accepted Einstein's special theory of relativity divided naturally into two different philosophical groups. On the one hand, many representational realists and Kantians, led by Planck and later by Max Born, emphasized the importance of the principle of the constancy of the velocity of light and how most of the startling features of Einstein's theory were simply logical consequences of it.[15] These men considered the "relativistic" implications of the theory as secondary and without epistemological significance.[16] Einstein's great merit was adding a new constant to physics, not making things more "relative."

On the other hand, many positivists and presentational realists, led by Philipp Frank, Joseph Petzoldt, and Anton Lampa, reversed priorities and accepted Einstein's special theory precisely because of its emphasis on relativity, and particularly, its compatibility or seeming compatibility with epistemological relativity.[17] These men regarded Einstein's theory as a positive continuation and fulfillment of Mach's criticism of Newton's ideas of "absolute" space, time, and motion. Einstein had revolutionized physics and based it on Mach's phenomenalistic epistemology.[18] Physics and positivism were now inseparable.[19] To complete the picture, both Frank and Petzoldt were disturbed by Einstein's principle of the constancy of light in a vacuum, and tried in different ways to eliminate, modify, or trivialize this inappropriate "absolute" out of his theory.[20] (Many nonphenomenalists were also troubled by light constancy, but their objections were physical, whereas those of Frank, Petzoldt, and other Machists were primarily epistemological.)

v

The brilliance of Einstein's 1905 papers, which was evident even to the numerous physicists who had trouble understanding them, soon resulted in his appointment as a privatdozent at the University of Bern and in 1909 as an *extraordinarius* professor at Zürich (not at the Technical *Hochschule* but at the regular University). This last promotion was made possible by Mach's socialist ally, Friedrich Adler.

At that time the professorship of theoretical physics at the University of Zürich became vacant, but the board of education of the Canton of Zürich, which was in charge of the university, had its own plans for this position. The majority of the board of education belonged to the Social Democratic Party, and they had in Zürich a party comrade who appeared to be a suitable candidate from both the political and the scientific viewpoint. This man was Friedrich Adler, Einstein's former fellow student at the Zürich Polytechnic, who was then a privatdozent at the Univerity of Zürich. As the son of the leader of the Austrian Social Democrats, he was held in high esteem by the party members in Zürich. Friedrich Adler was a man imbued with a fanatical love of truth and was interested in physics chiefly because of its philosophical aspects. He was in every respect a man who would not shrink from uttering what he regarded as the truth even if it was to his own disadvantage. Learning that it was possible to obtain Einstein for the university, he told the board of education: "If it is possible to obtain a man like Einstein for our university, it would be absurd to appoint me. I must quite frankly say that my ability as a research physicist does not bear even the slightest comparison to Einstein's. Such an opportunity to obtain a man who can benefit us so much by raising the general level of the university should not be lost because of political sympathies.[21]

Two other Machists, Anton Lampa and Georg Pick, as members of a faculty selection board, were equally instrumental in bringing Einstein less than two years later to the German University of Prague, this time as a regular or *ordinarius* professor.[22] By then, however, Einstein had already received what might easily be interpreted as direct private and public support from Ernst Mach himself.

VI

A few weeks before Einstein was to give an eagerly awaited lecture on relativity in Salzburg in September 1909 he received a book from Ernst Mach in the mail.[23] It was a new German edition of his *Conservation of Energy,* and it included the following reference to relativity and recent work by Minkowski, who had placed Einstein's special theory within a four-dimensional context: "Space and time are not here conceived as independent entities, but as forms of the dependence of the phenomena on one another. I subscribe, then, to the principle of relativity, which is also firmly upheld in my *Mechanics* and *Wärmelehre* (H. Minkowski, *Raum und Zeit,* Leipzig, 1909)." [24]

We do not know if Einstein or many readers of the book noticed Mach's attempt to link Minkowski with Mach's own epistemological theory of relativity, but at the very least the passage did suggest that Mach was interested in and very likely was kindly disposed toward Einstein's and Minkowski's notions of physical relativity.[25] Einstein thanked Mach for the book in a letter dated August 9, 1909, and declared that he had already read Mach's *Conservation of Energy* with care as well as his *Mechanics.* He added that Mach had great influence among the younger generation of physicists and that he personally sympathized with him in his current dispute with Max Planck.[26] (That Mach's influence among older physicists was also large at this time is confirmed by Ernst Lecher, Mach's successor at Prague, who wrote in January 1910 that "Natural scientists are for the most part followers of Mach, but not so the professional philosophers.") [27]

Mach replied in a letter which has since become lost. (All the Mach side of the Mach-Einstein correspondence is missing.) The letter, however, must have included something favorable about the theory of relativity because on August 17, only eight days after his first letter, Einstein wrote to Mach again, thanking him, among other things, for his favorable attitude toward the theory: "Your friendly letter has pleased me enormously as has your treatise. . . . I admire your great energy. It seems that I forgot to send you my treatises [which had been promised in the previous letter], but they will now accompany this [post]card. It pleases me greatly, that you take pleasure [*Vergnügen*] in the theory of relativity. . . ." [28]

The exact nature of Mach's "pleasure" is unclear, but two of Mach's articles, both published in 1910, *did* express a brief if rather cryptic admiration for the work of Einstein and Minkowski:

Similarly, one will have to distinguish between metrical and physical (time containing) space, as has already been suggested in my *Conservation of Energy* and in *Knowledge and Error*. . . . Essential progress in this direction has been instituted and carried out by A. Einstein and H. Minkowski. [29]

If the kinetic version of the physical world picture, which in any case I consider hypothetical, without intending thereby to degrade it, were to "explain" all physical appearances, I would still not consider the manifoldedness of the world to be exhausted, since for me matter, time, and space would still be problems, a view which the physicists (Lorentz, Einstein, Minkowski) are gradually approaching. [30]

Philipp Frank visited Mach in Vienna during that same year (1910) and departed with the feeling that he definitely accepted the theory of relativity: "I had the impression at that time that he agreed completely with Einstein's special theory and especially with its philosophical basis." [31] Einstein also visited Mach, but the meeting was short and the exact date unclear, though it was probably around 1910. Einstein vainly tried to persuade the older man to accept Boltzmann's approach to atomism. [32] Einstein never publicly recalled that their conversation had touched on the question of relativity, which suggests either that the subject was not discussed or that Mach tended to be evasive or noncommittal. If Mach had announced any strong opinion, favorable or unfavorable, Einstein would surely have remembered it. On the other hand, there is no evidence to believe that Einstein's notion that Mach at least sympathized with the special theory was in any way challenged or destroyed. Einstein clearly continued to imagine that on the more important points Mach was and remained his scientific and philosophical ally. [33]

Einstein was not unhappy at the University of Prague. In spite of having to dress "like a Brazilian admiral" for his oath of allegiance ceremony on becoming an Austrian professor, working in an office overlooking a park for the insane, and living in a city with so much unpleasantness between nationalities and culture groups, he seems to have been reasonably satisfied. [34] His wife, however, and an offer from the Technical University of Zürich weaned him back to Switzerland in 1912. Three semesters later he transferred again, this time to Berlin where he became a colleague of Max Planck and a regular member of the Prussian Academy of Science.

VII

Albert Einstein couched the essential insight of his theory of general relativity, the equivalence of inertial and gravitational mass, within a number of Machian ideas. Indeed, he considered the theory as a natural consequence of Mach's earlier work and believed that except for accidental factors Mach quite likely would have discovered and elaborated the theory himself.

Einstein shared Mach's desire to eliminate the notion of force from physics, that is, he wanted to solve dynamic problems using a merely kinematic approach.[35] He reasoned that if gravitation were completely understandable in geometric terms, and if gravitational and inertial acceleration were equivalent, then perhaps even inertia could be understood without appealing to traditional force explanation, particularly if inertial mass itself could be made dependent on the gravitational attraction of the totality of the stars in the universe as determined by a mere functional relation. In other words, Einstein, rejecting Planck's warning about the misuse of kinematics, attempted to apply Mach's relativistic "solution" of Newton's bucket experiment to support his theory of equivalence. Einstein called Mach's notion, which was partly based on reviving philosophical assumptions underlying Ptolemy's astronomy, *Mach's Principle*.[36]

Einstein wrote an enthusiastic letter to Mach on the subject, dated June 25, 1913:

Recently, you have probably received my new publication on relativity and gravitation which I have at last finished after unending labor and painful doubt. Next year at the solar eclipse it will turn out whether the light rays are bent by the sun, in other words whether the basic and fundamental assumption of the equivalence of the acceleration of the reference frame and of the gravitational field really hold. If so, then your inspired investigations into the foundations of mechanics—despite Planck's unjust criticisms—will receive a splendid confirmation. For it is a necessary consequence that inertia has its origin in a kind of mutual interaction of bodies, fully in the sense of your critique of Newton's bucket experiment.[37]

Einstein referred to Mach's principle again in another letter to Mach, which is undated, but according to Joseph Petzoldt was probably sent in early 1914: "I can't quite understand how Planck has so little understanding for your efforts. His stand on my [general relativity] theory is also one of refusal. But I can't take it amiss; so far, that one single epistemological argument is the only thing which I can bring forward in favor of my theory." [38]

The history of Einstein's general theory is a long and complicated one, but suffice it to say that Einstein changed and amended several features of it, that it is widely accepted today (1970), and that it still has not been conclusively proved or refuted. Einstein's goal of eliminating force from physics has not been accomplished. His understandings of mass and inertia still have their questionable aspects, and later versions of his theory have left out Mach's principle altogether.[39]

The common sense objection to Einstein's theory of general relativity is not directed against his somewhat startling attempt to make inertial and gravitational mass equivalent, but against the curious opinion that gravitational attraction is more understandable than inertial acceleration and that geometry is capable of explaining inertial mass. Nor will common sense tolerate any abandonment or redefinition of force which in any way is likely to reduce the successful application of force in practical life, the utopian hopes of Mach and Einstein notwithstanding.

VIII

Einstein's adulation of Mach reached a high point in his obituary on the latter, published in the April 1, 1916, edition of the *Physikalische Zeitschrift*.

The fact is that Mach by his historical writings, in which he followed the development of the individual sciences with so much love . . . has had a great influence on our generation of natural scientists. . . . The significance of such spirits, as Mach, in no way merely lies in having satisfied certain philosophical needs of the time. . . . I request the reader to take in hand Mach's work *The Science of Mechanics*, chapter two, sections six and seven. . . . One will find there a masterful presentation of thoughts, which by no means have yet become the common property of all physicists. . . . It is not improbable that Mach would have come across the theory of relativity, if at the time when his mind was still young and fresh, the question of the constancy of the speed of light had already moved physicists. . . . His thoughts on Newton's bucket experiment show how near his spirit lay to the demand for relativity in the general sense (relativity of accelerations).

Einstein began to adopt a more realistic attitude toward Mach's philosophy and contributions to physics during the following year, partly as the result of a rather bizarre series of circumstances. Friedrich Adler, the good friend of both Mach and Einstein, shot and killed Count Stürgkh, the Austrian prime minister, in a Viennese restaurant on October 21, 1916, in an effort to shock the Habsburg government directly into reopening the Austrian parliament and indirectly into halting World War I and making peace. The Habsburg ruler, the revered and grief-burdened Franz Josef, died exactly a month later, the parliament was reopened, but the war continued, and Adler was sent to prison. Einstein tried to help Adler, wrote an article on him as a physicist, and was somewhat annoyed by Adler's opposition to a critical aspect of the special theory of relativity.[40]

Like other Machists, Adler was enthusiastic about the "relativistic" features of Einstein's theory, but was disturbed by the principle of the constancy of the velocity of light in a vacuum, but unlike Frank and Petzoldt, who looked for ways to bypass it or explain it away, Adler considered this *Naturwunder,* as he called it, sufficiently dubious to justify rejecting the special theory itself, at least in its "uncorrected" form.[41]

Gerald Holton has described Einstein's reaction:

In the Spring of 1917 Einstein wrote to Besso and mentioned a manucript which Friedrich Adler had sent him. Einstein commented, "He rides Mach's poor horse to exhaustion." To this Besso, almost always the loyal Machist, responds on 5 May 1917: "As to Mach's little horse, we should not insult it, did it not make possible the infernal journey through the relativities? And who knows—in the case of the nasty quanta, it may also carry Don Quixote de la Einsta through it all!"

Einstein's answer of 13 May 1917 is revealing: "I do not inveigh against Mach's little horse, but you know what I think about it. It cannot give birth to anything living, it can only exterminate harmful vermin." [42]

Einstein had frowned on Mach's hostility to "hypotheses" and attempts to shackle scientific investigation to the millstone of sensations for several years, but Einstein's general theory of relativity made the disagreement even more acute. To many Machists, and especially to Hugo Dingler, from whom Mach expected more in the future than from any other of his followers, the general theory was simply too speculative; it had lost all touch with sensory experience and certainty, let alone practical application.

Einstein was now faced with a double dilemma, first, he had to choose between Mach's phenomenalistic epistemology (which implied the rejection of the light constancy principle) and the special theory of relativity, and second, between a major plank in Mach's phenomenalistic methodology of science (no theory or hypothesis could have more than provisional value in science) and the special and general theories of relativity (as at least potentially indispensable additions to science).

On both counts Einstein stood by his own theories and intentionally rejected Mach's ideas, and increasingly through the years, actually abandoned more and more particular aspects of Mach's epistemology and methodology of science. In positive terms, Einstein made a special effort to approach the semi-Kantian, semi-representationalist position of his Berlin colleague, Max Planck.[43] The new drift, or rather the more pronounced current, in Einstein's movement away from Mach's ideas, became increasingly evident in his correspondence:

A similar divergence appears in a letter of 4 December 1919 to [Paul] Ehrenfest. Einstein writes: "I understand your difficulties with the development of relativity theory. They arise simply because you want to base the innovations of 1905 on epistemological grounds (non-existence of the stagnant ether) instead of empirical grounds (equivalence of all inertial systems with respect to light). . . ." What we see emerging lowly is Einstein's view, later frequently expressed explicitly, that the fundamental role played by experience in the making of fundamental physical theory is not through the "atom" of experience, not through the individual sensation or protocol sentence, but through "die gesammten Erfahrungstatsachen," namely the *totality* of physical experience.[44]

IX

Strong evidence of a reciprocal disenchantment finally surfaced with the posthumous and long-delayed publication of the first part of Mach's *The Principles of Physical Optics* in 1921. Einstein was bitterly surprised to read the following in Mach's preface, dated July 1913:

I am compelled, in what may be my last opportunity to cancel my views of the relativity theory.

I gather from the publications which have reached me, and especially from my correspondence, that I am gradually becoming regarded as the forerunner of relativity. I am able even now to picture approximately what new expositions and interpretations many of the ideas expressed in my book on mechanics will receive in the future from this point of view. . . . I must, however, as assuredly disclaim to be a forerunner of the relativists as I personally reject the atomistic doctrine of the present-day school or church. The reason why, and the extent to which, I repect the present-day relativity theory, which I find to be growing more and more dogmatical, together with the particular reasons which have led me to such a view—considerations based on the physiology of the senses, epistemological doubts, and above all the insight resulting from my experiments—must remain to be treated in the sequel. . . .[45]

Einstein soon recovered from the psychological blow of Mach's flat opposition, but his own published comments took on a very mixed tone:

Mach was a good experimental physicist but a miserable philosopher.[46]

Mach's system studies the existing relations between data of experience; for Mach, science is the totality of these relations. That point of view is wrong, and in fact, what Mach has done is to make a catalog not a system.[47]

According to my belief, the greatest achievement of Newton's mechanics lies in the fact that its consistent application has led beyond this phenomenological representation (of John St. Mill and E. Mach).[48]

In general your [Moritz Schlick's] presentation fails to correspond to my conceptual style insofar as I find your whole orientation so to speak too positivistic. . . . I tell you straight out: Physics is the attempt at the conceptual construction of a model of the *real world* and of its lawful structure. You will be astonished about the "metaphysicist" Einstein. But every four- and two-legged animal is *de facto* in this sense metaphysicist.[49]

Einstein began to see the light around 1917 and Mach's 1913 preface, which was published in 1921, made the philosophical differences conspicuous to everyone; nonetheless, the fact remains that Mach had noticed the incompatibility well before Einstein. Epistemological relativity and physical relativity had nothing but the mere word in common. In spite of Einstein's considerable debt to Mach, Einstein was neither Mach's philosophical nor scientific "successor," nor, as Einstein himself increasingly realized, was Einstein's theory of relativity "positivistic" or even compatible with positivism.[50]

"Positivistic" relativity insisted that "all sensations were dependent on all other sensations," but Einstein argued that the velocity of light in a vacuum was independent of other phenomena, that physical phenomena should not be identified with sensations, and that physical laws were not mere "economical descriptions of the appearances," but had a constant validity independent of all sensations and conscious data. In other words, Mach's epistemological theory of relativity and Einstein's physical theory of relativity were dissimilar to the point of contradicting each other such that no rational person could or should hold both.

CHAPTER 17

Did Mach Finally Accept Einstein's Theory of Relativity?

I

Ernst Mach not only admitted that one could postulate a space of more than three dimensions, but as a young scientist, he had even anticipated Riemann in describing such a geometry.[1] The point was that while one could mathematically construct multidimensions, the sensory world, or what Mach as a presentationalist considered the external world, could never have more than the three dimensions of simple geometry. Mach's book *Space and Geometry,* which was published in 1906, expressed this point in very clear language.

Seldom have thinkers become so absorbed in revery, or so far estranged from reality, as to imagine for our space a number of dimensions *exceeding the three of the given space of sense,* or to conceive of representing that space by any geometry that departs appreciably from the Euclidean. Gauss, Lobachevski, Bolyai, and Riemann were perfectly clear on this point, and cannot be held responsible for the grotesque fictions which were subsequently constructed in this domain.[2]

Two years later, on September 21, 1908, Hermann Minkowski challenged Mach's view by giving a well-publicized lecture on his theory of four dimensions. Mach reacted by seeking a copy of the lecture and making a determined effort to understand Minkowski's argument.[3] He soon decided to keep silent about differences and treat Minkowski as a negative ally as he had done earlier with Ostwald, Driesch, and Haeckel, that is, as a man who opposed much that Mach opposed but who held different positive views. In particular, Mach appreciated Minkowski's implied attack on Newtonian "absolute" space and time, two fundamental pillars of "classical" mechanics.

Mach published three very brief references to Minkowski (1909–1910). One linked Minkowski with Mach's epistemological theory of relativity, one praised him for helping to clarify Mach's distinction between "metric" and "physical" space, and one complimented him on approaching Mach's position that space and time were still problems. There was no real mention of Minkowski's four-dimensional theory at all.

In point of fact, however, Mach was well acquainted with four-dimensional theories and tended to have a prejudice against them.[4] Some years earlier (1878–1881) the "scientist," Johann Karl Friedrich Zöllner, had deposited four works in the local University of Leipzig "Transactions." Two titles were: *History of the Fourth Dimension* (1879) and *Natural Science and Christian Revelation: A Popular Contribution to the History of the Fourth Dimension* (1881).[5] Professor Edwin G. Boring wrote on the scandal:

[Helmholtz] . . . raised the question as to what geometry would be developed by beings who lived in another kind of space than ours. There might, for example, be "sphere dwellers." . . . Beings who lived in an egg-shaped surface. . . . Dwellers in a pseudosphere. . . . So effectively were these pictures drawn that in certain limited circles they became the vogue of the time. Zöllner, the astronomer at Leipzig, came out with the theory that space must be curved and finite (a theory that has a modern ring), or else, he said, since time is finite, all matter would already have been volatilized. This theory is interesting, but thereafter Zöllner was drawn into a consideration of the performances of the great American medium, Slade. . . . As has always been the case when psychic research is in question, the result was a violently emotional and personal controversy. Helmholtz was criticized as having laid the ground for a great scientific scandal. One of Helmholtz's accusers was even dismissed from Berlin on account of the nature of the accusations.[6]

Mach never did publish an opinion specifically on the soundness of Minkowski's theory, but his own writings of 1906 and his memories of the Zöllner scandal leave no doubt that Mach no more favored the positive views of Minkowski than he earlier had the opinions of any of his other negative allies.[7]

II

One of the great hopes of science at the turn of the century was to relate gravitation and electromagnetism. Since the work of Hertz around 1890, a great many physicists, including Mach, imagined that future physical theories would discard the atomic hypothesis and concentrate on the electromagnetic "field." Since both magnetism and gravitation seemed to act at a distance and in inverse proportion to it, surely there had to be a close relation between them.

It was with this background in mind that Mach in the middle of 1909 became interested in the ideas of Paul Gerber and Albert Einstein. Gerber had written a manuscript relating gravitation and electromagnetism.[8] Mach's limited grasp of mathematics prevented him from judging its reliability and ultimate plausibility, hence, he asked a number of physicists to give their opinions on it. At the same time (1909–1910) Mach asked for opinions on Einstein's special theory of relativity. Some of the physicists complied and some of them passed Mach's requests on to young lecturers or privatdozents who they felt were more competent to handle contemporary highly technical, mathematical treatises. We do not have Mach's side of the large correspondence that followed, but in spite of that, some of the letters to Mach are interesting, even if somewhat cautious. As will be noticed, two of the privatdozents later became very prominent, and in differing degrees followers of Mach's philosophy of science. Hence, it is quite possible that this incidental contact contributed substantially to the spread of Mach's philosophical ideas. Professor Wilhelm Wirtinger gave the following account of Einstein's Salzburg lecture to Mach in a letter dated October 5, 1909: "A. Einstein has indeed held a lecture here (in Salzburg). Unfortunately, I could not understand the first part in physical terms and therefore I left. I was told, that in what followed he developed the idea of light as a quantity, but I wasn't able to get anything more precise on it. On the other hand, your colleague Anton Lampa was here, and he may be able to give you a more exact account."

Several months later, Wirtinger handed on Mach's request about Paul Gerber's theory to Dr. Erwin Schrödinger (July 28, 1910): "I have given Gerber's paper to a young electron man, who otherwise seems quite reasonable, and he offered to give me a detailed opinion in return. Dr. E. Schrödinger has now written that detailed letter, and what seems striking to me is his objection that the whole thing [the relation between gravity and electromagnetism] is quite different when another kind of radioactive material is taken under serious consideration."

Schrödinger found parts of Gerber's treatise very difficult to understand (July 25, 1910): "Regrettably, I could not carry out my task in a very satisfactory way, since some of the essential points in Gerber's paper remain completely unclear."

August Föppl, a Machian whose textbook, *Introduction into Maxwell's Theory of Electricity* (1894), may well have influenced Einstein, wrote to Mach about Einstein on January 11, 1910:[9]

I still can't seem to come to a definite conclusion on the work of Einstein and Minkowski. I can clearly see that provisionally the question is merely one of an hypothesis, whose confirmation by experience, that is, of the movement of perceivable bodies, is completely lacking at least for the moment. The thought which I cannot suppress is directed more against their ability to carry the thing through at all. . . . Whether this can be done, seems very doubtful, or more exactly expressed, I consider it very improbable. . . .

Gustav Jäger, a Vienna physicist and philosophical ally of Mach, wrote to him on Gerber's essay (June 5, 1910):

It is not my fault for first answering you today concerning Gerber's treatise. In the belief that Professor [Friedrich] Hasenöhrl, who has a much better judgment on such matters than I, would look through the work, I gave it to him since he stated a willingness to read it. After fourteen days, however, he gave it back—after having briefly looked through and declaring it worthy of attention—and said that at present he had no time to study it. I also believe the work deserves notice. . . . [Nonetheless] the good agreement between the calculated constant of gravitation and what has been measured is purely accidental. . . .

As a precaution I would like to allow privatdozent [Philipp] Frank to look through the work, a man who I think is the best qualified of any of the Vienna physicists to render a judgment on the matter.

Philipp Frank gave his opinion eight days later in a letter to Mach:

Concerning Gerber's work which you were friendly enough to send me: It is somewhat confused, such that in spite of considerable efforts I have not been able to understand it. . . . The basic thought is that while the electrical and magnetic strength of the field is dependent on the fluctuations of the vector potential, the value of this vector potential is itself the gravitational constant, which agrees with observation. Nevertheless, the deductions which lead to this result are so unsatisfactory that no exact conclusion can be rendered as to the validity of the result.

Philipp Frank then visited Mach and later reported: "He especially wanted to know more about the application of four-dimensional geometry. . . . He requested me to prepare a printed or handwritten representation [of my ideas] and leave a copy with him. I did that. . . ." [10]

An undated letter from Frank to Mach, but clearly also in 1910, gave more details: "I would like to mention further, that I am now working on a representation of the theory of relativity which is understandable to nonmathematicians, as you requested in your letter Herr Hofrat and as Herr Professor Lampa has also asked for. I will especially try to represent Minkowski's thoughts on space and time in an understandable way."

Philipp Frank strongly believed not only that Mach then accepted Einstein's theory of relativity but that it had even been Frank's own account and interpretation of it which the older man had adopted: "I did that also [i.e., wrote the book] and as a result the representation of *Einstein's* theory, which *Mach* accepted, appeared in print." [11]

III

Several weeks earlier, however, Mach had found a brief suggestion of what he thought was a very promising argument which in no way favored the pretensions of Einstein, Minkowski, Frank, or theoretical physics. The man was Hugo Dingler, the book was *Outlines of a Critique and Exact Theory of the Sciences, Especially Mathematics* (1907), and the argument concerned geometry and the relations of physics to sense-reality.

Mach immediately wrote to Dingler's publishers (March 24, 1910) in order to obtain his address and especially to get hold of a copy of Dingler's specific treatise on geometry, *On the Foundations of Euclidean Geometry* (1907). On receiving the young author's address Mach wrote to him asking for help in obtaining the work on geometry which had been published in the quite obscure *Report of the Aschaffenburg Scientific Society*, Vol. VI.[12]

Dingler replied and by April 11, 1910, Mach had received several publications in the mail. Dingler's position on geometry was further clarified in his *Limits and Goals of Science* (1910) which Mach finished reading during the summer of that year.[13]

Mach believed that Newtonian physics was basically sound if interpreted in phenomenalistic terms and if augmented by his own phenomenalistic redefinitions of space, time, motion, mass, and force.[14]

He further held that Newton was completely right in limiting himself to three dimensional geometry in attempting to describe the three dimensions of the external world. Nonetheless, Mach retained nagging doubts about both space and time which he hoped Dingler could put to rest.

Mach was especially attracted to Dingler's arguments that logical simplicity and descriptive certainty both demanded that physics confine itself to Euclidean geometry. More than three dimensions added unnecessary logical and mathematical complications, falsified nature, and opened the door to speculative chaos. If physicists were allowed to play with unlimited dimensions, certainty would never be possible in physics or in the natural sciences, and all would revert to fashion and subjectivity.[15] Dingler rejected Einstein's theory, and in a later article (1925) imagined how future scientists would look back on Einstein's approach: "But the theory of relativity will retain its great and lasting importance in the history of philosophy as the first concrete attempt to apply a non-Euclidean geometry to practical physics (and may this path soon be abandoned forever)."[16]

Armed with Dingler's ideas, Mach rejected Einstein's theory on precisely the same grounds that Einstein used to try to persuade Mach to accept the atomic theory in physics: logical economy! Mach and Dingler disagreed on many things. The young mathematician rejected Mach's biological theory of economy and Mach opposed Dingler's a priorism with respect to logic and mathematics, but on the use of multidimensional theories in physics they thought as one.[17] Einstein and Minkowski not only were wrong to introduce non-Euclidean geometry into physics, but by doing so, and glorifying theoretical physics, they were seriously compromising both the immediate future of physics and the overall development of the natural sciences.

Seen in this light, Mach's three published references to Minkowski and two on Einstein reveal themselves not even as genuine negative praise, but simply as opposition. Just as Mach had hoped in 1906 that the development of electron theory would so disintegrate the atomic theory as to make clear once again the uncertain nature of matter, space, and time, so four years later, Mach hoped that the speculations of Einstein and Minkowski would so undermine the "absolute" space and time of "classical" physics as to bring about, not a new or reformed theoretical physics, but the refutation of theoretical physics itself, so that once again, physicists would focus their attention on the sensory character of the natural world and on the ambiguous status of idealized relations such as "physical" space and time.

Mach's certainty as to the three-dimensional nature of sensory or "physiological" space was matched by his uncertainty as to the full character of "physiological," "metric," and "physical" space. "Physiological" space had never been thoroughly investigated without idealization; "metric" space was only limited by human imagination and mathematical ingenuity, and "physical" space was a mere relation, but Mach never defined what he meant by relations. Furthermore, whatever "physical" space was, it was both idealized and subject, unlike "metric" space, to the need for scientific "economy," hence Mach's inclination to restrict "physical" space to the three dimensions of physiological or "nativistic" space.[18]

Boltzmann had once despaired over the immediate future of his kinetic theory of gases (1898), but remained confident that in the more distant future physicists would come to their senses and accept his contributions. It was now Mach's turn (1910), though from an opposite point of view, to see "folly" control his discipline, but like Boltzmann he remained optimistic with respect to the remote future.[19]

In short, Mach was sustained during his last years by his fundamental belief in the soundness of phenomenalistically oriented experimental physics and by his confidence in human progress, his faith that the "stupidities" of undisciplined theoretical physics would eventually shatter the field into the understanding that describe-and-relate-the-appearances physics was not only a desirable scientific goal, but was also a reliable scientific method, and the only appropriate method for experimental physics.

By the end of 1910 an acute observer could suspect that Einstein's theory was well on its way to becoming a new physical orthodoxy. Einstein and Minkowski were attracting too much attention to be used simply as negative allies against earlier physical views. Furthermore, Einstein had just obtained a chair at the University of Prague, which Mach had hoped would go to Gustav Jaumann. His response was never to mention Einstein again in any of his publications during his lifetime.

Mach revised his *Science of Mechanics* in 1912. He repeated his opposition to the use of multidimensional geometries in physics in the following unmistakable words:

The space of sight and touch is *three-dimensional;* that, no one ever yet doubted. If, now, it should be found that bodies vanish from this space, or new bodies get into it, the question might scientifically be discussed whether it would facilitate and promote our insight into things to conceive experiential space as part of a four-dimensional or multi-dimensional space. . . . Everyone is free to set up an opinion and to adduce proof in support of it. Whether, though, a scientist shall find it worth his while to enter into serious investigations of opinions so advanced, is a question which his reason and instinct alone can decide. If these things, in the end, should turn out to be true, I shall not be ashamed of being the last to believe them.[20]

In his revision, Mach discussed Paul Gerber's attempt to relate gravitation and electromagnetism, and he praised Hugo Dingler in the most flattering terms: "I myself—seventy-four years old and struck down by a grave malady—shall not cause any more revolutions. But I hope for important progress from a young mathematician, Dr. Hugo Dingler, who judging from his publications, has proved that he has attained to a free and unprejudiced survey of *both* sides of science [i.e., the empirical and logical]." [21]

But not a word was mentioned about Einstein, Minkowski, Philipp Frank, or the theory of relativity.

IV

Einstein's letters to Mach on August 9 and 17, 1909, the articles accompanying them, and even his personal visit to Mach, all apparently failed to influence Mach away from supporting his former assistant, Gustav Jaumann, for the open chair in theoretical physics at the University of Prague. Jaumann, who was still teaching at the Brünn Technical University, suggested that the selection committee ask for outside evaluations from other physicists.[22] Anton Lampa, a member of the commission, obliged and wrote to Mach in February 1910:

I don't have to assure you that Jaumann's mental gifts seem to me to be beyond question and that his entire way of thinking is quite sympathetic from my point of view. I consider the pure phenomenological representation of theoretical physics as ideal, as it approximately exists in thermodynamics. Jaumann starts from the desire to construct such a phenomenological representation for the theory of electricity. . . . He therefore rejects the atomic and electron theories and tries to extend Maxwell's field equations. . . .[23]

Lampa and Georg Pick, the two Machists on the commission, strongly favored Jaumann, but Philipp Frank, writing some years later (1917), questioned how closely Jaumann actually followed Mach's philosophy in his scientific work:

It will perhaps be instructive, as a comparative case, to recall a theoretical physicist who, as an immediate student of Mach, really tried to construct a system of physics and chemistry in which no hypothetical corpuscles, whether atoms or electrons, occur, and which embraces all of the phenomena known at present. It cannot be denied that Gustav Jaumann in numerous works has undertaken this task with great constructive force. I do not believe, however, that the result has turned out to be really in the spirit of Mach's teachings. To be sure it corresponds to the surface requirement that all atomistics be omitted, but it hardly corresponds to the requirements of economy.[24]

Meanwhile, Lampa received letters from Max Planck and Woldemar Voigt, which offered only disappointing, mixed support for Jaumann. Planck openly praised Einstein as the superior candidate: "If Einstein's theory should prove to be correct, as I expect it will, he will be considered the Copernicus of the twentieth century." [25]

A somewhat shaken Anton Lampa was therefore doubly appreciative of Mach's letter strongly recommending Jaumann, and with this encouragement he and Pick won over the rest of the commission: "Your exposition concerning Jaumann's methodological approach put my mind so much at ease that I was able to give much warmer support for Jaumann before the commission than otherwise would have been possible. . . . Thus in this last commission meeting we unanimously decided to raise the question with Jaumann whether he would accept a call to Prague." [26]

Jaumann, however, surprised everyone. Philipp Frank, who would soon be teaching in Prague himself, wrote the following account of what finally happened:

Since the regulations provided that the names of the proposed candidates be listed on the basis of their achievements, Einstein, whose writings in the years from 1905 to 1910 had already made a strong impression on the scientific world was placed first and Jaumann second. Nevertheless, the Ministry of Education first offered the post to Jaumann. The Austrian government did not like to appoint foreigners and preferred Austrians. But the Ministry had not taken Jaumann's vanity and touchiness into account. He said: "If Einstein has been proposed as first choice because of the belief that he has greater achievements to his credit, then I will have nothing to do with a university that chases after modernity and does not appreciate true merit." Upon Jaumann's rejection of the offer, the government overcame its aversion to foreigners and offered the position to Einstein.[27]

In spite of Mach's active support of Jaumann, however, it has been widely imagined since then that Mach, as well as Pick and Lampa, had favored Einstein and helped him to obtain the post.[28] It is possible that even Einstein believed this. In fact, all three men initially preferred Jaumann. In addition, Prague was now thought to be more of a stronghold of Mach's philosophy than ever. In fact, far from identifying Prague with Machist philosophy, Anton Lampa, Mach's chief disciple in the Bohemian city, felt deeply annoyed by the presistent influence of Brentano and especially his philosophical followers Anton Marty and Oskar Kraus. He wrote to Mach about the situation on December 30, 1913: "There is nothing pleasing in the fact that Prague has served as Brentano's emporium for a very long time. I am only curious to know who Marty will choose as his successor. Our latest *Extraordinarius,* [Oskar] Kraus is a complete Brentanoid. . . . He considers Brentanoism as religion and even possesses a priest's haughtiness."

Strangely enough, however, Mach shared almost exactly the same objection that Oskar Kraus, the "Brentanoid," had against Einstein's theory of relativity. Philipp Frank in his biography of Einstein gave the following somewhat unsympathetic picture of Oskar Kraus and his point of view:

Einstein remained in Prague another evening to participate in a discussion of his theories that was to take place in the Urania before a large audience. Einstein's main opponent was a philosopher of the Prague University, Oskar Kraus, an acute thinker in the philosophy of law. . . . I presided at this discussion and endeavored to direct it in half-way quiet paths. . . .

Professor Kraus was a typical proponent of the idea that one can learn various things about the geometrical and physical behavior of bodies through simple "intuition". Anything that contradicted this intuition he considered absurd. Among these absurdities he included Einstein's assertion that Euclid's geometry, which we all learned in school, might not be strictly correct. Since in Kraus's opinion the truths of ordinary geometry must be clear to every normal person, it was a puzzle to him how a person like Einstein could believe the opposite.[29]

Mach never informed Frank or Lampa how close his own thinking was to that of Kraus with respect to Einstein's theory of relativity. The result was an ever-widening gap between Mach and many of the more vocal among his "supporters." They followed Einstein under the impression that he was Mach's "successor." Their mistake has helped to confuse the history of science even up to the present. Mach believed in experimental physics. He rejected theoretical physics, all theoretical physics.[30] No theory could ever have more than provisional value in science.

V

Let us now digress for a few pages in order to place Mach's thoughts on relativity within the context of the other concerns that were on his mind, and which, as we shall soon discover, normally took precedence.

Sometimes happy things just happen. Robert H. Lowie dropped into Mach's life from nowhere. He was born in Vienna, brought up on tales about American Indians, emigrated to America when he was ten years old, and received his doctor's degree in ethnology from Columbia University in 1908. Lowie's enthusiasm, and we must add naïve exaggeration, was the perfect tonic to perk up a determined but battle-weary Ernst Mach.

Lowie first wrote to Mach on March 8, 1911, informing him that the latter's books had become a center of interest among a group of graduate students at Columbia University.[31] A second letter was accampanied by an article, "A New Conception of Totemism," in which Lowie "had attempted to indicate the psychological affinity of modern American ethnological criticism with Mach's aspirations in the field." [32] Meanwhile, the exuberant young man sent two letters to Paul Carus praising Mach in the highest terms. Carus then sent Mach the letters. They were dated November 10 and 14, 1911: One letter said, "I greatly envy you the privilege of meeting Mach, whom I revere as the leader of a school that is at the same time uncompromisingly radical and punctiliously critical of its own assumptions. . . . The other included: "My admiration for Mach is indeed very great, and I feel under the greatest obligations to him for clarifying my views as to scientific concepts and method."

A month later, Lowie proposed Mach's name for honorary membership in the New York Academy of Science.[33] Lowie concluded his nominating speech with the following words: "In presenting to your notice the name of Ernst Mach, I propose not merely the greatest historian of physics, not only an original experimenter and thinker in the field of psychology and a keen logician of scientific method, but the founder and leader of a new and genuine scientific liberalism." [34]

Mach thanked Lowie for successfully obtaining the honorary membership for him but was most pleased by the articles and books that the Austro-American sent him. Robert H. Lowie was then an assistant curator at the American Museum of Natural History in New York and his special interest was traveling among Indian tribes, especially in Canada and the Far West. Lowie sent Mach articles on the Assiniboine and particularly on the Crow Indians, certain that the old physicist would enjoy reading about the tribes as much as Lowie enjoyed traveling among them and writing about them. And he was right! Mach developed a whole new set of interests!

Lowie's tendency to take things for granted finally went a step too far. In May 1912, Mach had to decline Lowie's request that he represent the New York Academy of Science at the International Anthropology Congress soon to be held in Geneva. The seventy-four-year-old physicist had no choice but to tell the ethnologist that he was half paralyzed, could not leave his house and garden, and had not traveled anywhere for over thirteen years.[35]

During 1911 and most of 1912 Mach was busy revising his *Mechanics* and *Analysis of Sensations* and working on his *Principles of Physical Optics*. At the same, however, his sister Marie was finishing and publishing her autobiography, *Remembrances of a Governess*.[36] Her book, besides discussing her own adventures and interest in animals, also went into some detail on the customs and habits of Slavic minorities in Montenegro, Bukovina, and other out-of-the-way places. In other words, her book further aroused Mach's interests in sociology and anthropology, especially of primitive culture groups.

By the spring of 1913 Mach had put his unfinished *Optics* aside and was actively engaged in a new direction. Ludwig Mach would do research in museums and libraries, Felix Mach would prepare the diagrams and drawings, Victor Mach would give his father the benefit of his knowledge about hand and machine tooling of everyday utensils, Mach's wife, Louise, would bathe, clothe, and help feed the seventy-five-year-old "project coordinator," and Mach himself would write the book on the pre-history of mechanics. Mach wanted to describe how primitive man gradually learned to shape and use instruments and utensils. He deplored the lack of accurate information on such matters, but relying heavily on Ludwig Mach's research, his own reading, and extensive use of Lamarck's theory of the inheritance of acquired habits and characteristics he completed the preface in August 1915 and published the book, *Culture and Mechanics,* in the same year.

Robert H. Lowie eventually became a professor of anthropology at the University of California at Berkeley (1921–1950) and even chairman of the department. He retained his admiration for Mach and later became friends with Ludwig Mach, but it is possible he was never cognizant of the extent to which his amiable enthusiasm had brightened the wintertime of Ernst Mach's last years.[37]

VI

Ernst Mach was tenacious, but even he could never have triumphed so long over his paralytic condition, numerous illnesses, and a weakening heart had it not been for the assistance of his wife and family in general and his son Ludwig in particular. The history of the last eighteen (and to some extent the last thirty) years of Mach's life has to be a joint account of the efforts of both Ernst and Ludwig Mach. This son equaled the firm purpose of both his father and grandfather. The physician-inventor carried out experiments for his father, answered correspondence for him when he was sick, treated both Mach and his wife during their very frequent illnesses, or called in a specialist, and he made sure that his father kept up with his correspondence, scientific journals, and with current developments in physics and other scientific disciplines.[38] Ludwig Mach was the giant behind the scenes, and it is now time for him to take his bow.

Ludwig Mach, who became wealthy through his patents on "magnalium," his interferometer, and other inventions, built a house-laboratory for his father in Bavaria in 1912. At first Ernst Mach was reluctant to leave Vienna; then when he became eager to go, he fell sick and was confined to his bed. Without remembering the incident at all, Mach had fallen and injured his hip. From August 1912 well into 1913 he remained bedridden.[39] He also suffered from prostatitis and bladder trouble.[40]

In May 1913 Ernst Mach finally left the Danube city for his last home near Munich by the town of Haar (literally in an isolated forest in part of what was becoming known as the village of Vaterstetten).

Soon after the move, Mach's wife, Louise, became very sick and generally remained in poor health until her death in 1919. Ludwig, however, was not only undaunted by the increasing burden upon himself, but even looked forward to renewed and expanded cooperation with his father on optical and other physical experiments. Ernst Mach enjoyed humoring his son, but could not develop any confidence at all in such a prospect at his age. On leaving Vienna, Mach wrote a farewell letter to the Austrian Academy of Science: "Should this letter be my last, please merely assume that Charon the Rogue has carried me off to a station which has not yet joined the postal union." [41]

As Mach reminded several of his correspondents, the trip from Vienna to Vaterstetten had not been a pleasant one. He traveled as far as Munich on a train and from there to his forest home by ambulance. "No one who has journeyed in this [horizontal] manner will envy me." [42]

Quite unexpectedly, Ernst Mach's health enjoyed a considerable improvement. By July 1913 he was back to serious writing and took conspicuous pleasure in welcoming his many visitors.[43] He also began to work in close cooperation again with his son on optical experiments.[44] Indeed, if they had an especially hard problem to solve, they would sometimes lock themselves in the laboratory, live on chocolate, and not emerge until the problem was solved.[45] Once they are supposed to have stayed inside working uninterruptedly for two days.

It was at this time that Ludwig Mach urged his father to permit at least the first half of *The Principles of Physical Optics* to be published.[46] Mach, however, was very reluctant. He finally acceded, but only under the condition that a number of additional experiments on light be carried out.[47] In point of fact, however, the publication was further delayed. Printing began in 1916, but was put off once more, only to be completed in 1921.[48] The importance of July 1913 is that it was then that Ernst Mach wrote his controversial preface to his *Optics* attacking Einstein's theory of relativity. Let us return to the adventure surrounding the title of this chapter: Did Mach finally accept Einstein's theory of relativity?

VII

Joseph Petzoldt, the long-time friend and correspondent of both Richard Avenarius and Ernst Mach, developed a strong interest in Einstein's theory of relativity. His letters to Mach focused more and more on this one issue. Both sides of the correspondence have now been located as well as a number of relevant letters from Albert Einstein and Ludwig Mach to Petzoldt.[49] Unfortunately, there is one conspicuous gap, namely, Ernst Mach's letters to Petzoldt from 1906 to 1913. All are missing.

Petzoldt's letters to Mach during 1910 and 1911 reveal that both men still held major objections to the theory of relativity. Petzoldt was especially disturbed by the principle of the constant velocity of light, and Mach, by epistemological considerations. "You wrote me last that on the epistemological side there seemed to be some deficiencies in the principle of relativity; I also believe that. . . . The constant speed of light seems to play a peculiarly 'naïve' role. It is constant for different space-time-systems only by definition. . . ."[50]

On the other hand, even at this time Petzoldt was attracted to the theory's "relativism" as if it were related to Mach's epistemological brand or a physical development from it. Mach, however, had already begun urging Petzoldt to read Hugo Dingler's books, as if he had started to notice the epistemologically alien nature of what Einstein meant by "relativity." Petzoldt continued: "But in any case, in theoretical physics as well as in mathematics, I find the modern development wonderful. Because of it, all absolutism and a priorism are finished. Old Protagoras is rising from his grave, a rebirth, now that the gushing current of the holy spirit of relativism is once again being followed."[51]

In 1912 Petzoldt published the first of many articles relating Mach's epistemology with Einstein's theory. He also republished a 1906 book, added fifty-eight pages to it, and inserted the word "relativistic" into the old title, so that it now read *The World Problem from the Standpoint of Relativistic Positivism* (1912). Petzoldt had struck a popular vein. This retitled book became by far his best-known publication and helped place him in the van among the numerous writers attempting to establish Mach as Einstein's forerunner.

In May and June of 1913 Petzoldt sent three letters to Mach on the theory of relativity, each more favorable than the last.[52] He was especially impressed with the fact that Einstein's new theory of general relativity rested on Mach's suggestion concerning Newton's bucket experiment, that is, on what we now call Mach's principle. Petzoldt also believed that the general theory should be able to eliminate the "absolute" constancy of the velocity of light, which had long been an epistemological annoyance to Mach and his friends. Here is part of one of Petzoldt's letters to Mach, dated June 6, 1913: "The day before yesterday, I spoke to Professor [Max von] Laue. . . . Einstein is said to be essentially finished with his explanation of gravitation and declares that this is his best work so far. According to Laue, he makes the centrifugal events of the relative rotations of masses dependent on each other, that is, exactly as you have done."

Less than three weeks later, on June 25, 1913, an enthusiastic Albert Einstein wrote directly to Mach about his new theory and repeated what Petzoldt had said about Mach's notion that local inertia may be dependent on the totality of the stars.[53] Mach had criticized Newton's bucket experiment in order to place epistemological relativity, the notion that "all phenomena are dependent on one another," at the core of Newtonian physics. He had no intention of employing Mach's principle in such a way as to replace Newtonian physics or to encourage a new speculative system. Mach had opposed Minkowski's four-dimensional theory; hence, one can easily imagine his reaction to Einstein's latest copious use of non-Euclidean geometry. Einstein's 1913 preliminary version of his general theory, which would not be fully worked out until 1916, probably was the most important factor in provoking Mach into writing his 1913 preface to his book on optics. Einstein's ideas too closely resembled those of Zöllner, both with respect to the use of multidimensions in physics and in its appeal to a so-called curved space.[54]

Mach's preface was dated "July 1913," which has suggested that it was written only days after receiving Einstein's letter. On the other hand, Mach received numerous visitors during July and August, including both Dingler and Petzoldt, hence, we should be cautious in our conclusion, since other people besides Einstein may have influenced the writing of the preface against the theory of relativity.[55]

Mach seems to have written the preface, not because he thought his book on optics was ready to be published or because he wanted to publish it at that time, but apparently, in order to have his opposition to Einstein's theory of relativity on record in case of his death. The main point in his preface was to deny the claim of Frank, Petzoldt, and at that time of Einstein himself that he was a forerunner of Einstein's theory of relativity or (by implication) of any form of theoretical physics at all.[56]

There is evidence that Mach became more sympathetic to Einstein's approach during late 1913 and early 1914. The evidence is not conclusive, but it must be recognized that it does exist.[57] There are three different groupings of relevant information of which the first two are quite brief and nebulous. An undated letter from Einstein to Mach, written probably in late 1913 or early 1914, started off with the comment: "I am very pleased by the friendly interest which you have shown in my new theory," as if Mach had earlier written a sympathetic letter to Einstein.[58] Another piece of evidence comes in a letter from Leo Gilbert (alias Leo Silberstein), an "energeticist" and notorious opponent of Einstein, who wrote to Mach on December 1, 1913: "The day before yesterday I permitted myself to send you a paper against the principle of relativity." Two months later, Gilbert wrote to Mach again and made the following interesting remark: "With respect to that, it is not important if we are not agreed on the matter of the principle of relativity." If Mach and Gilbert were not agreed, and Gilbert opposed the theory, then Mach presumably favored it. The problem, of course, is that too much rests on conjecture. For example, they may have disagreed over Mach's theory of relativity, rather than over that of Einstein.

The next grouping of evidence in favor of the notion that Mach became more sympathetic to Einstein's theory of relativity is considerably more substantial, but is, nonetheless, subject to different interpretations, and thus must also be regarded as ambiguous and inconclusive. Even though many of Petzoldt's letters to Mach explicitly refer to Einstein's theory of relativity, only two of the twenty-one extant letters from Mach to Petzoldt refer to that theory or to Einstein as a person. These two letters, however, while they do not state Mach's approval of any of Einstein's ideas, certainly seem sympathetic, at the very least. The first letter was sent in early 1914: "The accompanying letter from Einstein is proof of the penetration of positivistic philosophy into physics; you can take satisfaction in that. A year ago philosophy was still a mere stupidity.—The details confirm this. A year ago the paradox with the clock had not even occurred to Einstein." [59]

The second Mach-to-Petzoldt letter was posted a few days later: "I have meanwhile received a copy of the *Zeitschrift für positivistische,*

Philosophie, which includes your article on relativity [i.e., "The Theory of Relativity of Physics" (1914)], which pleases me not only because it acknowledges my modest contributions to this theme, but for other reasons also." [60]

The major question is whether Mach wrote these letters merely to please Petzoldt or also because he himself now felt more sympathetic to Einstein's theory of relativity. If indeed, Mach did become more sympathetic, then the reason was probably that Mach had come to share Petzoldt's view that the general theory was consistent with the "relativization" of the constancy of the velocity of light. If, on the other hand, Mach was trying to make Petzoldt happy, and in no way changed his opposition to Einstein's theories, then Mach had only himself to blame for the eventual consequences.

Mach's two letters, in addition to the one from Einstein, caused Petzoldt to believe that both Mach and Einstein supported his interpretation of Mach as an epistemological and scientific forerunner of Einstein, an interpretation which in fundamental terms was false, and which Mach at the time, and Einstein somewhat later, knew was false.[61] The consequences were that Petzoldt, along with numerous allies, strenuously advocated this misinterpretation until it became the majority opinion, as it may still well be today (1971).

IX

Joseph Petzoldt, in his elation over the letters, decided to visit Ernst Mach in Vaterstetten and have a long discussion with him concerning the whole question of Einstein's theory of relativity and its development from the special to the general theory. Unfortunately, however, while his psychological timing might have been right, his historical timing could hardly have been worse. He planned to make the trip in late July 1914, that is, during the tense days immediately preceding World War I when reservists had to keep in mind the imminent likelihood of mobilization. Petzoldt also noticed a rather cool reaction from Vaterstetten. Ludwig Mach, writing for his father, pointed out the following aspects of the situation: "Under the present conditions you will want to return home [to Berlin] soon. I'm sorry that you have not been able to speak with Dr. Dingler. . . . My father is not well. . . ." [62] Petzoldt reacted by coming to Munich anyway, but there was no one to meet him and conduct him to Vaterstetten. Ludwig

Mach apologized in a letter dated July 21, 1914: "Your telegram came yesterday evening and your card today. I'm sorry that it was no longer possible for me to arrange my departure. You and Dr. Dingler must definitely discuss the matter at your leisure."

The war broke out and Petzoldt never saw Ernst Mach again.[63] Later he believed that he could have talked Mach into accepting the theory of relativity if in fact he did not already accept it at that time.[64] In arguing this way, he blamed Ludwig Mach for being overly protective with respect to his father, and he appealed to the following letter from Ernst Mach, dated several weeks later, which expressed disappointment that Petzoldt had been unable to visit him: "When I asked my son whether he had been able to meet you, he told me that you had unexpectedly departed . . . I am very sorry that you left without visiting me. I wanted to say something to you." [65]

This letter strongly suggested to Petzoldt that either Ludwig or Ernst Mach had not been telling the truth. Petzoldt concluded that it was Ludwig Mach.[66] From our perspective too much has remained concealed to give a final answer. Nonetheless, we might do well to keep in mind that Joseph Petzoldt was already publicly committed to linking Mach with Einstein's theory of relativity, and in this sense had a vested interest in the matter, that Ernst Mach was willing to go to great lengths not to alienate influential partial allies such as Joseph Petzoldt, and that Ernst Mach's only known attacks specifically directed against Einstein's theory of relativity (he never criticized Einstein by name) were both published posthumously under the supervision of Ludwig Mach. In other words, there is enough evidence to raise suspicions against the veracity of all three men, but not enough evidence either to settle the matter or to justify undermining the reputation of any of these able and well-intentioned gentlemen. Let it suffice for our purposes simply to mention that a problem does exist, namely, whether Mach accepted, or was vulnerable to being persuaded to accept, the theory of relativity during late 1913 and early 1914, and the jury is still out on the entire situation, including the veracity of the participants.

x

All the meager evidence available from late 1914 until Mach's death a year and a half later has suggested that he continued to oppose Einstein's theory. Three letters from Mach to Petzoldt in the fall of 1914 emphasized Mach's respect for Hugo Dingler, and again, Petzoldt was requested to talk to Dingler.[67] Ludwig Mach in his foreword to the ninth edition of his father's *Science of Mechanics* (1933) remembered: "I [Ludwig Mach] can only refer to the situation as it existed at the end of 1915 and only in so far as his writings on the subject are available to me. . . . 'I [Ernst Mach] do not consider the Newtonian Principles as completed and perfect; yet in my old age, I can accept the theory of relativity just as little as I can accept the existence of atoms and other such dogma.' " [68]

Our last piece of significant evidence comes in a letter from Čeněk Dvořák dated August 19, 1915, clearly in reply to one by Mach: "The best contemporary physicists would agree with you about the exaggerated speculation, mass suggestion, and modish tendencies in modern physics."

Six months later, during a lull on the Western Front, Ernst Mach died, to the end a pacifist who had heard about the outbreak of World War I only belatedly, and who never commented on it, either in public or in his known correspondence.[69]

Paul Carus pictured the cremation ceremony in lasting chiaroscuro: "Lying among the branches of the fir-trees under which of late he had loved to spend his time, in his left hand his cane which was his faithful companion for sixteen years, and on his head a laurel wreath woven by the hands of his daughter, Professor Mach's body was given to the flame in utter stillness on the morning of February 22." [70]

XI

After the war was over, Joseph Petzoldt, who was still trying to find a theoretical way to prove that the constancy of the velocity of light was "relative," continued to publish books and articles emphasizing the close epistemological and scientific relation between the ideas of Mach and Einstein.[71] He was even able to add a relativistic "afterword" to the 1921 edition of Mach's *Mechanics,* which he titled "The Relation of Mach's Ideas to the Theory of Relativity." [72]

In early 1914 Ludwig Mach had expressed his agreement with Petzoldt's understanding and acceptance of Einstein's theory of relativity, but sometime between 1914 and 1919 he turned decidedly against it.[73] Ludwig Mach wrote the following letter to Petzoldt from Augs-

279

burg on December 14, 1919: "Dr. Dingler once visited me in Haar, and I learned a great deal from that conversation. Dingler does not draw the same consequences as Einstein does from the deviation of light rays in the gravitational field of the sun, a deviation which is said to have been established beyond objection."

According to Ludwig Mach, his father did not want any of his books revised after his death, but he had no objection to special "forewords" or "afterwords" by people interested in his ideas.[74] For this reason Ludwig Mach had no initial objection to Petzoldt's pro-Einstein afterword but on discovering its contents Ludwig tried to balance it with a foreword by Hugo Dingler.[75] Petzoldt, who believed that Ernst Mach still intended that he, Petzoldt, should continue to be the literary executor of his works (as Petzoldt had earlier been with the books of Avenarius) disregarded Ludwig Mach's suggestion.[76]

Mach's son allowed the afterword to appear, but at the same time pointed out that in a supplemental contract his father had made him responsible for the publication of all of Ernst Mach's books.[77] In addition, Ludwig Mach had his father's *The Principles of Physical Optics* (Part I) published in the same year as Petzoldt's afterword appeared, that is, in 1921. Readers around the world were now faced with two simultaneously published books by Mach, one with his own preface in which he denounced Einstein's theory, and another with an afterword written by a longtime philosophical ally which favored the theory and asserted that Mach was a forerunner of it.

Petzoldt was upset by the anti-Einstein preface and threatened to bring the 1914 correspondence problem into the open if Ludwig Mach attempted to publish a disclaimer he wished to add to the next edition of Mach's *Mechanics* to undermine the effectiveness of Petzoldt's afterword.[78] As it turned out, Ludwig Mach waited until Joseph Petzoldt's death in 1929 and then removed the pro-Einstein afterword and inserted his own anti-Einstein foreword to the 1933 edition of his father's *Science of Mechanics*.

During the early years after the war, Petzoldt and Ludwig Mach kept up an extensive correspondence. The following excerpts from two letters by Ludwig Mach reflect his attempt to persuade the Berlin professor that Ernst Mach never accepted Einstein's theory of relativity. The second excerpt is from the final letter between the two men and was dated June 4, 1923.

I can only repeat once again, my father was not a relativist as that term is *currently understood.*[79]

If you want to prove out of my 1914 correspondence Ernst Mach's shortcomings at that time, so should you already know today that I was specifically ordered to deny your visit because of his persistently painful bodily condition.

Regrettably, however, in the interest of truth, I must tell you today, that his fundamental reason was so as not to have to talk to you about relativity any more.

XII

Albert Einstein and Hans Reichenbach reacted to the hostile preface to Mach's *Optics* by blaming it on his age and presumed intellectual senility, as if he had become too old to change his mind. They also were inclined to the view that a young Ernst Mach would have accepted the theory of relativity.[80] Hugo Dingler, however, thought otherwise.

The same man who rejected the theory of relativity, wrote his *Physical Optics,* wrote *Culture and Mechanics,* and wrote a whole series of popular articles. They were all written entirely by the old Ernst Mach himself. There is not the slightest sign of any diminution in his mental powers. His extensive correspondence and the testimony of those around him also confirm this point. . . . Reichenbach thinks that the young Mach without doubt would have been a convinced friend of the theory of relativity. Naturally, one has no absolute proof of such things, neither for nor against. But I think I am able to say from my knowledge of Mach, that at that time he would already have taken the position which he held later.[81]

Ernst Mach rejected the atomic theory and the use of multidimensions in physics during the 1860s.[82] Dingler was probably right in that Mach would have had to have been at least in his middle twenties or younger in order to have been favorably disposed toward Einstein's theory at first glance. Whether he could have overcome an initial distaste for it during his earlier years is of course something which cannot be determined with accuracy.

If Joseph Petzoldt found a Tartar in Ludwig Mach, he soon discovered an equally implacable foe on his other flank as well, namely, Albert Einstein. The latter was adamant in refusing to accept Petzoldt's "relativistic" interpretation of the constancy of the velocity of light. Petzoldt argued and argued, but Einstein would not give in.

What you say about circumference measures and clocks is completely untenable. I am talking about the unjustifiable *transfer* of propositions from the special theory of relativity to referential systems which are accelerated relative to inertial systems. Freundlich and Schlick are completely right here. According to your way of forming conclusions one could reason just as well, that every ray of light must extend in a straight line relative to any rotating system etc. Your misunderstanding is quite fundamental.[83]

In other words, even if Petzoldt was correct that in 1914 Ernst Mach either did favor Einstein's theory of relativity or Petzoldt could have persuaded him to accept it, had he been allowed to visit him, still, there is no evidence that Mach ever abandoned his opposition to either theoretical physics or the use of multidimensional geometries in physics. Furthermore, even if Mach was briefly carried away, it was only into sympathizing with or accepting Petzoldt's understanding, which Einstein considered to be a false understanding of the theory of relativity, primarily because of Petzoldt's effort to "relativize" the constancy of the velocity of light. If we mean by accepting the theory of relativity, accepting a version compatible with Einstein's understanding of his own theory, then we are now ready to give a flat unequivocal answer to the leading question in this chapter: Did Mach finally accept Einstein's theory of relativity? No, he did not!

Joseph Petzoldt eventually faced facts, but it was hard. Undaunted by Einstein's earlier opposition, he tried again in 1927, this time to draw the great scientist into an updated version of his earlier positivistic society, now called: The International Society for Empirical Philosophy. Einstein refused to join both because of its positivistic background and what he imagined was its "empirical," "antitheoretical" orientation.[84] Petzoldt finally blurted out in his written reply what he had tried not to recognize for so many years: "You assume that . . . [our society] serves a 'special philosophical tendency'. . . . But our name has only historical and tactical significance, very much like the name 'relativity theory', which because of your insistence on the constancy of natural laws is really an absolute theory." [85]

XIII

The remainder of Ludwig Mach's life was devoted to carrying out the specific instructions of his father with respect to conducting experiments to determine the exact, measurable nature of light, and completing the second half of *The Principles of Physical Optics*.[86] "We hoped by means of clarifying the problem of the nature of light to at least dampen relativistic speculation, when the war intervened and death . . . ended my father's suffering. . . . My father advised me above all to complete his treatises and to publish them individually and only then to concentrate on enlarging and arranging part II of the *Optics*." [87]

Mach's eldest son saw to the 1921 publication of part I of the *Optics,* to the 1923 publication of the *Popular Scientific Lectures* which included several previously unpublished articles, and to the 1933 reprinting of the *Mechanics*.[88] He also allowed unchanged reprintings of several other of his father's books. Through the years, Ludwig Mach worked on revising and enlarging *Culture and Mechanics,* conducted hundreds of experimental observations of solar and celestial light rays, and planned a short biography of his father.[89] Serious difficulties, however, stood in the way of completing part II of the *Optics*. First, he was no longer young; in 1920 he was fifty-two years old. Second, while he was a skilled inventor and experimentalist, his knowledge of both physics and philosophy was limited. Third, there were serious financial difficulties which hampered efforts to buy equipment and limited the time he could spend on experimentation. And fourth, and probably most important, several publishing rebuffs, a continuing series of illnesses and deaths in his immediate family, and the apparently inconclusive nature of his experimental results so depressed his spirits as to translate his lingering mental determination into experimental impotence and sloth, occasionally broken by ever rarer bursts of energy and high hopes.[90]

As a result of the loss of my hard-earned fortune in the war I regrettably have had to mortgage my house. . . .[91]

Increasing age, unfavorable living conditions, and the more than twelve-year-long illness of my wife who died in October 1931 has made everything more difficult and gnaws away at my life's goal.[92]

Since the death of my brother in 1933 there has been no one to help me in my experimental work. . . .[93]

In 1936, Robert H. Lowie, who had been in correspondence with Ludwig Mach, led a campaign to help Mach's son get back on his feet and finish the many tasks he had promised his father that he would accomplish or at least try to accomplish. Lowie published the following note in the magazine *Science:*

Dr. Ludwig Mach, the only surviving son of the late Ernst Mach, is threatened by economic pressure with the prospect of having to abandon the house and laboratories in which he has for years endeavored to complete his father's physical researches. The premises contain a complete archive with Ernst Mach's notebooks and diaries, on the basis of which Dr. Ludwig Mach had hoped to prepare a memoir of his father's life. Eviction from the valuable but heavily mortgaged property would mean the destruction of all the material assembled. 3000 to 4000 marks would stave off the immediate difficulty. Since the case is urgent, remittances of those interested should be addressed directly to Dr. Ludwig Mach, Vaterstetten bei München Landstrasse 61, Germany.[94]

The campaign, which somewhat ironically included a financial contribution from Albert Einstein himself, was successful and so encouraged Mach's son that he sent to Professor Lowie a prospectus of all Ernst Mach's writings that he intended to finish and have published. As the document is unique and as accuracy has some value, I quote it at length in German.[95]

Neuzuveröffentlichende Schriften
1. Grundzüge der physikalischen Optik Band II.
2. Neuausgabe von "Kultur und Mechanik" (in etwa 3–4 fachem Umfange das bisherigen und mit maschinentechnischem Anhang.)
3. Im Zusammenhang mit dem 2. Band der "Optik" sollen Abhandlungen über die Lichtgeschwindigkeit und den Ablauf der Lichtemission zur Veröffentlichung kommen. Ein Teil diesser Arbeiten steht mit der Vollendung einer jahrelangen Versuchsreihe unmittelbar vor dem Abschluss. Über sekundäre Interferenzen u.s.w.
4. Ein Bändchen technologischer Untersuchungen mit Betrachtungen über die Konstitution der Materie. Zum teil enthält diese Schrift ebenfalls eine Reihe optischer Untersuchungen von Ernst und Ludwig Mach.
5. Ein Bändchen soziologischer Studien.
6. Ein Bändchen enthaltend eine illustrierte biographische Lebenskizze über Ernst Mach von Ludwig Mach.

It is unlikely anyone will ever know how close Mach's son came to finishing his task before the catastrophe took place. Ludwig Mach had set up a 500-meter-long series of "light lines" in the forest and open country around his house in order to carry out his experiments on the nature of light.[96] He hoped that the isolation of his house and apparatus would keep electrical interference to a minimum. During the winter of 1944, however, the German army strung high-tension wires through the area where the experiments were conducted. All protests shattered against specific military instructions and the desperate needs of the failing German war effort.[97] Ernst Mach had specified that if the light experiments proved fruitless, then the second half of his *Optics* should be destroyed.[98] According to Frau Anna Karma Mach, Ludwig's wife since 1940, her seventy-six-year-old husband in a fit of despair and unrelieved weeping destroyed all the remaining unpublished articles and books by Ernst Mach.[99] Ludwig Mach had dedicated himself to aiding his father in any and every possible manner, but on the question of light and relativity he had failed. He died on August 22, 1951.[100]

Joseph Petzoldt had tried to find a theoretical way to replace the principle of the constant velocity of light. Ernst and Ludwig Mach sought an experimental determination of the nature of light. Einstein defined its characteristics; Mach wanted to know what light actually was.

If Ludwig Mach, or anyone else, could have experimentally proved Einstein's principle of the constant velocity of light in a vacuum, then Ernst Mach would surely have accepted at least that aspect of Einstein's theory of relativity, but theoretical physics aims at verification rather than proof. Hugo Dingler argued that empirical verification could never constitute proof.[101] If Mach accepted Dingler's point of view, then perhaps there was neither a theoretical nor experimental way to persuade Mach to accept the above principle and Einstein's theory of relativity.

On the larger question of Mach's influence on Einstein, one can hardly avoid the conclusion that in spite of the extent of that influence, there is something grotesque in considering Ernst Mach, the leading opponent of theoretical physics, as the "forerunner" of Albert Einstein, the most successful of all recent proponents of theoretical physics.

Mach and Buddhism

I

Mach developed an early interest in Chinese and Indian culture.[1] He was especially pleased by Chinese art, at least partly because it tended to ignore shading in the same way as he himself had done in his own drawings during his childhood: "I remember quite well that, in my childhood, all shadows of a drawing appeared to me an unjustifiable disfigurement, and that an outline drawing was much more satisfactory to me. It is likewise well-known that whole peoples, for instance, the Chinese, despite a well-developed artistic technique, do not shade at all, or shade only in a defective way."[2]

Mach was equally impressed by Chinese sight-see characters and social ethics:

In Chinese writing, we have an actual example of a true ideographic language, pronounced diversely in different provinces, yet everywhere carrying the same meaning. Were the system and its signs only of a simpler character, the use of Chinese writing might become universal. The dropping of unmeaning and needless accidents of grammar, as English mostly drops them, would be quite requisite to the adoption of such a system. But universality would not be the sole merit of such a character; since to read it would be to understand it. Our children often read what they do not understand; but that which a Chinaman cannot understand, he is precluded from reading.[3]

But *healthier* [than Christian morality] is an ethics, which, like the Chinese is based only on *facts*. Ethics and justice belong to social cultural training, and stand the higher the more rational thinking replaces vulgar thought in both fields.[4]

Mach's closest friend, Josef Popper-Lynkeus, was also an enthusiastic admirer of Chinese civilization. In particular, he believed that Confucian ethics could benefit the Western world: "I indicated in my work *Das Individuum* the usefulness of Confucian ethics in raising the level of civilization in Arian Europe (and America)." [5]

Mach's interest in Indian literature and science ranged from an acquaintance with classical Indian drama, through familiarity with the Hindu pantheon, to an attraction toward Indian mathematics and logic:

The old Hindu mathematicians wrote their theorems in verses, and lotus flowers, roses, and lilacs, beautiful sceneries, lakes, and mountains figured in their problems. [6]

The Hindus make use of the principles of symmetry and similarity . . . with a generality which is totally foreign to the Greeks. Hankel's proposal to unite the rigor of the Greek method with the perspicacity of the Indian in a new mode of presentation is well worthy of encouragement. [7]

II

From his earliest years, Mach showed a Buddhist respect for the life and feelings of animals. The first explicit declaration, however, of his "Buddhist conscience" came in his 1875 book *Outlines of the Theory of the Motor Sensations* in which he rejected the scientific necessity of vivisection. [8] Two of Mach's friends, Paul Carus and Theodor Beer, seem to have influenced him toward greater awareness of the epistemological and ontological similarities of his philosophy with Buddhism. On hearing about the suicide of Mach's son, Heinrich, Carus wrote the following letter to Ernst Mach (September 28, 1894): "Pure Buddhism is a serious religion which possesses its advantage precisely by looking death and the evils of existence straight in the eye. Buddhism is the religion which will become the next religion of science. . . . In the course of the following fourteen days to three weeks you will receive the next fruit of my labor, *The Gospel of Buddha.*"

Mach showed his appreciation for Carus's sympathy and books in the following footnote which he added to the first American edition of his *Analysis of Sensations*:

But to ask that the observer should imagine himself as standing upon the sun instead of upon the earth, is a mere trifle in comparison with the demand that he should consider the Ego to be nothing at all, and should resolve it into a transitory connexion of changing elements. It is true that on various sides, the way has long been prepared for this conception. . . . Cp. the standpoint of Hume and Lichtenberg. For thousands of years past Buddhism has been approaching this conception from the practical side. Cp. Paul Carus, *The Gospel of Buddha,* Chicago, 1894. Cp. also the wonderful story unfolded by the same writer in *Karma, A Story of Early Buddhism,* Chicago, 1894.[9]

Theodor Beer, a physiologist who attempted to introduce "physicalistic" language into psychology, and who wrote a "non-critical" book on Mach in 1903, was tried and convicted on a morals charge shortly after the book was published.[10] While in jail he turned to Buddhism. He subsequently wrote to Mach about his beliefs (February 18, 1908):

I find it necessary to speak to you on your 70th birthday and to thank you. Some of your suggestions have led me to the study of pure Buddhist literature, which without my becoming a complete, unconditional Buddhist, has nevertheless, yielded enormous stimulation, peace of mind, and continuing pleasure. . . . In the healing loneliness of prison I found a wealth of opportunity for the deepest self-examination. I also learned to treasure the practical-moralistic value of your teaching and from it, as out of the teaching of Buddhism, has developed the greatest consolation.

Beer journeyed to Ceylon in 1911, presumably to learn more about Buddhism. He may also have helped to spread Mach's ideas in that region. Two more quotations, one from Popper-Lynkeus and another from W. Fred, both testify to the fact that Mach's works were used in parts of Asia to give a measure of scientific authority to Buddhist doctrines, especially concerning the nonexistence of the "I" or "self":

The elimination of the "ego" manifestly reminds one of the analogous basic conception of Buddhism, and as Mach has told me, it was his treatment of this most important of all philosophical problems which is being used in India itself to support the Buddhist world view. . . .[11]

I had been on top of the great pagoda in Rangoon where the many thousands of gods stand, objects of prayer worshipped by Buddhists of all description, simple and cultivated, native and proselyte. . . . Then, as the sun no longer burned with such brazen heat, I passed through the narrow, bazaar-lined alleys of the city. . . . There . . . under books printed in all dialects spoken and written from the Nile delta and the Ganges to Mongolia, I saw something European. On the reverse side of a small, yellow book stood the name of the author written out in the language of his homeland: Ernst Mach. But the book itself had been published by the Buddhists in Ceylon, in their own language. I could not read it. Some weeks later in the main quarters of the *New Buddhist Society* in Columbo I first discovered that a whole series of writings of the Viennese philosopher, Ernst Mach, had been translated, and because of the similarity in point of view to Buddhist teachings, they were being disseminated as educational material and as a means of attracting followers in the various lands and islands of the East.[12]

III

Mach never wrote extensively on Buddhism or on his attitude toward it. His strongest statement was included in an autobiographical fragment written for Wilhelm Ostwald in 1913 which both he and Ostwald agreed should not be published. "After I recognized that Kant's 'thing-in-itself' was nonsense, I also had to acknowledge that the 'unchanging ego' was also a deception. I can scarcely confess how happy I felt, on thus becoming free from every tormenting, foolish notion of personal immortality, and seeing myself introduced into the understanding of Buddhism, a good fortune which the European is rarely able to share." [13]

Mach's correspondence and writings during his last years were filled with references to his approaching departure into "Nirvana." [14] One or two references might be considered incidental or even humorous, but his frequent use of the expression and the absence of any known reference to the Christian term "heaven" force us to take the matter a little more seriously. The natural conclusion would be, not that Mach became a "true believer" in Buddhism or in any organized religion, but that he did anticipate a future state of personal "nothingness," and tried to use the most accurate word available in referring to it.

On the other hand, Mach's grandson, Dr. Ernst Anton Lederer vividly remembers how religiously Ernst Mach tried to enforce Buddhist doctrine concerning the humane treatment of animals:

Beginning in 1899 my parents and grandparents lived in the same apartment house in Vienna (XVIII, Hofstattg. 3). In the rear of the 4 story house was a small space, the so-called garden, where I spent much time digging holes in the soil and closing them again. At the age of about 5, I snapped up from a conversation between grown-ups, that earthworms when cut each section will live, going its own way.

Determined to test this statement and equipped with my wooden toy-wheelbarrow and spade, I dug an especially deep hole near the plank fence. Soon I found several wiggling earthworms that I placed in the wheelbarrow. Their writhing motions were more obvious on the light wooden background than on the earth. Using the spade as a knife I cut one worm, then another and really the sections went their own way; remarkably there was no blood flowing. "What are you doing here?" boomed a deep voice from behind me. It was grandfather who observed my activity from the window of his first floor study and came out to get a close view.

Somewhat intimidated I explained my experiment. "Now suppose my boy a big giant would come and cut you in half to see how long you could survive; what would you say to that?"

"Put the worms back where they were and cover them with earth!" grandfather ordered. Of course I complied for I felt bad and sheepish that I angered my beloved good grandfather. The episode left a lasting impression for from then on I have never willingly harmed an earthworm or any other animal.[15]

IV

The shift toward Buddhism which many positivists made around the turn of the century has seemed very odd to numerous observers. Carl T. Jackson has described his own curiosity (1968):

It is fascinating that a man such as Carus, the highly educated product of XIXth century positivistic currents who prided himself on his modern scientific views should have inclined toward the ancient religion of a non-scientific culture. Nor was he the only example of this peculiar attraction. Lafcadio Hearn and Ernest Fenalosa, Carus's better known contemporaries likewise gravitated toward Buddhism from positivism; both were lifelong enthusiasts of Herbert Spencer. Like Carus they seemed to regard Buddhism and positivism as compatible and in many respects even identical systems. . . . More recently Aldous Huxley and Gerald Heard followed somewhat the same path. Both moved in the 1930's from views heavily colored by science to a mysticism deeply indebted to the Oriental religions.[16]

Mach, of course, did not share this mysticism, and unlike Carus and many other philosophical Buddhists who sought to reconcile the "essentials" of the great religions into an all-embracing pantheism, he felt an uncompromising antagonism toward several aspects of Christianity, its sects, dogma, and practice. Or to put the matter another way, his emotions ran much deeper against clerical "hypocrisy" than in favor of Buddhism. Mach never tired of abusing the "Christian" foundation of Western "superiority."

As soon as the Christians had won great influence, they turned against the dissenters both inside and outside of their own community. In 415 A.D.

under the leadership of the patriarch Chrillus, the outstanding Alexandrine mathematician and philosopher, Hypatia, . . . was gruesomely murdered.

The role of Judeo-Greek philosophy in helping to bring about the endless conflicts which divided the Christians into numerous sects is well-known.[17]

I consider the philosophical point of view of the common man with all of its prehistoric superstitions as more of a natural than an artificial development. It seems to me that Jesus and Plato have taken more from the common man than the reverse.[18]

I am not in a position to deal from a scientific point of view with such a self-contradictory, unscientific thing as the [Pope's] syllabus.[19]

Such disgusting stupidities as those of the Jesuits, how well I know them. . . . One even finds such nonsense with Faraday. With Newton there is documentary proof, and Brewster admires this sort of thing as much as he does science.[20]

You [Ernst Mach] do Luther and me [Marie Mach] an injustice. He has not, as you say, believed 997 of every 1000 stupidities, but 999.[21]

The fear of spirits is the true mother of religions.[22]

When a chemist who is famous for wonderful discoveries in his specialty yields to spiritualism . . . the intellectual damage runs deep, and not only with the lay public.[23]

Mach's hostility, his version of "écrasez l'infâme," while generally kept hidden from public view, was quite marked in his correspondence. It also resulted in at least one strongly worded, lingering controversy with an old friend, Mach's former student and assistant at Prague, Čeněk Dvořák. The latter, who had known Mach before he became a famous philosopher, was a strong Christian who defended his position with energy (October 12 and 18, 1905):

It pleases me that Flammarion did not bore you. He would have viewed your interesting observation from the year 1868 as proof of continued existence after death. . . .

I believe, that from this point of view, *Flammarion's* announcement has greater importance than all of the achievements of science. For the consolation which present-day science offers to mankind is as good as none at all. One pleasantly refers to the *bad* consequences of belief in immortality, and indeed, of belief itself; to that I would reply, that infinitely more people have been brought down and destroyed by mistaken theories and unskillful application of medical science than by all the witch hunts and religious wars put together.[24]

Mach's answer to Dvořák's argument has not survived, but there is some evidence that he knew how to turn his anticlerical thoughts into action. We have already mentioned his conspicuous role in helping to prevent the construction of a "free Catholic university" in Salzburg in 1902 and his front-page denunciation of the Pope's new syllabus in 1907. In addition, he was the only Vienna professor, albeit a "retired" one, who signed the 1912 manifesto of an international "Non-Denominational Committee" which had called on all Catholics to leave their church.[25]

V

It is doubtful if any one explanation could answer why so many positivists have leaned toward or adopted Buddhism. Each case has its own peculiarities and unique factors, its own history; nonetheless, there were at least a few common features of both positivism and Buddhism which probably have been operative in many of these "conversions."

Both positivism and Buddhism rested on epistemological phenomenalism; both reduced the "self" or "ego" to a mere "grouping of sensations"; and both rejected the common sense notion of "force" as a reality, as a causal determinant, and as an instrument for achieving human goals.[26]

Ernst Mach's rejection of Christianity and partial acceptance of Buddhism were logical consequences of his stand on the question of "force," and most likely numerous other Buddhist "converts" have reasoned or been influenced in a similar way.[27]

The Crusades, Reformation, and Counterreformation were referred to by Mach as evidence that Christianity was not really opposed to force itself but merely to the misuse of force or to its employment by the wrong people. This was not good enough for him. Mach, as a Utopian, believed that in an ontological sense force was unreal and that in a practical sense all violence could be eliminated from human existence. Peace could become a natural human condition where policemen and soldiers were superfluous, as if lions and wolves could be educated to see the advantages of coexistence with sheep and lambs, even in the absence of shepherds.

Mach accepted the anarchist position of Buddhism on force, at least in principle, but he denied its rejection of scientific progress. According to traditional Buddhist "lore," it was futile to try to solve human problems by active or scientific means. There would always be more problems, and there would always be more unhappiness than happiness.

The only true or "Eastern" solution was to eliminate conscious desires. "For he who never hopes [or desires] can never despair." [28] In spite of Mach's rejection of force he still believed that science could progress to the "Western" extent that happiness could be made to prevail over unhappiness. Expresssed in "East-West" terms, Mach's phenomenalism and "internal" purpose of science were "Oriental" and his Darwinism and "external" purpose of science "Occidental." Regrettably, the two hemispheres in Mach's "world" did not fit together very well, and giving priority to his repudiation of "force" as it was normally understood by practical people, then Mach was logically a Buddhist and illogically a believer in science.[29]

VI

Richard Hönigswald in 1903 seems to have been the first critic to point out the several resemblances between Mach's philosophy and Buddhism. Nor was he gentle in referring to the inconsistencies in Mach's point of view:

No less rich in relations is the practical side of his philosophy. Buddhist contempt for individual existence and vigorous life affirmation, anti-occultist free thought and mystical will-metaphysics all co-exist in peaceful harmony and offer welcome points of association for the most diverse tendencies of his readers. . . . Mach's Indian teaching of renunciation, the Buddhist belief in the nothingness of individual existence, includes no ethical principle, for it contains no principle of action.[30]

Mach's death year, 1916, saw a number of articles referring to Mach's restoration of Buddhist doctrine on the "self" or "ego." An article by Hermann Bahr was critical, one by Carl Haas, neutral, but those by Kurt Schmidt and W. Fred were conspicuously pro-Mach and pro-Buddhist.[31] The most enthusiastic observer of Mach's connection with the Oriental philosophy was Anton Lampa in Prague. His book *Ernst Mach*, published in 1918, ended as a paean to Mach and Buddhism:

Already at the age of sixteen to eighteen he [Mach] had had an experience . . . like that of the youthful Buddha on his first journey into the world where he saw the truth of suffering and discovered the way to end it.[32]

For Mach the moral order of the world is not the result of theoretical speculation, but is a demand stemming out of the warm feeling of his heart, from his "Buddhist conscience." [33]

Mach's thought shows a remarkable agreement in its main characteristics with those of Buddha in the exclusion of metaphysics and the concept of substance.[34]

The brief flirtation of many of Mach's followers with Buddhism at this time seems to have been closely connected with their opposition to World War I. For Austrian patriots the war was caused by the assassination of Archduke Ferdinand, heir to the Austrian throne, and the refusal of Serbian authorities to allow a thorough investigation into the matter on Serbian soil.[35] For German patriots their declaration of war on France and Russia and the resulting invasion of Belgium were caused by Russia's refusal to stop mobilizing troops and was strictly preemptive in nature, that is, it was forced by the need to avoid the disastrous consequences that most likely would have resulted had a fully mobilized France and Russia simultaneously attacked Germany.[36]

Many German and Austrian socialists, however, as well as numerous intellectuals, pacifists, and Jews, disliked war in principle and believed that actual wars were examples of "types" which in modern times were caused by egoism, militarism, armament industry greed, and economic and political imperialism.[37]

By 1917 strong civilian leadership under Clemenceau, Lloyd George, and Woodrow Wilson had developed to unify and strengthen the allied war effort. In Germany and Austria, however, the situation was entirely different. Civilian leadership continued to be weak, parliamentary opposition to the war grew in strength, and the frequent German efforts to set up a peace conference and the rejection of those efforts by the allies helped demoralize German and Austrian public opinion.

Central European "Machists" were split on the war, but several of them became conspicuous figures in the opposition. Friedrich Adler, as already mentioned, shot the Austrian prime minister in 1916. Anton Lampa and Wilhelm Jerusalem wrote pacifistically inclined books.[38] Philipp Frank tried to remain mentally neutral, and Albert Einstein, who still considered himself closely allied with many of Mach's ideas, refused to support the country of his birth, a nation that had recently granted him a privileged academic status in Berlin.[39]

Regardless of how well intentioned "Machist" pro-Buddhism and opposition to the conflict were, there can be little doubt that this attitude did not endear "Machism" to German and Austrian patriots, and that eventually there would be a reckoning, one that would restrict

Mach's conspicuous influence to ivory tower circles, uncorrupted by political realism.

VII

Robert Bouvier read Lampa's sympathetic account of Mach and Buddhism and devoted a section of his own work, *The Thought of Ernst Mach* (Paris, 1923) to an analysis of the entire relationship.[40] He concluded "Mach was a Buddhist without pessimism." He meant that while Mach's theory of economy and desire to eliminate problems were compatible with Buddhism, the Buddhist rationale for "simplicity" was missing. Mach believed that human feelings could not yet be examined with enough scientific accuracy to be able to make scientifically reliable statements about them, hence, he was unable to accept Buddhist claims about the predominance of "unhappiness" over "happiness" in life. Mach, the philosopher, accepted epistemological, ontological, and ethical Buddhism, but Mach, the scientist, had no place for the emotional justification for his choice. He did not regard the misery of life as in any way inevitable.[41]

Bouvier's book and Hermann Keyserling's once popular *The Travel Diary of a Philosopher* (1919) represented an end to a period of concern with Mach's attraction toward Buddhism.[42] Most writers since the early 1920s have ignored the entire matter. They have been concerned primarily with Mach as a philosopher of science, and honestly have not seen the relevance of this or any Oriental religion to his work in that field. They could not have been more wrong.

VIII

Since the Crusades, Western Civilization has been based on the judicious use and mixture of three different sets of values: the humane, the practical, and the heroic.[43] In general, they have represented Christian, mercantile, and aristocratic interests. Two of these sets of values, the practical and the heroic, have necessitated a realistic understanding of force and causal explanation. By the end of the seventeenth century, science, philosophy, and common sense had reached an agreement.[44] To "see" or "experience" the external or physical world no longer meant that sensory impressions or objects were the external world or even a part of it, but that noticed primary qualities such as size, shape, extension, number, density, and texture closely resembled or represented similar characteristics in the external cause of our sensory impressions. Secondary qualities such as color, sound, smell, taste, balance, and touch as well as tertiary or emotional qualities became entirely mental with no analogies in the physical world at all. Furthermore, mass, weight, and potential or actual force were added as qualities to all physical objects, even though it was freely admitted that they had no reliable resemblance to the feeling of pressure which probably first suggested them, or to any other sensory characteristic.[45]

Berkeley, Hume, and Kant during the eighteenth century destroyed the above synthesis of science, philosophy, and common sense by returning to presentationalism, that is, to the pre-Galilean view that noticed sensory impressions or objects were parts or aspects of the external world itself and not mere mental symbols or representations of it. The nineteenth and twentieth centuries have seen a continuation of presentationalist philosophy in positivism, logical positivism, pragmatism, idealism, phenomenology, and in a return to the most consistent form of phenomenalism and most extreme ideological opponent of force-oriented common sense—Buddhism.

The last two centuries have also seen a gradual decline in respect for the heroic values, a natural consequence of the elimination of the aristocracy from power in most Western countries.[46] This has left humane and practical values in a dominant position, one antiforce and the other force oriented.

Science developed in the seventeenth century on a force-oriented "knowledge is power" foundation. Scientific knowledge and understanding would enable men to become stronger and better able to influence or control their surroundings. Properly used, force could benefit man by helping him to solve problems and to become happier. The nineteenth-century attempt of Auguste Comte in the social sciences and Ernst Mach in the natural sciences to shift the basic assumptions of science from a representationalist to a presentationalist epistemology, and from a common sense to a Buddhist conception of force, has reintroduced the question of the desirability of science itself.

Almost all contemporary philosophy is presentationalist, and its most consistent form seems to be Buddhism, but if Buddhism is the final answer, then why have science at all? Buddhism does not need science, and Buddhistic, that is, kinematic, science will never satisfy common sense.[47]

Modern scientists, such as Mach and Einstein, who continued to live, speculate, and do research because other people who had not lost all practical and heroic values cared for and protected them could allow themselves the luxury of Buddhistic or pacifistic opinions, that is, reject two-thirds of the traditional Western triad of value systems. But how could such an attitude benefit science over the long run? How could a presentationalist, kinematic science serve the best interests of the business and laboring community and of policemen and soldiers who by necessity have to be representationalist and in large measure force oriented? [48] The answer is that it could not. Presentationalist, kinematic science was just as much a hothouse product as Buddhism and pacifism. They could survive only through the good fortune that at least a few humane and practical and heroic leaders have still retained political control in many intellectually significant countries. If "humane" values were ever to prevail to the full exclusion of practical and heroic ways of thinking among political leaders, then heaven help the human race.

If Buddhism were to prevail as a world religion, then science would have to go. If common sense with its triad of basically inconsistent value systems were to prevail, then many scientists would have to reform their purposes, beliefs, and methodologies. In particular, "understand-reality" or dynamic science would once again have to take precedence over "describe-and-relate-the-appearance" or kinematic science as it did almost four hundred years ago when Galileo during the original scientific revolution helped overthrow Ptolemy's kinematic approach to astronomy and corrected Aristotle's quasi-dynamic understanding of force.[49]

IX

The Buddhist theory of economy holds that desires cause problems and problems cause unhappiness and that if desires were eliminated problems would cease and unhappiness would vanish. Mach's theory of economy argued that problems should be eliminated and that, as a result, at least scientific unhappiness should vanish. Both approaches agreed in an economy of thought, since presumably thinking was responsible for a good many "unnecessary" of "superfluous" problems.

Max Born, perhaps unconsciously, pointed out the compatibility of Mach's *Denkökonomie* with Buddhist doctrine in the following critical attack: "If we want to economize thinking the best way would be to stop thinking at all." [50]

In spite of Mach's recognition of having a "Buddhist conscience" and of sharing a Buddhist rejection of the "self" or "ego," there is no evidence that he was aware of how close some uses of his theory of economy were to the Buddhist "cure" for human unhappiness. The drift in Mach's thinking, however, was unmistakable:

> Not all problems, which arise in the course of the development of science, can be solved; on the contrary, many will fall away because one recognizes them as *null* [*nichtig*]. By the *annihilation* [*Vernichtung*] of problems, which rest upon an inverted false manner of asking questions . . . science takes a fundamental step forward.[51]

> If one is able to demonstrate the unsolvability or meaninglessness of problems which many generations have tried to solve without success, then one has accomplished something which cannot be praised too highly.[52]

> Still less can I allow "motion" the right to create a world problem where none exists, and thereby to conceal the real point of attack in the investigation of reality.[53]

> Everything that we can want to know is given by the solution of a problem in mathematical form, by the ascertainment of the functional dependence of the sensational elements on one another. This knowledge exhausts the knowledge of 'reality'.[54]

Mach was saved, even if illogically, by his Darwinian "biological needs" purpose of science and life, but how did his followers escape from Buddhistic nihilism and its "final solution" of the human achievement problem? The answer was twofold: they did not fully escape (witness Lampa, W. Fred, and others), and while accepting Mach's "describe-and-relate-the-appearances" approach as an end-purpose of science, they rejected it as a methodology in favor of the Boltzmann-Einstein emphasis on theories, imaginative construction, and interest in new problems. Boltzmann saw that careful use of some theories could "describe-and-relate-the-appearances" in a logically simpler and less arbitrary way than could some direct applications of "mathematical functions." Einstein emphasized the occasional scientific necessity of speculation. Even though he himself had a personality sympathetic to Buddhism, pacifism, and a kinematic rejection of force, Einstein insisted on the rejection of "Mach-Buddhist reductionism" in favor of what he thought were those values most beneficial to the continued development of science.

I see Mach's greatness in his incorruptible skepticism and independence; in my younger years, however, Mach's epistemological position also influenced me very greatly, a position which today appears to me to be essentially untenable. For he did not place in the correct light the essentially constructive and speculative nature of thought and more especially of scientific thought; in consequence of which he condemned theory on precisely those points where its constructive-speculative character unconcealably comes to light, as for example in the kinetic atomic theory.[55]

CHAPTER 19

Mach's Influence on Early Logical Positivism and on Quantum Theory

I

The end of World War I brought socialist governments to power in Germany and Austria. They did not last long, but during their brief months of control several of Mach's friends and followers acquired a measure of political influence or advanced in rank in their academic professions. Anton Lampa entered the Austrian Education Ministry where he energetically promoted adult education. Wolfgang Pauli, the elder, became a regular professor in Vienna, and four other Mach allies were promoted from privatdozent to *extraordinarius* professor: Hugo Dingler in Munich, Joseph Petzoldt at the Technical University of Berlin, and Wilhelm Jerusalem and Heinrich Gomperz at the University of Vienna.

Mach's influence also expanded on the publishing front. All his major books reappeared in new German editions, his *Principles of Physical Optics,* Vol. I, added to his reputation as an historian of science, and his anti-Planck and anti-Stumpf articles were published in book form for the first time.

These last two were reprinted on the recommendation of the hero of the hour, Friedrich Adler.[1] Almost simultaneously with the death of Adler's father, he was released from prison and shortly afterward helped arouse Viennese workers to oppose a communist putsch of the type that had briefly succeeded in neighboring Hungary and Bavaria at the time (spring 1919). Adler then attempted to mediate between the 2d and 3d Internationals (the so-called $2\frac{1}{2}$ International), and on his failure permanently left for Zürich to become general secretary of what remained of the socialist Second International.[2]

His last contribution to Machist philosophy was his book *Ernst Mach's Overcoming of Mechanistic Materialism,* which had been put together from previous articles and was published in 1918 while he was still in prison.

II

F. A. von Hayek has described Mach's influence in Vienna immediately after the war:

I studied in Vienna exactly three years, 1918 to 1921, and as far as philosophical discussion went it essentially revolved around Mach's ideas. Vienna even at this time was extraordinarily focused toward scientific philosophy. Outside of Heinrich Gomperz, whom we have already mentioned, there were Adolf Stöhr, who thought along similar lines, and Robert Reininger [a Kantian idealist], who at least stood in a friendly relation to this orientation. . . .

For the young student interested in philosophy . . . who felt a distaste for orthodox thought, Mach was the only alternative. . . . I would also add that Ernst Mach's role was great not only in the narrow realm of the natural sciences, but especially in those fields where there were serious problems with respect to the methodological or scientific character of their theories. . . .

Today, I can no longer remember why I turned to Mach almost at once after returning from the field in 1918. My surviving list of classes unfortunately starts with 1919 and includes the remark: "and next *Knowledge and Error"* which presupposes that I was already familiar with other books by Ernst Mach. . . .

It is not easy to say why there was so much interest in Mach's philosophy. Already before the war the situation must have been quite similar.[3]

III

The major impact of Mach's influence in Vienna during the 1920s, however, was not transmitted by Mach's old followers, but by a new group whose first members largely came from Germany and who had especially strong interests in mathematics, physics, and symbolic logic.

Hans Hahn, a mathematician-educator who had long been influenced by Mach's ideas, began to teach at the University of Vienna in 1921.

The following year he invited Moritz Schlick, who in 1918 had written an impressive book on scientific methodology, to come to Vienna to fill Ernst Mach's old chair in the philosophy of the inductive sciences.[4]

Moritz Schlick (1882–1936) was born in Berlin, studied under Max Planck, and received his doctor's degree in 1904. Before coming to Vienna he had taught at Rostock and Kiel. His philosophy of nature from about 1910 to 1925 was close to that of Hermann Helmholtz in that he believed that sensory objects gave symbolically informative clues about the nature of the real world outside experience.[5]

Schlick, who had an agreeable conversational personality, started with small informal chats and by 1925 had collected a number of gifted professors and students into a circle which met every Thursday. Some of those who attended the sessions included Viktor Kraft, Herbert Feigl, Friedrich Waismann, and later the mathematicians Karl Menger, Kurt Gödel, and Gustav Bergmann.[6]

Bela Juhos, a member of the Vienna Circle who, with Viktor Kraft, became a leader of what remained of the movement in Vienna after World War II, has described Schlick's intellectual transformation from "realism" to "phenomenalism" and from an interest in ontology to one in linguistic philosophy:

> Schlick's starting point was the analyses carried out by Ernst Mach, Hermann von Helmholtz, and Henri Poincaré of the basic concepts and presuppositions of the individual sciences. . . .
>
> Under the influence of Wittgenstein and Carnap, Schlick's philosophical views underwent a profound modification, which he later characterized by saying that he no longer saw the goal of philosophy as acquiring knowledge and presenting it as a system of presuppositions but rather as the applications of a method. . . . Schlick no longer treated realism and idealism as factually contradictory theses but, rather, as alternative ways of speaking.[7]

The arrival of Rudolf Carnap (1891–1970) for a short stay in Vienna in 1925 and permanently the following year added another Mach-oriented physicist-philosopher to Schlick's circle. Carnap had studied at Jena and Freiburg and had been a student of Hugo Dingler at Munich. The latter had hoped that Carnap would become a disciple or follower, but this notion was rudely shattered when Carnap accepted Einstein's theory of relativity and firmly opposed Dingler's stand:

> My strongly conventionalist attitude in this article (1924) and in (1923) was influenced by Poincaré's books and by Hugo Dingler. However, I did

not share Dingler's radical conventionalism and still less his rejection of Einstein's general theory of relativity.[8]

Poincaré had already proven that the question of whether nature is Euclidean or non-Euclidean is meaningless.[9]

Carnap's debt to Mach came out clearly in his first major work, *The Logical Structure of the World* (1928): "Thus the analysis led to what Ernst Mach called the elements. My use of this method was probably influenced by Mach and phenomenalist philosophers. But it seemed to me that I was the first who took the doctrines of these philosophers seriously. I was not content with their customary statements like 'a material body is a complex of visual, tactile, and other sensations,' but tried actually to construct these complexes in order to show their structure." [10]

Rudolf Carnap was a classic example of a widespread contemporary limitation. He was simply unable to distinguish between presentationalist and representationalist philosophy with the result that he interpreted all philosophy in presentationalist terms, thereby distorting representationalist philosophy and making it literally impossible for him to understand the history of ideas or any point of view significantly different from his own. Under the influence of Wittgenstein's approach to language during the middle 1920s he completed his intellectual solipsism by declaring that all philosophy was merely a "linguistic variation" of his own approach, that is, of his own epistemological presentationalism. But since for him his position had no "nonlinguistic" alternative he felt safe in concluding that he held no ontology or epistemology at all! [11] In this sense he agreed with Auguste Comte that he was advocating a methodology and not a philosophy. And it is for this reason along with the Circle's "scientism" that one may correctly consider "logical positivism" to be a historical extension of "positivism" as it was understood in the nineteenth century.

The primary reason for Carnap's inability to understand representationalist points of view was his theory of reference, his phenomenalistic opinion that reference implied existence, at least phenomenal or conscious existence.[12] He insisted on treating reference as a form of experience as if we could not refer to or talk about what we could not consciously notice. For most people reference is not a form of experience but allows for characteristics which could or do exist outside possible consciousness. Sensations and ideas are normally not what people refer to, but merely symbolize or imperfectly represent the object of reference. In this way representationalist theories of reference differ drastically from presentationalist theories of reference. Carnap, like so many contemporary philosophers, failed to master the philosophical assumptions of common sense, and in particular the theory of reference which most practical people employ.

Given Carnap's presentationalist theory of reference it was only natural that he would be attracted to Wittgenstein's "verification theory of meaning," an approach that attempted to formalize presentationalist reference and place it at the core of scientific methodology.

Ernst Mach attempted to help "unify science" by means of his mind-matter parallelism and belief in the applicability of physical methods to all the sciences. Rudolf Carnap, however, wanted to go beyond this by eliminating all vestiges of pluralistic, mind-matter languages as well. In conjunction with Neurath he adopted "physicalism," which he originally understood as the thesis that "every concept of the language can be explicitly defined in terms of observables." In his first book (1928) he described those observables in a unitary "phenomenalistic" language, and later, he shifted to a "realistic" form of expression.[13] In this way he "abandoned" phenomenalism and "overcame" mind-matter dualism.

Otto Neurath (1882–1945) had become imbued with Mach's ideas as early as 1910 in his Vienna coffeehouse conversations with Hans Hahn and Philipp Frank.[14] During the war he corresponded with Mach and may have been allowed to read part of his manuscript on optics as a way of preparing himself for his own work on the same subject.[15] Neurath was a left-wing socialist who had briefly worked as a civil servant in the Bavarian Communist regime of 1919.[16] He was also deeply interested in sociology.

Otto Neurath not only wanted to abolish the distinction between "mind" and "matter" but also that between what the Germans call the *Geisteswissenschaften* and the *Naturwissenschaften*.[17] In this respect, he followed directly in the tradition of Jacques Loeb and the latter's pupil John Watson; indeed, he even called his approach "behavioristics."

Mach had engaged in a unitary "physicalistic" language when he called sensations "elements" and psychology "physiology," but warned by Jacques Loeb's epistemological confusions he thereafter tried to avoid ordinary language "physicalism." Indeed, it was precisely for this reason that Mach was reluctant to call microsensations "atoms." He feared that this identification would result in attributing ideas to the sensations which properly belonged to the historical or physical use of the word "atom" and not to the sensations at all.[18]

On top of the above difficulty the notion of "physicalism" was plagued by ambiguity. Sometimes it meant the definition of concepts in terms of observables, sometimes the applicability of the methods of physics to all the sciences, sometimes the reduction of "mental" to "materialistic" reality, sometimes it referred to a "realistic" as opposed to an "idealistic," "phenomenalistic," or "dualistic" language, and in its normal undefined use it vaguely suggested all the above by no means always compatible notions.[19]

It cannot be said that Neurath fully solved the "physicalism" problem any more than Loeb or Watson had, but Carnap's decision to avoid everyday "physicalistic" language in favor of an ideal, symbolic "physicalistic" form of expression at least met Mach's objection.

IV

The weak background of most members of Schlick's circle in the history of both science and philosophy and their presentationalist theory of reference helped to confine their thinking within narrow epistemological limits, but within those limits they also helped to bring about a continuing evolution and sophistication as they gradually learned much that they should have understood in the first place. This evolution has made it increasingly difficult to spell out their "system" in an unequivocal form which would do justice to their movement as a whole from 1922 to 1936 or in a larger sense until the present. When such attempts have nonetheless been made, however, they have usually focused on the magnetic influence of Ludwig Wittgenstein and on some of his better-known contributions. This approach of course has not done justice either to the variety of thinking in the circle, to its evolution, or to the few members who refused to be completely mesmerized by the inspired one, but it was correct in concentrating on the single doctrine most closely associated with the circle and most responsible for arousing the majority of practical scientists against the entire movement, namely, Wittgenstein's notorious "verifiability theory of meaning."

We have already discussed Mach's influence on Wittgenstein and the latter's influence in turn on Bertrand Russell.[20] We will ignore our mystic's pastoral existence after World War I in an Austrian village and concentrate first on his principle and then on his contact with Schlick's group. The "verifiability principle" in its most widely recognized form asserted that only those statements which were in principle empirically verifiable or falsifiable had meaning.[21] The problem, even apart from clarifying the expressions "empirical" and "verifiable," was that it arbitrarily limited the scope of understandability, encouraged premature dismissal as "meaningless" or "nonsense" of much that in fact could be understood, especially in terms of other theories of meaning and reference, and it tended to glorify ignorance as if the less one understood the better.

Its overt purpose was to provide a methodological instrument to help remove "metaphysics" from scientific investigation. In practice, it denied "intelligible" reference to what most representational realists meant by physical reality and all practical people understood by causes, namely, particular mental or physical forces located at particular places and times. It was not true, however, that every time a believer in Wittgenstein's principle used the term "metaphysics" or "nonsense" he was specifically attacking what Galileo, Descartes, and practical people considered common sense, but it was true that when such presentationalists were consistent they had to reject traditional common sense as well as all representationalist philosophy as "meaningless."

To allow rules, any rules, to determine meaning restricts communication by condemning all violations of the rules to nonunderstandability. To avoid unnecessary ignorance and misunderstanding most people in practical life have tried to keep communication open by subordinating expressed words and rules to what other people are most likely driving at, that is, they focus on intentions. In this way all philosophies and points of view, presentationalist and representationalist, have remained at least conceivably capable of being understood by everyone. Indeed, even when other people speak in a foreign language or use no expressed words or symbols at all, it is still frequently possible to understand them by focusing on what people in their situation or with their beliefs and background most likely intend to communicate and plan to achieve by communication. To be sure, the common sense approach lacks "certainty" and what is more vague or nonempirical than the notion of an "intention"? Nonetheless, intention-oriented communication works, avoids the arrogance of rule-determined meaning, and is so practical that the likelihood of it ever being abandoned by people who want reliable communication and who insist on correctly understanding the views of other people is next to nonexistent.

Presentationalist theories of reference as well as the "verifiability principle" oscillate between "strong" and "weak" versions or interpretations. The "strong" version identifies both the process or relation of reference and the referent in presentationalist terms; reference must be consciously immediate and the referent cannot have other than consciously experienceable characteristics. The "weak" version, which since the 1930s has been the dominant one, relaxes the presentationalist strictures on reference but not on the referent. Reference may now be representationalist and extend beyond what is immediately conscious, but the referent is still shackled and may not possess characteristics other than what in principle could be consciously experienced. Needless to say, this referential bondage still makes it impossible to understand representationalist epistemologies in a reliable way, and equally serious, means either that the history of philosophy (and much science as well) will not be understood at all or will be misunderstood in presentationalist terms as if such were merely a different "linguistic approach."

v

Ludwig Wittgenstein first published his *Tractatus Logico-Philosophicus* in Wilhelm Ostwald's journal, *Annalen der Naturphilosophie,* in 1921. A revised version was published in book form the following year in London with an introduction by Bertrand Russell. Also during 1922 Hans Hahn conducted a seminar in Vienna on the *Tractatus* which aroused Schlick's interest, so that by 1926 the circle was reading the book aloud sentence by sentence and analyzing it in detail.[22] Both Schlick and Carnap were especially impressed by it. The latter has described how the circle first came into direct contact with Wittgenstein himself:

In 1927 Schlick became personally acquainted with Wittgenstein. Schlick conveyed to him the interest of our circle in his book and his philosophy and also our urgent wish that he meet with us and explain certain points in his book which puzzled us. But Wittgenstein was not willing to do this. . . . Wittgenstein finally agreed to meet Waismann and me. Thus the three of us met several times with Wittgenstein during the summer of 1927. Before the first meeting, Schlick admonished us urgently not to start a discussion of the kind to which we were accustomed in the circle, because Wittgenstein did not want such a thing under any circumstances. We should even be cautious in asking questions, because Wittgenstein was very sensitive and easily disturbed by a direct question. . . .

His point of view and his attitude toward people and problems, even theoretical problems, were much more similar to those of a creative artist than to that of a scientist, one might almost say, similar to those of a religious prophet or seer. . . . [He] tolerated no critical examination by others, once the insight had been gained by an act of inspiration. . . .

I found the association with him most interesting, exciting and rewarding. Therefore I regretted it when he broke off the contact. From the beginning of 1929 on, Wittgenstein wished to meet only with Schlick and Waismann, no longer with me or Feigl, who had also become acquainted with him in the meantime, let alone with the circle. Although the difference in attitudes and personalities expressed itself only on certain occasions, I understand very well that Wittgenstein felt it all the time and, unlike me was disturbed by it. . . .

Neurath was from the beginning very critical of Wittgenstein's mystical attitude, of his philosophy of the "ineffable", and of the "higher things". . . .[23]

F. A. von Hayek has added:

They [Schlick and Friedrich Waismann], in turn, came to regard themselves as little more than the expositors of Wittgenstein's ideas, and to many of Schlick's friends in particular it became a matter of surprise that this fertile and mature mind should come to be so completely dominated by Wittgenstein that he would often hesitate to pronounce a philosophical question until he had heard Wittgenstein's latest views on the subject.[24]

Wittgenstein returned to England in 1929 where he finally received a doctor's degree and soon began teaching at Cambridge. At the same time he became increasingly dissatisfied both with the *Tractatus* and with the interpretation which the Vienna Circle, in line with Russell's introduction, had placed on it. Rudolf Carnap later described the situation:

When we found in Wittgenstein's book statements about "the language," we interpreted them as referring to an ideal language; and this meant for us a formalized symbolic language. Later Wittgenstein explicitly rejected this view. He had a sceptical and even negative view of the importance of a symbolic language for the clarification and correction of the confusions in ordinary language and also in the customary language of philosophers which, as he had shown himself, were often the cause of philosophical puzzles and pseudo-problems. On this point, the majority of British analytic philosophers shared Wittgenstein's view, in contrast to the Vienna Circle and to the majority of analytic philosophers in the United States.[25]

Stephen Toulmin, who has chosen to defend Wittgenstein on many points, seems to believe that Mach's influence was responsible for the Vienna Circle's "distorted understanding" of Wittgenstein's *Tractatus:*

> The argument of the *Tractatus* had employed the notion of "atomic facts" to correspond with the "unit propositions" of an idealized formal language. . . . But Wittgenstein had said nothing to indicate, how in practice, one was to recognize "atomic facts" or "unit propositions": this had not been his purpose. The logical positivists now remedied his omission. Taking a hint from Mach and from Russell's own doctrine of "knowledge-by-acquaintance" they equated Wittgenstein's "atomic facts" with the indubitable and directly known "hard data" of Mach's and Russell's epistemologies. . . .
>
> [But for Wittgenstein] definitions can have a logical force only or between one set of words and another; thus the ambition to establish formal relationships between words and the world, whether of "ostensive" definitions or otherwise, was unacceptable. Yet for Mach, that ambition had been fundamental if epistemology was to give the kinds of guarantees for natural science that he required.
>
> This was the breaking point . . . between Wittgenstein and the logical positivists. They would have to choose between him and Mach; and by and large they chose Mach. Yet they did so at first without consciously renouncing Wittgenstein, for as they saw it, there was nothing incompatible between the insights of the two *maestri*. . . . The idea of "atomic facts" lent itself at once to an epistemological use, if these facts were simply identified with the evidence of Mach's "sensations". And a dozen other gnomic remarks in the *Tractatus* thrown out in passing could be reinterpreted in the same sense. . . . Thus was born the hybrid system of logical positivism which professed to put an end to all metaphysics [i.e., non-experiential ontology] but succeeded, rather, in rewriting the metaphysics [i.e., experiential ontology] of Hume and Mach in the symbolism of Russell and Whitehead.[26]

Wittgenstein's repudiation of the Vienna Circle included both its use of ideal symbolic language and its particular type of phenomenalism, but he did retain a presentational realism with respect to the "external" or "physical world," nor should this realism be confused with older, more traditional uses of the term.[27] The "ordinary language philosophy" of Wittgenstein and his numerous English and American followers differed from both naïve and causal realism in rejecting force-explanation and from causal and Platonic realism in being presentationalist rather than representationalist in epistemology. He did, however, adopt a representationalist theory of reference in his opposition to "the private language theory" which went back to Locke. In other words, even though Wittgenstein gradually came to consciously oppose the phenomenalism of Mach and the Vienna Circle and especially their theory of reference he still fell far short, even in his later "language-game" years, of fully adopting causal, representational realism, that is, the realism of traditional (i.e., Galilean) common sense.

VI

In view of Mach's opposition to the atomic theory and his ferocious controversy with Max Planck, the recognized founder of quantum physics, it would seem out of the question that Mach could have significantly influenced the development of quantum theory. Yet, two different arguments or cases have been advanced to suggest just that; namely, Ernst Mach anticipated and may have influenced Max Planck's discovery of discontinuous phenomena; and Mach's use of a multidimensional mathematical theory of atoms preceded by fifty years and helped open the way for a similar methodological approach in quantum mechanics.

Heinrich Löwy published an article in 1933, "An Historical Note on Quantum Theory," in which he held that Mach had written in favor of discontinuous phenomena in a letter to Popper-Lynkeus dated five years before Planck's discovery.[28] Mach also included similar remarks in his 1896 *Principles of Heat Theory*, a book that Planck is known to have read with some care.[29] On the basis of Löwy's article and the letter to Popper-Lynkeus one of Mach's followers in the field of balistics and shock waves, General Viktor von Niesiolowski, wrote a scathing indictment of Max Planck in a letter to Ludwig Mach (February 14, 1941): "The above shows that Joseph Popper and Ernst Mach were undoubtedly precursors of Max Planck's quantum theory. *'By their fruits ye shall know them'* wrote Planck at the end of his lecture 'The Unity of the World Picture' in Leyden on December 9, 1908 against Ernst Mach. And now *this* must happen to him!! Oh 'the irony of world history'!!! Professor Bibl recently (1940) wrote a whole book on the matter."

Mach's "anticipation" concerned a phenomenalistic contrast of physics with chemistry. Physical appearances, such as in mechanics, moved or changed continuously, but chemical appearances, such as from a gas to a liquid, discontinuously evolved into something very different.[30] Oxygen and hydrogen gases, for example, were qualitatively quite remote from water, that is, when noticed as sensations rather than understood as groupings of atoms or molecules.

On the face of it, Mach's chemical theory was irrelevant to Planck's physical quantum discovery, which concerned energy emission, nevertheless, one could conceive that Planck in his search to understand black body radiation and spectrum intensities did consciously or unconsciously recall Mach's notion of discontinuity in such a way as to suggest energy quanta. Carlton Berenda Weinberg (1937) and Joachim Thiele (1968) have attempted to revive a measure of interest in Mach's theory of chemical discontinuity. Whether it should be regarded as a genuine "anticipation" of or as a significant "influence" on Max Planck's quantum discovery, however, may best be left to the reader's discretion.

VII

C. B. Weinberg pointed out in 1937 how Mach's pre-1870 ideas on using "n-dimensions" in atomic theory anticipated the later work of Erwin Schrödinger and other recent quantum physicists:

> [There is] substantial evidence . . . that Mach anticipated, by about half a century, some of the basic, methodological notions of present day quantum mechanics of the atom. For it is within the domain of *spectroscopy* of the elements, that modern quantum mechanists find it very convenient to talk about "n-dimensional space". . . . In comparing Mach's views upon n-dimensional atomic theory with those of modern writers, the difficulty of interpretation does not arise with Mach, but rather, with Schrödinger, Heisenberg and others. Mach's theory is set within a clear philosophical context—and that can scarcely be said of contemporary atomic theories. . . .
>
> From what has already been said, it should be evident that the purpose which lies behind Mach's introduction of n-space, is the desire to permit interatomic functions the greatest number of *degrees of freedom* necessary, for a correct representation of what can be observed and measured (e.g. atomic spectra). The ascription of n-space or of n-degrees of freedom is determined and controlled by the observable facts which are to be represented and placed within a convenient comprehensive symbolism. That is,

the assignment of the *number* of degrees of freedom is determined by the successful representation or correct description of the experimental material. This procedure is also characteristic of Schrödinger's quantum mechanics. . . .

For both the moderns and Mach, the mathematical postulates of the calculus and of the multiplicity of dimensions, ultimately serve to describe what is actually observed in experiment, namely, the complexity of lines in the spectra of elements. There is no doubt whatsoever in my mind, that had Mach lived to see the rise of Schrödinger's theory and the associated non-commutative mathematics, he would have claimed (and with considerable justification) that the quantum mechanics of the atom was merely a further substantiation of his doctrine that mathematical physics is an economic ordering of observable things (e.g. spectral lines), and that the *n*-dimensional space (e.g. six dimensions or degrees of freedom for two interacting electrons) *within* the atom has precisely the same significance as his *n*-dimensional space or *n*-degrees of freedom *between* the atoms. In both cases, there is provided an economical hypothesis capable of embodying, in convenient mechano-mathematical form, the equations or functions necessary for providing a satisfactory or correct description of the observed spectrum. . . .

If the present discussion has demonstrated anything at all, it has clearly shown that we would be quite justified in regarding Mach as the father of the modern quantum mechanics of the atom, so far as the *general methodology* of atomic physics is concerned.[31]

Mr. Weinberg also added, however, that Mach himself failed to explain line spectra by means of "the atomic hypothesis" and rejected the necessity of introducing multidimensional geometries into physics.[32] Indeed, shortly after Mach's speculation during the 1860s on the use of "*n*-dimensions" he abandoned and discouraged all further atomic theorizing.

VIII

But if Mach failed where Bohr and his colleagues succeeded in relating line spectra and the behavior of atoms and molecules, we still should not forget that several of Mach's ideas, particularly on the methodology and philosophy of science, have wormed their way, though admittedly often in distorted form, into the very entrails of quantum theory, indeed, to such an extent as once again to provoke the wrath of Max Planck.

Mach significantly influenced all quantum theorists through his criticisms of Newton's definitions of mass and force and his rejection of "absolute" motion, space, and time, but as with Mach's impact on Albert Einstein there was a confusion of physical and epistemological considerations. Einstein finally separated some of these factors out and at least tried to reject Mach's phenomenalistic point of view. Many quantum theorists, however, continued to employ an ambiguous conceptual mixture in both their methodological theorizing and in the "physical meaning" which they attached to their increasingly abstruse and complicated mathematical formalism. Opponents of this approach, and they have been very numerous among both philosophers and physicists, have labeled it "the Copenhagen interpretation of quantum physics."[33] Its chief advocates have been Niels Bohr, Werner Heisenberg, and Wolfgang Pauli, and its principal opponents Albert Einstein, Max Planck, Erwin Schrödinger, and Louis de Broglie.[34]

The Copenhagen interpretation, formulated by Niels Bohr and his institute friends and allies in 1926/1927, insisted that all micronature was necessarily both particle and wave in character, that this view would not be overthrown in the future, and that quantum physics was necessarily statistical and noncausal since it was impossible to understand the characteristics of particular particle-waves which of necessity were significantly altered by all observational or experimental attempts to measure them.[35]

This interpretation made use of a number of phenomenalistic ideas but not in the way that Mach intended them. There was talk, for example, about "describing and relating sensory appearances," but what was meant was the description and relation of highly mediated photographs and instrument data. Similarly, the Mach-sounding Copenhagen restriction on "meaningful" reference to observables was compromised in a variety of ways: by the particle-wave ambiguity of observables, by the un-Machian appeal to "theories," and by the act rather than content nature of the phenomenalism.

Mach believed that all sensations could be known with certainty and that ambiguities and paradoxes (such as the particle-wave nature of microsensations) reflected a verbal, conceptual, or methodological confusion. Heisenberg's "uncertainty principle," on the other hand, while admittedly phenomenalistic, was not compatible with this approach.

Mach opposed theories in "end-science" but made occasional use of them in "becoming-science" as transitional or methodological aids. All Copenhagen theorists and many of their opponents rejected Mach's position by introducing theories into both "becoming" and "end-science" as if theories could be indispensable even in the final formalistic stages of science. Quantum physicists also tended to be skeptical of Mach's theory of economy, especially in its biological form.

Mach was of the opinion that sensations were real even when unperceived or unconscious and when not in the presence of observational or measuring instruments. Copenhagen physicists, however, rejected this view as "metaphysical." [36]

The Copenhagen attempt to out-Mach Mach however, ran afoul of two major objections: it overly narrowed the methodological approach to be used in quantum investigation, and to numerous opponents holding a variety of different epistemologies and ontologies particle-wave duality seemed neither fully rational nor a final stage of human understanding. Mach's objection to the methodological narrowness would probably have been that the Copenhagen group unwisely transferred restrictions which legitimately applied to "end-science" and imposed them instead on "becoming-science," which in Mach's opinion should be left comparatively free and unrestricted.

The Copenhagen instrument-oriented, perceptual act phenomenalism irritated *content phenomenalists* who believed that unambiguous microsensations existed when unperceived and perhaps even when unperceivable, *presentational realists* who accepted the reality of microsensory objects, and *representational realists* who believed that unobservable microphysical objects were just as real as unobservable macrophysical objects, and at least in principle could be just as reliably understood.

But if advocates of all major epistemological persuasions could be found who opposed the "Copenhagen interpretation of quantum theory," then what philosophical position or positions did the Copenhagen theorists themselves accept?

IX

Niels Bohr (1885-1962) encountered epistemological phenomenalism in the writings of Søren Kierkegaard and a positivistic approach to science in the books of Harold Høffding, a family friend and noted historian of philosophy.[37] Mach's influence was conjectural, but may have come through Bohr's colleague at the University of Copenhagen, Anton Thomsen, or more likely, through his long friendship with Georg von Hevesy, who between 1900 and 1910 had, like Thomsen, corresponded with Mach.[38] Max Jammer has supposed that Bohr's sympathy with causal indeterminism could be traced back to the influence of Charles Renouvier and William James.[39] In later years, Niels Bohr became attracted to a form of relational "holism" as if particle-wave duality might be reconciled by means of a Hegelian or teleological "synthesis." [40]

Wolfgang Pauli, the younger, (1900–1958), perhaps the most acute and skeptically minded of the Copenhagen theorists, was the son of an active supporter of Ernst Mach, and indeed, Mach was his legal godfather.[41] Young Pauli became attracted to Einstein's argument that thought could not be deduced from sensations but possessed a measure of imaginative freedom. This notion encouraged him to reject Mach's mind-matter parallelism, and while he continued to use a positivistic approach in science, his philosophy as a whole drifted away from Mach through the years until in his old age Pauli became actively interested in Kepler's "archtypes," Plato's "forms," and Jung's unconscious "world soul." [42]

Erwin Schrödinger (1887–1961), the long-time opponent of the Copenhagen interpretation, who nonetheless made essential contributions to it, like Pauli grew up in Vienna and took Mach's phenomenalism and Boltzmann's methodology of science for granted.[43] Even in his later years (1959) Schrödinger still wrote in a pure Machian style: "It is the same elements that go to compose my mind and the world. The subject and object are only one." [44]

Werner Heisenberg (1901———) was a positivist in his scientific work, but like Bohr and Pauli has increasingly been unable to resist the lush jungles of traditional German nature philosophy. In his latest book, *The Part and the Whole* (1969), he is on the lookout for a "world purpose." In light of Heisenberg's "uncertainty principle" one might have suspected that he sympathized with Mach's philosophy, but he has explicitly denied this (1962):

No. I must say that I never have read Ernst Mach quite seriously. I have later on studied it a little bit, but that was much later. And in some way I was never much impressed by Mach. I was impressed by Einstein's way of doing things, but not by Mach's. And why was that? I would say Mach was always a bit formal for me. It was too—I would say not too negative, but too modest in what he wanted. It was perhaps I should say, too little poetical. I mean, Plato is, of course, a poet; that's obvious. Kant is not a poet, but still he has some poetry even in the way he writes, but Mach, I would say is very little poetical. I mean the positivist is very frequently not practical with perhaps the exception of Wittgenstein who is in some way also a poet.[45]

Pascual Jordan (1902———) has probably been the most outspoken Machist among all the quantum theorists who have contributed to or accepted the Copenhagen interpretation: "Yes, he [Mach] strongly influenced me. Basically, even today I am still a follower of Mach, though of course I am critical on points of detail. But fundamentally I have constructed my physical thinking an Mach's conceptions, which have later proved most helpful in the understanding of quantum mechanics and the theory of relativity." [46]

Jordan was one of the very few followers of Mach who dared publish articles and books honoring the Austrian professor and *Judenfreund* in Nazi Germany.[47] Most Austrian and German celebrations of the hundredth anniversary of Mach's birth, which were to take place in 1938, were discouraged or canceled, but Jordan in *Festung* Rostock continued to sing Mach's praises.

x

Ernst Mach rejected Einstein's theory of relativity partly because of its reliance on multidimensional geometries.[48] It is more than likely that he would have rejected much of quantum theory on the same grounds. Both Mach and Dingler predicted that the use of *"n-*dimensions" and the like would result in logical paradoxes and serious problems of interpretation. Dingler at least lived long enough to conclude "I told you so" and Mach would surely have joined the chorus.[49] Mach believed that all mathematical symbolism should have a clear "physical meaning," but neither multidimensionality nor particle-wave duality allow this. Nor would Mach have been amused by causal indeterminism.

Multidimensionality made force-oriented causal explanation literally unimaginable, but this was not a problem for Mach since he rejected forces as causes in any case, but the Copenhagen statistical approach with its refusal to allow that particular particle-waves could be understood in causal fashion of any kind, would have been a most provocative red flag for him. Mach believed that causes were mathematical functions and that such functions could be found to relate all "phenomena." The notion that particle-waves were exempt from functional determinism except on a statistical basis conflicted with his positivistic belief that all problems were either solvable or "meaningless." If particular particle-waves were real, then they had to be understandable in functional terms, and if they were not real, then such an ambiguously defined notion should be abandoned in favor of what did less violence to conceptual rationality. Mach wanted clarity, but even though the Copenhagen interpretation was largely phenomenalistic in epistemology, it has not yet provided this.

XI

As might have been expected, quantum theory in general and the Copenhagen interpretation in particular proved godsends to a number of previously rejected "scientific" ideas. Gustav Jaumann, for example, and his "Brünn school" of continuum physics now had at least a partial defense in the continuity aspects of the quantum statistical approach, to the extent that even after Jaumann's death in 1924 his colleague Erwin Lohr was still able to keep this lingering version of antiatomism alive.[50] Indeed, in a sense, it was fitting that Mach's birthplace should have been the last stronghold of "pure" Machist science.[51] In 1945 with the Russian "liberation," another philosophical orientation, of course, took charge. In a philosophical sense, it might be interesting to note that Czechoslovakia, with its long history of "Machism" and "Brentanoid" thought (it was the last major European bastion of Machist philosophy after Hitler's rise to power) was probably the least prepared of any nation for an invasion of "dialectical materialism." But be that as it may, Lenin had finally gained yet another measure of revenge against "Machism."[52]

Speaking of Communist philosophy, it too has recently become grateful for the Copenhagen interpretation. The notion of a "dialectical process in nature" used to be an embarrassment for Soviet and other left-wing scientists, but now, the particle-wave duality seemed to prove that there really were "contradictions in nature." And who knows, perhaps still cleverer quantum physicists will eventually discover a "dialectical synthesis" to "reconcile" the duality and thus help further "the inevitable course of world history."

But seriously, lest one be carried away by the implausibility of the Copenhagen interpretation of quantum physics, one must at least admit, that regardless of how uninformative its "physical meaning" may be, quantum theory as a mathematical system does work.[53] And if one merely seeks a convenient symbolic tool, and not understanding, much less a common sense interpretation, then that should suffice. Bohr and Heisenberg may have thought their interpretation permanent, but even if one is inclined to doubt this, one should not confuse either their methodological narrowness or any kind of "physical meaning" with the mathematical system itself. The latter will surely be extended and perhaps some of its multidimensional geometry modified or abandoned, but total revision is probably much less likely than for "the thousand year Copenhagen interpretation" itself.

Planck argued "By their fruits ye shall know them," but should the current "physical meaning" of quantum theory be blamed on Ernst Mach? Or perhaps even on Max Planck himself? Or has this particular fruit rotted only since its stay in Denmark? Hamlet wondered "to be or not to be," a very profound question. Niels Bohr and Polonius Heisenberg have labored long and skillfully to find a solution. But in spite of all their mathematical and methodological wisdom is particle-wave duality really the final answer?

Appendix

DID MACH FINALLY ACCEPT THE REALITY OF ATOMS?

Until 1950 it was generally believed that Mach never altered his opposition to the reality of atoms. Many people tried to persuade him, but he would always answer: "Have you seen one?" And that ended the discussion.[1] But Stefan Meyer, a former assistant of Boltzmann, published an article in that year in which he claimed to have been present when Mach changed his mind and accepted the reality of atoms.

According to Meyer, shortly after the invention of the spinthariscope, an instrument that detected alpha ray scintillations, he invited Ernst Mach, who was then retired, to take a look through the instrument and judge the reality of what he saw for himself. Mach entered the darkened room and then looked at the screen. Stefan Meyer continued: "It remains one of my most striking remembrances, when Mach after the introduction of the spinthariscope did not make obstinate objections, but simply declared: 'Now I believe in the existence of atoms.' An entire world view had changed in a few minutes."[2]

Did Mach really change his mind? In the rest of this appendix I marshal evidence pro and con and then add my own analysis and conclusion.

To help corroborate Meyer's story I have tried to contact people who knew him. This is part of a letter from a well-known Viennese scientist, Karl Przibram:

I shall try to answer your questions to the best of my ability. 1) Do you remember this story (about St. Meyer's meeting with Ernst Mach)? Yes, I do remember Meyer relating it several times, always in the same way. 2) Do you accept Stefan Meyer's account of it? Of course I do, knowing from long friendship Meyer's upright, truthful character. 3) Do you think Mach changed his attitude towards atoms? Yes I do. But I also think that Meyer's words about "ein ganzes Weltbild" being changed is not to be taken too literally. I do not think that Mach will have given up his positivistic views, but only conceded that atoms now fitted into them. 4) When did the meeting happen? I don't know, but I do not think that Meyer would have hesitated long to show Mach the spinthariscope when it became known in 1903.[3]

Fritz Chmelka published an article in 1966 which supported Meyer's contention and which may have been based on an independent source: "Mach's student, Anton Lampa, reported, however (in his lecture), that Mach had been greatly shaken when shown scintillations for the first time, flashes of light, which originate by the impingement of alpha particles from a radioactive preparation on a zinc sulfide screen, and which made the effects of atom nuclei immediately visible."[4]

Meyer, Przibram, and Chmelka have surely presented a strong case for the affirmative, that the spinthariscope episode did take place, and that Mach was strongly affected by it; nonetheless, the evidence against both the episode and its impact is also considerable. In particular, Mach never mentioned the episode either in his published writings or in his known correspondence. Furthermore, he wrote extensively on the reality of atoms after 1903, the year the spinthariscope was introduced into Vienna, and he continued to deny their existence until his death. Also, a former student and long-time friend specifically asked Mach whether recent discoveries had changed his mind, and according to Bohuslav Brauner the answer was negative:

As one of the oldest pupils of Mach who worked with him on fluorescence in 1877 and enjoyed his warm friendship since 1876, I often had an opportunity of discussing atomism with him. Not long before the War, I was sitting with him in his garden in Vienna, and I remember that he said to me: "Atomism is a good working hypothesis for the study of chemistry; it must be used with great care on studying and working in science; but it is extremely dangerous as a noetic theory." . . . At the beginning of the War, I asked him in a letter whether he considered the results of all the observations in radioactivity as a proof of the existence of atoms, and he replied to me verbally: "I do not make myself a proselyte of my ideas—

do not make yourself a proselyte on atomism." He never changed his ideas up to his death.[5]

Here are some quotations published by Mach after 1903 including several originally written between 1910 and 1915. They all support Brauner and the contention that Mach did not change his attitude toward the reality of atoms. To be precise, the first two quotations were written before 1903 but retained in all editions after that time. The third quotation was originally written and published in 1910. The fourth, fifth, and sixth quotations were written in the late 1890s, 1913, and 1915, respectively, and were published for the first time in 1905, 1921, and 1933 (see notes 6–11, bibliography, and Joachim Thiele, "Ernst Mach-Bibliographie," *Centaurus*, 8 (1963), 189–237).

Atoms cannot be perceived by the senses; like all substances they are things of thought. Furthermore, atoms are invested with properties that absolutely contradicted the attributes hitherto observed in bodies.[6]

Still less, therefore, will the monstrous idea of employing atoms to explain psychical processes ever get possession of us, seeing that atoms are but the symbols of those peculiar complexes of sensational elements which we meet with in the narrow domains of physics and chemistry.[7]

The results of the atomic theory can be just as manifold and useful if one is not in such a hurry to treat atoms as realities. Therefore all honor to the beliefs of physicists! But I myself cannot make this particular belief my own.[8]

Our geometry always refers to objects of sensuous experience. But the moment we begin to operate with mere things of thought like atoms and molecules, which from their very nature *can never be made the objects of sensuous contemplation,* we are under no obligation whatever to think of them as standing in spatial relationships which are peculiar to the Euclidean three-dimensional space of our sensuous experience. This may be recommended to the special attention of thinkers who deem atomistic speculations indispensable.[9]

I must, however, as assuredly disclaim to be a forerunner of the relativists as I withhold from the atomistic belief of the present day.[10]

I do not consider the Newtonian principles as completed and perfect; yet in my old age, I can accept the theory of relativity just as little as I can accept the existence of atoms and other such dogma.[11]

One explanation would be that perhaps Mach did observe the spinthariscope scintillations but was not as impressed as Meyer thought. As another explanation one might speculate that Mach was only temporarily persuaded.[12] A third explanation would be to identify Mach's reaction with that of his ally and follower Joseph Petzoldt. The latter managed to retain his phenomenalism and yet accept the reality of atoms by redefining "atoms" as "complexes of microsensations."[13] But if Mach agreed with Petzoldt, how are we to explain the above quotations explicitly directed against the reality of atoms in any form, except as ideas? The best answer would be that we cannot explain them in terms of Petzoldt's solution at all. Indeed, there is every evidence from Mach's published works that few if any of his followers properly understood Mach's position on the reality of atoms.

If we go directly to Mach's *Analysis of Sensations* which he personally checked and revised in 1912, we read: "If ordinary 'matter' must be regarded merely as a highly natural, unconsciously constructed mental symbol for a relatively stable complex of sensational elements, much more must this be the case with the artificial hypothetical atoms and molecules of physics and chemistry."[14]

Both the spinthariscope episode and Mach's stand on the nature and reality of atoms should now be clear. The spinthariscope episode did occur and Mach was shocked, shocked by the existence of extremely minute microsensations as represented in magnified form on a screen, and he may have briefly called those sensations "atoms" before reflecting on their actual character. The microsensations existed, but they were not "atoms," first, because all "material objects" including "atoms" were merely "mental symbols" for groups of sensations, and second and most important, because "atoms" as they were understood in physics could only be properly understood in a space of more than three dimensions, but the space of sensations, including microsensations, was only three-dimensional and could never be more than three-dimensional.[15]

Mach had held this position on the reality of atoms from the early 1860s, and the spinthariscope episode did not change it at all.[16] The only change was that Mach now accepted the existence of extremely small complexes of microsensations, which some phenomenalists such as Joseph Petzoldt and Anton Lampa, but not Mach, identified with "atoms." One may add that Mach's position on the need to understand "atoms" in a space of more than three dimensions anticipated aspects of recent quantum theory as has already been discussed in chapter 19.

Did Mach finally accept the reality of atoms? No, he did *not!* Atoms required a space of more than three dimensions for satisfactory explanation, but the real world, that is, the world of sensations, could never have more than three dimensions, hence, atoms were unreal.

Mach the phenomenalist and ally of David Hume doomed the understanding of Mach the scientist. Mach's form of phenomenalism was not compatible with belief in the reality of atoms.

Notes

I. CHILDHOOD

1. Karl Kühn, "Ernst Machs Herkunft und Abstammung," *Heimatbildung*, 19 (1938), 269.
2. Liebenau/Hodkovice.
3. Richard W. Eichler, *Liebenau in Sudetenland* (Munich, 1966, pp. 119-120.
4. 1880 Auto., p. 1.
5. Kühn, *op. cit.*
6. František Kavka, *The Caroline University of Prague* (Prague, 1962), p. 46.
7. Kühn, *op. cit.*
8. A private communication from Frau Anna Karma Mach (1967).
9. *Ibid.*
10. (Marie Mach), *Erinnerungen einer Erzieherin* (Vienna, 1913), p. 5.
11. Kühn, *op. cit.*, p. 268. Brünn/Brno, Chirlitz/Chrlice, Turas/Tuřany. I am indebted to Dr. Josef Sajner of Brno for helping to clear up the confusion concerning Mach's birthplace.
12. 1913 Auto., p. 1.
13. Lundenburg/Břeclav. 1910 Auto., p. 1.
14. *AOS* (New York, 1959), p. 96.
15. *PSL* (La Salle, Ill., 1943), pp. 76-77.
16. *Ibid.*, p. 82.
17. *E & I* (Leipzig, 1917), p. 102.
18. *AOS*, p. 15.
19. (Marie Mach), *op. cit.*, p. 10.
20. *CAOS* (Chicago, 1897), p. 37.
21. *COE* (Chicago, 1911), pp. 64-65.
22. Floyd Ratliff, *Mach Bands* (San Francisco, 1965), p. 9.
23. Robert H. Lowie, "Letters from Ernst Mach to Robert H. Lowie," *Isis*, 37 (1947), 66.
24. Carl Haas, *Hofrat Dr. Ernst Mach* (Vienna, 1916), p. 2.
25. 1880 Auto., pp. 1-2.
26. 1910 Auto., p. 1.
27. 1913 Auto., p. 1.
28. *Ibid.*

29. Wilhelm Jerusalem, "Erinnerungen an Ernst Mach," *Neue Freie Presse* (Vienna), no. 18509, Morgenblatt, March 2, 1916, p. 1, col. 1.

30. (Marie Mach), *op. cit.*, pp. 11 and 13.

31. Ernst Mach to Paul Carus, Prague, Oct. 21, 1892.

32. 1910 Auto., p. 2.

33. *AOS*, p. 30.

34. *Ibid.*

35. Kremsier/Kronměříž. 1910 Auto., p. 3.

36. 1880 Auto., p. 2.

37. *Ibid.*, pp. 2-3.

38. (Marie Mach), *op. cit.*, pp. 14-26.

2. YOUNG SCIENTIST

1. Ernst Mach to Hugo Dingler, Vienna, March 16, 1911.

2. Josef Gicklhorn, "Josef Petzval," *Österreichische Naturforscher und Techniker* (Vienna, 1951), p. 134.

3. Ernst Mach to Hugo Dingler, Vienna, Nov. 20, 1912.

4. Ernst Mach, *Compendium der Physik für Mediciner* (Vienna, 1863).

5. *AOS* (New York, 1959), p. 370.

6. Ernst Mach, "Vorträge über Psychophysik," *Zeitschrift für praktische Heilkunde*, 9 (1863), 146-148, 167-170, 202-204, 225-228, 242-245, 260-261, 277-279, 294-298, 316-318, 335-338, 352-354, 362-366.

7. See photograph of handbill advertising these lectures.

8. Ernst Mach, "Über die Verwerthung der Mikrophotographie," *Photographische Correspondenz*, 13 (1876), 227-228.

9. Ernst Mach, "Vorträge über Psychophysik," pp. 8-9 (preprint pagination).

10. *AOS*, p. 109.

11. J. W. S. Rayleigh, *The Theory of Sound*, Vol. II (New York, 1945), p. 155.

12. Ernst Mach, "Neue Versuche zur Prüfung der Doppler'schen Theorie der Ton und Farbenänderung durch Bewegung," *SW*, 77 (1878), 299-310.

13. Leo Gilbert to Ernst Mach, Aug. 1 and 18, 1913.

14. Anton Lampa, *Ernst Mach* (Prague, 1918), p. 9.

15. Ernst Mach, "Untersuchungen über den Zeitsinn des Ohres," *SW*, 51 (1865), 133.

16. Ernst Mach, "Vorträge über Psychophysik," p. 22 (preprint pagination).

17. Ernst Mach, "Zur Theorie der Pulswellenzeichner," *SW*, 47 (1863), 43.

18. *COE* (Chicago, 1911), p. 87.

19. *PSL* (La Salle, Ill., 1943), p. 307.

20. Eduard Kulke, *Kritik der Philosophie des Schönen*, Foreword by Ernst Mach (Leipzig, 1906), p. xi.

21. Eduard Kulke, *Über die Umbildung der Melodie* (Prague, 1884), p. 2.

22. I am deeply obliged to Dr. Ernst Anton Lederer for sending me this story and to his mother Carolina Lederer for having transcribed it in the first place.

23. 1910 Auto., p. 6.

24. *COE*, p. 88.

25. Joachim Thiele, "Ernst Mach: Bibliographie," *Centaurus*, 8 (1963), 199-200.

26. Joachim Thiele, "Briefe von Gustav Theodor Fechner und Ludwig Boltzmann an Ernst Mach," *Centaurus*, 12 (1967), 222-226.

27. *Leitgedanken* (Leipzig, 1919), p. 3.
28. Wilhelm Jerusalem, "Ernst Mach," *Die Zukunft*, 95 (1916), 326.

3. PHILOSOPHICAL DEVELOPMENT

1. In later years Mach denied both that he was a philosopher and that he had a philosophy. This stand should be understood in terms of Mach's occasional identification of philosophy with "metaphysics" and his acceptance of Comte's "three stages of progress" with its identification of "metaphysics" with a pre-scientific stage.

2. K. R. Popper, "A Note on Berkeley as a Precursor of Mach," *British Journal for the Philosophy of Science*, 4 (1953), 26–36; John Myhill, "Berkeley's 'De Motu': An Anticipation of Mach," *University of California Publications in Philosophy*, 29 (1957), 141–157.

3. Ernst Mach, *The Science of Mechanics* (6th ed.; La Salle, Ill., 1960), p. xiii, introduction by Karl Menger.

4. *AOS* (New York, 1959), pp. 361–362.

5. *Ibid.*, pp. 37, 56.

6. *PW* (Leipzig, 1900), pp. 211, 365.

7. See chapter 12 for a discussion of Mach's "internal," "intermediate," and "external" purposes of science.

8. Gustav Fechner, *Elements of Psychophysics*, Vol. I, trans. Helmut E. Adler (New York, 1966), p. 7.

9. Thomas Case, "Metaphysics," *Encyclopaedia Britannica*, Vol. 18 (11th ed.; London, 1910–11), p. 234.

10. *AOS*, pp. 60–61.

11. *Ibid.*, p. 341.

12. Stephen F. Mason, *A History of the Sciences* (New York, 1962), p. 454: "From about 1820 to 1860 the atomic theory did not play a prominent part in chemistry. For the most part chemists preferred to use the directly determined equivalent weights of the elements, rather than the atomic weights which involved uncertain estimates as to the combining numbers of the atoms."

13. Mach did advocate what he called a "universal physical phenomenology," however (*PSL* [La Salle, Ill., 1943], p. 250). In this book I use "phenomenalism" as the general term and confine "phenomenology" to the philosophy of Edmund Husserl and his associates and followers.

14. *AOS*, p. 12: "The assertion, then is correct that the world consists only of our sensations. In which case we have knowledge *only* of sensations."

15. *Ibid.*, p. 363: "The external world, it is felt, is not adequately expressed as a sum of sensations; in addition to the actual sensations, we ought at least to bring in Mill's possibilities of sensation. In reply to this, I must observe that for me also the world is not a mere sum of sensations. Indeed, I speak expressly of functional relations of the elements."

16. E. A. Burtt, *The Metaphysical Foundations of Modern Science* (New York, 1954), pp. 233–239.

17. *AOS*, p. xl.

18. *COE* (Chicago, 1911), p. 17.

19. *S & G* (La Salle, Ill., 1960), p. 104.

20. *COE*, p. 87.

21. Ludwig Boltzmann, *Populäre Schriften* (Leipzig, 1925), p. 339.

22. Ernst Mach, *Compendium der Physik für Mediciner* (Vienna, 1863), p. 13.
23. *SOM* (La Salle, Ill., 1960), p. 599.
24. Stillman Drake, *Discoveries and Opinions of Galileo* (New York, 1957), pp. 166–167.
25. *Ibid.*, p. 163.
26. *PW*, p. 365.
27. *AOS*, p. 29.
28. *E & I* (Leipzig, 1917), p. 9.
29. *AOS*, pp. 24 & 27.
30. Case, *op. cit.*, p. 234.
31. *AOS*, p. 24.
32. See chapter 18.

4. PRAGUE PROFESSOR

1. K. D. Heller, *Ernst Mach: Wegbereiter der modernen Physik* (Vienna, 1964), p. 16.
2. *PWV* (Leipzig, 1923), p. 428.
3. *Ibid.*
4. Heller, *op. cit.*
5. *PWV*, p. 428.
6. Heller, *op. cit.*, pp. 16–17.
7. *Ibid.*, p. 17.
8. *Ibid.*
9. Ernst Mach to Johannes Purkyně, Prague, June 14, 1867.
10. Wilhelm Jerusalem, "Erinnerungen an Ernst Mach," *Neue Freie Presse,* (Vienna) no. 18509, Morgenblatt, March 2, 1916, p. 2, col. 3.
11. G. P. Gooch, *History and Historians in the Nineteenth Century* (Boston, 1959), p. 397.
12. Jerusalem, *op. cit.*
13. Ludovica "Louise" Marussig was the daughter of a Graz financial official (*Rechnungsrat*) and she probably first met Mach either at the Kienzl mansion in Graz, the *Paradeishof,* or at one of Mach's special lectures for women. The Marussig family was German speaking but had Italian connections. Several Marussigs were artists or teachers of art at this time (one in Graz and two in Italy). Mach's mother also had artistic inclinations and Mach's son, Felix, later became a professional artist. According to Mach's grandson, Ernst Anton Lederer, Louise Marussig is supposed to have been a happy bride who gradually became more serious through the years. In later life she was often in bad health.
14. *Ordnung der Vorlesungen an der K. K. Universität zu Prag . . . Personalstand dieser Universität* (Prague, yearly 1867–1895).
15. Otto Blüh, "Ernst Mach," *Tagesbote* (Brünn), Feb. 15, 1938.
16. Ernst Mach, "Mach's Vorlesungs-Apparate," *Carls Reportorium der Physik* (Munich), 4 (1868), 8–9.
17. *Ibid.*
18. Joachim Thiele, "Ernst Mach: Bibliographie," *Centaurus,* 8 (1963), 200–205.
19. Ernst Mach, *Optisch-akustische Versuche: Die spectrale und stroboskopische Untersuchung tönender Körper* (Prague, 1873); *Beiträge zur Doppler'schen Theorie der Ton- und Farbenänderung durch Bewegung* (Prague, 1874); *Grundlinien der Lehre von den Bewegungsempfindungen* (Leipzig, 1875).

20. I am indebted to Dr. Strouhal, the son of Dr. Čeněk Strouhal, for the following information on his father.

21. Václav Šebesta, "Strouhal jako, fysik, učitel a člověk," *Technické Listy* (Brno), n.v. (April, 1950), 1.

22. Irena Seidlerová, "Physics," in *Dějiny exaktních věd v českých zemích* (Prague, 1961), p. 381.

23. 1913 Auto., p. 9.

24. Čeněk Dvořák to Ernst Mach, Zagreb, Aug. 19, 1915.

25. Seidlerová, *op. cit.,* p. 380.

26. *Ibid.*

27. *Ibid.,* p. 381.

28. *Ibid.,* p. 380.

29. Wilhelm Kienzl, "Wilhelm Kienzl's Erinnerungen an Prag," *Deutsche Arbeit,* 6 (1907/1908), p. 62.

30. Wilhelm Kienzl, *Meine Lebenswanderung* (Stuttgart, 1926), p. 279.

31. Kienzl, *op. cit.,* p. 62.

32. *AOS* (New York, 1959), pp. 203–204.

33. Paul Carus to Ernst Mach, March 12, 1915.

34. Clemens Neumann to Ernst Mach, March 11, 1868.

35. *Ordnung der Vorlesungen an der K.K. Universität zu Prag . . . Personalstand dieser Universität* (Prague, 1875–1878).

36. Thiele, *op. cit.,* pp. 204–207.

5. PSYCHOLOGY

1. Rudolf Kindinger, ed., *Philosophenbriefe aus wissenschaftlichen Korrespondenz von Alexius Meinong* (Graz, 1965), p. 74.

2. Christian von Ehrenfels, "On Gestalt Qualities," *Psychological Review,* 44 (1937), 521.

3. Patrick J. Capretta, *A History of Psychology* (New York, 1967), p. 90.

4. *Ibid.*

5. *Ibid.,* p. 91.

6. *Ibid.*

7. Floyd Ratliff, *Mach Bands* (San Francisco, 1965), p. 41.

8. H. Haga and C. Wind, "Beugung der Röntgenstrahlen," *Wiedemann's Annalen,* 68 (1899), 866.

9. C. H. Wind, "Zur Demonstration einer von E. Mach entdeckten optischen Täuschung," *Physikalische Zeitschrift,* 1 (1900), 112–113.

10. *SW,* 115 (1906), 633–648.

11. Ratliff, *op. cit.,* p. v.

12. Alois Kreidl, "Ernst Mach," *Wiener Klinische Wochenschrift,* 28 (1916), 395.

13. Ernst Mach, *Outlines of the Theory of the Motor Sensations,* SLA Translation Center, John Crerar Library (Chicago, 1961), p. 2.

14. Anton Lampa, *Ernst Mach* (Prague, 1918), p. 19.

15. *PSL* (La Salle, Ill., 1943), p. 272.

16. *Ibid.,* pp. 272, 287.

17. See J. Ackeret, "Ernst Mach zum 50sten Todestag," *Schweizerische Bauzeitung,* 84 (1966), 140–141, for an interesting story of an unintended duplication of Mach's work half a century later.

18. *PSL,* p. 290.

19. *Ibid.*

20. Ernst Mach, *op. cit.*, p. 54.

21. Erna Lesky, *Die Wiener medizinische Schule im 19 Jahrhundert* (Graz and Cologne), 1965), p. 535.

22. Ernst Mach, *Grundlinien der Lehre von den Bewegungsempfindungen* (Leipzig, 1875), p. 54.

23. *AOS* (New York, 1959), p. 126.

24. *CAOS* (Chicago, 1897), pp. 68–69.

25. Ernst Mach, *Einleitung in die Helmholtz'sche Musiktheorie: Populär für Musiker dargestellt* (Graz, 1866).

26. *AOS*, pp. 297, 305.

27. *Ibid.*

28. Edwin G. Boring, *A History of Experimental Psychology* (New York, 1957), p. 309.

29. *SW*, 54 (1866), 143.

30. Ernst Mach, "Bemerkungen über intermittirende Lichtreize," *Archiv für Anatomie, Physiologie, und wissenschaftliche Medicin*, n.v. (1865), 634.

31. *Ibid.*

32. R. Jung, "Ernst Mach als Sinnesphysiologe," Symposium (Freiburg im Breisgau, 1967), p. 134.

33. *SOM* (La Salle, Ill., 1960), p. 560.

34. Boring, *op. cit.*, p. 352.

35. *Ibid.*, p. 354.

36. Jung, *op. cit.*

37. Ernst Mach, "Some Sketches in Comparative Animal and Human Psychology," *Open Court*, 32 (1918), 363.

38. Ewald Hering, *On Memory and the Specific Energies of the Nervous System* (Chicago, 1902), p. 21.

39. *Ibid.*, p. 27.

40. Ernst Mach, "Einige vegleichende tier-und menschenpsychologische Skizzen," *Naturwissenschaftliche Wochenschrift*, 15 (1916), 241–247.

41. Edwin G. Boring considered Hering's theory of "unconscious memory" as "trite" (*op. cit.*, p. 354), but be that as it may, as a "scientific" link with traditional German *Naturphilosophie* it and devolpments from it have continued to have a remarkable influence in German contemporary thought, especially among relapsed quantum theorists (see chap. 19).

42. According to Theodor Ackermann Antiquariat, *Bibliothek Ernst Mach, Teil II, Katalog 636* (Munich, 1960), the only book by Brentano in Mach's library was *Untersuchungen zur Sinnespsychologie* (Leipzig, 1907). Mach's aversion to reading Brentano's books was probably based on his identification of him as a Catholic "theologian" and of his ideas as "metaphysical."

43. Wilhelm Wundt, *Grundzüge der physiologischen Psychologie* (Leipzig, 1874); Franz Brentano, *Psychologie vom empirischen Standpunkt* (Leipzig, 1874).

44. Boring, *op. cit.*, pp. 360–361.

45. *Ibid.*, p. 361.

46. *COE* (Chicago, 1911), p. 91.

47. *AOS* (New York, 1959), p. 18.

48. *Leitgedanken* (Leipzig, 1919), p. 16.

49. *AOS*, p. 340.

50. Mach's basic problem with respect to space and time was to reconcile the "nativism" of Müller and Hering with the "psychophysical parallelism" of Fechner, and later, with his own version of parallelism. Mach never really succeeded.

51. For Mach the *physical world* was the most "economical" mathematical description of the "real," i.e., the physiological, world. The *metric world* included all the idealized mathematical possibilities of which the physical world was only one.

52. The science of physiology was "physical" in that it employed "economical" mathematical description to describe sensations related to or within the human body, but the physiological world as something nonmathematical and nonidealized was not "physical" for Mach.

53. To turn "psychology" into "physiology" meant to turn elusive, not-yet-measured sensations related to or within the human body into measurable sensations capable of being described in economical, mathematical (i.e., "physical") terms. A serious problem in Mach's approach was that "physical," besides meaning "employing the methods of physics," also sometimes meant "relating sensations to other than the human body."

54. As a notion sensation in the "larger sense" included everything that could be referred to with the possible exception of relations. In the "narrower sense" sensation as a notion referred to what could be reliably measured as opposed to "psychological" phenomena that were not yet capable of being so measured.

55. *AOS*, p. 10.

56. *COE*, p. 87.

57. *Ibid.*, p. 94.

58. *S & G* (La Salle, Ill., 1960), p. 10.

59. *Ibid.*, pp. 30–31.

60. *Ibid.*, p. 31.

61. For a rather sharp criticism of Mach's theory of time, see Mario Bunge, "Mach's Critique of Newtonian Mechanics," *American Journal of Physics,* 34 (1966), 586–588.

62. *AOS*, pp. 246–249.

63. *Ibid.*, pp. 248, 249.

64. *E & I* (Leipzig, 1917), p. 433.

65. *PWV* (Leipzig, 1923), p. 495.

66. *AOS*, p. 82.

67. *Ibid.*, p. 100.

68. *Ibid.*, p. 7.

69. Ernst Mach to Joseph Petzoldt, Vaterstetten, March 20, 1914.

70. *AOS*, p. 46. "I differ from Comte in holding that the psychological facts are, as sources of knowledge, at least as important as the physical facts."

71. Watson rejected "psychophysics" because of its reliance on introspection and ignored the "mind," "consciousness," and the "ego." But ignoring such entities was quite a different matter from Mach's drastic phenomenalistic treatment of them. To claim that the "self" could not be scientifically treated was one thing, but to deny that "I" exist was farther than most people, especially Christians, were willing to go.

72. Boring, *op. cit.*, p. 645: "Watson . . . failed to provide his case with a rigorous epistemology."

73. *Ibid.*

74. Archibald Edward Heath, *Scientific Thought in the Twentieth Century* (London, 1951), p. 170.

75. *AOS,* p. 340: "I . . . think it a great mistake to reject so-called 'introspective' psychology entirely. For self-observation is not only an important means, but in many cases is the only means of obtaining information as to fundamental facts."

76. *Ibid.,* pp. 207, 208.

77. See Josef Breuer to Ernst Mach, Vienna, April 1, 1908.

78. Sigmund Freud, "My Contact with Josef Popper-Lynkeus," *The Complete Psychological Works of Sigmund Freud,* Vol. 22 (London, 1953–1954), p. 224.

79. *AOS,* introduction by Thomas S. Szasz, p. xviii.

6. MACH'S TWO RECTORATES

1. *Die Deutsche Karl-Ferdinands-Universität in Prag* (Prague, 1899), p. 25.

2. Paul Molisch, *Politische Geschichte der Deutschen Hochschulen in Österreich von 1884 bis 1918* (Vienna and Liepzig, 1939), pp. 50–51.

3. Prague police report no. 7020 to the *Statthalterei,"* Dec. 10, 1879.

4. Oskar Hackel, "Die Geschichte der Burschenschaft 'Carolina'," *Deutsche Arbeit,* 9 (1909–1910), 492–493.

5. *Ibid.*

6. Prague police report to the *Statthalterei,* May 17, 1880.

7. Hackel, *op. cit.,* p. 493.

8. Friedrich Adler, "Zur Geschichte der Lese- und Redehalle," *Deutsche Arbeit,* 9 (1909–1910), 546.

9. Prague police report no. 3272 to the *Statthalterei,* May 16, 1880.

10. *Ibid.*

11. *Politik* (Prague), no. 135, May 16, 1880, p. 5, col. 1.

12. *Ibid.,* p. 2, col. 2.

13. *Wer Ist's,* Vol. VII (Leipzig, 1914), p. 1053.

14. The death of the botanist Eduard Fenzl (1808–1880) made the chair in the academy available. It is not clear whether Mach's notoriety as rector at Prague influenced his selection. The timing strongly suggests, however, that Mach's reputation as a champion for the German side helped him to receive this overdue honor.

15. *Die Deutsche Karl-Ferdinands-Universität in Prag* (Prague, 1899), p. 404.

16. Theodor Gomperz to Ernst Mach, Vienna, May 25, 1882.

17. Henry James, ed., *The Letters of William James,* Vol. I (Boston, 1920), pp. 211–212.

18. Ernst Mach, *Populärwissenschaftlichen Vorlesungen* (3d ed.; Leipzig, 1903).

19. Richard Avenarius to Ernst Mach, Zürich, June 28, 1895.

20. See Oskar Ewald, *Richard Avenarius als Begründer der Empirio-Kritizismus* (Berlin, 1905), and V. I. Lenin, *Materialism and Empirio-Criticism* (New York, 1927).

21. *AOS* (New York, 1959), pp. 28, 49–56.

22. *Die Deutsche Karl-Ferdinands-Universität in Prag,* p. 16.

23. Wilhelm Jerusalem, "Ernst Mach zum 70. Geburtstag," *Deutsche Arbeit,* 7 (1907–1908), 394.

24. František Kavka, *The Caroline University of Prague* (Prague, 1962), p. 59.

25. Ernst Plener, *Erinnerungen,* Vol. II (Leipzig, 1911–1921), p. 248.

26. *Neue Freie Presse* (Vienna), no. 6896, Nov. 7, 1883, p. 2, col. 3.

27. Anticipating trouble, Mach contacted a pastor in Liebenau who returned a letter to him affirming the Christian background of his parents, grandparents, and great-grandparents, as attested in city records and birth certificates (Franz Plaíñík to Ernst Mach, Liebenau, Nov. 6, 1883).

28. *Neue Freie Presse,* no. 6897, Nov. 8, 1883, p. 7, col. 3.

29. *Ibid.*

30. *Bohemia* (Prague), no. 48, Feb. 18, 1908, p. 1, col. 2.

31. *Ibid.*

32. *Neue Freie Presse,* no. 6965, Morgenblatt, Jan. 17, 1884, p. 2, col. 3.

33. *Bohemia,* no. 48, Feb. 18, 1908, p. 1, col. 2.

34. *Neue Freie Presse,* no. 6970, Abendblatt, Jan. 22, 1884, p. 3, col. 3.

35. *Ibid.,* no. 6917, Nov. 28, 1883.

36. K. Korischka to Ernst Mach, Prague, April 18, 1884.

37. Molisch, *op. cit.,* p. 122.

38. Hermann L. Strack, "Anti-Semitism," *Encyclopedia of Religion and Ethics,* Vol. I (Edinburgh, 1926), p. 597.

39. There are two relevant documents in the Ernst-Mach-Institut in Freiburg on this Rohling-Mach controversy, a circular sent to Mach supporting him in the controversy with signatures from twenty-two Prague professors attached, dated March 1889, and a letter from Mach to an unknown "Hochgeehrte Herrn!" dated March 21, 1889. Mach wrote: "Ich kann nicht unterlassen Ihnen für die Richtigstellung des Rohlingschen Referates über meinen am 18 October 1883 gesprochenen Toast herzlichst zu danken."

40. *Neue Freie Presse,* no. 6893, Nov. 4, 1883, p. 7, col. 3, p. 8, col. 1.

41. Molisch, *op. cit.,* pp. 126–127.

42. Hackel, *op. cit.,* p. 496.

43. I am deeply grateful to Dr. Julius Kroczek for this explanation and to Professor Otto Blüh for the further information that the *Ewigelandfriede* of 1495 prohibited Jews (and others) from wearing arms, hence, making them *Satisfactionsunfähig.*

44. Molisch, *op. cit.,* p. 181.

45. Josef Mayerhöfer, "Ernst Machs Berufung an die Wiener Universität 1895," *Clio Medica,* 2 (1967), 53.

46. Molisch, *op. cit.,* p. 128.

7. THEORETICAL PHYSICS

1. Mario Bunge, "Mach's Critique of Newtonian Mechanics," *American Journal of Physics,* 34 (1966), 585.

2. *PSL* (La Salle, Ill., 1943), p. 248.

3. *COE* (Chicago, 1911), p. 74.

4. *AOS* (New York, 1959), pp. 103, 105.

5. *COE,* p. 47.

6. *Ibid.,* p. 48.

7. *Ibid.*

8. *Ibid.,* p. 49.

9. *Ibid.,* p. 61.

10. Josip Boncelj, *Jožef Stefan* (Ljubljana, 1960), pp. 132–133.

11. Ludwig Boltzmann, *Populäre Schriften* (Leipzig, 1925), pp. 243–244.

12. Ludwig Flamm, "Die Persönlichkeit Boltzmanns," *Österreichische Chemiker-Zeitung*, 47 (1944), 28.

13. *Ibid.*, p. 29.

14. Friedrich Herneck, "Wiener Physik vor 100 Jahren," *Physikalische Blätter*, 17 (1961), 459.

15. *PSL*, pp. 245–248.

16. Stephen F. Mason, *A History of the Sciences* (New York, 1962), p. 499.

17. In particular, Pierre Duhem and Georg Ferdinand Helm.

18. Karl R. Leistner, *Professor und Prolet: Kurzweilige und Vollständige Widerlegung des Hassbuches Lenins gegen die Machisten* (Karlsbad, 1932), p. 62; Alois Höfler, "Ludwig Boltzmann als Mensch und Philosoph," *Süddeutsche Monatshefte*, Vol. 3, Heft 10 (Oct., 1906), unpaginated.

19. For a different point of view on Newton's philosophy see Howard Stein, "Newtonian Space-Time," *Texas Quarterly*, 10 (1967), 174, and other articles in the same issue.

20. E. A. Burtt, *The Metaphysical Foundations of Modern Science*, (New York, 1954), pp. 233–239.

21. Isaac Newton, "Absolute and Relative Space, Time, and Motion," *Philosophy of Science*, Arthur Danto and Sidney Morgenbesser, eds. (Cleveland, 1964), p. 325.

22. *AOS*, p. 12.

23. A. Wolf, *A History of Science, Technology, and Philosophy in the 16th and 17th Centuries*, Vol. II (New York, 1959), p. 672: "The introduction of 'mass' among the primary qualities of matter appears to have been suggested to Newton by Boyle's experiments on the density of air. The concept made it possible to work out the mechanical theory of nature more satisfactorily than it was possible to do with the Cartesian vortices."

24. *SOM* (La Salle, Ill., 1960), p. 298.

25. *Ibid.*, p. 299.

26. Newton, *op. cit.*, pp. 322–329.

27. *Ibid.*, pp. 322–323.

28. *Ibid.*, p. 323.

29. *Ibid.*

30. *Ibid.*

31. *Ibid.*, p. 322.

32. *Ibid.*

33. *Ibid.*, p. 323.

34. *Ibid.*

35. *Ibid.*, pp. 323, 326.

36. *Ibid.*

37. In order to grasp what Newton meant by "relative" and "absolute" let me use an example that probably came to Newton's mind many times, namely, the "retrograde" motion of Mars.

In terms of Newton's causal, representative realism and mind-matter dualism, the observed retrogression was a *relative apparent motion,* and the unobserved but scientifically measurable retrogression was a *relative physical* motion. The *absolute physical motion* of Mars, however, was an ellipse around the sun with no retrogression: first, because only that ellipse "in itself" could satisfy all measurements from all perspectives; second, because only that ellipse was presumably measurable from the edge of the universe, and third, because only that ellipse was able to explain the causal behavior and influence of Mars.

38. For Newton everything "absolute" was also "relative" in that (1) measurement from the edge of the universe involved a relation, (2) there were normally local perspectives that gave a "relative" picture closely in accord with what could be measured from the "fixed stars," (3) everything "absolute" could be "related," that is, compared or contrasted, with any number of other things, (4) all "absolutes" had numerous historical and causal relations, and (5) all "absolutes" had various relations with God. In short, by "absolute" Newton did not mean free from relations. Free from *observable* (i.e., sensuous, noticeable) constant relations, yes, but then for Newton *all* physical reality, both "absolute" and "relative," was free from those kinds of relations, i.e., mental or epistemological relations.

39. Karl R. Popper, "A Note on Berkeley as a Precursor of Mach," *British Journal for Philosophy of Science*, 4 (1953), 26–36; John Myhill, "Berkeley's 'De Motu': An Anticipation of Mach," *University of California Publications in Philosophy*, 29 (1957), p. 141–157.

40. *SOM*, pp. 272, 280.

41. *Ibid.*, p. 237.

42. Frederick Coppleston, *A History of Philosophy* (New York, 1964), Vol. 5, part 1, p. 162.

43. *Ibid.*

44. *COE*, p. 82.

45. *SOM*, p. 237.

46. Boltzmann, *op. cit.*, pp. 256–257.

47. *COE*, pp. 84–85.

48. *SOM*, p. 341.

49. Bunge, *op. cit.*, p. 594. "In short, as Newton had discovered, kinematics is deducible from dynamics but not as D'Alembert, Kirchhoff, and Mach wanted, conversely. In other words, the inverse problem of experimental mechanics— deriving masses, stresses and forces from a knowledge of motions alone—is in general as unsolvable as the problem of inferring postulates from theorems in a unique way."

50. *Ibid.*, p. 588.

51. *SOM*, p. 272.

52. *Ibid.*, p. 273.

53. *Ibid.*

54. *Ibid.*, p. 280.

55. *Ibid.*

56. *Ibid.*

57. *Ibid.*, p. 337.

58. *S & G* (La Salle, Ill., 1960), p. 139.

59. *PW* (Leipzig, 1900), p. 56.

60. Newton, *op. cit.*, p. 327.

61. *Ibid.*, p. 325.

62. *Ibid.*, p. 327.

63. *SOM*, pp. 279–284; Theodor Häbler, "Ein Brief von Ernst Mach," *Zeitschrift für Mathematischen und Naturwissenschaftlichen Unterricht*, 49 (1918), 96–98.

64. *SOM*, p. 279.
65. *Ibid.*, p. 284.
66. *Ibid.*
67. Bunge, *op. cit.*, pp. 585–596.
68. *Ibid.*, p. 589.
69. *SOM*, pp. 279, 286.
70. *Ibid.*, pp. 336–337.
71. Boltzmann, *op. cit.*, p. 256.

8. MACH SHOCK WAVES

1. Josip Boncelj, "Josef Stefan und seine Tätigkeit auf dem Gebiete der Elektrotechnik," *E und M: Elektrotechnik und Maschinenbau*, 75 (1958), 666–667.
2. *PSL* (La Salle, Ill., 1943), p. 310.
3. Wolfgang F. Merzkirch, "Mach's Contribution to the Development of Gas Dynamics," *Boston Studies in the Philosophy of Science*, 6 (1970), 53.
4. *SW—Anzeiger*, 13 (1876), 144–145.
5. Anton Lampa, *Ernst Mach* (Prague, 1918), pp. 10–13.
6. Ernst Mach, C. Tumlirz, and C. Kögler, "Über die Fortpflanzungsgeschwindigkeit der Funkwellen," *SW*, 77 (1878), 7–32.
7. Merzkirch, *op. cit.*, p. 52.
8. Wolfgang F. Merzkirch, "Die Beiträge Ernst Machs zur Entwicklung der Gasdynamik," *Symposium* (Freiburg im Breirgau, 1967), p. 116.
9. *Ibid.*
10. Wolfgang F. Merzkirch, *op. cit.*, p. 52.
11. Walker Bleakney, "Review of Significant Observations on the Mach Reflection of Shock Waves," *Proceedings of Symposia in Applied Mathematics*, 5 (1953), 41–47.
12. *PSL*, p. 317.
13. *Ibid.*, p. 318.
14. Floyd Ratliff, *Mach Bands* (San Francisco, 1965), p. 17.
15. *SW—Anzeiger*, 23 (1886), no. 15.
16. *PSL*, p. 320.
17. *Ibid.*, pp. 327–328.
18. Ernst Mach and Josef Wentzel, "Ein Beitrag zur Mechanik der Explosionen," *SW*, 92 (1885), 625–638.
19. J. Ackeret, "Der Luftwiderstand bei sehr grossen Geschwindigkeiten," *Schweizerische Bauzeitung*, 94 (1929), 179.
20. *Grande Larousse*, Vol. XVI (Paris, 1962), p. 937.
21. Private communication from Professor J. Ackeret.
22. Merzkirch, *op. cit.* p. 56.
23. *Ibid.*
24. Ludwig Mach, "Über ein Interferenzrefraktometer," *Zeitschrift für Instrumentenkunde* (March, 1892), p. 89.
25. *POPO* (New York, 1953), p. 170.
26. Merzkirch, *op. cit.* p. 50.

9. EARLY PHILOSOPHICAL INFLUENCE

1. Wilhelm Tobias, *Grenzen der Philosophie* (Berlin, 1875), pp. 168–169.

2. Anton von Leclair, *Der Realismus der modernen Naturwissenschaft im Lichte der von Berkeley und Kant angebahnten Erkenntniskritik* (Prague, 1879), pp. 176, 252.

3. Theodor Ackermann Antiquariat, *Bibliothek Ernst Mach, Teil II, Katalog 636* (Munich, 1960), p. 14.

4. *COE* (Chicago, 1911), p. 10.

5. Wilhelm Oswald, *Vorlesungen über Naturphilosophie* (Leipzig, 1902), p. 4.

6. Milič Čapek, "Wilhelm Ostwald," *The Encyclopedia of Philosophy,* Vol. VI (New York, 1967), p. 5.

7. Wilhelm Ostwald, *Lebenslinien,* Vol. II (Berlin, 1926), pp. 243–244, 310.

8. 1913 Auto., p. 10.

9. Ostwald, *op. cit.,* p. 310.

10. Wilhelm Ostwald, "Ernst Mach," *Neue Freie Presse* (Vienna), no. 15684, Morgenblatt, April 19, 1908, p. 6, col. 2.

11. Stephen Brush, "Mach and Atomism," *Synthèse,* 18 (1968), 204.

12. Friedrich Herneck, *Bahnbrecher des Atomzeitalters* (Berlin, 1966), p. 49.

13. Heinrich Hertz, *Die Prinzipien der Mechanik* (Leipzig, 1894), p. xxvi.

14. *COE,* p. 11.

15. Henri Poincaré, "Hertz on Classical Mechanics," *Philosophy of Science,* Arthur Danto and Sidney Morgenbesser, eds., and Arnold Miller, trans. (Cleveland, 1964), pp. 366, 373; Ludwig Boltzmann, *Populäre Schriften* (Leipzig, 1925), p. 218.

16. Joachim Thiele, "Briefe von Gustav Theodor Fechner und Ludwig Boltzmann an Ernst Mach," *Centaurus,* XI (1967), 228; Hans-Günther Körber, ed., *Aus dem wissenschaftlichen Briefwechsel Wilhelm Ostwalds,* Vol. I (Berlin, 1961), p. 3.

17. Boltzmann, "Über die Unentbehrlichkeit der Atomistik in der Naturwissenschaft," in *op. cit.,* pp. 141–157.

18. Carl Stumpf, *Deutsche Litteraturzeitung,* 27 (July 3, 1886), cols. 947–948; Theodor Lipps, *Göttingsche Gelehrte Anzeigen,* 2 (Jan. 15, 1887), 47–53.

19. *AOS* (New York, 1959), p. 354.

20. 1913 Auto., p. 10.

21. Hans Henning, "Ernst Mach," *Frankfurter Zeitung,* erstes Morgenblatt, Feb. 14, 1916, p. 1, col. 4.

22. Joachim Thiele, "Ernst Mach: Bibliographie," *Centaurus,* 8 (1963), 230.

23. *Leitgedanken* (Leipzig, 1919), p. 4.

24. *Ibid.,* p. 5.

25. "Briefe von Richard Avenarius und Ernst Mach an Wilhelm Schuppe," *Erkenntnis,* 6 (1936), 73–80.

26. K. D. Heller, *Ernst Mach: Wegbereiter der modernen Physik* (Vienna, 1964), pp. 69–71.

27. Friedrich Nietzsche, *Gesammelte Werke,* Vol. XXI (Munich, 1926), p. 13.

28. Philipp Frank, *Between Physics and Philosophy* (Cambridge, Mass., 1941), p. 51.

29. Leszek Kolakowski, *The Alienation of Reason* (Garden City, N.Y., 1968), p. 105.

30. *AOS*, p. 25.
31. Anthony Quinton, "British Philosophy," *Encyclopedia of Philosophy,* Vol. I (New York, 1967), p. 389.
32. *SOM* (La Salle, Ill., 1960), p. 592.
33. Joachim Thiele, "Karl Pearson, Ernst Mach, John B. Stallo: Briefe aus den Jahren 1897 bis 1904," *Isis,* 60 (1969), 538.
34. L. C. Dunn, *A Short History of Genetics* (New York, 1965), pp. 84–85.
35. *Ibid.*
36. Josiah Royce, *The Spirit of Modern Philosophy* (New York, 1955), p. 398; (Charles Peirce), *The Nation,* 57 (1893), 251–252.
37. Joachim Thiele, "William James und Ernst Mach," *Philosophia Naturails,* 9 (1966), 308.
38. *PSL* (London, 1898), p. 419.
39. R. B. Perry, *The Thought and Character of William James,* Vol. I (London, 1936), pp. 586–587.
40. *Ibid.,* II, 462.
41. Thiele, *op. cit.,* pp. 301–302.
42. R. B. Perry, *In the Spirit of William James* (Bloomington, Ind. 1958), pp. 80, 94.
43. *Ibid.,* p. 92.
44. Edward C. Hegeler to Ernst Mach, Aug. 11, 1888.
45. Paul Carus to Ernst Mach, May 31, 1892.
46. Carl T. Jackson, "The Meeting of East and West," *Journal of the History of Ideas,* 29 (1968), 76.
47. *Ibid.,* p. 80.
48. W. J. V. Osterhout, *The Journal of General Physiology,* 8 (Sept. 15, 1928), x.
49. Heller, *op. cit.,* p. 81.
50. Jacques Loeb to Ernst Mach, Dec. 23, 1900.
51. Jacques Loeb, *The Mechanistic Conception of Life* (Chicago, 1912), p. 26.
52. Osterhout, *op. cit.,* p. liii.
53. Loeb, *op. cit.,* p. 26.
54. *Ibid.,* pp. 30–31.
55. *Ibid.,* p. 30.
56. *Ibid.,* pp. 55–56.
57. *Ibid.,* p. 80.
58. *Ibid.,* p. 79.
59. *Ibid.,* p. 103.

10. EDUCATIONAL THEORY AND TEXTBOOKS

1. Ernst Mach, *Der relative Bildungswert der philologischen und der mathematisch-naturwissenschaftlichen Unterrichtsfächer der höheren Schulen* (Leipzig, 1886); "Über den Unterricht in der Wärmelehre," *Zeitschrift für den physikalischen und chemischen Unterricht,* 1 (1887/1888), 3–7; "Über das psychologische und logische Moment im naturwissenschaftlichen Unterricht," *Zeitschrift für den physikalischen und chemischen Unterricht,* 4 (1890), 1–5.
2. *PSL* (La Salle, Ill., 1943), p. 191.
3. *Ibid.,* p. 364.
4. *PW* (Leipzig, 1900), p. 376.
5. *Ibid.,* p. vii. For Mach's influence on contemporary German educational

theorists see Joachim Thiele, "Schulphysik vor 70 Jahren Hinweis auf Ernst Machs Lehrbücher der Physik anlässlich des 50. Todestages Machs am 19. Februar 1966," *Zeitschrift für Mathematische und naturwissenschaftliche Unterricht,* 19 (1966), 15.

6. 1880 Auto., p. 2.

7. *K & M* (Stuttgart, 1915), p. 24.

8. Ernst Mach. "Über den Interricht in der Wärmelehre," p. 3.

9. *PSL*, p. 369.

10. *Ibid.*, p. 366.

11. *Ibid.*, p. 367.

12. Friedrich Paulsen, *Friedrich Paulsen: An Autobiography,* Theodor Lens, trans. and ed. (New York, 1938), pp. 280–281.

13. Friedrich Paulsen, *Geschichte des gelehrten Unterrichts,* Vol. II (Berlin and Leipzig, 1921), p. 765.

14. *PSL*, p. 338.

15. *Ibid.*, pp. 365–371.

16. *Ibid.*

17. M. F. Schwiedland, "Le Latin et des études scientifiques en Allemagne d'après M. Mach," *Revue Scientifique,* n.v. (Jan. 1, 1887), 18–21.

18. Eduard Maiss, *Zeitschrift für das Realschulwesen,* 12 (1886), 620–625.

19. Ernst Mach and Johann Odstrčil, *Grundriss der Naturlehre für die unteren Classen der Mittelschulen* (Prague, 1886).

20. *Zeitschrift für den physikalischen und chemischen Unterricht.*

21. Paulsen, *op. cit.,* II, 595.

22. Friedrich Eby, *The Development of Modern Education* (New York, 1952), pp. 535–536.

23. Paulsen, *op. cit.,* II, 765, 772–773.

24. Joachim Thiele, "Ernst Mach: Bibliographie," *Centaurus,* 8 (1963), 208–213.

25. Ernst Mach, "Über den Unterricht in der Wärmelehre," pp. 3–7.

26. *Ibid.*, p. 3.

27. *Leitgedanken* (Leipzig, 1919), p. 18.

28. Alois Höfler, "Ernst Mach," *Zeitschrift für den physikalischen und chemischen Unterricht,* 29 (1916), 63.

29. *S & G* (La Salle, Ill., 1960), p. 113.

30. Anon., "Briefe von Richard Avenarius und Ernst Mach an Wilhelm Schuppe," *Erkenntnis,* 6 (1936), 76–77.

31. Alois Höfler, "Alois Höfler," *Philosophie der Gegenwart in Selbst Darstellungen,* Vol. II (Leipzig, 1921), p. 139.

32. *Ibid.*

33. Paulsen, *op. cit.,* II, 719.

34. Ernst Mach, *Compendium der Physik für Mediciner* (Vienna, 1863); and the following coauthored books: *Grundriss der Naturlehre für die unteren Classen der Mittelschulen* (Prague, 1886); *Leitfaden der Physik für Studierende,* (Leipzig, 1891).

35. Ernst Mach, *Leitfaden der Physik für Studierende* (Leipzig, 1891), p. 1.

36. *Ibid.*

37. *Ibid.*, p. 8.

38. Ernst Mach, *Machs Grundriss der Physik,* II Teil (Leipzig, 1894), p. 122. For a different point of view on the philosophical ideas presented in Mach's

textbooks see Otto Blüh, "Ernst Mach as Teacher and Thinker," *Physics Today,* 20 (June, 1967), 34.

39. Albert Einstein, "Ernst Mach," *Physikalische Zeitschrift,* 17 (1916), 102.

II. RETURN TO VIENNA

1. *Die Deutsche Karl-Ferdinands Universität in Prag* (Prague, 1899), pp. 40–41.
2. Viktor Niesiolowski to Ludwig Mach, Vienna-Mödling, Feb. 14, 1941.
3. Ernst Mach, document dated 1894, now in the possession of the Ernst-Mach-Institut.
4. *Ordnung der Vorlesungen an der Universität zu Prag . . . und Personalstand dieser Universität* (Prague, yearly from 1886–1893).
5. Ernst Mach, *op. cit.*
6. *Ibid.*
7. *Ibid.*
8. Georg Pick to Ernst Mach, Prague, July 15, 1895.
9. This letter was found among Mach's papers, hence, was probably either a copy or was not sent.
10. Eduard Krischek to Ernst Mach, Vienna, Jan. 14, 1893.
11. Erna Lesky, *Die Wiener medizinische Schule in 19 Jahrhundert* (Graz and Cologne, 1965), p. 530.
12. Gustav Tschermak to Ernst Mach, Vienna, March 2 and 20, 1893.
13. Ernst Mach, *op. cit.*
14. W. Voigt, "Ludwig Boltzmann," *Physikalische Zeitschrift,* 7 (1906), 650.
15. Gustav Jaumann to Ernst Mach, Salzburg, July 21, 1894.
16. Ludwig Mach to Ernst Mach, Prague, March 15, 1894.
17. Heinrich Mach, *Beiträge zur Kenntniss der Abietinsäure, II Abhandlung* (Göttingen, 1894), p. 11.
18. A private communication from Frau Anna Karma Mach.
19. 1913 auto., p. 12.
20. Ernst Mach to Joseph Petzoldt, Vaterstetten, Aug. 19, 1914.
21. Josef Mayerhöfer, "Ernst Machs Berufung an die Wiener Universität 1895," *Clio Medica,* 2 (1967), 47.
22. Josef Popper-Lynkeus to Ernst Mach, Vienna, May 3, 1895.
23. Mayerhöfer, *op. cit.*
24. PSL (La Salle, Ill., 1943), pp. 236–259.
25. "Ernst Mach," *Neue Freie Presse* (Vienna), no. 18500, Feb. 22, 1916, p. 3, col. 2.
26. Alois Höfler to Ernst Mach, Vienna, Jan. 24, 1895.
27. Heinrich Gomperz, "Ernst Mach," *Archiv für Geschichte der Philosophie,* 29 (1916), 325–326.
28. Gustav Tschermak to Ernst Mach, Vienna, Oct. 11, 1894.
29. *Ibid.,* Nov. 2, 1894.
30. Mayerhöfer, *op. cit.,* p. 48.
31. Theodor Gomperz to Ernst Mach, Vienna, Nov. 27, 1894.
32. Heinrich Gomperz, *op. cit.,* p. 326.
33. Mayerhöfer, *op. cit.,* p. 51.
34. Josef Mayerhöfer, "Ernst Mach as a Professor of the History of Science," *Proceedings of the Tenth International Congress of History of Science,* Vol. I (Paris, 1964), p. 338.
35. Theodor Gomperz to Ernst Mach, Vienna, Jan. 26, 1895.

36. Wilhelm von Hartel to Ernst Mach, Vienna, Jan. 26, 1895. I am indebted to Josef Mayerhöfer for determining the authorship of this letter and of the following letters by Von Hartel.

37. Mayerhöfer, "Ernst Machs Berufung an die Wiener Universität 1895," pp. 52–53.

38. Ernst Mach to Paul Carus, Prague, May 15, 1895.

39. *Die Feierliche Inauguration des Rectors der Wiener Universität für das Studienjahr 1895/96* (Vienna, 1895), pp. 14–15.

40. D. J. Bach, "Ernst Mach," *Frankfurter Zeitung,* erstes Morgenblatt, Feb. 18, 1908, p. 1, col. 1–2.

41. Hermann Bahr, *Bilderbuch* (Vienna, 1921), p. 37.

42. W. Fred, "Ernst Mach," *Die Aktion,* 6 (1916), cols. 431–432.

43. *PSL,* pp. 259–281.

44. Viktor Niesiolowski, "Erinnerung an Ernst Mach," an unpublished article intended to commemorate the twenty-fifth anniversary of Mach's death (1941). The manuscript is now in the Ernst-Mach-Institut.

45. *Ibid.*

46. *PSL,* pp. 282–337.

47. Verein zur Verbreitung naturwissenschaftlicher Kenntnisse in Wien.

48. Joachim Thiele, "Ernst Mach: Bibliographie," *Centaurus,* 8 (1963), 212 and 222.

49. J. E. Trevor, *Journal of Physical Chemistry,* I (1897), 431.

50. Ludwig Boltzmann, *Populäre Schriften* (Leipzig, 1925), pp. 141–157.

51. Lise Meitner, "Looking Back," *Bulletin of the Atomic Sciences,* 20 (Nov., 1964), 2–7.

52. Anton Lampa, *Ernst Mach* (Prague, 1918), pp. 60–64.

53. Wilhelm Jerusalem, *Gedanken und Denker: Neue Folge,* (Vienna, 1925), p. 23.

54. Wilhelm Jeralusalem, "Ernst Mach," *Die Zukunft,* 95 (1916), 327.

55. Wilhelm Jerusalem, "Erinnerungen an Ernst Mach," *Neue Freie Presse* (Vienna), No. 18509, Morgenblatt, March 2, 1916, p. 3, col. 2.

56. Jerusalem, *Gedanken und Denker,* pp. 25 and 30.

57. *Ibid.,* p. 28.

58. Heinrich Gomperz, "Autobiographical Remarks," *The Personalist,* 24 (1943), 266–267.

59. *Ibid.,* p. 264.

60. Professor H. Feigl to John Blackmore, Minneapolis, March 31, 1969.

61. Gomperz, *op. cit.,* p. 258.

62. Lesky, *op. cit.,* pp. 340–341.

63. Austrian National Library, Vienna, Handschrift Abteilung, doc. 257/100.

64. Document in the possession of Dr. Ernst Anton Lederer.

65. *AOS* (New York, 1959), pp. 174–175.

66. Jerusalem, "Erinnerungen an Ernst Mach," *Neue Freie Presse* (Vienna), no. 18,509, Morgenblatt, March 2, 1916, p. 3, col. 3, and p. 4, col. 1.

67. Thiele, *op. cit.,* pp. 212–213.

12. PHILOSOPHY OF SCIENCE

1. *Sinnliche Elemente* (Leipzig, 1919), p. 31.

2. Ernst Mach to Philip Jourdain, Vienna, May 14, 1912.

3. *AOS* (New York, 1959), p. 47.

4. *E & I* (Leipzig, 1917), p. vii.

5. *AOS*, p. 46.

6. It was precisely the compatibility of positivism with religion which stirred Lenin to distinguish between materialism and positivism and to accuse the latter of being "idealistic" in a Berkeleyan sense.

7. *AOS*, p. 369.

8. Peter Alexander, "Ernst Mach," *The Encyclopedia of Philosophy*, Vol. V (New York, 1967), pp. 115–119.

9. *AOS*, p. 56.

10. *E & I*, p. 13.

11. *Sinnliche Elemente*, pp. 19–20.

12. *E & I*, p. 283.

13. Herbert Feigl succeeded Philipp Frank as director.

14. *AOS*, p. 316.

15. *COE* (Chicago, 1911), p. 63.

16. *PSL* (La Salle, Ill., 1943), p. 270.

17. *Ibid.*, p. 205.

18. *PW* (Leipzig, 1900), p. 366.

19. *AOS*, p. 37.

20. *Ibid.*, p. 23.

21. See F. A. von Hayek, *The Counter-Revolution of Science* (London, 1964).

22. Max Jammer, *The Conceptual Development of Quantum Physics, Mechanics*, (New York, 1966), pp. 379–382.

23. See chapters 14–17.

24. *Sinnliche Elemente*, p. 26.

25. See Ernst Mach, *Erkenntnis und Irrtum* (Leipzig, 1905).

26. *PSL*, p. 198.

27. *AOS*, p. 32.

28. Oswald Külpe, *The Philosophy of the Present in Germany*, trans. M. L. Patrick and G. T. W. Patrick (London, 1913), p. 37. Külpe quotes a passage from Mach.

29. *PW*, p. 391.

30. *PSL*, p. 254.

31. *Ibid.*, p. 206.

32. *SOM* (La Salle, Ill., 1960), p. 579.

33. Ernst Mach, "Über das psychologische und logische Moment in naturwissenschaftlichen Unterricht," *Zeitschrift für den physikalischen und chemischen Unterricht*, 4 (1890) 5.

34. Ernst Mach to Ernst Haeckel, Vienna, October 5, 1905.

35. *PW*, p. 393.

36. *SOM*, p. 578.

37. Edmund Husserl, "Das Princip der Denkökonomie und die Logik," *Logische Untersuchungen*, Part I, (Halle, 1900), pp. 192–210.

38. *S & G* (La Salle, Ill., 1960), p. 98.

39. *SOM*, pp. 585–586.

40. William Jerusalem, *Introduction to Philosophy* (New York, 1910), p. 51.

41. *E & I*, p. 449.

42. *Leitgedanken* (Leipzig, 1919), p. 9.

43. Husserl, *op. cit.*

44. *E & I*, p. 454.

45. *PSL*, p. 254.
46. *PWV* (Leipzig, 1923), p. 476.
47. Ernst Mach, "Resultate einer Untersuchung zur Geschichte der Physik," *Lotos*, 23 (1873), 189.
48. Ludwig Boltzmann, "Models," *Encyclopaedia Britannica*, 11th ed., Vol. 18 (Cambridge, England, 1911), p. 640.
49. *E & I*, pp. 164, 183, 203, & 210.
50. *AOS*, p. 57.
51. *E & I*, p. 187.
52. *Ibid.*, p. 197.

13. WORLD INFLUENCE: PHILOSOPHY

1. Ernst Mach to Auguste Forel, Vienna, Aug. 7, 1912.
2. Émile Bertrand to Ernst Mach, Sept. 14, 1903; Wilhelm Jerusalem, "Ernst Mach," *Neue Freie Presse* (Vienna), no. 18501, Abendblatt, Feb. 23, 1916, p. 3, col. 3; K. D. Heller, *Ernst Mach: Wegbereiter der modernen Physik* Vienna, 1964), p. 137.
3. 1913 Auto., pp. 12–13.
4. Ernst Mach to Jacques Loeb, Vienna, July 3, 1904.
5. Josef Eisenmeier to Ernst Mach, Florence, Feb. 8, 1901.
6. Joachim Thiele, "Karl Pearson, Ernst Mach, John B. Stallo: Briefe aus den Jahren 1897 bis 1904," *Isis*, 60 (1969), 537.
7. Heller, *op. cit.*, p. 97.
8. Friedrich Adler, *Ernst Machs Überwindung des mechanischen Materialismus* (Vienna, 1918), p. 27.
9. Joachim Thiele, "Ernst Mach: Bibliographie," *Centaurus*, 8 (1963), 213–220.
10. Ernst Mach, *Die Leitgedanken meiner naturwissenschaftlichen Erkenntnislehre und ihre Aufnahme durch die Zeitgenossen. Sinnliche Elemente und ihre naturwissenschaftliche Begriffe.* (Leipzig, 1919). Two essays.
11. Thiele, *op. cit.*, pp. 213–220.
12. Private communication from Viktor Kraft (1967).
13. Private communication from Hans Thirring (1967).
14. Hans Thirring, "Ernst Mach als Physiker," *Almanach der Österreichischen Akademie der Wissenschaften*, 116 (1966), 368–371.
15. *Ibid.*, p. 371.
16. Philipp Frank, *Modern Science and its Philosophy* (New York, 1955), p. 1.
17. Philipp Frank, *Between Physics and Philosophy* (Cambridge, Mass., 1941), pp. 6–7.
18. Rudolf Carnap, "Intellectual Autobiography," in *The Philosophy of Rudolf Carnap*, Paul Arthur Schilpp, ed. (La Salle, Ill., 1963), p. 20.
19. Georg Henrik von Wright, "Biographical Sketch," in Norman Malcolm, *Ludwig Wittgenstein: A Memoir* (London, 1959), p. 10; F. A. von Hayek, unfinished draft of a sketch of a biography of Ludwig Wittgenstein (1953), p. 3.
20. Carnap, *op. cit.*, p. 27.
21. Ludwig Wittgenstein to Bertrand Russell, Jan. 16, 1913.
22. Von Hayek, *op. cit.*, p. 44.
23. Philip P. Wiener, "Method in Russell's Work on Leibniz," in *The Philosophy of Bertrand Russell*, Paul Arthur Schilpp, ed. (Chicago, 1944), p. 274.
24. Stephen F. Mason, *A History of the Sciences* (New York, 1962), p. 501.

25. Nicola Abbagnano, "Positivism," *The Encyclopedia of Philosophy,* Vol. VI (New York, 1967), p. 223.

26. Ludwig Wittgenstein, *Tractatus Logico-Philosophicus,* (London, 1958), p. 189.

27. Bertrand Russell, *My Philosophical Development* (London, 1959), pp. 116–117.

28. Gershon Weiler, "Ludwig Wittgenstein," *The Encyclopedia of Philosophy,* Vol. V (New York, 1967), p. 223.

29. Heller, *op. cit.,* p. 81.

30. *Ibid.*

31. Von Hayek, *op. cit.,* p. 43.

32. A document in the possession of Dr. Ernst Anton Lederer.

33. Friedrich Adler, "Ernst Machs Überwindung des mechanischen Materialismus," *Die Neue Zeit,* 35 (1916), 111.

34. Adler, *Ernst Machs Überwindung des mechanischen Materialismus,* p. 137.

35. Sol Liptzin, *Arthur Schnitzler* (New York, 1932), p. 4.

36. Private communication from Frau Anna Karma Mach (1967).

37. Joachim Thiele, "Zur Wirkungsgeschichte der Methodenlehre Ernst Machs," *Symposium* (Freiburg im Breisgau, 1967), p. 87.

38. Hermann Bahr, *Bilderbuch* (Vienna, 1921), p. 38.

39. Thiele, *op. cit.,* p. 87.

40. Hans Siegbert Reiss, "Robert Musil," *Encyclopaedia Britannica,* Vol. XVI (Chicago, 1963), p. 22B.

41. Wilfried Berghahn, *Robert Musil* (Hamburg, 1967), p. 55.

42. *Ibid.,* p. 56.

43. Bruno Altmann, "Die Zürcher Machkolonie: Zur Vorgeschichte der Relativitätstheorie," *Allgemeine Zeitung* (Munich), Dec. 3, 1922, p. 2, col. 1–2.

44. *Ibid.,* p. 2, cols. 3–4.

45. Rudolf Holzapfel, *Panideal: Psychologie der sozialen Gefühle* (Leipzig, 1901); Rudolf Laemmel, *Die Reformation der nationalen Erziehung* (Zürich, 1910).

46. Friedrich Herneck, *Bahnbrecher les Atomzeitalters* (Berlin, 1966), p. 236.

47. A biographical document located in the Technical University of Berlin Archive.

48. Joseph Petzoldt to Ernst Mach, Berlin-Spandau, May 8, 1904.

49. Hugo Dingler to Ernst Mach, March 23, 1912.

50. *SOM* (La Salle, Ill., 1960), p. xxviii.

51. Alf Nyman, "Hugo Dingler: Die Exhaustions Methode und das Prinzip der Einfachstheit," *Hugo Dingler Gedenkbuch zum 75 Geburtstag* (Munich, 1956), pp. 170–171.

52. Ernst Mach to Ernst Haeckel, Vienna, Oct. 5, 1905.

53. Benno Erdmann, *Über den Modernen Monismus* (Berlin, 1914), p. 31.

54. Wilhelm Ostwald to Ernst Mach, Grossbothen, Feb. 24, March 10 and 13, 1912.

55. Ernst Mach to Wilhelm Ostwald, Vienna, Nov. 26, 1912.

56. E. T. Bell, *Men of Mathematics* (New York, 1962), p. 527.

57. G. J. Whitrow, "Albert Einstein," *The Encyclopedia of Philosophy,* II (New York, 1967), 469.

58. Henri Poincaré, *Science and Method* (New York, 1958), pp. 15–24.

59. Peter Alexander, "The Philosophy of Science, 1850–1910," *A Critical History of Western Philosophy,* D. J. O'Conner, ed. (London, 1964), p. 414.

60. *SOM*, p. 306.

61. Alexander, *op. cit.*, p. 416.

62. Poincaré, *op. cit.*, p. 22.

63. Pierre Duhem, *The Aim and Structure of Physical Theory*, trans. Philip P. Wiener (New York, 1962), p. 307.

64. *Ibid.*, p. 43.

65. *Ibid.*, pp. 42–43.

66. *Ibid.*, pp. 21–23, 39, 53–54, 268, 317, and 327.

67. *Ibid.*, p. 21.

68. Pierre Duhem to Ernst Mach, Aug. 10, 1909.

69. Duhem, *op. cit.*, p. 285.

70. *Ibid.*, p. 273.

71. Henri Bergson to Ernst Mach, Sept. 3, 1909; Ernst Mach to Paul Carus, Vienna, Jan. 27, 1911.

72. Gian N. G. Orsini, *Benedetto Croce* (Carbondale, Ill., 1961), pp. 18–19.

73. Russell, *My Philosophical Development*, p. 36.

74. *Ibid.*, p. 39.

75. Bertrand Russell, "On the Nature of Acquaintance," *The Monist*, 24, (1914), p. 162.

76. *Ibid.*

77. *Ibid.*, p. 187.

78. Russell, *My Philosophical Development*, p. 134.

79. Bertrand Russell, "Reply to Criticisms," in *The Philosophy of Bertrand Russell*, ed. Paul Arthur Schilpp (Chicago, 1944), p. 704.

80. Russell, *My Philosophical Development*, p. 139.

81. Bertrand Russell, *An Outline of Philosophy* (London, 1927), p. 303.

82. Russell, *My Philosophical Development*, p. 114.

83. *Ibid.*, p. 117.

84. *Ibid.*, p. 118.

85. Bertrand Russell, "Reply to Criticisms," p. 702.

86. Edwin G. Boring, *A History of Experimental Psychology* (New York, 1957), p. 413.

87. *Ibid.*, p. 420.

88. *Ibid.*, p. 417.

89. *Ibid.*, p. 419.

90. Syed Zafarul Hasan, *Realism* (Cambridge, 1928), p. 69.

91. The six writers were, besides Perry and Holt, William Pepperell Montague, W. T. Marvin, W. B. Pitkin, and E. G. Spaulding. In addition to appearing in the *Journal of Philosophy* the manifesto was also reprinted in the group's collectively written book: *The New Realism* (1912).

92. Frederick Coppleston, *A History of Philosophy*, Vol. VIII, part 2 (New York, 1967), p. 149.

93. For a clear analysis of the differences between *presentationalist* and *representationalist* epistemologies see Syed Zafarul Hasan's *Realism*.

94. See Herbert Feigl, "The Origin and Spirit of Logical Positivism," *The Legacy of Logical Positivism*, Peter Achinstein and Stephen F. Barker, eds. (Baltimore, 1969), pp. 3–24.

95. Karl Popper has reputedly become interested in representationalist epistemology, but one may argue that he was not "really" a member of the "Vienna Circle," in spite of Carnap's opinion to the contrary.

14. MACH VS. BOLTZMANN, PLANCK, STUMPF AND KÜLPE

1. G. H. Bryan, "Ludwig Boltzmann," *Nature*, 74 (1906), 570.
2. Hans-Günther Körber, ed., *Aus dem wissenschaftlichen Briefwechsel Wilhelm Ostwalds*, Vol. I (Berlin, 1961), pp. 20–21.
3. Arnold Sommerfeld, "Ludwig Boltzmann zum Gedächtnis," *Wiener Chemiker Zeitung*, 47 (1944), 25.
4. Erwin Hiebert, "The Conception of Thermodynamics in the Scientific Thought of Mach and Planck," a manuscript soon to be published.
5. Robert A. Millikan, *The Autobiography of Robert A. Millikan* (New York, 1950), pp. 21–22.
6. Ludwig Boltzmann, *Populäre Schriften* (Leipzig, 1925), pp. 141–157.
7. *Ibid.*, pp. 338–339.
8. *Ibid.*, p. 175.
9. *PW* (Leipzig, 1900), p. 425.
10. *AOS* (New York, 1959), p. 372.
11. Ludwig Boltzmann, *Lectures on Gas Theory*, Stephen G. Brush, trans. (Berkeley and Los Angeles, 1964), p. 216.
12. Alois Höfler, "Ludwig Boltzmann als Mensch und als Philosoph," *Süddeutsche Monatshefte*, 3 (Oct., 1906), unpaginated.
13. Ludwig Flamm, "Die Persönlichkeit Boltzmanns," *Wiener Chemiker Zeitung*, 47 (1944), 30.
14. Lise Meitner, "Looking Back," *Bulletin of the Atomic Scientists*, 20 (Nov., 1964), 3.
15. Gabriele Rabel, "Mach und die 'Realität der Aussenwelt,'" *Physikalische Zeitschrift*, 21 (1920), 433.
16. D. J. Bach, "Ernst Mach," *Frankfurter Zeitung*, No. 59, Feb. 18, 1908, p. 2, col. 1.
17. Meitner, *op. cit.*, p. 3.
18. Anon., "Der Lebenslauf Boltzmanns," *Die Zeit* (Vienna), No. 1420, Sept. 7, 1906, p. 2, col. 2.
19. Ludwig Flamm, "Zum 50. Todestag von Ludwig Boltzmann," *Physikalische Blätter*, 12 (1956), 410.
20. Stephen Brush, "Mach and Atomism," *Synthèse*, 18 (1968), 207.
21. Meitner, *op. cit.*, p. 3.
22. Millikan, *op. cit.*, pp. 84–85.
23. Engelbert Broda, *Ludwig Boltzmann* (Berlin, 1957), pp. 102–103.
24. Boltzmann, *Populäre Schriften*, pp. 370–371.
25. *Ibid.*, p. 371.
26. *Ibid.*, p. 368.
27. *Analyse* (Leipzig, 1922), pp. 304–305.
28. Boltzmann, *op. cit.*, p. 385.
29. Broda, *op. cit.*, p. 106.
30. George Jaffé, Recollections of Three Great Laboratories," *Journal of Chemical Education*, 29 (1952), 235.
31. Bryan, *op. cit.*, p. 570.
32. Private communication from Dieter Flamm.
33. Anon., "Der Tod des Hofrates Boltzmann," *Die Zeit*, No. 1421, Morgenblatt, Sept. 8, 1906, p. 5, col. 1.

34. Flamm, "Die Persönlichkeit Boltzmanns," p. 30.
35. Private communication from Dieter Flamm.
36. Höfler, *op. cit.,* unpaginated.
37. Ernst Mach, "Ludwig Boltzmann," *Die Zeit,* no. 1420, Abendblatt, Sept. 7, 1906, p. 1, col. 3.
38. Anon. "Weitere Nachrichten die letzten Tage," *Die Zeit,* No. 1420, Abendblatt, Sept. 7, 1906, col. 2.
39. Private communication from Frau Dr. Lili Hahn.
40. *Die Zeit,* no. 1420, Abendblatt, Sept. 7, 1906, p. 1, col. 3.
41. Brush, *op. cit.,* p. 207.
42. Paul K. Feyerabend, "Ludwig Boltzmann," *Encyclopedia of Philosophy,* Vol. I (New York, 1967), p. 336.
43. *Ibid.,* pp. 334–335.
44. Broda, *op. cit.,* 39.
45. Philipp Frank, *Einstein: His Life and Times* (New York, 1947), p. 68.
46. Sommerfeld, *op. cit.,* p. 26.
47. Feyerabend, *op. cit.,* p. 334.
48. Wilhelm Ostwald, "Wilhelm Ostwald," *Philosophie der Gegenwart in Selbstdarstellungen,* Vol. II (Leipzig, 1921), p. 17.
49. Friedrich Herneck, "Die Beziehungen zwischen Einstein und Mach, dokumentarisch dargestellt," *Wissenschaftliche Zeitschrift der Friedrich-Schiller-Universität Jena,* 15 (1966), 6.
50. Max Planck, "Zur Machschen Theorie der physikalischen Erkenntnis: Eine Erwiderung," *Vierteljahrschrift für wissenchaftliche Philosophie,* 34 (1910), 498.
51. Erwin Hiebert, "The Conception of Thermodynamics in the Scientific Thought of Mach and Planck," *Symposium* (Frieburg im Breisgau, 1967), p. 186.
52. Max Planck, "Naturwissenschaft und reale Aussenwelt," *Die Naturwissenschaften,* 28 (1940), 779.
53. Körber, *op. cit.,* p. 35.
54. Planck, "Zur Machschen Theorie der physikalischen Erkenntnis: Eine Erwiderung," p. 492.
55. *Ibid.,* p. 502.
56. Max Planck, "Gegen die neuere Energetik," *Annalen der Physik,* 57 (1896), 72–78.
57. Max Planck, *Vorträge und Erinnerungen* (Darmstadt, 1965), pp. 24–25.
58. *Ibid.,* p. 13.
59. Erwin Hiebert, "The Conception of Thermodynamics in the Scientific Thought of Mach and Planck," a manuscript soon to be published.
60. Planck, *Vorträge und Erinnerungen,* pp. 45–51.
61. *Ibid.,* p. 50.
62. *Ibid.,* p. 49.
63. *Ibid.*
64. Max Planck, "The Unity of the Physical Universe," *A Survey of Physical Theory,* R. Jones and D. H. Williams, trans. (New York, 1960), pp. 25–26.
65. *Ibid.,* p. 26.
66. Friedrich W. Adler, "Die Einheit des physikalischen Weltbildes," *Naturwissenschaftliche Wochenschrift,* 8 (1909), no. 52; Joseph Petzoldt, "Die vitalistische Reaktion auf die Unzulänglichkeit der mechanischen Naturan-

sicht," *Zeitschrift für allgemeine Physiologie,* 10 (1910), 69–119; Philipp Frank, "Die Bedeutung der physikalischen Erkenntnistheorie Machs für das Geistesleben der Gegenwart," *Naturwissenschaften,* 5 (1917), 65–72.

67. Philipp Frank, *Between Physics and Philosophy* (Cambridge, Mass., 1941), p. 31.

68. Joachim Thiele, "Ein zeitgenössiches Urteil über die Kontroverse zwischen Max Planck und Ernst Mach," *Centaurus,* 13 (1968), 87.

69. Herneck, *op. cit.,* p. 6.

70. Carl Cranz to Ernst Mach, Berlin, Oct. 9, 1910.

71. *Leitgedanken* (Leipzig, 1919 , p. 10.

72. *Ibid.,* p. 11.

73. *Ibid.,* pp. 11–12.

74. Brush, *op. cit.,* p. 208.

75. Plank, "Zur Machschen Theorie der physikalischen Erkenntnis: Eine Erwiderung," pp. 497–498.

76. *Ibid.,* p. 502.

77. *Ibid.,* p. 504.

78. *Ibid.,* p. 505.

79. *Ibid.*

80. *Ibid.,* p. 500.

81. *Ibid.,* p. 506.

82. Albert von Schrenk-Notzing to Ernst Mach, June 4, 1896.

83. E. Forster to Ernst Mach, Berlin, undated (1900–1910?).

84. Edwin G. Boring, *A History of Experimental Psychology* (New York, 1957), pp. 369–370.

85. *Ibid.,* 366.

86. *Sinnliche Elemente* (Leipzig, 1919), p. 24.

87. *Ibid.,* pp. 19–21, 31.

88. *Ibid.,* p. 31.

89. Boring, *op. cit.,* pp. 397, 409.

90. Oswald Külpe, *The Philosophy of the Present in Germany,* trans. M. L. Patrick and G. T. W. Patrick (London, 1913), p. 48.

91. Patrick J. Capretta, *A History of Psychology* (New York, 1967), p. 89.

92. Boring, *op. cit.,* p. 404.

93. *Ibid.,* p. 407.

15. POLITICS, RUSSIA, AND VLADIMIR LENIN

1. *PSL* (La Salle, Ill., 1943), p. 336.

2. *AOS* (New York, 1959), p. 25.

3. *PSL,* p. 372.

4. *Ibid.,* pp. 373–374.

5. *E & I* (Leipzig, 1917), p. 81.

6. *AOS,* p. 255.

7. *CAOS* (Chicago, 1897), p. 40.

8. K. D. Heller, *Ernst Mach: Wegbereiter der modernen Physik* (Vienna, 1964), pp. 17–18.

9. *PSL,* p. 373.

10. *E & I,* p. 79.

11. *Ibid.,* p. 81.

12. *K & M* (Stuttgart, 1915), p. 86.

13. Friedrich Adler, *Ernst Machs Überwindung des mechanischen Material-ismus* (Vienna, 1918), p. 24.

14. *Ibid.*, p. 27.

15. *Ibid.*

16. Friedrich Funder, *Vom Gestern ins Heute* (Munich, 1953), pp. 286–287.

17. Karl Leistner, *Professor und Prolet* (Karlsbad, 1932), pp. 144–148.

18. See Mach's newspaper articles in bibliography.

19. Ernst Mach to Čeněk Dvořák, Vienna, March 2, 1909.

20. *SW—Anzeiger*, no. 10, (1875), 82.

21. G. V. Osnobschin to Ernst Mach, Moscow, Jan. 19, 1883.

22. Bruno Kolbe to Ernst Mach, St. Petersburg, Nov. 28, 1891.

23. Lieutenant Colonel Alexandre Zindeberg to Ernst Mach, Simbirsk, Oct. 5, 1892. (Simbirsk/Ulianovsk)

24. Bruno Kolbe to Ernst Mach, St. Petersburg, March 13, 1895.

25. Sergei von Koschljakow to Ernst Mach, St. Petersburg, April 24, 1895.

26. Joachim Thiele, "Ernst Mach: Bibliographie," *Centaurus*, 8 (1963), 214.

27. *Ibid.*, pp. 214–218.

28. P. K. von Engelmeyer to Ernst Mach, Moscow, Jan. 31, 1910.

29. *Ibid.*, Jan. 14, 1912.

30. Dr. W. Scharwin to Ernst Mach, Moscow, Feb. 27, 1906.

31. Alexander Jollos to Ernst Mach, Moscow, Feb. 16, 1908.

32. Löwintoff to Ernst Mach, Odessa, Oct. 8 and Dec. 24, 1901.

33. Hans Kleinpeter to Ernst Mach, Bologna, May 5, 1911.

34. P. K. von Engelmeyer to Ernst Mach, Moscow, June 6, 1912.

35. Vladimir Nochotowitsch to Ernst Mach, Ekaterinoslav, Feb. 26, 1910.

36. Alexander Bogdanov, "Ernst Mach und die Revolution," *Die Neue Zeit* (Stuttgart), 26 (1908), 695–700.

37. George Katkov, "Lenin as Philosopher," in *Lenin: The Man, the Theorist, the Leader*, Leonard Schapiro and Peter Reddaway, eds. (New York, 1967), p. 73.

38. V. I. Lenin, *Materialism and Empirio-Criticism* (New York, 1927), p. 357.

39. Leszek Kolakowski, *The Alienation of Reason* (Garden City, N.Y., 1968), pp. 127–128.

40. *Ibid.*, pp. 127 and 131.

41. Katkov, *op. cit.*, p. 74.

42. *Ibid.*, p. 73.

43. Louis Fischer, *The Life of Lenin* (New York, 1964), p. 64.

44. *Ibid.*, p. 69.

45. Dietrich Grille, *Lenins Rivale: Bogdanov und seine Philosophie* (Cologne, 1966), pp. 63 and 211.

46. Fischer, *op. cit.*, p. 63.

47. *Ibid.*, p. 495.

48. Lenin, *op. cit.*, p. 13. The terms "Machian," "Machist," and "Machism" suggest a double meaning in Russian, namely, to blunder or miss the target, hence, calling Bogdanov a "Machist" identified him as both a blunderer and a follower of Ernst Mach. See Wolfgang Yourgrau and Alwyn van der Merve, "Did Ernst Mach 'Miss the Target'?" *Synthèse*, 18 (1968), 234.

49. Lenin, *op. cit.*, p. 51.

50. *Ibid.*, p. 40.

51. Thiele, *op. cit.*, p. 222.
52. Grille, *op. cit.*, p. 250.
53. Fischer, *op. cit.*, pp. 67 and 492.
54. Robert Payne, *The Life and Death of Lenin* (New York, 1964), p. 230.
55. Fischer, *op. cit.*, p. 493.
56. Grille, *op. cit.*, p. 119.
57. Payne, *op cit.*, 230.

16. MACH AND EINSTEIN

1. Philipp Frank, *Einstein: His Life and Times* (New York, 1947), p. 13.
2. Frederick Copleston, *A History of Philosophy*, Vol. VII, part 2 (New York, 1965), pp. 126–127.
3. Frank, *op. cit.*, p. 13.
4. Barbara Lovett Cline, *The Questioners* (New York, 1965), pp. 77–78.
5. Friedrich Herneck, *Albert Einstein* (Berlin, 1967), p. 58.
6. Frank, *op. cit.*, p. 20.
7. Gerald Holton, "Mach, Einstein, and the Search for Reality," *Daedalus,* 97 (1968), 640.
8. Albert Einstein, *Einstein: Essays in Science* (New York, 1934), p. 15.
9. Cornelius Lanczos, *Albert Einstein and the Cosmic World Order* (New York, 1965), p. 14.
10. Albert Einstein, *Out of My Later Years* (New York, 1950), p. 63.
11. Holton, *op. cit.*, pp. 636–637.
12. Albert Einstein, "Autobiographical Notes," in *Albert Einstein: Philosopher-Scientist*, Vol. I, Paul Arthur Schilpp, ed. (New York, 1959), p. 53.
13. G. J. Whitrow, "Albert Einstein," *The Encyclopedia of Philosophy*, Vol. II (New York, 1967), pp. 470–471.
14. Holton, *op. cit.*, p. 641.
15. Max Planck, *A Survey of Physical Theory* (New York, 1960), p. 85.
16. Paul Volkmann, "Studien über Ernst Mach vom Standpunkt eines theoretischen Physikers der Gegenwart," *Annalen der Physik,* 4 (1924), 309.
17. Joseph Petzoldt, "Die Relativitätstheorie der Physik," *Zeitschrift für positivistische Philosophie,* 2 (1914), 3.
18. Anton Lampa to Ernst Mach, Prague, May 1, 1910.
19. Philipp Frank, *Between Physics and Philosophy* (Cambridge, Mass., 1941), p. 38.
20. Laszlo Tisza, "Philipp Frank and Physics," *Philipp Frank 1884–1966* (printed as a pamphlet by Harvard University, 1966), p. 8.
21. Frank, *Einstein: His Life and Times*, p. 75.
22. *Ibid.*, pp. 78–79.
23. Friedrich Herneck, "Die Beziehungen zwischen Einstein und Mach, dokumentarisch dargestellt," *Naturwissenschaftliche Zeitschrift der Friedrich-Schiller-Universität Jena*, 15 (1966), 6.
24. *COE* (Chicago, 1911), p. 95.
25. In brief, *Machian relativity* meant the functional dependency of all sensations. *Physical relativity* meant the equivalence of all physical systems (i.e., none privileged). *Einstein's physical relativity* meant the equivalence of all physical systems with respect to the constant velocity of light in a vacuum.
26. Herneck, *op. cit.*, p. 6.

27. Ernst Lecher, "Hofrat Professor Dr. Ernst Mach," *Neue Freie Presse* (Vienna), no. 16313, Morgenblatt, Jan. 21, 1910, p. 8, cols. 1–2.

28. Herneck, *op. cit.,* p. 7.

29. *Sinnliche Elemente* (Leipzig, 1919), p. 20.

30. *Leitgedanken* (Leipzig, 1919), p. 15.

31. Herneck, *op. cit.,* p. 7.

32. Frank, *Einstein: His Life and Times,* pp. 104–105. Einstein at first believed that he had successfully persuaded Mach to accept the indispensable utility of the atomic theory, at least on a conditional basis. Later, Einstein changed his mind and realized that he had failed. Mach's "agreement" had been based on a conditional assumption which in fact Mach rejected. According to Philipp Frank, Mach answered Einstein: "If with the help of the atomic hypothesis one could actually establish a connection beetween several observable properties which without it would remain isolated, then I should say that the hypothesis was an 'economical' one. . . ."

33. Albert Einstein, "Ernst Mach," *Physikalische Zeitschrift,* 17 (1916), 101–104.

34. Frank, *op. cit.,* p. 98–99.

35. Whitrow, *op. cit.,* p. 470.

36. James W. Felt, "Mach's Principle Revisited," *Laval Théologique et Philosophique,* 20 (1964), 44.

37. Herneck, *op. cit.,* p. 9.

38. *Ibid.,* p. 8.

39. Felt, *op. cit.,* p. 44.

40. Albert Einstein, "Friedrich Adler als Physiker," *Vossische Zeitung* (Berlin), Morgenblatt, May 23, 1917, p. 2.

41. Hans Reichenbach, "Der gegenwärtige Stand der Relativitätsdiskussion: Eine kritische Untersuchung," *Logos,* 10 (1921/1922), 340–341.

42. Holton, *op. cit.,* p. 657.

43. *Ibid.,* pp. 660–661.

44. *Ibid.,* p. 646.

45. *POPO* (New York, 1953), pp. vii–viii. Professor Gerald Holton has retranslated Mach's preface and it is his that I have used (see Holton, *op. cit.,* p. 647).

46. Holton, *op. cit.,* p. 647.

47. *Ibid.,* p. 656.

48. Einstein, *Out of My Later Years,* p. 73.

49. Holton, *op. cit.,* p. 660.

50. Albert Einstein, "Reply to Criticisms," in *Albert Einstein: Philosopher Scientist,* Vol. II, Paul Arthur Schilpp, ed. (New York, 1959), p. 669.

17. DID MACH FINALLY ACCEPT
EINSTEIN'S THEORY OF RELATIVITY?

1. Carlton B. Weinberg, *Mach's Empirio-Pragmatism in Physical Science* (New York, 1937), pp. 104–110.

2. *S & G* (La Salle, Ill., 1960), p. 135.

3. Kurt Geissler to Ernst Mach, Ebikon bei Luzern, March 5 and June 11, 1909.

4. Čeněk Dvořák to Ernst Mach, Zagreb, Dec. 28, 1888; *SOM* (La Salle, Ill., 1960), pp. 589–591.

5. Wilhelm Kienzl, *Meine Lebenswanderung* (Stuttgart, 1926), p. 53.

6. Edwin G. Boring, *A History of Experimental Psychology* (New York, 1957), pp. 306–307.

7. *SOM*, pp. 589–591.

8. Paul Gerber, *Gravitation und Elektrizität* (ca. 1910).

9. See Gerald Holton, "Influences on Einstein's Early Work in Relativity Theory," *American Scholar*, 37 (1967/1968), 59–79.

10. Friedrich Herneck, "Die Beziehungen zwischen Einstein und Mach, dokumentarisch dargestellt," *Naturwissenschaftliche Zeitschrift der Friedrich-Schiller-Universität Jena*, 15 (1966), 7.

11. *Ibid.*

12. Ernst Mach to Hugo Dingler, Vienna, April 4, 1910.

13. *Ibid.*, Sept. 4, 1910.

14. *Mechanik* (Leipzig, 1933), pp. xviii–xx.

15. Hugo Dingler, *Der Zusammenbruch der Wissenschaft und der Primat der Philosophie* (Munich, 1926).

16. Hugo Dingler, "Bilanz der Relativitätstheorie," *Süddeutsche Monatshefte*, 23 (1925), 218.

17. Ernst Mach to Hugo Dingler, Vienna, Sept. 4, 1910, and Jan. 26, 1912.

18. See chap. 5.

19. Ernst Mach to Wilhelm Ostwald, Vaterstetten, July 23, 1913.

20. *SOM*, pp. 589–591.

21. *Ibid.*, pp. xxviii and 234–235.

22. Anton Lampa to Ernst Mach, Prague, Feb. 9, 1910. The exact date of Einstein's visit to Mach is not clear. Carlton B. Weinberg has written (*op. cit.*, p. 104) that the meeting occurred in "1910–1911." Gerald Holton believes that they probably met in 1911. If 1911 is correct, then the meeting probably had little or nothing to do with Einstein's effort to be appointed at Prague.

23. Anton Lampa to Ernst Mach, Prague, Feb. 9, 1910.

24. Philipp Frank, *Between Physics and Philosophy* (Cambridge, Mass., 1941), pp. 42–43.

25. Philipp Frank, *Einstein: His Life and Times* (New York, 1947), p. 101.

26. Anton Lampa to Ernst Mach, Prague, Feb. 18, 1910.

27. Frank, *Einstein: His Life and Times*, p. 78.

28. Carl Seelig, *Albert Einstein* (Zurich, 1954), p. 138.

29. Frank, *Einstein: His Life and Times*, pp. 172–173.

30. *SOM*, pp. 589–590; Mario Bunge, "Mach's Critique of Newtonian Mechanics," *American Journal of Physics*, 34 (1966), 585.

31. Joachim Thiele, "Briefe Robert H. Lowies an Ernst Mach," *Isis*, 59 (1968), 85.

32. *Ibid.*

33. *Ibid.*

34. Robert H. Lowie, "Letters from Ernst Mach to Robert H. Lowie," *Isis*, 37 (1947), 66.

35. *Ibid.*

36. (Marie Mach), *Erinnerungen einer Erzieherin* (Vienna, 1912).

37. Lowie's book *Are We Civilized?* (New York, 1929) was dedicated to Mach.

38. K. D. Heller, *Ernst Mach: Wegbereiter der modernen Physik* (Vienna, 1964), pp. 137–139.

39. Ernst Mach to Paul Carus, Vienna, Oct. 14, 1912; Ernst Mach to Wilhelm Ostwald, Vienna, March 9, 1913.

40. Heller, *op cit.*, p. 137.

41. Franz Exner, "Ernst Mach," *SW—Almanach*, 66 (1916), 334.

42. Ernst Mach to Wilhelm Ostwald, Vaterstetten, May 29, 1913.

43. Ernst Mach to Josef Popper-Lynkeus, Vaterstetten, Aug. 11, 1913.

44. Frau Anna Karma Mach, "Ernst Mach," *Bibliothek Ernst Mach,* Theodor Ackermann Antiquariat, *Katalog #634* (Munich, 1959), p. 1.

45. Private communication from Frau Anna Karma Mach (1967).

46. Ludwig Mach to Paul Carus, Vaterstetten, Feb. 28, 1913.

47. *POPO* (New York, 1953), p. vii.

48. *Ibid.*

49. The letters from Ernst and Ludwig Mach and Einstein to Joseph Petzoldt are located in the archive of the Technical University of Berlin.

50. Joseph Petzoldt to Ernst Mach, Berlin-Spandau, June 1, 1911. (See also Petzoldt's letter to Mach, dated Sept. 22, 1910).

51. *Ibid.*, June 1, 1911.

52. *Ibid.*, May 25, June 6, and June 15, 1913.

53. Herneck, *op. cit.*, p. 9.

54. *SOM*, pp. 589–591.

55. Ernst Mach to Josef Popper-Lynkeus, Vaterstetten, Aug. 11, 1913.

56. *POPO*, p. vii.

57. Joachim Thiele already suspected as much in his article "Bermerkungen zu einer Äusserung im Vorwort der 'Optik' von Ernst Mach," *Schriftenreihe für Geschichte der Naturwissenschaften, Technik und Medizin,* 2 (1965), 10–19.

58. Herneck, *op. cit.*, p. 8.

59. There are problems concerning the correct dates for this and the following letter. The dates on Mach's letters do not correspond with the dates mentioned in Petzoldt's letters to Mach. (See Joseph Petzoldt to Ernst Mach, Berlin-Spandau, March 5, 1914).

60. See Joseph Petzoldt, "Die Relativitätstheorie der Physik," *Zeitschrift für positivistische Philosophie,* 2 (1914), 1–56.

61. Joseph Petzoldt, "Das Verhältnis der Machschen Gedankenwelt zur Relativitätstheorie," Anhang zu: Ernst Mach, *Mechanik* (Leipzig, 1921), p. 494.

62. Ludwig Mach to Joseph Petzoldt, Vaterstetten, July 20, 1914.

63. Joseph Petzoldt to Albert Einstein, Berlin-Spandau, March 3, 1927.

64. *Ibid.*

65. Ernst Mach to Joseph Petzoldt, Vaterstetten, Aug. 19, 1914.

66. Joseph Petzoldt to Albert Einstein, Berlin-Spandau, March 3, 1927.

67. Ernst Mach to Joseph Petzoldt, Vaterstetten, Sept. 30, October 20, and 24, 1914.

68. *Mechanik* (Leipzig, 1933), pp. xviii–xx.

69. See Ludwig Mach to Joseph Petzoldt, Vaterstetten, Aug. 20, 1914.

70. Paul Carus, "Professor Ernst Mach," *Open Court,* 30 (1916), 257.

71. See Joseph Petzoldt, "Verbietet die Relativitätstheorie Raum und Zeit als etwas Wirkliches zu denken?" *Verhandlungen der Deutschen Physikalischen Gesellschaft,* 20 (1918), 189–201.

72. Other articles by Petzoldt on "relativity" included: "Mechanistische Naturauffassung und Relativitätstheorie," *Annalen der Philosophie,* 2 (1921), 447–462; "Kausalität und Relativitätstheorie," *Zeitschrift für Physik,* 4 (1921),

467-474; "Postulat der absoluten und relativen Bewegung," *Zeitschrift für Physik*, 21 (1924), 143-150.

73. Ludwig Mach to Joseph Petzoldt, Vaterstetten, May 11, 1914.

74. *Ibid.*, Augsburg, Dec. 14, 1919.

75. *Ibid.*, June 29, 1920.

76. Joseph Petzoldt to Albert Einstein, Berlin-Spandau, March 3, 1927.

77. Ernst Mach to Paul Carus, Vienna, Nov. 12, 1912; Ludwig Mach to Joseph Petzoldt, Augsburg, June 29, 1920.

78. Joseph Petzoldt to Albert Einstein, Berlin-Spandau, March 3, 1927.

79. Ludwig Mach to Joseph Petzoldt, Augsburg, June 29, 1920.

80. Hans Reichenbach, "Die gegenwärtige Stand der Relativitätsdiskussion," *Logos*, 10 (1921-1922), 378; Bohuslav Brauner, "Einstein and Mach," *Nature*, 113 (1924), 927.

81. Hugo Dingler, *Das Problem des absoluten Raumes* (Leipzig, 1923), p. 43.

82. Erwin Hiebert, "Mach's Early Views on Atomism," *Boston Studies in the Philosophy of Science*, 6 (1970), 102-103.

83. Albert Einstein to Joseph Petzoldt, Berlin, Aug. 23, 1919.

84. Joseph Petzoldt to Albert Einstein, Berlin-Spandau, March 3, 1927.

85. *Ibid.*

86. Ludwig Mach to Joseph Petzoldt, Augsburg, Feb. 14, 1920.

87. Ludwig Mach to Robert H. Lowie, Vaterstetten, Oct. 18, 1922.

88. Joachim Thiele, "Ernst Mach: Bibliographie," *Centaurus*, 8 (1963), 222-223.

89. Ludwig Mach to Robert H. Lowie, Vaterstetten, Oct. 30, 1923, Jan. 29 and Feb. 25, 1936.

90. See Ludwig Mach to Robert H. Lowie, Vaterstetten, Feb. 28 and Oct. 30, 1936.

91. Ludwig Mach to Robert H. Lowie, Vaterstetten, Jan. 29, 1936.

92. *Ibid.*, March 17, 1936.

93. *Ibid.*, May 31, 1947.

94. Robert H. Lowie, *Science*, 83 (May 22, 1936), 499.

95. Using Ludwig Mach's numbers: no 1 was never finished or published; no. 2 was written and finished by Ludwig Mach but never published; no. 3 was never published and the nature of it remains mysterious; no. 4 especially concerning "the constitution of matter" remains most mysterious; no. 5 may have originally included some essays published in the 1923 German edition of Mach's *Popular Scientific Lectures*, but beyond that nothing is known; no. 6 may have been finished by Ludwig Mach with assistance from Marie Mach.

96. Private communication from Frau Anna Karma Mach (1967).

97. Ludwig Mach to Robert H. Lowie, Vaterstetten, May 25, 1947.

98. *Ibid.*, April 6, 1923, and April 20, 1936.

99. Among the mansucripts that were probably destroyed the most important most likely were: (*a*) Ludwig Mach's second experimental notebook (1911-1944); (*b*) The biography of Ernst Mach by Ludwig and Marie Mach; (*c*) The manuscript(s) on "the constitution of matter"; (*d*) Ernst Mach's referred to (1908-1911) but never published manuscript on "electron theory."

100. At the end of his life Ludwig Mach described himself as follows: "Ich kämpfte für einen Toten, dessen Schatten ich immer war" (Ludwig Mach to Robert H. Lowie, Vaterstetten, Aug. 6, 1947).

101. Dingler, "Bilanz de Relativitätstheorie," *Süddeutsche Monatshefte, 23* (1925), p. 212.

18. MACH AND BUDDHISM

1. Mach's interest in Schopenhauer, who was popular during the 1860s, probably attracted Mach toward Eastern philosophy.

2. *AOS* (New York, 1959), p. 209.

3. *SOM* (La Salle, Ill., 1960), p. 578.

4. *E & I* (Leipzig, 1917), pp. 104–105.

5. Josef Popper-Lynkeus, *Mein Leben und Wirken* (Dresden, 1924), pp. 50–51.

6. *PSL* (La Salle, Ill., 1943), p. 30.

7. *AOS,* p. 120.

8. Ernst Mach, *Outlines of the Theory of the Motor Sensations* (Chicago, 1961), p. 54.

9. *AOS,* p. 356.

10. Theodor Beer, *Die Weltanschauung eines modernen Naturforschers: Ein nicht-kritisches Referat über Mach's "Analyse der Empfindungen"* (Dresden, 1903).

11. Josef Popper-Lynkeus, "Ernst Mach," *Die Vossische Zeitung* (Berlin), Sonntags Beilage, April 2, 1916, p. 104.

12. W. Fred, "Ernst Mach (nach seinem Tod)," *Die Aktion,* 6 (1916), cols. 430–431.

13. 1913 Auto., p. 10; Friedrich Herneck, "Über eine unveröffentlichte Selbstbiographie Ernst Machs," *Wissenschaftliche Zeitschrift der Humboldt-Universität zu Berlin,* 6 (1956–1957), 213.

14. Ernst Mach to Wilhelm Ostwald, Vaterstetten, May 29, 1913; Ernst Mach, "Some Sketches in Comparative Animal and Human Psychology," *Open Court,* 32 (1918), 374; Friedrich Adler, *Ernst Machs Ueberwindung des mechanischen Materialismus,* (Vienna, 1918), pp. 28–29.

15. This story titled "The Earthworm" is part of a manuscript by Dr. Ernst Anton Lederer about his grandfather, Ernst Mach. It was written at the beginning of 1969.

16. Carl T. Jackson, "The Meeting of East and West," *Journal of the History of Ideas,* 29 (1968), 91.

17. Ernst Mach, "Der Kampf um die Universität," *Neue Freie Presse* (Vienna), no. 15, 732, Morgenblatt, June 7, 1908, p. 2, col. 3.

18. Ernst Mach to Josef Popper-Lynkeus, Vienna, July 6, 1900.

19. Ernst Mach, "Einige Worte über den neuen Syllabus," *Neue Freie Presse* (Vienna), no. 15, 413, Morgenblatt, July 21, 1907, p. 1, col. 2.

20. Ernst Mach to Josef Popper-Lynkeus, Vienna, Oct. 8, 1900.

21. Marie Mach to Ernst Mach, undated.

22. *AOS,* p. 75.

23. *PW* (Leipzig, 1900), pp. 371–372.

24. Čeněk Dvořák to Ernst Mach, Zagreb, Oct. 12, 1905. Camille Flammarion was a scientist and fashionable religious writer whose book, *La Fin du Monde,* fitted into the "heat death" tradition started by William Thomson who had interpreted the second law of thermodynamics in such a way as to prophesy that the sun was rapidly losing heat so that in a few million years life on earth would perish. (See Stephen Brush, "Thermodynamics and History," *Graduate*

Journal, 7 (1967), 477–565.) We do not know what Mach's "interesting observation from the year 1868" was.

25. Herneck, *op. cit.,* p. 216.

26. Robert Bouvier, *La Pensée d'Ernst Mach* (Paris, 1923), p. 245.

27. The fundamental weakness of all presentationalist philosophies, including Buddhism and positivism, has always been defective causal explanation. Common sense "force" explanation works in both narrative history and everyday life. The use of "laws" or "functional relations" as "causes" may have value in helping to understand ideal types of behavior, but in the practical world they lead to distortion by oversimplification and irrelevance. In the real, that is, in the world of historical events, sufficient and variable causes are more important than necessary causes; particular come before universal considerations. Napoleon did not lose the battle of Waterloo because of "the law of falling bodies" or because "all phenomena are relative." He lost it because General Grouchy failed to keep the Prussians away from the battlefield, because he started the battle too late in the day, because he had not carefully examined the "typical" way that Wellington organized and used his forces, and because he failed to exercise sufficient supervision over General Ney who authorized too many unwise cavalry attacks. Realistic explanation looks for agents as causes, that is, particular forces at particular places and times. To be sure, "General laws" are assumed and taken for granted, but they tend to be simple and obvious e.g., generals who try to take advantage of interior lines in fighting battles had better be quick about it or they will get crushed between opposing forces, a "maxim" known to all generals since Thucydides the Greek thousands of years ago.

It is precisely defective causal explanation which is responsible for the inability of presentationalists to solve practical problems in an effective way and which tempts them to reject practical life itself in favor of Buddhist escapism. The price of rejecting force in physics or redefining it in presentationalist terms is failure to understand dynamic behavior in a plausible way. The price of rejecting particular forces as causal determinants in practical life is practical failure.

28. The immediate quotation is from George Bernard Shaw, but presumably, it was used by others before him.

29. Bouvier, *op. cit.,* p. 242.

30. Richard Hönigswald, "Empirist. und kritisch. Idealismus," *Allgemeine Zeitung: Beilage* (Munich), Sept. 5, 1903, pp. 449 and 453.

31. Hermann Bahr, "Mach," *Berliner Tageblatt,* no. 116, March 3, 1916; Carl Haas, *Hofrat Dr. Ernst Mach* (Vienna, 1916), p. 13; Kurt Schmidt, "Die Lehre des Buddha," *Das Freie Wort,* 16 (1916), 43; Fred, *op. cit.,* col. 431.

32. Anton Lampa, *Ernst Mach* (Prague, 1918), p. 53.

33. *Ibid.,* p. 58.

34. *Ibid.,* p. 60.

35. For a more adequate analysis see Sidney Bradshaw Fay, *The Origins of the World War* (New York, 1936).

36. The Israeli preemptive attack on its Arab neighbors in 1967 resembled the German World War I situation closely enough that more sympathy for the German response should gradually develop. On the other hand, it may be argued that Germany had not exhausted all her options in trying to persuade Russia to demobilize.

37. The limitations of presentationalist causal explanation, especially its de-

pendence on so-called mathematical functions, are nowhere better demonstrated than in trying to understand diplomatic or military affairs. A positivistic or presentationalist military historian is almost a contradiction in terms.

38. Lampa, *op. cit.;* Wilhelm Jerusalem, *Der Krieg im Lichte der Gesellschaftslehre* (Stuttgart, 1915).

39. Philipp Frank, *Einstein: His Life and Times* (New York, 1947), pp. 119–121.

40. Bouvier, "Rapprochement avec le Bouddhisme," in *op. cit.*, pp. 240–247.

41. *Ibid.*, pp. 241–242.

42. I am indebted to Theodore Kneupper for mentioning Keyserling's identification of Mach's ideas with aspects of Buddhist thought.

43. I am generalizing in a broad way here. Tommaso Campanella (1568–1639), who wrote a defense of Galileo in 1616, emphasized not unrelated sets of values under the expressions *power, wisdom,* and *love.*

44. This is something of an exaggeration. By "agreement" I mean the gradual acceptance of Isaac Newton's *Principia Mathematica.*

45. I am again relying on Newton, but on his physical rather than mathematical conceptions of mass, weight, and force. For details see chap. 7, especially Newton's distinction between physical and mathematical causes.

46. I do not mean to imply that it is impossible to be "heroic" in a "nonaristocratic" society. States under siege or surrounded by hostile neighbors frequently develop a sense of heroism regardless of their form of government, and each system of values defines "humanity," "practicality," and "heroism" in its own terms, i.e., Aristotle, for example, who often thought in practical terms, defined "heroism" differently than the notion appeared to be defined in an "heroic" poem such as the *Iliad.*

47. Causal, representational realists understand "dynamics" in terms of force as an ontological primary quality neither consciously experienceable nor analogous to what can be consciously experienced and moving physical bodies as ontological realities which while not consciously experienceable are analogous in many respects to consciously experienceable primary qualities.

Phemomenalists, positivists, and Buddhists understand "dynamics" in terms of force as a particular type of relation between groups of sensations or appearances and moving physical bodies as the groups of sensations themselves. For representationalists what presentationalists call "dynamics" is merely a form of mentalistic kinematics. For presentationalists what representationalists call "dynamics" is merely a form of "metaphysics."

48. A good way of distinguishing between presentational and representational understanding would be to remember that what presentationalists consider physical is rejected as mental by representationalists and what representationalists consider physical is rejected as metaphysical by presentationalists, that is, when they are capable of understanding what representationalists mean at all.

49. Alexandre Koyré, "Influence of Philosophic Trends on the Formulation of Scientific Theories," *The Validation of Scientific Theories,* Philipp Frank, ed., (Boston, 1956), p. 202.

50. Max Born, *Natural Philosophy* (Oxford, 1951), p. 207.

51. *E & I*, p. 265.

52. *Ibid.*

53. Ernst Mach, "Some Questions of Psycho-Physics," *The Monist,* I (1890–1891), 398–399.

54. *AOS*, p. 369.

55. Albert Einstein, "Autobiographical Notes," *Albert Einstein: Philosopher-Scientist*, Vol. I, Paul Arthur Schilpp, ed. (New York, 1959), p. 21.

19. MACH'S INFLUENCE ON EARLY LOGICAL POSITIVISM
AND ON QUANTUM THEORY

1. *Leitgedanken* (Leipzig, 1919), p. 2.

2. *Encyclopaedia Britannica*, Vol. I (New York, 1929), p. 168.

3. F. A. von Hayek, "Diskussionsbemergungen über Ernst Mach und das sozialwissenschaftliche Denken in Wien," *Symposium* (Freiburg, 1967), pp. 41–44.

4. Philipp Frank, *Between Physics and Philosophy* (Cambridge, Mass., 1941), p. 9.

5. Herbert Feigl, "Moritz Schlick," *Erkenntnis*, 7 (1938), 399.

6. Rudolf Carnap, "Intellectual Autobiography," *The Philosophy of Rudolf Carnap*, Paul Arthur Schilpp, ed. (La Salle, Ill., 1963), p. 20. Heinrich Gomperz also held "at homes" at this time which met on Saturdays and included many of the same people who attended Schlick's "conversations."

7. Bela Juhos, "Moritz Schlick," *The Encyclopedia of Philosophy*, Vol. 7 (New York, 1967), pp. 319–321.

8. Carnap, *op. cit.*, p. 15.

9. Rudolf Carnap, "Über die Aufgaben der Physik," *Kant Studien*, 28 (1923), 91.

10. Carnap, "Intellectual Autobiography," p. 16.

11. Rudolf Carnap, "The Rejection of Metaphysics," *The Age of Analysis*, Morton White, ed. (New York, 1959), pp. 213–214.

12. Private communication from Rudolf Carnap (1969). During a conversation at his house I asked him: "But you don't believe that reference implies existence?" "But I do!" replied Carnap "Exactly that! Only I do not believe that reference determines meaning as you seem to think." I did not press the subject further.

13. Carnap, "Intellectual Autobiography," pp. 18, 44, 863. Ludwig Boltzmann was the true predecessor of both Wittgenstein and Carnap with respect to linguistic reductionism: ". . . die Ausdrucksweise des Realismusist zweckmässiger als die des Idealismus." See his *Populäre Schriften* (Leipzig, 1925), p. 180.

14. Frank, *op. cit.*, p. 6–7.

15. Otto Neurath to Ernst Mach, 2 AEK Feldpost 20, undated but during World War I.

16. Robert S. Cohen, "Otto Neurath," *The Encylopedia of Philosophy*, Vol. 5 (New York, 1967), p. 477.

17. Carnap. "Intellectual Autobiography," p. 23.

18. See Appendix.

19. For four different definitions of "physicalism" see *PSL* (La Salle, Ill., 1943), p. 210, and Carnap, "Intellectual Autobiography," pp. 50 and 59.

20. See chap. 13.

21. Wittgenstein's original version may be found in his *Tractatus Logico-Philosophicus* (London, 1958), pp. 187 and 189.

22. Carnap, "Intellectual Autobiography," pp. 24 and 29.

23. *Ibid.,* pp. 25–28.

24. F. A. von Hayek, "Unfinished Draft of a Sketch of a Biography of Ludwig Wittgenstein," p. 44.

25. Carnap, "Intellectual Autobiography," pp. 28–29.

26. Stephen Toulmin, "From Logical Analysis to Conceptual History," *The Legacy of Logical Positivism,* Peter Achinstein and Stephen Barker, eds. (Baltimore, 1969), pp. 34, 39–40. For a different point of view see Norman Kretzmann, "History of Semantics," *The Encyclopedia of Philosophy,* Vol. VII (1967), p. 402.

27. Ludwig Wittgenstein, *Philosophical Investigations* (New York, 1963), p. 34.

28. Heinrich Löwy, "Historisches zur Quantentheorie," *Naturwissenschaften,* 21 (1933), 302–303.

29. See chap. 14.

30. See Carlton Berenda Weinberg, *Mach's Empirio-Pragmatism in Physical Science* (New York, 1937), p. 52.

31. *Ibid.,* pp. 104–109.

32. *Ibid.,* pp. 106 and 108.

33. See Norwood Russell Hanson, "The Copenhagen Interpretation of Quantum Theory," *Philosophy of Science,* Arthur Danto and Sidney Morgenbesser, eds. (Cleveland, 1964), pp. 450–470.

34. Broglie has switched more than once. He first opposed the Copenhagen interpretation, then for twenty-five years he accepted it (1927–1962), and then he renewed his opposition to it (Louis de Broglie, *New Perspectives in Physics* [New York, 1962], p. 153).

35. Max Jammer, *The Conceptual Development of Quantum Mechanics* (New York, 1966), pp. 351–352.

36. For a defense of the Copenhagen position see Hanson, *op. cit.*

37. S. Rozental, *Niels Bohr* (New York, 1964), pp. 13 and 25.

38. Anton Thomsen corresponded with Mach between 1910 and 1913 and was enthusiastic about his theory of economy. Georg von Hevesy corresponded with Mach between 1904 and 1906 and with Bohr between 1913 and 1922. Von Hevesy won a Nobel prize in chemistry in 1943.

39. Jammer, *op. cit.,* pp. 167, 176–179.

40. Niels Bohr, *Essays 1958–1962 on Atomic Physics and Human Knowledge* (London, 1963), pp. 2 and 7.

41. Wolfgang Pauli, *Collected Scientific Papers,* Vol. I (New York, 1964), p. v.

42. Wolfgang Pauli, "Der Einfluss archtypischer Vorstellungen auf die Bildung naturwissenschaftlichen Theorien bei Kepler," *Naturerklärung und Psyche,* 4 (1952), 109.

43. See Erwin Schrödinger, *My View of the World* (Cambridge, 1964), p. vii.

44. Erwin Schrödinger, *Mind and Matter* (Cambridge, 1959), p. 51.

45. Thomas S. Kuhn, *Sources for History of Quantum Physics* (Philadelphia, 1967), p. 45.

46. *Ibid.,* p. 51.

47. See Karl Groos, "Rückkehr zu Mach? Über den Positivismus Pascual Jordans," *Blätter für deutsche Philosophie,* 11 (1937), 117–129.

48. See chap. 17.

49. See Hugo Dingler, *Max Planck und die Begründung der sogenannten modernen theoretischen Physik* (Braunschweig, 1939).

50. Erwin Lohr, "Gustav Jaumann," *Physikalische Zeitschrift,* 26 (1925), 189–198; Erwin Lohr, "Mach als Physiker," *Zeitschrift für die gesamte Naturwissenschaft,* 4 (1938–1939), 108–116.

51. Dr. Julius Kroczek, who studied under both Jaumann and Lohr, does not believe that the atomic theory was taught in the Brünn physics department before World War II (private communication, 1967).

52. See chap. 15.

53. See P. Feyerabend, "The Quantum Theory of Measurement," *Observation and Interpretation* (London, 1957).

APPENDIX: DID MACH FINALLY ACCEPT
THE REALITY OF ATOMS?

1. Stefan Meyer, "Die vorgeschichte der Gründung und das erste Jahrzehnt des Institutes für Radiumforschung," *SW,* 159 (1950), 5; Alois Höfler, "Ernst Mach," *Zeitschrift für physikalischen und chemischen Unterricht,* 29 (1916), 61.

2. Meyer, *op. cit.*

3. Private communication (Vienna, Dec. 12, 1967).

4. Fritz Chmelka, "Ernst Mach: Physiker und Philosoph," *Universum,* 21 (1966), 79.

5. Bohuslav Brauner, "Einstein and Mach," *Nature,* 113 (1924), 927.

6. *SOM* (La Salle, Ill., 1960). p. 589.

7. *AOS* (New York, 1959), pp. 311–312.

8. *Leitgedanken* (Leipzig, 1919), pp. 10–11.

9. *S & G* (La Salle, Ill., 1960), p. 138.

10. *POPO* (New York, 1953), p. viii.

11. *Mechanik* (Leipzig, 1933), pp. xviii–xx.

12. Stephen Brush, "Mach and Atomism," *Synthèse,* 18 (1968), 208.

13. Joseph Petzoldt, "Die Existenz der Atome," *Chemiker-Zeitung,* 40 (1916), 846; Joseph Petzoldt, "Mach und die Atomistik," *Die Naturwissenschaften,* 10 (1922), 230–231.

14. *AOS,* p. 311.

15. *COE* (Chicago, 1911), pp. 53, 87.

16. Erwin Hiebert, "The Genesis of Mach's Early Views on Atomism," *Boston Studies in the Philosophy of Science,* 6 (1970), 101–102.

A Select Bibliography

A. OTHER BIBLIOGRAPHIES

Thiele, Joachim, "Ernst Mach: Bibliographie," *Centaurus,* 8 (1963), 189–237. *Bibliographie der deutschen Zeitschriften-Literatur.* Leipzig, 1896——. *Bibliographie der fremdsprachigen Zeitschriften-Literatur.* Leipzig, 1911——. *Deutsche Arbeit.* Prague, 1901–1910.

B. DOCUMENTS AND LETTERS

1. *Berkeley, Calif.:* Bancroft Library, University of California, Robert H. Lowie Papers, Ludwig Mach to Robert H. Lowie, Vaterstetten, Oct. 18, 1922, April 6, 1923, Feb. 28, 1923, Oct. 30, 1923, Jan. 29, 1936, Feb. 15, 1936, March 17, 1936, April 20, 1936, May 13, 1947, May 25, 1947, Aug. 6, 1947, and a manuscript listing Ernst Mach's unpublished articles and books.
2. *Berlin—East:* Akademie-Archiv, Deutsche Akademie der Wissenschaft, Wilhelm-Ostwald-Archiv: Ernst Mach to Wilhelm Ostwald, Vienna, Nov. 18, 1897, Jan. 27, 1902, Dec. 25, 1902, Nov. 26, 1912, Mar. 9, 1913, April 13, 1913, Vaterstetten, May 29, 1913, and an autobiographical manuscript by Ernst Mach with thirteen typed pages and dated 1913.
3. *Berlin—West:* Hochschularchiv, Universität-Bibliothek der Technischen Universität, Joseph-Petzoldt-Archiv: Albert Einstein to Joseph Petzoldt, Berlin, Aug. 23, 1919; Ernst Mach to Joseph Petzoldt, Vaterstetten, March 18, 1914, March 20, 1914, April 27, 1914, Aug. 9, 1914, Aug. 19, 1914, Oct. 24, 1914, Oct. 20, 1914, Sept. 30, 1914, Dec. 3, 1914; Ludwig Mach to Joseph Petzoldt, Vaterstetten, May 11, 1914, July 20, 1914, July 21, 1914, Augsburg, Dec. 14, 1919, Feb. 14, 1920, June 29, 1920, Vaterstetten, June 4, 1923.
4. *Cambridge, Mass.:* Houghton Library, Harvard University, William James Collection: Ernst Mach to William James, June 10, 1902.
5. *Carbondale, Ill.:* University Library, Southern Illinois University, Open Court Archive: Ernst Mach to Paul Carus, Vienna, Oct. 21, 1892, May 15, 1895, July 28, 1896, Oct. 27, 1897, July 17, 1906, Oct. 4, 1907, July 30, 1910, Nov. 11, 1910, Jan. 27, 1911, June 7, 1912, Oct. 14, 1912, Nov. 12, 1912; Ludwig Mach to Paul Carus, Vaterstetten, Feb. 28, 1913, and a seven-page typed autobiographical manuscript by Ernst Mach, dated 1910.
6. *Essex Fells, N.J.:* Ernst Anton Lederer, Ernst Mach's grandson, who lives

at 195 Fells Road, has a number of documents from his mother which describe conditions in Prague and Vienna while Mach was there. She also collected useful newspaper articles about him. Dr. Lederer has also written out his reminiscences of Ernst Mach in manuscript form.

7. *Frieburg im Breisgau:* Ernst-Mach-Institut der Fraunhofer-Gesellschaft, Eckerstrasse 4: Ernst Mach to Philip Jourdain, Vienna, May 4, 1912 (copy); Ernst Mach to Ludwig Mach, Vienna, April 19, 1901, Seebenstein, July 22, 1902; Ernst Mach to Josef Popper-Lynkeus, Prague, Dec. 30, 1883, Jan. 13, 1884, March 14, 1895, July 6, 1900, Oct. 8, 1900, Vaterstetten, Aug. 11, 1913 (copies); Ernst Mach to "Verehrter Herr College!" Prague, Oct. 11, 1877; Viktor Niesiolowski to Ludwig Mach, Vienna-Mödling, Feb. 14, 1941; a three-page unpublished article by Victor Niesiolowski titled "Erinnerung an Ernst Mach" and dated 1941; four short testaments by Ernst Mach on current and former employees in his Prague Physical Institute; the first testament is dated 1886 and the last three 1894.

The following Freiburg letters are all *to* Mach. Friedrich Adler, July 13, 1906, July 23, 1909, Dec. 5, 1911; Richard Avenarius, Feb. 22, 1895, June 28, 1895; Theodor Beer, Aug. 1, 1906, Feb. 18, 1908; Henri Bergson, Sept. 3, 1909; Alfred Binet, Dec. 6, 1905; Bohuslav Brauner, March 21, 1909; Franz Brentano, Jan. 31, 1908; Josef Breuer, April 1, 1908; Paul Carus, May 31, 1892, March 30, 1896, June 2, 1897, Dec. 8, 1898, Nov. 18, 1899, Oct. 2, 1903, Aug. 13, 1907, Jan. 1910, Nov. 8, 1910, April 26, 1911, April 2, 1912, March 12, 1915; Louis Couturat, Feb. 10, 1903; John Cox, Jan. 14, 1902; Carl Cranz, Oct. 9, 1910; George Davison, April 29, 1891; Eugene Dietz-gen, July 20, 1906; Hugo Dingler, March 23, 1912; M. Dufour, Sept. 13, 1912; Pierre Duhem, Aug. 10, 1909; Čeněk Dvořák, Dec. 28, 1888, May 19, 1889, Oct. 21, 1895, Oct. 12, 1905, Oct. 17, 1905, Oct. 18, 1905, Aug. 19, 1915; Josef Eisenmeir, Feb. 8, 1901; Peter Klementitsch von Engelmeyer, Jan. 22, 1894, Nov. 23, 1895, March 28, 1900, March 2, 1906, Jan. 31, 1910, Feb. 10, 1911, Jan. 14, 1812, June 6, 1812; Andreas Ritter von Ettinghausen, Vienna, 1863; E. Forster, Berlin, undated; Kurt Geissler, March 5, 1909, June 11, 1909; Leo Gilbert, Aug. 1, 1913, Aug. 18, 1913; Heinrich Gomperz, Feb. 17, 1908; Theodor Gomperz, May 25, 1882, Nov. 27, 1894, Jan. 26, 1895; Wilhelm von Hartel, Feb. 11, 1895, Feb. 12, 1895, Feb. 14, 1895, Feb. 22, 1895; Georg von Hevesy, June 29, 1906; Alois Höfler, Jan. 24, 1895; Makoto Ischihara, March 13, 1906; Gustav Jaumann, July 21, 1894, Oct. 27, 1906; Alexander Jollos, Feb. 16, 1908; Josef Kareis, March 31, 1895; M. R. Kaufmann, Oct. 31, 1894; Hans Kleinpeter, Sept. 4, 1904, May 5, 1911, Nov. 25, 1911, Dec. 22, 1911, Nov. 9, 1912, Nov. 14, 1912; Bruno Kolbe, Nov. 28, 1891, March 13, 1895; K. Korischka, April 18, 1884; Sergei von Koschljakow, April 24, 1895; Eduard Krischek, April 25, 1863, Feb. 17, 1882, Jan. 14, 1893, Oct. 2, 1894, Dec. 19, 1894; Rudolf Laemmel, Oct. 10, 1906, Oct. 29, 1906, May 7, 1910; Anton Lampa, Feb. 9, 1910, Feb. 18, 1910, May 1, 1910; Viktor von Lang, July 15, 1913; Jacques Loeb, Dec. 23, 1900, Dec. 28, 1902, Feb. 21, 1903; Löwentoff, Oct. 8, 1901, Dec. 24, 1901; Carl Ludwig, May 14, 1864; Thomas J. McCormack, June 16, 1893, Nov. 24, 1897, June 12, 1903; Anton Marty, Sept. 26, 1908; Ludwig Mach, March 15, 1894, Nov. 27, 1897, Dec. 3, 1897; Marie Mach, Dec. 22, 1894, May 25, 1895; H. Münsterberg, July 16, 1895; Clemens Neumann, March 11, 1868; Vladimir Nochotowitsch, Feb. 26, 1910; G. V. Osnobschin, Jan. 19, 1883; Wilhelm Ostwald, May 31, 1901,

Feb. 24, 1912, March 10, 1912, March 13, 1912, Nov. 26, 1912; Wolfgang Pauli (Sr.), Feb. 17, 1913; Karl Pearson, July 1897, Dec. 20, 1902; Joseph Petzoldt, May 8, 1904, Aug. 8, 1907, Sept. 22, 1910, June 26, 1912, Sept. 1, 1912, May 25, 1913, June 6, 1913, June 15, 1913, March 5, 1914; Georg Pick, July 15, 1895; Franz Plaíník, Nov. 6, 1883; Victor Pierre, April 16, 1867; Josef Popper-Lynkeus, May 3, 1895; Edmund Reitlinger, July 12, 1867, May 19, 1880; E. Reusch, May 30, 1884; Alois Riehl, Jan. 2, 1902; Rignano, Jan. 10, 1912; W. Rossicky, July 21, 1914; Van Schaik, April 29, 1891; W. Scharwin, Feb. 27, 1906; Schlesinger, May 17, 1895; Albert von Schrenk-Notzing, June 4, 1896; Hugo von Seeliger, Jan. 7, 1885, Sept. 30, 1906; J. P. Y. Smith, Sept. 1, 1883, Sept. 18, 1883; J. B. Stallo, Oct. 20, 1897; Adolf Stöhr, April 14, 1915; Simon Subic, Sept. 21, 1877; Gustav Tschermak, March 2, 1893, March 20, 1893, Jan. 22, 1894, Oct. 11, 1894, Nov. 2, 1894; František Wald, July 2, 1900; Auer von Welsbach, Feb. 20, 1860; Alexandre Zindeberg, Oct. 5, 1892.

8. *Jena:* Ernst-Haeckel-Haus: Ernst Mach to Ernst Haeckel, Vienna, Oct. 5, 1905.

9. *Knebworth, Herefordshire:* The Karl Pearson Papers are in the hands of his daughter Helga S. Hacker of 12 Lytton Fields, Corner Croft: Ernst Mach to Karl Pearson, Vienna, July 12, 1897.

10. *Munich:* Hugo Dingler Institut für methodologische Forschung, Eidos Verlag, Postfach 23: Ernst Mach to Hugo Dingler, Vienna, April 4, 1910, Sept. 4, 1910, March 16, 1911, Jan. 26, 1912, Nov. 20, 1912, June 29, 1913, July 21, 1913, Oct. 8, 1915.

11. *Prague:* Central State Archive, Karmelitska 2: Prague police reports to the governor of Bohemia ("Statthalter"), no. 7020 Dec. 10, 1879, May 17, 1880, no. 3272 May 15, 1880, May 19, 1880, July 2, 1885, Aug. 8, 1895.

   Archive of Czech Literature: Ernst Mach to Johannes Purkyně, Prague, June 14, 1867.

12. *Princeton, N. J.:* Institute for Advanced Study, Princeton University, Einstein Archive: Joseph Petzoldt to Albert Einstein, Berlin-Spandau, March 3, 1927.

13. *Vaterstetten bei München:* Frau Anna Karma Mach, the daughter-in-law of Ernst Mach, has preserved a great many documnts by Johann, Ernst, Marie, and Ludwig Mach. She lives with her sister, Frau Irma Tauber, at Münchenerstrasse 28. We have utilized Johann Mach's university course completion certificates, Ludwig Mach's university diploma, and have read through the latter's optical experiment book which was used by Ernst Mach in Volume One of his book on optics. Ernst Mach's library still retains thousands of books as well as many manuscripts of his own publications.

14. *Vienna:* Die Österreichische Akademie der Wissenschaft: a four-page handwritten autobiographical manuscript by Ernst Mach, dated 1880.

   Österreichische Nationalbibliothek, Handschrift Abteilung: Ernst Mach to Franz Exner, Vienna, June 14, 1903, and a newspaper clipping from an unknown newspaper: Philipp Frank, "Zum 100. Geburtstag Ernst Machs."

   Österreichisches Staatsarchiv: Ernst Mach to Wilhelm von Hartel, Vienna, April 22, 1901, and numerous documents from Mach's file from the old Imperial education ministry ("K. K. Ministerium für Cultus und Unterricht").

15. *Washington, D.C.:* The Library of Congress, Manuscript Division: Ernst Mach to Jacques Loeb, Vienna, July 3, 1904, Aug. 13, 1904, Nov. 11, 1906.
16. *Zagreb:* University of Zagreb, Physics Department Library: Ernst Mach to Čeněk Dvořák, Prague, May 10, 1878, Vienna, March 2, 1909.
17. *Zürich:* Universität Zürich, Medizinhistorisches Institut: Ernst Mach to Auguste Forel, Vienna, Aug. 7, 1912.

C. BOOKS BY ERNST MACH

Compendium der Physik für Mediciner. Vienna, 1863. 274 pp.
Zwei populäre Vorlesungen über musikalische Akustik. Graz, 1865. 31 pp.
Einleitung in die Helmholtz'sche Musiktheorie: Populär für Musiker dargestellt. Graz, 1866. 98 pp.
Zwei populäre Vorträge über Optik. Graz, 1867. 39 pp.
Optisch-akustische Versuche: Die spectrale und stroboskopische Untersuchung tönender Körper. Prague, 1873. 110 pp.
Beiträge zur Doppler'sschen Theorie der Ton- und Farbenänderung durch Bewegung: Gesammelte Abhandlungen. Prague, 1874. 34 pp.
Grundlinien der Lehre von den Bewegungsempfindungen. Leipzig, 1875. 127 pp.
(Coauthored with Johann Odstrčil). *Grundriss der Naturlehre für die unteren Classen der Mittelschulen.* Prague, 1886. 194 pp.
(Coauthored with Gustav Jaumann). *Leitfaden der Physik für Studierende.* Leipzig, 1891. 372 pp.
Machs Grundriss der Physik für die höheren Schulen des Deutschen Reiches. Reworked by Ferdinand Harbordt and Max Fischer, Part 2. Leipzig, 1894. 346 pp.
Contributions to the Analysis of the Sensations. Trans. C. M. Williams. Chicago, 1897. 208 pp.
Die Principien der Wärmelehre: Historisch-kritisch entwickelt. 2d ed. Leipzig, 1900. 484 pp.
Die Geschichte und die Wurzel des Satzes von der Erhaltung der Arbeit. 2d ed. Leipzig, 1909. 60 pp.
Kultur und Mechanik. Stuttgart, 1915. 86 pp.
Erkenntnis und Irrtum: Skizzen zur Psychologie der Forschung. 3d ed. Leipzig, 1917. 483 pp.
Die Leitgedanken meiner naturwissenschaftlichen Erkenntnislehre und ihre Aufnahme durch die Zeitgenossen. Sinnliche Elemente und naturwissenschaftliche Begriffe. Leipzig, 1919. 31 pp. Two essays.
Die Prinzipien der physikalischen Optik: Historisch und erkenntnis-psychologisch entwickelt. Leipzig, 1921. 443 pp.
Die Analyse der Empfindungen und das Verhältnis des Physischen zum Psychischen. 9th ed. Jena, 1922. 323 pp.
Populär-wissenschaftliche Vorlesungen. 5th ed. Leipzig, 1923. 628 pp.
Die Mechanik in ihrer Entwicklung historisch-kritisch dargestellt. 9th ed. Leipzig, 1933. 493 pp.
Popular Scientific Lectures. 5th ed. Trans. Thomas J. McCormack. La Salle, Ill., 1943. 411 pp.
The Principles of Physical Optics: An Historical and Philosophical Treatment. 2d ed. Trans. John S. Anderson and A. F. A. Young. New York, 1953. 324 pp.
The Analysis of Sensations and the Relation of the Physical to the Psychical.

Trans. C. M. Williams and Sydney Waterlow. 3d ed. New York, 1959. 380 pp.
Space and Geometry in the Light of Physiological, Psychological and Physical Inquiry. 2d ed. Trans. Thomas J. McCormack. La Salle, Ill., 1960. 148 pp.
The Science of Mechanics: A Critical and Historical Account of Its Development. 6th ed. Trans. Thomas J. McCormack. La Salle, Ill., 1960. 634 pp.
Outlines of the Theory of the Motor Sensations. SLA Translation Center, John Crerar Library. Chicago, Ill., 1961. 162 pp.
Arbeiten über Erscheinungen an fliegenden Projektilen. Hamburg-Altona, 1966. 69 pp. Five articles on shock waves arranged and published by Joachim Thiele.

D. JOURNAL AND BOOK ARTICLES BY ERNST MACH

"Vorträge über Psychophysik," *Zeitschrift für praktische Heilkunde,* 9 (1863), 146–148, 167–170, 202–204, 225–228, 242–245, 260–261, 277–279, 294–298, 316–318, 335–338, 352–354, 362–366.
"Zur Theorie der Pulswellenzeichner," *SW,* 47 (1863), 43–48.
"Untersuchungen über den Zeitsinn des Ohres," *SW,* 51 (1865), 133–150.
"Bemerkungen über intermittirende Lichtreize," *Archiv für Anatomie, Physiologie, und wissenschaftliche Medicin* (1865), 629–635.
"Mach's Vorlesungs-Apparate," *Carls Reportorium der Physik,* 4 (1868), 8–9.
"Resultate einer Untersuchung zur Geschichte der Physik," *Lotos,* 23 (1873), 189–191.
"Über die Verwerthung der Mikrophotographie," *Photographische Correspondenz,* 13 (1876), 227–228.
"Über wissenschaftliche Anwendungen der Photographie und Stereoskopie," *Photographische Correspondenz,* 14 (1877), 10–11.
(Coauthored with C. Tumlirz and C. Kögler.) "Über die Fortpflanzungsgeschwindigkeit der Funkwellen." *SW,* 77 (1878), 7–32.
"Neue Versuche zur Prüfung der Doppler'schen Theorie der Ton und Farbenänderung durch Bewegung," *SW,* 77 (1878), 299–310.
(Coauthored with Josef Wentzel.) "Ein Beitrag zur Mechanik der Explosionen," *SW,* 92 (1885), 625–638.
"Über den Unterricht in der Wärmelehre," *Zeitschrift für den physikalischen und chemischen Unterricht,* 1 (1887), 3–7.
"Über das psychologische und logische Moment im naturwissenschaftlichen Unterricht," *Zeitschrift für den physikalischen und chemischen Unterricht,* 4 (1890), 1–5.
"Some Questions of Psycho-Physics," *The Monist,* 1 (1891), 394–400.
"An Account of Scientific Applications of Photography," *Journal of the Camera Club,* 6 (1893), 110–112.
"Durchsicht-Stereoskopbilder mit Röntgenstrahlen," *Zeitschrift für Elektrotechnik,* 14 (1896), 359–361.
"On the Stereoscopic Application of Roentgen's Rays," *The Monist,* 6 (1896), 321–323.
"Über Gedankenexperimente," *Zeitschrift für den physikalischen und chemischen Unterricht,* 10 (1896), 1–5.
"The Notion of a Continuum," *Open Court,* 14 (1900), 409–414.
"Leben und Erkennen," *Neue Gesellschaft Sozialistische Wochenschrift,* 1 (1905), 371–372.

"Sur le rapport de la physique avec la psychologie," *L'Année Psychologique,* 12 1906), 303–318.

"Inventors I Have Met," *The Monist,* 22 (1912), 230–242.

"Einige vergleichende tier- und menschenspychologische Skizzen," *Naturwissenschaftliche Wochenschrift,* 15 (1916), 241–247.

"Some Sketches in Comparative Animal and Human Psychology," *Open Court,* 32 (1918), 363–376.

"Die Rassenfrage." In K. D. Heller, *Ernst Mach: Wegbereiter der modernen Physik.* Vienna, 1964. Pp. 99–102.

"The Significance and Purpose of Natural Laws." Trans. Frederic Schick. In *Philosophy of Science.* Arthur Danto and Sidney Morgenbesser, eds. Cleveland, 1964. Pp. 266–273.

"On the Effect of the Spatial Distribution of the Light Stimulus on the Retina." Trans. Floyd Ratliff. In F. Ratliff, *Mach Bands.* San Francisco, 1965. Pp. 253–271.

"On the Physiological Effect of Spatially Distributed Light Stimuli." Trans. Floyd Ratliff. In F. Ratliff *Mach Bands.* San Francisco, 1965. Pp. 272–284. First of three articles.

"On the Physiological Effect of Spatially Distributed Light Stimuli." Trans. Floyd Ratliff and included in his *Mach Bands.* San Francisco, 1965. Pp. 285–298. Second of three articles.

"On the Physiological Effect of Spatially Distributed Light Stimuli." Trans. Floyd Ratliff and included in *Mach Bands.* San Francisco, 1965. Pp. 299–306. Third of three articles.

"On the Dependence of retinal points on one another," Trans. Floyd Ratliff and included in his *Mach Bands.* San Francisco, 1965. Pp. 307–320.

"On the Influence of Spatially and Temporally Varying Light Stimuli on Visual Perception." Floyd Ratliff and included in his *Mach Bands.* San Francisco, 1965. Pp. 321–332.

"Über der relative Bildungswert der philologischen und der mathematisch-naturwissenschaftlichen Unterrichtsfächer der höheren Schulen", *Physikalische Blätter,* 22 (1966), 49–67.

E. NEWSPAPER ARTICLES BY ERNST MACH (VIENNA)

"Ludwig Boltzmann," *Die Zeit,* no. 1420, Abendblatt, Sept. 7, 1906.

"Ludwig Boltzmann," *Neue Freie Presse,* no. 15,103, Morgenblatt, Sept. 8, 1906.

"Einige Worte über den neuen Syllabus," *Neue Freie Presse,* no. 15,413, Morgenblatt, July 21, 1907.

"Morsens Angriff auf die Universitäten," *Neue Freie Presse,* no. 15,416, Morgenblatt, July 24, 1907.

"Josef Popper-Lynkeus," *Die Zeit,* no. 1944, Feb. 19, 1908.

"Der Kampf um die Universität," *Neue Freie Presse,* no. 15,732, Morgenblatt, June 7, 1908.

"Erinnerungen an Darwin und die Entwicklungslehre," *Neue Freie Presse,* no. 16109, Morgenblatt, June 27, 1909.

"Die Organisierung der Intelligenz," *Neue Freie Presse,* no. 16,494, Morgenblatt, July 24, 1910.

"Ein Ersuchen von Ernst Mach an die 'Neue Freie Presse' in seinem letzten Willen," *Neue Freie Presse,* no. 18,500, Abendblatt, Feb. 22, 1916.

F. FOREWORDS BY ERNST MACH

Stallo, J. B. *Die Begriffe und Theorien der modernen Physik.* Trans. Hans Kleinpeter. Leipzig, 1901. Pp. iii–xiii.

Kulke, Eduard. *Kritik der Philosophie des Schönen.* Leipzig, 1906. Pp. x–xiii.

Laemmel, Rudolph. *Die Reformation der nationalen Erziehung.* Zürich, 1910. P. iii.

Jacob, Josef. *Praktische Methodik des mathematischen Unterrichts.* Vienna, 1913. Pp. iii–vii.

G. BOOKS ON ERNST MACH, HIS BACKGROUND, OR INFLUENCE

Achinstein, Peter, and Stephen F. Barker eds. *The Legacy of Logical Positivism.* Baltimore, 1969.

Ackermann Antiquariat, Theodor. *Bibliothek Ernst Mach, Teil I, Katalog 634.* Munich, 1959.

———. *Bibliothek Ernst Mach, Teil II, Katalog 636,* Munich, 1960.

Adler, Friedrich. *Ernst Machs Überwindung des mechanischen Materialismus.* Vienna, 1918.

Avenarius, Richard. *Kritik der reinen Erfahrung.* 2 vols. Leipzig, 1888–1890.

Boltzmann, Ludwig, *Populäre Schriften.* Leipzig, 1925.

———. *Lectures on Gas Theory.* Trans. Stephen G. Brush. Berkeley and Los Angeles. 1964.

Boncelj, Josip. *Jožef Stefan.* Ljubljana, 1960.

Boring, Edwin G. *A History of Experimental Psychology.* New York, 1957.

Bouvier, Robert. *La Pensée d'Ernst Mach.* Paris, 1923.

Broda, Engelbert. *Ludwig Boltzmann.* Berlin, 1957.

Cohen, Robert S., and Raymond J. Seeger, eds. *Ernst Mach: Physicist and Philosopher.* Boston Studies in the Philosophy of Science, Vol. 6. Dordrecht, The Netherlands, 1970.

Dingler, Hugo. *Die Grundgedanken der Machschen Philosophie.* Leipzig, 1924.

———. *Der Zusammenbruch der Wissenschaft und der Primat der Philosophie.* Munich, 1926.

Druce, Gerald. *Two Czech Chemists.* London, 1944. On Bohuslav Brauner and Franktišek Wald.

Duhem, Pierre. *The Aim and Structure of Physical Theory.* trans. Philip P. Wiener. New York, 1962.

Easton, Loyd D. *Hegel's First American Followers.* Athens, Ohio, 1966. Includes four letters from Ernst Mach to J. B. Stallo.

Eichler, Richard W. *Liebenau im Sudetenland.* Munich, 1966.

Einstein, Albert, *Einstein: Essays in Science.* New York, 1934.

———. *Out of My Later Years.* New York, 1950.

Ewald, Oskar. *Richard Avenarius als Begründer der Empirio-Kritizismus.* Berlin, 1905.

Fechner, Gustav. *Elements of Psychophysics.* Vol. I. Trans. Helmut E. Adler. San Francisco, 1966.

Frank, Philipp. *Between Physics and Philosophy.* Cambridge, Mass., 1941.

———. *Einstein: His Life and Times.* New York, 1947.

Frank, Philipp, ed. *The Validation of Scientific Theories.* Boston, 1956.

Grille, Dietrich. *Lenins Rivale: Bogdanov und seine Philosophie.* Cologne, 1966.
Hasan, Syed Zafarul. *Realism: An Attempt To Trace Its Origin and Development in Its Chief Representatives.* Cambridge, 1928.
Heller. K. D., *Ernst Mach: Wegbereiter der modernen Physik.* Vienna, 1964.
Henning, Hans. *Ernst Mach als Philosoph, Physiker und Psycholog.* Leipzig, 1915.
Herneck, Friedrich. *Bahnbrecher des Atomzeitalters.* Berlin, 1966.
Hertz, Heinrich. *Die Prinzipien der Mechanik.* Leipzig, 1894.
Hönigswald, Richard. *Zur Kritik der Machschen Philosophie.* Berlin, 1903.
Husserl, Edmund. *Logische Untersuchungen.* Part I. Halle, 1900.
James, Henry, ed. *The Letters of William James.* Vol. I. Boston, 1920.
Jammer, Max. *Concepts of Space.* New York, 1960.
————.*Concepts of Force.* New York, 1962.
————. *Concepts of Mass.* New York, 1964.
————.*The Conceptual Development of Quantum Mechanics.* New York, 1966.
Jerusalem, Wilhelm. *Gedanken und Denker: Neue Folge.* Vienna, and Leipzig, 1925.
Kienzl, Wilhelm. *Meine Lebenswanderung.* Vienna, 1953.
Kindinger, Rudolf, ed. *Philosophenbriefe aus der wissenschaftlichen Korrespondenz von Alexius Meinong. . . .* Graz, 1965.
Kleinpeter, Hans. *Der Phenomenalismus.* Leipzig, 1913.
Körber, Hans-Günther, ed. *Aus dem wissenschaftlichen Briefwechsel Wilhelm Ostwalds.* Vol. I. Berlin, 1961.
Kolakowski, Leszek. *The Alienation of Reason: A History of Positivist Thought.* Trans. Norbert Gutterman. Garden City, N.Y., 1968.
Kraft, Viktor. *The Vienna Circle.* Trans. Arthur Pap. New York, 1953.
Kuhn, Thomas S. *Sources for History of Quantum Physics.* Philadelphia, 1967.
Külpe, Oswald. *The Philosophy of the Present in Germany.* Trans. M. L. Patrick and G. T. W. Patrick. London, 1913.
Lampa, Anton. *Ernst Mach.* Prague, 1918.
Leclair, Anton von. *Der Realismus der modernen Naturwissenschaft im Lichte der von Berkeley und Kant angebahnten Erkenntniskritik.* Prague, 1879.
Leistner, Karl R. *Professor und Prolet: Kurzweilige und vollständige Widerlegung des Hassbuches Lenins gegen die Machisten.* Karlsbad, 1932.
Lenin, Vladimir Il'ich, *Materialism and Empirio-Criticism.* New York, 1927.
Lentze, Hans. *Die Universitätsreform des Ministers Graf Leo Thun-Hohenstein.* Vienna, 1962.
Lesky, Erna. *Die Wiener medizinische Schule im 19 Jahrhundert.* Graz and Cologne, 1965.
Mach. Heinrich. *Beiträge zur Kenntnis der Abietensäure.* Göttingen, 1894.
(Mach, Marie.) *Erinnerungen einer Erzieherin.* Foreword by Ernst Mach. Vienna, 1913.
Merzkirch, Wolfgang, and Frank Kerkhof. eds. *Symposium aus Anlass des 50. Todestages von Ernst Mach.* Freiburg im Breisgau, 1967.
Millikan, Robert A. *The Autobiography of Robert A. Millikan.* New York, 1950.
Molisch. Paul. *Politische Geschichte der deutschen Hochschulen in Österreich von 1848 bis 1918.* Vienna and Leipzig, 1939.
Musil, Robert. *Beitrag zur Beurteilung der Lehren Machs.* Wilmersdorf, 1908.
Økland, Fridthiof. *The Structure of Nature.* Oslo, 1950.
Pearson, Karl. *Grammar of Science.* London, 1900.

Planck, Max. *Vorträge und Erinnerungen.* Darmstadt, 1965.

Poincaré, Henri. *Science and Method.* New York, 1958.

Ratliff, Floyd, *Mach Bands.* San Francisco, 1965. Includes six previously untranslated articles by Ernst Mach.

Russell, Bertrand. *My Philosophical Development.* London, 1959.

Schilpp, Paul Arthur, ed. *The Philosophy of Bertrand Russell.* Chicago, 1944.

———. *Albert Einstein: Philosopher-Scientist.* 2 vols. New York, 1959.

———. *The Philosophy of Rudolf Carnap.* La Salle, Ill., 1963.

Stallo, John Bernard. *The Concepts and Theories of Modern Physics.* Cambridge, Mass., 1960.

Tobias, Wilhelm. *Grenzen der Philosophie.* Berlin, 1875.

Weinberg, Carlton B. *Mach's Empirio-Pragmatism in Physical Science.* New York, 1937.

Wlassak, Rudolf. *Ernst Mach.* Leipzig, 1917.

H. JOURNAL AND BOOK ARTICLES ON OR RELATING TO ERNST MACH

Ackeret, J. "Der Luftwiderstand bei sehr grossen Geschwindigkeiten," *Schweizerische Bauzeitung,* 94 (1929), 179–183.

Alexander, Peter. "Ernst Mach," in *The Encyclopedia of Philosophy,* Vol. V. New York, 1967. Pp. 115–119.

———. "The Philosophy of Science, 1850–1910," *A Critical History of Western Philosophy.* Daniel J. O'Conner, ed. London, 1964. Pp. 402–425, 568–569, 589.

Anon. "Briefe von Richard Avenarius und Ernst Mach an Wilhelm Schuppe," *Erkenntnis,* 6 (1936), 73–80.

Blüh, Otto. "Ernst Mach as Teacher and Thinker," *Physics Today,* 20 (June, 1967), 32–42.

———. "Ernst Mach as an Historian of Science," *Centaurus,* 13 (1968), 62–84.

Bogdanov, Alexander. "Ernst Mach und die Revolution," *Die Neue Zeit* (Stuttgart), 26 (1908), 695–700.

Boltzmann, Ludwig. "Models," in *Encyclopedia Britannica,* Vol. 18, 11th ed. Cambridge, 1911. Pp. 638–640.

Brauner, Bohuslav. "Einstein and Mach," *Nature,* 113 (1924), 927.

Bridgman, Percy W. "The Mach Principle," in *The Critical Approach to Science and Philosophy.* Mario Bunge, ed. London, 1964. Pp. 224–233.

Brush, Stephen. "Mach and Atomism," *Synthèse,* 18 (1968), 192–215.

Bunge, Mario. "Mach's Critique of Newtonian Mechanics," *American Journal of Physics,* 34 (1966), 585–596.

Cafiero, Luca. "Cinque lettere di G. Vailati a E. Mach," *Rivista Critica di Storia della Filosofia,* 17 (1962), 68–74.

Carnap, Rudolf. "Intellectual Autobiography," *The Philosophy of Rudolf Carnap.* Paul Arthur Schilpp, ed. La Salle, Ill., 1963.

Carus, Paul. "Some Questions of Psycho-Physics," *Fundamental Problems.* Chicago, 1903. Pp. 336–349.

———. "Professor Mach and His Work," *The Monist,* 21 (1911), 19–42.

———. "Professor Ernst Mach," *Open Court,* 30 (1916), 257.

Case, Thomas. "Metaphysics," in *Encyclopaedia Britannica.* Vol. 18. 11th ed. Cambridge, 1911. Pp. 224–253.

Chmelka, Fritz. "Ernst Mach: Physiker und Philosoph," *Universum,* 21 (1966), 74–80.

Cohen, I. B. "An Interview with Einstein," *Scientific American,* 193 (1955), 71.

Dicke, R. H., and C. Brans. "Mach's Principle and a Relativistic Theory of Gravitation," *Physical Review,* 124 (1961), 925–935.

Dingler, Hugo. "Ernst Mach," *Monatshefte für den naturwissenschaftlichen Unterricht,* 9 (1916), 321–329.

Einstein, Albert. "Ernst Mach," *Physikalische Zeitschrift,* 17 (1916), 101–104.

———. "Autobiographical Notes," *Albert Einstein: Philosopher-Scientist.* Paul Arthur Schilpp, ed. Vol. I. New York, 1959. Pp. 2–95.

Elek, Tibor. "Zur Geschichte der Beziehungen zwischen Physik und Philosophie: Die Philosophische Diskussion zwischen Ernst Mach, Max Planck und Albert Einstein zu Beginn des 20. Jahrhunderts," *Periodica Polytechnica* (Budapest), 1 (1967), 135–157.

Exner, Franz. "Ernst Mach," *Almanach der kaiserlichen Akademie der Wissenschaft* (Vienna), 66 (1916), 328–334.

Feigl, Herbert. "The Origin and Spirit of Logical Positivism," in *The Legacy of Logical Positivism.* Peter Achinstein and Stephen F. Barker, eds. Baltimore, 1969. Pp. 3–24.

Felt, James W. "Mach's Principle Revisited," *Laval Théologique et Philosophique,* 20 (1964), 35–49.

Flamm, Ludwig. "Die Persönlichkeit Boltzmanns," *Österreichische Chemiker Zeitung,* 47 (1944), 28–30.

Frank, Philipp. "Die Bedeutung der physikalischen Erkenntnistheorie Machs für des Geistesleben der Gegenwart," *Naturwissenschaften,* 5 (1917), 65–72.

———. "Ernst Mach: The Centenary of His Birth," *Erkenntnis,* 7 (1937/1938), 247–256.

———. "Einstein, Mach, and Logical Positivism," in *Albert Einstein: Philosopher-Scientist.* Vol. I. Paul Arthur Schilpp, ed. New York, 1959. Pp. 271–286.

Fred, W. "Ernst Mach (nach seinem Tod)," *Die Aktion,* 6 (1916), cols. 430–435.

Gomperz, Heinrich. "Ernst Mach," *Archiv für Geschichte der Philosophie,* 29 (1916), 321–328.

———. "Autobiographical Remarks," *The Personalist,* 24 (1943), 254–270.

Groos, Karl. "Rückkehr zu Mach– Über den Positivismus Pascual Jordans," *Blätter für Deutsche Philosophie,* 11 (1937), 117–129.

Häber, Theodor. "Ein Brief von Ernst Mach," *Zeitschrift für mathematischen und naturwissenschaftlichen Unterricht,* 49 (1918), 96–98.

Hayek, F. A. von. "Diskussionsbemerkungen über Ernst Mach und das sozialwissenschaftliche Denken in Wien," in *Symposium aus Anlass des 50. Todestages von Ernst Mach,* Freiburg im Breisgau, 1967. Pp. 41–44.

Henning, Hans. "Ernst Mach," in *Deutsches Biographisches Jahrbuch 1914/1916.* Berlin and Leipzig, 1925. Pp. 233–237.

Herneck, Friedrich, "Über eine unveröffentlichte Selbstbiographie," *Wissenschaftliche Zeitschrift der Humboldt-Universität,* 6 (1956/1957), 209–220.

———. "Wiener Physik vor 100 Jahren," *Physikalische Blätter,* 17 (1961), 455–461.

———. "Die Beziehungen zwischen Einstein und Mach, dokumentarisch dargestellt," *Naturwissenschaftliche Zeitschrift der Friedrich-Schiller-Universität Jena,* 15 (1966), 1–14.

———. 'Ernst Mach und Albert Einstein," in *Symposium aus Anlass des 50. Todestages von Ernst Mach.* Freiburg, 1967. Pp. 45–61.

Herrmann, Dieter. "Ernst Mach zur Doppler-Theorie," *Die Sterne,* 40 (1964), 155–156.

————. "Ernst Mach und seine Stellung zur Doppler-Theorie," *Forschungen und Fortschritte*, 40 (1966), 362–365.

Hiebert, Erwin N. "The Genesis of Mach's Early Views on Atomism," *Boston Studies in the Philosophy of Science*, 6 (1970), 79–106.

Höfler, Alois. "Ernst Mach," *Zeitschrift für den physikalischen und chemischen Unterricht*, 29 (1916), 57–63.

Holton, Gerald. "Influences on Einstein's Early Work in Relativity Theory," *American Scholar*, 37 (1967/1968), 59–79.

————. "Mach, Einstein, and the Search for Reality," *Daedalus*, 97 (1968), 636–673.

Hönl, Helmut. "Ein Brief Albert Einsteins an Ernst Mach," *Physikalische Blätter*, 16 (1960), 571–581.

————. "Zur Geschichte des Machschen Prinzips," *Wissenschaftliche Zeitschrift der Friedrich-Schiller-Universität Jena*, 15 (1966), 225–236.

Jackson, Carl T. "The Meeting of East and West," *Journal of the History of Ideas*, 29 (1968), 73–92.

Jaffé, George. "Recollections of Three Great Laboratories," *Journal of Chemical Education*, 29 (1952), 230–238.

Juhos, Bela. "Ernst Mach und die moderne Philosophie," *Österreichische Hochschulzeitung*, 18 (April 15, 1966), 3–4.

Katkov, George. "Lenin as Philosopher," in *Lenin: The Man, the Theorist, the Leader*. Leonard Schapiro and Peter Reddaway, eds. New York, 1967. Pp. 71–86.

Kleinpeter, Hans. "Über Ernst Mach's und Heinrich Hertz' principiell Auffassung der Physik," *Archiv für systematische Philosophie*, 5 (1899), 159–184.

————. "On the Monism of Professor Mach," *The Monist*, 16 (1906), 161–168.

Koyré, Alexandre. "Influence of Philosophic Trends on the Formulation of Scientific Theories," in *The Validation of Scientific Theories*. Philipp Frank, ed. Boston, 1956.

Kraft, Viktor. "Ernst Mach als Philosoph," *Almanach der Österreichischen Akademie der Wissenschaften*, 116 (1966), 373–387.

Kreidl, Alois. "Ernst Mach," *Wiener Klinische Wochenschrift*, 28 (1916), 394–396.

Kühn, Karl. "Ernst Machs Herkunft und Abstammung," *Heimatbildung*, 19 (1938), 268–269.

Kutterer, R. E. "Zur ballistischen, elektrischen Momentphotographie: Der Weg von E. Mach über C. Cranz zu H. Schardin," *Wehrtechnische Monatshefte*, n.v. (1966), 25–33.

Lampa, Anton. "Moderne Ergebnisse der Atomistik," *Deutsche Arbeit*, 12 (1912/1913), 686–690 and 739–745.

————. "Ernst Mach," *Chemiker-Zeitung*, 40 (1916), 445–448.

Löwy, Heinrich. "Die Erkenntnistheorie von Popper-Lynkeus und ihre Beziehung zur Machschen Philosophie," *Naturwissenschaften*, 20 (1932), 770–772.

————. "Historisches zur Quantentheorie," *Naturwissenschaften*, 21 (1933), 302–303.

Lohr, Erwin. "Gustav Jaumann," *Physikalische Zeitschrift*, 26 (1925), 189–198.

————. "Mach als Physiker," *Zeitschrift für die gesammte Naturwissenschaft*, 4 (1938), 108–116.

Lowie, Robert H. "Scientists' Scientist," *New Republic*, 6 (1916), 335.

————. "Dr. L. Mach," *Science*, 83 (1936), 499.

————. "Letters from Ernst Mach to Robert H. Lowie," *Isis*, 37 (1947), 65–68.

Lübbe, Hermann. "Positivismus und Phänomenologie: Mach und Husserl," in *Beiträge zur Philosophie und Wissenschaft, Wilhelm Szilasi zum 70. Geburtstag.* Munich, 1969. Pp. 161–184.

Mach, Anna Karma. "Ernst Mach," in Theodor Ackermann Antiquariat, *Bibliothek Ernst Mach, Teil I, Katalog #634.* Munich, 1959. P. 1.

———. "Begrüssungsansprachen," in *Symposium aus Anlass des 50. Todestages von Ernst Mach.* Freiburg, 1967. Pp. 8–11.

Mach, Johann. "Beschreibung der hiesigen Aufzucht des Japanischen Seidenspinners der Eiche Yama-mai," *Allgemeine Deutsche Zeitschrift für Seidenbau,* 1 (1867), 83–84.

———. "Der Eichenspinner Bombyx Yama-Mai," *Allgemeine Deutsche Zeitschrift für Seidenbau,* 3 (1868), 54–56.

———. "Die Zucht der Yama-Main Raupe (des Eichenspinners)," *Allgemeine Deutsche Zeitschrift für Seidenbau,* 4 (1869), 12–13.

———. "Kurze Anleitung zur Zucht des Eichenseidenspinners," *Zeitschrift für Akklimatisation,* 9 (1871), 23–30.

Mach, Ludwig. "Über ein Interferenzrefraktometer," *Zeitschrift für Instrumentenkunde,* n.v. (March, 1892), 89.

———. "Erkenntnis und Irrtum," *Naturwissenschaften,* Oct. 8, 1926, p. 933.

———. "Vortwort," in Ernst Mach, *Die Mechanik in ihrer Entwicklung historisch-kritisch dargestellt.* 9th ed. Leipzig, 1933. Pp. xviii–xx.

Mayerhöfer, Josef. "Ernst Mach as a Professor of the History of Science," in *Proceedings of the Tenth International History of Science.* Vol. I. Paris, 1964. Pp. 337–339.

———. "Ernst Machs Berufung an die Wiener Universität 1895," *Clio Medica,* 2 (1967), 47–55.

Meitner, Lise. "Looking Back," *Bulletin of the Atomic Scientists,* 20 (Nov., 1964), 2–7.

Merzkirch, Wolfgang F. "Die Beiträge Ernst Machs zur Entwicklung des Gasdynamik," in *Symposium aus Anlass des 50. Todestages von Ernst Mach.* Freiburg, 1967. Pp. 114–131.

———. "Mach's Contribution to the Development of Gas Dynamics," *Boston Studies in the Philosophy of Science,* 6 (1970), 42–59.

Meyer, Stefan. "Die Vorgeschichte der Gründung und das erste Jahrzehnt des Institutes für Radiumforschung," *Sitzungsberichte der Österreichischen Akademie der Wissenschaft,* 159 (1950), 5.

Myhill, John. "Berkeley's 'De Motu': An Anticipation of Mach," *University of California Publications in Philosophy,* 29 (1957), 141–157.

Osterhout, W. J. V. "Jacques Loeb: A Biographical Sketch," *Journal of General Physiology,* 8 (Sept. 15, 1928), ix–xcii.

Pachner, Jaroslav. "Machs Kritik an der Newtonschen Mechanik und ihre Weiterentwicklung zum Machschen Prinzip," *Symposium aus Anlass des 50. Todestages von Ernst Mach.* Freiburg im Breisgau, 1967. Pp. 216–226.

(Peirce, Charles.) (A review of Mach's *Mechanics*), *Nation,* 57 (1893), 251–252.

Peter, Gustav. "Kant und Mach: Ein Erkenntnistheoretischer Briefwechsel mit F. C. Müller-Lyer," *Annalen der Naturphilosophie,* 14 (1921), 97–111.

Petzoldt, Joseph. 'Die Relativitätstheorie der Physik," *Zeitschrift für Positivistische Philosophie,* 2 (1914), 3.

———. "Die Existenz der Atome," *Chemiker-Zeitung,* 40 (1916), 846.

———. "Das Verhältnis der Machschen Gedankenwelt zur Relativitätstheorie."

Anhang zu: Ernst Mach, *Die Mechanik in ihrer Entwicklung historisch-kritisch dargestellt*. 8th ed. Leipzig, 1921. Pp. 490–517.

———. "Mach und die Atomistik," *Die Naturwissenschaften*, 10 (1922), 230–231.

Planck, Max. "Gegen die Neuere Energetik," *Annalen der Physik*, 57 (1896), 72–78.

———. "Die Einheit des physikalischen Weltbildes," *Physikalische Zeitschrift*, 10 (1909), 62–75.

———. "Zur Machschen Theorie der physikalischen Erkenntnis: Eine Erwiderung," *Physikalische Zeitschrift*, 11 (1910), 1186–1190. Also in *Vierteljahrschrift für wissenschaftliche Philosophie*, 34 (1910), 497–507.

Popper, Karl R. "A Note on Berkeley as a Precursor of Mach," *British Journal for Philosophy of Science*, 4 (1953), 26–36.

Rabel, Gabriele. "Mach und die 'Realität der Aussenwelt,'" *Physikalische Zeitschrift*, 21 (1920), 433–437.

Reichenbach, Hans. "Die auf Mach zurückgehenden Auffassungen," *Logos*, 10 (1921/1922), 328–341.

Reimann, Dora. "Historische Studie über Ernst Machs Darstellung des Hebelsatzes," *Quellen und Studien zur Geschichte der Naturwissenschaften und der Medizin*, 3 (1936), 554–592.

Russell, Bertrand. "On the Nature of Acquaintance: Neutral Monism II," *The Monist*, 24 (1914), 161–187.

Seaman, F. "Mach's Rejection of Atomism," *Journal of the History of Ideas*, 29 (1968), 381.

Seidlerová, Irena. "Fysika," *Dějiny exaktních věd v českých zemích*. Prague, 1961. Pp. 277–314, 380–381.

Sommerfeld, Arnold. "Nekrolog über Ernst Mach," in *Jahrbuch der Königlich Bayerischen Akademie der Wissenschaften*. Munich, 1917. Pp. 58–67.

Stöhr, Adolf. "Ernst Mach," *Die Feierliche Inauguration des Rektors der Wiener Universität für das Studienjahr 1916/17*. Vienna, 1916. Pp. 37–46.

Stumpf, Carl. (A review of Mach's *Analysis of Sensations*), *Deutsche Literaturzeitung*, n.v. (July 3, 1886, 947–958.

Thiele, Joachim, "Ein Brief Edmund Husserls an Ernst Mach," *Zeitschrift für philosophische Forschung*, 19 (1965), 134–139.

———. "Bemerkungen zu einer Äusserung im Vorwort der 'Optik' von Ernst Mach," *Schriftenreihe für Geschichte der Naturwissenschaften, Technik und Medizin*, 2 (1965), 10–19.

———. "Schulphysik vor 70 Jahren Hinweis auf Ernst Machs Lehrbücher der Physik anlässlich des 50. Todestages Machs am 19. Februar 1966," *Zeitschrift für mathematischen und naturwissenschaftlichen Unterricht*, 19 (1966), 15–17.

———. "William James and Ernst Mach," *Philosophia Naturalis*, 9 (1966), 298–310.

———. "Briefe von Gustav Theodor Fechner und Ludwig Boltzmann an Ernst Mach," *Centaurus*, 12 (1967), 222–235.

———. "Briefe Robert H. Lowies an Ernst Mach," *Isis*, 59 (1968), 84–87.

———. "Ernst Mach und Heinrich Hertz," *Schriftenreihe für Geschichte der Naturwissenschaften, Technik und Medizin*, 5 (1968), 132–134.

———. "Ein zeitgenössisches Urteil über die Kontroverse zwischen Max Planck und Ernst Mach," *Centaurus*, 13 (1968), 85–90.

———. "'Naturphilosophie' und 'Monismus' um 1900," *Philosophia Naturalis*, 10 (1968), 295–315.

————. "Briefe deutscher Philosophen an Ernst Mach," *Synthèse*, 18 (1968), 285–301.

Thirring, Hans. "Ernst Mach als Physiker," *Almanach der Österreichischen Akademie der Wissenschaften*, 116 (1966), 361–372.

Titchener, E. B. "Mach's 'Lectures on Psychophysics,'" *American Journal of Psychology*, 32 (1922), 213–222.

Toulmin, Stephen E. "From Logical Analysis to Conceptual History," in *The Legacy of Logical Positivism*. Peter Achinstein and Stephen F. Barker, eds. Baltimore, 1969. Pp. 25–56.

Volkmann, Paul, "Studien über Ernst Mach vom Standpunkt eines theoretischen Physikers der Gegenwart," *Annalen der Philosophie*, 4 (1924), 303–312.

Wind, C. H. "Zur Demonstration einer von E. Mach entdeckten optischen Täuschung," *Physikalische Zeitschrift*, 1 (1900), 112–113.

Wright, Georg Henrik von, "Biographical Sketch," in Norman Malcolm, *Ludwig Wittgenstein: A Memoir*. London, 1959.

I. NEWSPAPER ARTICLES ON ERNST MACH
(ARRANGED CHRONOLOGICALLY)

Berlin

Petzoldt, Joseph. "Ernst Mach," *Berliner Tageblatt*, no. 98, Feb. 23, 1916.

Bahr, Hermann. "Mach," *Berliner Tageblatt*, no. 116, March 3, 1916.

Popper-Lynkeus, Josef. "Ernst Mach," *Die Vossische Zeitung, Sonntagsbeilage*, 26 March 1916 and 2 April 1916.

Brünn/Brno

Blüh, Otto. "Ernst Mach," *Tagesbote*, Feb. 15, 1938.

Frankfurt

Bach, D. J. "Ernst Mach," *Frankfurter Zeitung*, no. 49, Erstes Morgenblatt, Feb. 18, 1908.

Munich

Altmann, Bruno. "Die Zürcher Machkolonie: Zur Vorgeschichte der Relativitätstheorie," *Allgemeine Zeitung*, Dec. 3, 1922.

Dingler, Hugo. "25 Todestages von Ernst Mach," *Münchner Neuesten Nachrichten*, Feb. 29, 1941.

Vienna

Boltzmann, Ludwig. "Mach's Vorlesungen," *Neue Freie Presse*, Morgenblatt, no. 13789, Jan. 15, 1903.

Ostwald, Wilhelm. "Ernst Mach," *Neue Freie Presse*, no. 15684, Morgenblatt, April 19, 1908.

Lecher, Ernst. "Hofrat Professor Dr. Ernst Mach," *Neue Freie Presse*, no. 16313, Morgenblatt, Jan. 21, 1910.

Kleinpeter, Hans. "Ernst Mach und Friedrich Nietzsche," *Neue Freie Presse*, Morgenblatt, Feb. 23, 1913.

Adler, Friedrich. *Arbeiter-Zeitung*, Morgenblatt, Feb. 23, 1916.

Popper-Lynkeus, Josef. "Erinnerungen an Ernst Mach," *Neues Wiener Tageblatt*, Feb. 23, 1916.

Jerusalem, Wilhelm. "Erinnerungen an Ernst Mach," *Neue Freie Presse*, no. 18509, Morgenblatt, March 2, 1916.

Anon. "Josef Popper-Lynkeus und Ernst Mach," *Neue Freie Presse*, no. 19212, Nachmittagsblatt, Feb. 18, 1918.

Einstein, Albert. "Zur Enthüllung von Ernst Machs Denkmal," *Neue Freie Presse,* June 12, 1926.

Ehrenhaft, Felix. "Ernst Machs Stellung im wissenschaftlichen Leben," *Neue Freie Presse,* June 12, 1926.

Schlick, Moritz. "Ernst Mach, der Philosoph," *Neue Freie Presse,* June 12, 1926.

Thirring, Hans. "Ernst Mach und die theoretische Physik," *Neue Freie Presse,* June 12, 1926.

Index

Abb, Edmund: Zürich follower of Mach and Avenarius, 190
Absolute motion. *See* Motion, absolute
Absolute space. *See* Space, absolute
Absolute time. *See* Time, absolute
Absolute zero: Planck attacks Mach's understanding of, 225
Absolutes: Newton's understanding of, 95, 334–335; Machist criticisms of 99–104, 250–251, 274–275; as constancies, 168; as certainties, 31
Ach, N.: worked on imageless thoughts, 230
Ackeret, J.: coined expression "Mach number," 112, 336
Ackermann Antiquariat, Theodor (a Munich book store), sold part of Mach's library, 330, 337
Acoustics: Mach's books, lectures, and laboratory approach toward, 15, 21, 42, 43, 156, 328; acoustic waves, 106, 115; mentioned 85, 326
Act psychology: described, 61–62. *See also* Brentano, Franz
Adler, Friedrich (Austrian literary figure): mentioned, 332
Adler, Friedrich (Austrian socialist, physicist, and follower of Mach): as philosopher, 186–187, 235, 243; advises Mach on Lenin and Russia, 235–236; defended Mach against Planck, 222, 347–348; relations with Einstein, 251, 256, 351; assassination of Austrian prime minister, 256, 294; political activities in Austria and Switzerland, 300–301; mentioned, 344, 349, 355
Adler, Viktor (father of above, leader of

Austrian socialists): Mach's friend, 186, 235
Akselrod, Lyubov: wrote against Machism, 241
Alembert, Jean le Rond D': attempted to derive dynamics from kinematics, 335
Altmann, Bruno: described Mach colony (Zürich) and its influence on Einstein, 189–190, 344
America, the United States of: Mach's philosophical influence in, 126–131, 201–203, 270–271; mentioned, 10, 233
Analysis of Sensations (Mach's book on psychology and phenomenalism): first draft abandoned, 25; original title, 63; revised and enlarged, 180; late revision, 271; foreign translations, 181–182; Bogdanov's preface, 239; Stumpf and Lipps critical toward, 120–121, 227–229; footnote references to, 325–334, 337–338, 341–343, 346, 348, 355, 358, 360. *See also* *Contributions to the Analysis of Sensations*
Analogy: knowledge of other people by, 36, 122; reliability of, 168, 178
Analytic philosophy. *See* Vienna Circle; Logical Positivism; Wittgenstein, Ludwig
Analytic truth. *See* Truth, analytic
Ångström, Anders: trouble measuring Doppler effect, 17
Animal psychology: Mach's views on, 68–71
Animals: Mach's attitude and behavior toward, 41, 287, 289–290
Anthropology: Mach's interest in, 271.

Index

Index

160; identified logic with Mach's theory of economy, 175; pacifistically inclined, 294; mentioned, 9, 80, 116, 176, 300

Jevons, William Stanley: mentioned, 139

Jollos, Alexander: Russian follower of Mach, 238

Jordan, Pascual (German quantum theorist): strongly influenced by Mach, 316

Joseph II (Habsburg ruler and radical reformer): opposed nationalism, 40

Joule, James: mentioned, 84

Jouvenel, Bertrand de: mentioned, 195

Juhos, Bela: member of the Vienna Circle, 302

Jung, C. G.: his doctrine of an unconscious world soul, 60, 315

Jung, R.: discussed Mach's color theory, 60

Kafka, Franz: mentioned, 83

Kālidāsa: Indian dramatist admired by Mach, 44. See also Kienzl, Wilhelm

Kant Immanuel: influence on Mach, 10–11; his "Copernican revolution" as a return to Bellarmine's philosophy of science, 35, 171; not a referential phenomenalist, 32; definition of metaphysics, 33; in idealist tradition, 127; attacked by Boltzmann, 210; mentioned, xi, 26, 165, 190, 226, 250, 257, 289, 296, 301, 315

Karabaček, J. von: role in Mach's transfer to Vienna, 152

Kármán, Theodor von: mentioned, 22

Karpath, Ludwig: wrote about Mach's student life, 23

Keller, Helen: mentioned, 159

Kelvin, Lord (William Thomson): mentioned, 84

Kepler, Johannes: mentioned, 221, 222, 315

Kern, Berthold von: member of (Berlin) Society for Positivistic Philosophy, 192

Keyserling, Hermann: interested in Mach's attraction to Buddhism, 295

Kienzl, Wilhelm (Austrian opera composer): influenced by Mach to turn from acoustics to opera composing, 44

Kierkegaard, Søren: mentioned, 314

Kinematics (the study of physical motion without taking forces as causes into consideration): Mach's attempt to reduce dynamics to, 96, 98, 296–297, 357; Mach's kinematic approach to shock waves, 114; Einstein's attempt to reduce dynamics to kinematics, 254; Mach's influence on Pearson, 124; Planck attacks Mach's understanding of, 225; Bunge's criticism of Mach, 335; mentioned, 93, 245. See also Dynamics

Kinetic theory of gases. See Gases, kinetic theory of

Kirchhoff, Gustav Robert (prominent German physicist): atomic theory uneconomical, 89; mentioned, 218, 248

Klein, Felix (German mathematician): supported Boltzmann at Lübeck debate, 205; signed positivistic manifesto, 190; mentioned, 192

Kleinpeter, Hans (Austrian supporter of Mach): pointed out resemblances in the epistemologies of Mach and Nietzsche, 123; helped form (Berlin) Society for Positivistic Philosophy, 190

Kneupper, Theodore: called attention to Keyserling's interest in Mach and Buddhism, 357

Knowledge and Error (Mach's still largely untranslated book on the philosophy and methodology of science): based on 1895–1898 lectures, 181; dedicated to Wilhelm Schuppe, 122; distinguished between metrical and physical space, 253; read by F. A. von Hayek, 301; footnote references to, 325, 328, 342, 343, 348, 355, 357

Koffka, Kurt (Gestalt theorist): influenced by Stumpf, 228

Köhler, Wolfgang (Gestalt theorist): influenced by Stumpf, 228

Koláček, František (Czech physicist): influenced by Mach, worked on Maxwell's theory, 43

Kolakowski, Leszek: mentioned, 123

Kolbe, Bruno (Russian teacher): used Mach's textbooks in St. Petersburg, 236

Koranyi, Alexander von: mentioned, 130

Koschliakov, Sergei von: asked for Mach's advice on photography, 236

Koyré, Alexandre (French historian of science): careful thinker, 195

Kraft, Viktor (Vienna philosopher and historian): influenced by Mach, 182–183; leader of Vienna Circle after World War II, 302

Krasnopolski, Horaz: mentioned, 80, 83

Kraus, Oskar (Prague philosopher and student of Brentano): opposed Einstein's use of non-Euclidean geometry, 269–270

Index

Lenzen, Victor (Berkeley scientist-philosopher): theory of aspects based on Mach's theory of elements, 231

Le Roy, Edouard ("Modernist" Catholic and philosopher of science): part of a French reaction against positivism and the importance of science, 194

Lesevich, V. V.: student of Avenarius and teacher of Bogdanov, 239

Lichtenberg, Georg (German philosopher): Mach read, 26; influenced Mach toward Hume's ideas, 27; Mach accepted his rejection of the ego, 35, 288

Liebenau (Bohemia): Mach family's ancestral home, 3

Liebig, Justus: mentioned, 56

Light, theory of: Neumann's work on, 14; undulatory theory of, 221. *See also* Optics; Relativity

Light constancy, theory of (Einstein's principle): Einstein's youthful conception of, 248; Born and Planck supported Einstein's position, 250; not relativistic, 258; refusal of Mach and Petzoldt to accept unless interpreted in a "relativistic" way, 274–275, 277, 282, 285; Einstein's rejection of Petzoldt's "relativistic" interpretation of, 281–282; Ludwig Mach's attempt to determine experimentally or to refute, 282–285; mentioned, 249, 280. *See also* Relativity, Einstein's theory of; Absolutes

Light quanta. *See* Photons

Linguistic analysis: mentioned, xi

Linguistic reductionism (the notion that metaphysical, ontological, or epistemological differences are merely linguistic in character): Carnap's approach, 303–304; Wittgenstein's later approach, 310; presentationalist nature of, 303; failure to allow for representationalism, 303–304; mentioned, 307

Lipps, Theodor (German psychologist-philosopher): student of Brentano, 62; criticized Mach's book on psychology, 120, 227

Lobachevski, Nikolai Ivanovich: mentioned, 260

Locke, John: private language theory of, 310; mentioned, xi

Loeb, Jacques (German-American physiologist and philosopher): influenced by Mach's philosophical ideas, 129–130; not clear on differences between phenomenalism and materialism, 131; confused understanding, 186; approach

similar to that of Watson and Neurath, 304

Logic: Mach's lectures on, 156; subordination of to psychology, 138; subordination of to Darwinism, phenomenalism, and theory of economy, 175; less certain than sensations, 176; Jerusalem's definition of it in terms of Mach's theory of economy, 175; Mach's approach rejected as "psychologistic," 174–176; mentioned, 152, 202

Logic, symbolic: mentioned, 184, 199

Logical atomism (Russell's theory): based on Mach's theory of elements, 231; mentioned, 199

Logical positivism (a philosophical movement which attempted to combine phenomenalism with symbolic logic, scientism, and linguistic reductionism): defined and compared with Comte's Positivism, 164–169; mentioned, 159, 184, 203, 230, 296. *See also* Positivism; Vienna Circle

Lohr, Erwin: continued Brünn school of continuum physics, 317. *See also* Jaumann, Gustav

Loschmidt, Josef (Austrian physicist): associate of Stefan, 24; background and work on the size and density of molecules in gases, 87; claimed entropy was not reversible, 88; retired, 147

Loschmidt number: proportional to Avogadro's number, 87

Lotze, Rudolf Hermann: mentioned, 61, 126

Lovejoy, Arthur (American philosopher-historian): opposed phenomenalism and New Realism, 202–203

Lowie, Robert H. (American anthropologist and friend of Mach): interested Mach in anthropology, 270–272; helped raise financial aid for Ludwig Mach, 283–284

Löwy, Heinrich: wrote on Mach's anticipation of Planck's quantum discoveries, 310

Lübeck Scientific Conference (atomism vs. energeticism): Boltzmann's victory over Ostwald, 154, 204–205. *See also* Boltzmann, Ludwig; Ostwald, Wilhelm

Ludwig, Carl (German physiologist): work on blood pressure measuring instruments, 20; helped influence Mach toward physiology, 21

Lueger, Karl (mayor of Vienna): opposed Mach's atheism, 158–159; at-

Priessnitzian water cure: used on Mach, almost killed him, 5

Primary space. *See* Space, primary

Principles, Mach's methodological: principle of adjustment of thoughts to one another, of thoughts to facts, of broadest possible generalization, of compensation, of continuity, of permanence, of sufficient differentiation, of variation, 179. *See also* Science, methodology of

Principles of Heat Theory (Mach's book on thermodynamics): hurried into publication apparently to counter Boltzmann, 157; severely criticized for incompleteness, 158; criticized by Planck, 219; included Mach's theory of chemical discontinuity which purportedly influenced Planck's quantum theory, 310; footnote references to, 327, 328, 335, 338, 341, 342, 346, 355

Principles of Physical Optics, The (Mach's posthumously published history of optics): Mach's preface hostile to Einstein's theory of relativity, 257–258, 273, 280; publication of Part I, 181, 271, 300; Ludwig Mach worked on Part II but apparently destroyed his manuscript, 283–285; footnote references to, 336, 351, 353, 360; mentioned, 281

Professional philosophers (university professors of philosophy): mentioned, 193, 209, 247, 252

Prokop the Great: military leader during Hussite wars, 40

Proletcult (Russian cultural movement): opposed by Lenin, 246

Protagoras: mentioned, 274

Protocol statements (supposedly indubitable): mentioned, 230, 257

Przibram, Karl (Vienna scientist): supported Meyer's story about Mach's alleged acceptance of the reality of atoms, 319–320

Pseudosphere: Helmholtz's geometrical speculation about, 261

Psychological atomism. *See* Atomism, psychological

Psychologism: Husserl's label for attempts to understand logic in psychological and historical terms such as Mach attempted to do, 174–176; New Realism (and Logical Positivism) rejected Mach's understanding of logic because of, 202

Psychology: Mach's definitions of, 63–64; Mach's lectures on, 156; Mach's books on, 63, 69, 120; Mach's early interest in, 14, 16, 27; Mach's work in, 47–72; Fechner's ideas on, 28–29; William James, 126–128, 202; Mach's possible influence on Freud, 71; attacks of Stumpf, Lipps, and Külpe on Mach, 154, 227–231; Mach refused to attend psychology congress, 154, 227; mentioned, 207, 270–271, 304. *See also* Act psychology; Animal psychology; Behavioral psychology; Child psychology; Descriptive psychology; Gestalt psychology; Introspective psychology

Psychophysical (intraexperiential, i.e., ontologically monistic) interactionism: Müller, 55; William James, 55, 127

Psychophysical (transexperiential, i.e., ontologically pluralistic) interactionism: Descartes, 29; Stumpf, 227

Psychophysical (intraexperiential, i.e., ontologically monistic) parallelism: Fechner's version of, 20, 29–30, 129; Mach rejects Fechner's understanding of, 20, 29–30, 53; Mach's own rather nominal version of, 30, 36, 54, 227; relation of Fechner's version to Hering's "unconscious memory," 60; Bergson rejected Mach's position, 197; Stumpf attacked Mach's parallelism, 227; mentioned, 55, 127, 315

Psychophysics (the study of the relations between mind on the one side and body and matter on the other; for Mach this was an intraexperiential discipline): related to Fechner's law, 20; field created by Fechner, 29–30; Mach's definition of, 63; mentioned, 53, 54, 60, 126, 127, 227, 315

Ptolemaic theory: Mach's defense of, 102

Ptolemy: related to phenomenalistic purpose of science, 297

Purkyně, Jan Evangelista (Czech phsyiologist, better known under his German name Johannes Purkinje): Mach interested in his ideas on the adaptation of the human eye, 39, but Purkyně seemed more interested in bringing Mach over to Czech nationalism, 40; approach similar to Hering, 59

Purpose: Mach's definition of, 68

Quantum theory: Mach's relations to, 310–318; Mach methodological father of quantum mechanics (according to Weinberg), 312; Mach's anticipation of